Networking the Russian Diaspora

**MUSIC AND
PERFORMING
ARTS** OF ASIA
AND THE PACIFIC

Networking the Russian Diaspora

RUSSIAN MUSICIANS AND MUSICAL ACTIVITIES IN INTERWAR SHANGHAI

HON-LUN HELAN YANG
SIMO MIKKONEN
JOHN WINZENBURG

University of Hawai'i Press
Honolulu

25 24 23 22 21 20   6 5 4 3 2 1

Library of Congress Cataloging-in-Publication Data

Names: Yang, Hon-Lun, author. | Mikkonen, Simo, author. | Winzenburg, John, author.

Title: Networking the Russian diaspora : Russian musicians and musical activities in interwar Shanghai / Hon-Lun Helan Yang, Simo Mikkonen, John Winzenburg.

Other titles: Music and performing arts of Asia and the Pacific.

Description: Honolulu : University of Hawai'i Press, 2020. | Series: Music and performing arts of Asia and the Pacific | Includes bibliographical references and index.

Identifiers: LCCN 2020022863 | ISBN 9780824879662 (cloth) | ISBN 9780824882693 (pdf) | ISBN 9780824882709 (epub) | ISBN 9780824882716 (kindle edition)

Subjects: LCSH: Music—China—Shanghai—20th century—History and criticism. | Russians—China—Shanghai—History—20th century. | Shanghai Municipal Orchestra.

Classification: LCC ML336.8.S55 Y36 2020 | DDC 780.89/9171051132—dc23

LC record available at https://lccn.loc.gov/2020022863

Cover Art: (Front) A historic photo of the former Cathedral of the "Surety of Sinners," which was completed in 1934 and consecrated by Bishop John Maximovitch of Shanghai. The structure (no longer a church) is located at 55 Xinle Road, formerly Rue Paul Henry in the French Concession. (Back) Colonel Frizovsky's Russian-Ukrainian Choir in the late 1920s (Zhiganov 1936).

CONTENTS

ILLUSTRATIONS

Figures

Tables

PREFACE

In 2004, the British historian and Soviet music expert Neil Edmunds of the University of the West of England and Hon-Lun Helan Yang of this volume embarked on a quest to learn more about Russian musicians in interwar Shanghai. At the time, the best existing account of Russian contributions to Shanghai's musical life was a three-page journal article by Tszo Chzhenguan in Russian (2000), which merely summarized a brief chapter of Wang Zhicheng's history of the Russian émigré community in Shanghai in Chinese (1993). The lack of information on this unique page of human migration and its connection to the development of Western culture in Shanghai was what prompted Edmunds and Yang to pursue the initial research behind the present volume. In the summer of 2005 and 2006, Yang and Edmunds did archival research in Shanghai with funding from two small grants from Hong Kong Baptist University. Two papers were presented in Hong Kong and the United Kingdom in 2007 and early 2008, respectively. By then, Edmunds had secured a British Academy Fellowship to spend a semester in Shanghai to do further research in the spring of 2008.

But Edmunds' untimely death in January 2008 put the project almost to an end until the joining in 2013 of the other two authors of the present volume, Simo Mikkonen and John Winzenburg. Both Mikkonen and Winzenburg were a godsend to the project, each bringing their own expertise to the research. Mikkonen is a historian specializing in Soviet and Russian culture (see for instance 2007, 2009, 2011a, 2011b, and 2012), whereas Winzenburg is a conductor and musicologist specializing in Sino-Western intercultural compositions (2012, 2013, and 2015). Both helped to deepen the research far beyond what Edmunds had begun. With the support of a General Research Fund (GRF) of the University Grant Council of Hong Kong, we took an innovative approach toward the subject matter. We examined the impact of the Russian émigré musicians on

Shanghai's musical scene from both a diaspora as well as a network perspective. This was revealing not only from the viewpoint of what these musicians did for their own communities, but also how they interacted with and contributed to other communities. Finally, the research pointed out important influences of Russian émigrés on the trajectory of Chinese musical development.

Transliteration, Orthography, and Spelling

One of the challenges in writing this multiauthor volume has been to adopt a uniform and consistent approach toward structure as well as writing style. Different renditions of names in multilingual (Chinese, Russian, French, and many others) sources presents an additional challenge. Our objective has been to offer a reader-friendly text. Russian names are rendered according to English transliteration, disregarding how they were transliterated in original sources unless otherwise specified or in case of a direct quotation. Furthermore, Chinese names are presented as last name first, the two-syllable first name combined, and then Romanized using pinyin, disregarding their original rendition in old sources unless the old or alternative usage has long been established or is in a quotation. In such a case, clarification is provided in brackets in the first instance of the respective chapter. Names of places are generally presented as they were used historically, but accompanied by modern usage in brackets or explained in a note where necessary. American spelling is used throughout the book, but when quoting from an original source, its original spelling is kept for the sake of historical flavor. Titles of musical compositions that appear in concert programs, newspaper articles, and memoirs are presented in their proper form in English (or their most familiar form), disregarding how they were presented in the original source unless in a quotation. In the reference list, the use of simplified or complex Chinese characters follows the format used in the original source; that is, writings published prior to 1949 or published in Taiwan are rendered in complex Chinese characters, whereas writings published after 1949, particularly in the People's Republic of China (PRC), are rendered in simplified Chinese characters. Chinese names that appear in the chapters, however, are all rendered in simplified Chinese characters according to the practice of the PRC.

Whereas in-text citations (adhering to the author-date system and title-date without author) and a reference list of books and articles are used, details of archival records or other types of sources that are difficult to cite—such as newspaper clippings without dates, concert programs from a scrapbook, diaries, personal communications, employment contracts, unpublished articles in archive folders—are provided in the notes.

Sources

We have consulted a wide variety of primary sources, including unpublished personal correspondences, diaries, institutional records, musicians' contracts, repository files of individual musicians, and Shanghai newspapers in English, Chinese, Russian, and French, collected in the following archives and libraries: Paul Sacher Foundation (PSF) in Basel, the Shanghai Public Library and the Shanghai Municipal Archive, the Shanghai Symphony Archive, the Prague Slavonic Library, the UC Berkeley libraries, the Stanford Hoover Library, and the Helsinki University Library. We have also consulted secondary literature in Chinese, Russian, and English.

Acknowledgments

In general, we provide our own translations of foreign-language sources with the exception of some of the Russian sources used by Winzenburg and Yang, which were translated by Riikkamari Muhonen with funding provided by the GRF grant. An initial Excel file of all the programs of the SMO was compiled by Yang Ning, a former archivist of the Shanghai Symphony Orchestra, which was then checked and augmented by Amanda Liu, the research assistant for this project, both endeavors also funded by the GRF grant. In a span of two years, Liu worked first as a full-time and later as a part-time assistant for the project. Liu was responsible for identifying useful articles in various English and Chinese newspaper databases as well as compiling the integrated bibliography at the end of this volume. During the time she worked as a part-time assistant, Liu also compiled the tables included in chapters 3 and 4. Without Liu's help, this project would have taken much longer to come to fruition, and if there are mistakes and oversights, they are ours to bear.

Yang feels greatly indebted to her two coauthors for their multiple readings of this introduction as well as other parts of the volume. In particular, she would like to thank Mikkonen for checking Russian names and spellings, and Winzenburg for editing and proofing the entire initial manuscript. Naturally, all oversights and mistakes are Yang's. Without their commitments, this project would not have come to fruition.

All three authors of this volume would like to thank the numerous librarians at various libraries and archives who have helped us in so many ways in our research process. We would also like to thank the Shanghai Symphony Orchestra Archive and the Paul Sacher Foundation (PSF) in Basel for letting us reproduce images in their collections. We are also grateful to Fred Lau and Masako

Ikeda, the series editor of Music and Performing Arts of Asia and the Pacific and the executive editor of the University of Hawai'i Press for their feedback on the initial draft of the volume. Most of all, we would like to express our deepest gratitude to the two reviewers who have provided us with insightful comments and suggestions that no doubt have contributed to a better volume in the end. Naturally, nobody but us, the authors, are responsible for any of the mistakes and oversights remaining in the volume. Last we would like to acknowledge the financial support of the General Research Fund (HKBU248813) of the University Grant Council of Hong Kong as well as Hong Kong Baptist University's Department of Music.

Networking the Russian Diaspora

Networking the Musical Communities in Shanghai

SHANGHAI is often regarded as where modern China began. The first cosmopolitan city in China (Howard 2012, 240), it was the cradle of an array of new cultural forms,[1] including Chinese "new music" (*xin yinyue*), music by Chinese composers that combined both Chinese and Western musical mediums and idioms.[2] This music was rooted in Shanghai's colonial past as well as being influenced by the refugees from Europe during the interwar period, who came due to the city's no-passport or visa-control policy, both of which coincided with China's quest for modernity after the New Culture Movement in 1919. In Marcia R. Ristaino's study of refugees in Shanghai, she refers to the city as the port of last resort, an unlikely locale for European refugees to call home (2000, 2001). Yet the Russian-speaking community alone was estimated to be around thirty thousand in the mid-1930s, joined by more than eighteen thousand Central European Jews after 1937 (Ristaino 2001, 5). Refugee musicians brought with them their cultural heritage, musical skills, and practices that not only enriched Shanghai's cultural scene at the time but also made an impact on China's music development. A case in point can be gleaned from a concert report titled "Concert of the Young Pianist" in the Russian newspaper *Shanghai Zaria* dated May 12, 1935, devoted to the Chinese pianist Tin Shande's (Ding Shande 丁善德) recital at the New Asia Hotel held the day before (Kontsert molodogo kitaiskogo pianista 1935, 13).[3]

That a Russian newspaper reported Ding's concert is important, as it was a testimony to the impact of migration. Ding was a student of the National Conservatory studying with the renowned Russian pedagogue Boris Zakharov, a Russian émigré in Shanghai at the time. Being the first public piano recital by a Chinese in China, Ding's concert marked an important page in Chinese music history (Dai 1993, 2), and Ding was to become a key figure in China's musical scene a couple of decades later. In the newspaper report, Ding was regarded as technically at ease when playing the works of Beethoven, Chopin, and Liszt. The concert was reported to have "drawn the attention of the Chinese art circle of European inclination, and a large crowd of young Chinese" (Kontsert molodogo kitaiskoko pianista 1935, 13).

Ding's concert was a window into the intricate musical network in Shanghai in the 1930s and 1940s. As mentioned in the newspaper report, in addition to playing works of Western masters, Ding was said to be the first Chinese pianist to play compositions of Alexander Tcherepnin, a Russian émigré composer who had recently been in Shanghai. In addition, Ding also played two short compositions by Ho Rodin (He Luting 贺绿汀), a Chinese musician who had just won a competition organized by Tcherepnin.

The many reports like the one above demonstrate the interconnectedness of Russian émigré musicians with musical activities of other communities in Shanghai. We have thus chosen the notion of "network" to guide the scope and structure of this volume. Network as a theoretical construct has long been adopted by scholars of social research to understand objects that entail complexity,[4] as networks are seen to "defy narrative, chronology and thus also genealogy because they entail a multiplicity of traces" (Loon 2006, 307).[5] Scholars of other disciplines involving music have also used this approach to explore organizational structures, interpersonal connections, and knowledge flow.[6]

The word "network" carries a number of meanings in this volume. As a verb, "network" marks the volume's objective to link the Russian musical activities to its community, but also beyond. As a noun, as in the word's common usage, it means a group or a system of interconnected people or things, the different communities in Shanghai, namely the Russian community, the international community, and the Chinese community. Another usage of "network" draws on the notion of "actor/actant network" in Actor Network Theory; that is, "network" can be any entity, be it human or nonhuman, that can cause actions to take place (see Latour 1996, 2005).[7] This last understanding of "network" directs the volume's focus to two prominent musical institutions in Shanghai, the Shanghai Municipal Orchestra of the international community and the National Conservatory of Music of the Chinese community, which could be seen as two actor networks. At a smaller level, "actor/actant network" refers to the numerous musical events, particularly different types of concerts organized by different institutions and communities, that reveal not only cultural intersections and interactions but also racial relations and identity and power negotiations. Last but not least, the notion of actor network points to two case studies of Russian émigré composers, Alexander Tcherepnin and Aaron Avshalomov, both important human agents that reveal the impact of migration on creativity. Nonetheless, the purpose of this volume is not to test the applicability of network theory, but rather to address the following issues:

- What was music's role in the Russian community and how did it serve the émigrés and musicians alike?
- How did the Russian émigrés interact with the international and Chinese communities through music, with primary focus on two cases: the Shanghai Municipal Orchestra (international) and the National Conservatory (Chinese)?
- What was the impact of migration on creativity, especially the works of émigré composers and concerts highlighting Russian and Chinese musicians?
- What was the Russian émigré musicians' contribution to Shanghai's musical scene and the developmental trajectory of China's music?

Shanghai: The Port of Last Resort

Shanghai's developmental trajectory and its treaty port status were what contributed to the city's receptiveness toward newcomers. Migration as a human phenomenon has a long history, and even the transnational movement of people on a global scale dates back more than a century. For instance, as a result of colonialism, Europeans moved to Africa, Asia, Oceania, and the Americas, while approximately fifteen million slaves were taken from Africa to the Americas (Brickner 2013, 1). From 1870 to World War I, hundreds of thousands of Europeans moved to North America for better economic opportunities (Nugent 1992, 3). Thus the development of Shanghai is a part of the history of global migration connected to colonialism and Western expansion. The burgeoning of nonindigenous musical forms in Shanghai was made possible by this mobility,[8] while the arrival of Russian émigré musicians in the interwar period supplied the fuel for China's modernization in the cultural arena as a result of the New Culture Movement in 1919.

Shanghai, which means "upon the sea," is situated on the banks of the Huangpu (Whampoa) River, which merges with the Yangtze River before it enters the East China Sea about fifty-four miles away (*All About Shanghai and Environs*, 39). It was one of five Chinese treaty ports opened to foreign trade and settlement following the 1842 Treaty of Nanjing after Qing China lost the First Opium War to Great Britain.[9] In just a few years, China signed treaties with America and France, giving their nationals the same rights as those of Great Britain to trade and reside in Shanghai. In 1854, the Shanghai International Settlement overseen by a Municipal Council was formed by these three countries. In 1862, France withdrew from the International Settlement to form its own.[10] As a result, Shanghai in the first part of the twentieth century was governed by three different bodies—the International Settlement, the French Settlement, and the Chinese Settlement—each with quite different political systems, the Chinese Settlement overseeing the Chinese city and greater Shanghai (see figure I.1). The foreign settlements were not limited to settlers of their respective nations, but also those of their colonies as well as nationals of other countries. In fact, Chinese were also allowed to live in the settlements after the Taiping Rebellion (1850–1864) (Tang 2014, 29).

Between 1865 and 1935, Shanghai's census registered nationals of forty-six countries (Wei 1987, 104). Over the years, the foreign settlements grew not only in population, but also in physical size due to Shanghai's political stability and economic prosperity. Shanghai was China's first industrial city with more than 250 factories that included 58 cotton mills and 80 silk filatures as well as cigarette factories employing around three hundred thousand workers at the end of the 1920s (Hsia 1929, 118). For visitors of the 1920s and 1930s, the cityscape of Shanghai—the grand neoclassical buildings at the waterfront, the famous Bund, its busy streets containing vehicles of every possible type, illuminated by neon signs, crowded with cinemas and shops of all kinds, and people with varying ethnic and cultural backgrounds—was an astounding experience. Regarded by many as a haven for adventurers, a place to amass fortune quickly if one was smart enough, Shanghai attracted newcomers who went after opportunities hitherto unavailable elsewhere.[11]

Despite racial/ethnic segregation in early Shanghai (as discussed in Bickers 1998 and 1999), the city was to become more integrated and cosmopolitan after the 1920s. In 1920, the appointment of a Chinese Advisory Committee in the International Settlement was approved at the ratepayers' (taxpayers) meeting, followed by the formation of the Chinese Ratepayers' Association, and in 1925

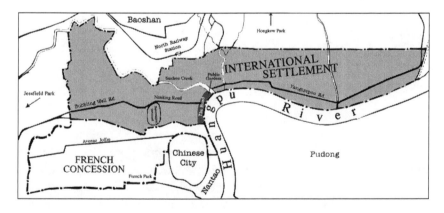

Figure I.1 Map of 1920s Shanghai

both the Town Hall of the Municipal Council and the concerts of the Municipal Orchestra were finally opened to Chinese.[12] In 1928, three Chinese councilors took seats in the Municipal Council, and that number increased to five in 1930. The public parks were also opened to Chinese on the same terms as foreigners in 1928 (*All About Shanghai and Environs*, 209–210).

This was the Shanghai that received hundreds of thousands of Russian émigrés after 1922. Although the Russian émigré community in Shanghai lasted for about a quarter of a century, it was part of a larger movement often referred to as the White Russian emigration, Russian Diaspora, and Russia Abroad (Raymond and Jones 2000, 1). When speaking of Russian emigration, post-1917 émigrés are often called the "first wave," distinguishing them from the émigrés of the World War II-era and the post-1989 emigrations. While many Shanghai Russians were "white Russians" who supported the Bolshevik-opposing White movement in Russia and considered themselves political exiles, many others were politically neutral, or even pro-Soviet. Even so, Shanghai Russians shared many features of what Marc Raeff (1990) called "Russia abroad" regarding the social and institutional structure of the Russian emigration and describing its rich cultural and intellectual life in Paris, Berlin, Prague, and many other European cities.

During the early history of Shanghai, however, the number of Russian residents was limited, only 28 in 1895 and 47 in 1900. Around 1905, 300 Russian Jews came to Shanghai following the pogroms (Wei 1987, 105–106), increasing the number of Russians to 354. This Russian community, which consisted largely of diplomatic personnel, bankers, well-off businessmen, and government officials representing Imperial Russia (Wang Zhicheng 1994, 59), was in stark contrast to the refugee community that expanded quickly after 1922. This large wave of émigrés arriving in Shanghai represented a later stage in Russian post-1917 emigration. The first wave started soon after the February Revolution of 1917, when aristocrats and former government officials left for Finland for fear of persecution,[13] followed by the affluent middle class when living conditions in Saint Petersburg deteriorated. A much-larger-scale emigration took place during the Civil War between 1918 and 1922 (Raymond and Jones 2000, 7). Those who left for Europe were often of a more affluent class, whereas the less well-off journeyed east across Siberia to Vladivostok, then crossed to Harbin when Vladivostok fell to the Bolsheviks in 1920, and some continued south to Chinese treaty ports such as Tianjin and Shanghai (Sergeant 2002, 31–32). When the Civil War began, however, few people residing in Siberia at the time were able to travel to Europe even if they were affluent, as Bolsheviks controlled the railroad. Typically, émigrés lost most of their wealth when they left Russia.

Shanghai was quite different from Harbin, the so-called Russian city in China. Their locations were very different, with Harbin situated close to the

Russian border. Harbin was essentially a Russian city. It developed as a result of Russian influx before 1917, as Harbin was the administrative center of the Chinese Eastern Railway built on the land granted to Imperial Russia in 1898 by the Qing government. Before Harbin became the most highly populated Russian émigré city in the East in the 1920s, 50 percent of Harbin's population, according to the 1913 census, was already Russian (Bakich 1986, 142). The Russian population of Harbin skyrocketed after 1917. According to a 1924 report, the Russian population reached 250,000 and boosted a vibrant city life with burgeoning restaurants, hotels, theaters, Russian-language schools, orthodox churches, and publishing houses (Raymond and Jones 2000, 49). Much of this vigor streamed to Shanghai in the late 1920s, with musicians, actors, ballet dancers, and opera singers moving in from Harbin.[14] These émigrés established orchestras, operas, theaters, ballet and other stage companies, and numerous private music schools that left an indelible mark on Shanghai's cultural scene during the interwar period.

Current Literature, Migration, and Diaspora

There is no doubt that Russian émigrés contributed to Shanghai's fascinating soundscape. Its hybridity, the coexistence of local and imported musical forms, has attracted scholarly attention. As described by Andrew Jones in his seminal work *Yellow Music* (2001):

> What would you hear as you move up and down the dial, sampling from the sonic world of Republican China? The crash of gongs, the plucked strings of a *sanxian*, the rhythmic recitation of drum song, the hypnotic drone of chanted sutras, the sharply nasal syllables of Peking opera? The warble of a Chinese sing-song girl? The lilt of Hawaiian steel guitar? The propulsive swing of big band jazz? Advertisements? Anthems? String quartets? Scholarly lectures? Official pronouncements? Symphony orchestras? In the cacophony of a multiply colonized metropolis of more than 3 million inhabitants, in which well above sixty radio stations operated by the mid-1930s, the answer would surely be all of the above, and much more (21–22).

A similar impression is presented in Joys Cheung's "Chinese Music and Translated Modernity in Shanghai, 1918–1937" (2008), in which she provides a hypothetical tour of the city's musical venues from the Bund to the French Concession, passing through the International Settlement and the Chinese City (84–124). On the Bund was the public park where the Municipal Band played several times a week in the summer. Near Nanking Road, there were two piano retail stores, Robinson Pianos and S. Moultrie & Co., Ltd., the first to sell pianos in China, and there were department stores such as Sincere and Wing On, in which both Western and Chinese instruments were sold. Throughout the city, there were movie theaters with bands that provided music to both imported and local films, and there were many dance halls in hotels, cafes, and restaurants that showcased big band jazz and popular songs. Naturally, there were tea houses and theaters for performances of Chinese music, and likewise, theaters such as the Grand, Carlton, and Lyceum also showcased Western classical music in addition to hosting other nonmusic performances.

Nonetheless, Russian émigrés' contribution to Shanghai's complex soundscape is overlooked in these two studies and likewise in almost all other studies on music in Shanghai, nor is it adequately discussed in studies of Russian emigration. For instance, Raymond and Jones' *The Russian Diaspora: 1917–1941* (2000), despite its broad scope, does not cover Russian emigration in Asia. Likewise, Marc Raeff's *Russia Abroad: A Cultural History* (1990) discusses a number of émigré communities, Harbin among them, but leaves Shanghai uncovered. As he emphasizes, between 1919 and 1939 Russians were residing in different parts of the world, with Chinese cities being among these hubs. Russian émigrés regarded themselves at the time as the other Russia, as opposed to Soviet Russia (Raeff 1990, vii–viii). Ristaino's two studies, "The Russian Diaspora Community in Shanghai" (2000) and *Port of Last Resort* (2001), do provide some information about Russian emigration in Shanghai. Nonetheless, as the sources of Ristaino's monograph rely heavily on the files of the Municipal Police of the International Settlement, her focus shies away from Russian émigrés' diaspora experience, let alone their contributions to Shanghai's cultural scene.

Other more recent studies have begun to emphasize the long-term impact of Russian émigrés on surrounding communities, as their legacies did not simply vanish as Russian émigrés integrated with their host communities or moved forward like the Shanghai Russians. The impact of Russian émigrés has been examined in the European context, especially their literary influences and politics. Part of the Russian emigration was politically active, keen on allying with anti-Soviet forces in their host countries. More culturally oriented émigrés created a flourishing publishing scene, authoring books, journals, and magazines (see for example Slobin 2013). Russian Jewish diaspora and its cultural and political clout in a number of European countries have also been examined in detail by Schulte, Tabachnikova, and Wagstaff (2012). There are also many similarities between this first-wave Russian emigration and the so-called third-wave that left the country after the collapse of the Soviet Union (see for instance Isurin 2011). Common to this body of literature is that it mostly disregards the Russians in China, instead focusing on those in Europe. Mikkonen's recent article (2018), collected in Flamm's (2018) edited volume *Transcending the Borders of Countries, Languages, and Disciplines in Russian Émigré Culture*, is the first English-language literature with Shanghai Russians as its focus.

A limited number of existing studies pertinent to Russian musicians in Shanghai are written in either Chinese or Russian. The three-page journal article by Tszo Chzhenguan in Russian (2000) on Russian musicians in Shanghai that prompted the initiative of this study has been joined by Wang Zhicheng's (2007) seminal volume in Chinese on Russian émigré musicians in Shanghai. Tszo Chzhenguan's (2014) recently published volume in Russian on a similar topic is an answer to the hiatus to an extent. Nonetheless, both have limited circulation serving mostly Russian and Chinese readers. Moreover, while Tszo's volume is largely based on secondary literature, Wang's volume, though it contains a great deal of useful information, falls short of addressing issues such as music's connection to migration, identity negotiation, cultural exchange, and the interconnectedness among different Shanghai communities. In conference proceedings on Sino-Russian musical exchange in Chinese (Tao 2011),[15] the Shanghai Russian émigré musicians are covered in a couple of chapters by scholars who have researched the subject matter, namely Bian Zushan 卞祖善 (2011), Tszo Chzhenguan (Zuo Zhenguan) 左貞观 (2011), Wang Yanli 王艳丽 (2011), and Luo Qin 洛秦 (2011).[16] Yang of this volume has written a survey on Russian musical life in Shanghai focusing on Russian musicians' contribution to Shanghai's musical soundscape (2013). Yet it fell short of examining émigrés' contributions in detail or examining the impact and implication of these activities.

In defining the scope and approach of this study, amid an array of possibilities, one important issue to address was the role of music in the Russian community—or diaspora—in Shanghai. The word "diaspora" (Greek διασπορά) means to scatter like seeds over a large area while retaining a common religion, language, and cultural heritage (Vertovec 2000, 2), an experience that has been associated with the dispersion of the Jewish people. Nonetheless, the term's usage is often conflated with "migration," "minority," and "transnationalism" (Tölölyan 1996, 3). "Diaspora" is not limited to the Jewish experience, but can be applied to any dispersed group of voluntary and involuntary migration that occurs as a result of, in James Clifford's (1994) words, "decolonisation, increased immigration, global communication and transport—a whole range of phenomena that encourage multi-locale attachments, dwelling, and travelling within and across nations" (306). The many émigré communities' adopting the term as a form of self-identification and also the significant amount of academic discourse the term has attracted have rendered it as "one of the buzzwords of the postmodern age" (Cohen 1999, 3).

Martin Baumann argues that "diaspora" can refer to three different dimensions of displacement: (1) the process of becoming scattered, (2) the community living in the foreign land, and (3) the *place* or *space* shared by the dispersed groups as a larger imagined community (Baumann 1995, cited in Vertovec 2000, 2). Robin Cohen has summarized nine features of diaspora as follows: (1) traumatic dispersal from an original homeland, (2) settlement in places beyond the homeland, (3) dispersed group(s) sharing a collective memory of the homeland and its past, (4) collective commitment to the maintenance of the memory of the homeland, (5) longing for a return to the homeland, (6) sustained consciousness of ethnic identity and distinctiveness, (7) troubled relationship with host society, suggesting a lack of acceptance, (8) a sense of empathy and solidarity toward coethnic members in other settlements, and (9) the possibility of a creative and enriching life in a tolerant host society (1997, 26).

In several studies on Russian emigration after the October Revolution, the word "diaspora" has been invoked. Titling their monograph *The Russian Diaspora: 1917–1941*, Raymond and Jones (2000, 3) define their subject matter as Russian citizens of the pre-1917 Russian Empire, educated in Russia, departing after 1917, and whose cultural self-definition and loyalty were primarily to the old Russia. Ristaino argues that, like the Central European Jews in Shanghai, the Russian community in Shanghai was a victim diaspora. Russian refugees suffered from nostalgia for their homeland and they made it their mission to ensure the preservation of Russian culture by "building churches, opening schools, and establishing newspapers and journals. They sponsored and participated in literary and musical societies, theater groups, and other cultural events" (2001, 4).

While there is no doubt that the Russian community in Shanghai was a part of the Russian diaspora, one must not overlook its complexities and the many factions within it. Not only was there a divide between the old and new émigrés, there were also ethnic divisions between Russians, Jews, and other Russian-speaking émigrés from Imperial Russia's neighboring states. These ethnic divisions grew in importance during the 1920s and 1930s. There were also political divides, like the pro-Empire émigrés versus the pro-Soviet ones.[17] Different professional and social backgrounds and places of origin could also set émigrés apart.[18] The Russian composers Alexander Tcherepnin and Aaron Avshalomov, to be examined in chapters 6 and 7, exemplify this variety. Avshalomov was a Russian Jew who grew up in Siberia, whereas Tcherepnin was an ethnic Russian, a short-term sojourner in Shanghai, who grew up in Saint Petersburg.

A recent study titled *Russian Émigré Culture: Conservatism or Evolution*, edited by Christoph Flamm, Henry Keazor, and Roland Marti (2013), also articulates the complexities of Russian emigration in relation to cultural production. Russian émigré cultures were defined by different waves of emigration. In each of the waves, artists of the same group from the same period, having been exposed to similar influences, tended to produce cultural products marked by uniquely identifiable features. Thus, Flamm, Keazor, and Marti's volume argues that whether to see "the Russian diaspora as an entity may depend on periodization" (3), as even though the Russians abroad during the interwar period, as pointed out by Raeff (1990, 5), were less willing to assimilate for fear of denationalization, later émigrés were more willing (3).

Our perception of Shanghai's Russian community does not concur with Raeff's (1990) observation. In addition, our research also leads us to question Cohen's (1997) notion of diaspora as a closely knit group sharing a common interest to the extent it may have troubles with its hosting society (26). While this may be true for some of the Shanghai Russians, we will argue that the majority of Shanghai Russians felt at ease in their adopted home, and, at the same time, they also felt they were a part of the larger worldwide Russian diaspora rather than an isolated group in an estranged locale.

Some of the issues raised in *Russian Émigré Culture* (Flamm, Keazor, and Marti 2013) are thought provoking. One is the need to define as well as redefine "Russian émigré culture," because what are taken as Russian boundaries have changed dramatically over the years and because "émigré culture" is itself an elusive concept (3). The other is the pitfall of taking Russian émigré culture to be just the study of Russian literature and the current research's overt focuses on its political implication. Such an approach, Flamm, Keazor, and Marti's volume argues, would result in a distorted understanding of what Russian émigré culture really is (4–5). While focusing on the various "texts" in literature, art, and music, the volume also brings up issues such as conservation versus evolution and émigré identity versus state identity (8–12).

Even though Shanghai is beyond the scope of the above volume, the sociopolitical function of culture, especially music, in defining and providing cohesion to Russian communities abroad is a theme overlooked. Various studies have underlined that music plays an important role in the formation and maintenance of diaspora (Myers 1998; Collins 2010). For example, Martin Stokes proclaims, "[music] provides means by which people recognize identities and places, and the boundaries which separate them" (1994, 5). Natalie Zelensky, in her study of the Russian diaspora in New York, regards music as crucial in the social processes of constructing a diaspora in four ways: "1) constructing an imagined community; 2) creating, negotiating, and dissolving social boundaries; 3) preserving 'authentic' culture; and 4) performing multiple and, potentially, contested diasporic identities" (2009, 3). Music is also a means for diaspora to engage in power negotiation, as in the case of Asian Americans living in New York (Wong 2004; Zheng 2010). For them, diaspora becomes "a new analytical category with which we take part in current discourses in cultural politics, and a new empowering consciousness for many people struggling in their everyday lives to live with, claim, and belong to multiple cultural identities" (Zheng 2010, 28).

For the Russian community in Shanghai, music served various purposes, and many different types of music were practiced by Russian musicians for different purposes. In a way, it is not too far-fetched to suggest that music has played a symbolic role in connecting Russians abroad within their own community as well as globally. On the one hand, music has served to hold the many diverse Russian groups in a particular community together. On the other hand, accomplished émigré musicians and well-recognized compositions by émigré composers have often been treated as symbols of Russian culture with which Russians abroad identified. Most of all, in the case of Shanghai, music also let Russian émigrés reach out to other communities, and they have left an impact on Chinese musical development, as the rest of this volume will show. Even though most of the émigrés' music activities were originally intended to serve the Russian community, they ended up attracting participants from other communities. For instance, a charity concert of Tchaikovsky's music was held for the benefit of the Union of Russian Army and Navy Men and the Russian Benevolent Society on February 23, 1929. Interestingly, in the concert, Russian soloists were accompanied by the Municipal Orchestra, not led by its regular conductor but instead by the Russian émigré A. G. Slutsky. Most of all, the concert drew a large audience and was reported in detail in Shanghai's English-language newspapers ("Russian Charity Concert" 1929, 12; "Tchaikovsky Memorial Concert" 1929, 17), suggesting its impact far beyond the diaspora.

In fact, the Russian émigrés were aware of their cultural capital. They often openly criticized Shanghai's cultural void or the Municipal Council's lack of support for musical endeavors despite the city's golden and silvery bank buildings (Kul'turnyia zadachi Shankaia 1929, 2). Increased public support for musical activities was potentially beneficial for the Russian community in general. Thanks to the arrival of Russian intelligentsia and musicians after 1929, Shanghai became a hub of Western culture in the 1930s. Even the renowned British ballerina Margot Fonteyn remembered fondly the cultural scene in Shanghai, where she spent part of her teenage years dancing under the tutelage of Russian ballet masters Georgy Goncharov and Eduard Elirov. As she recalled, there were several dancing schools, amateur dramatic societies, and occasional visiting artists (Fonteyn 1998, 101).

Fonteyn's memoir focused only on dance, which was only a small piece of the high cultural scene in Shanghai, largely dominated by Russians. There were many concerts and other forms of musical activities by the Municipal Orchestra as well as by other professional and amateur musicians. Most memoirs from interwar Shanghai take these features for granted and rarely bring them up.

While there have been a number of studies on the Shanghai Municipal Orchestra (SMO) (Han 1995; Enomoto 2009; Bickers 2001; Tang 2014; Pang 2015), but none pays extra attention to the importance of the Russian players. Wang Yanli's studies (2010, 2015) are an exception in that she provides an analysis of the proportion of Russian works in the SMO's repertoire.

Our archival research deepens our understanding of the role played by Russians in the SMO. The institution's hiring practices indicate that Russian musicians were sometimes treated unfairly. Intricacies of concert programming for the SMO also reveal the Russian factor. Most of all, the Russians' greatest musical impact was their teaching, as a handful of pedagogues were responsible for nurturing the first generation of the People's Republic of China's (PRC's) key musical figures. Even though the subject matter has been covered in Yang's earlier article (2012) on Russian pedagogues at the Shanghai Conservatory, further research in this volume underlines how important the Russian influence actually was.

The relationship between migration and culture is intricate. If we accept that culture(s) have indeterminate boundaries, that cultures are being constantly reinvented and renegotiated (Cohen and Jónsson 2011, xxvii), and that cultures are borderlands of contact zones (Clifford 1997, 8) in which migration plays an important part, we are able to see how culture and migration intersect. As suggested by Cohen and Jónsson, migrant imaginaries developed by the migrants could spread to the surrounding societies and communities. Migrants could use their own cultural forms as a means of authentication, through which they could perform and express their origins, journeys, and experiences and which could have an impact on the surrounding cultures in unexpected ways. As a result, culture becomes hybrid and shows fusions and mixings (2011, xxvii).[19] Cohen and Jónsson also note that "[b]ecause of the possibility of living in bilocal or transnational space, diasporic practices connecting home and away, origin and destination, established or newly acquired cultural practices, can thrive *simultaneously*" (2011, xxvii). In a way, the creative paths of the two émigré composers Tcherepnin and Avshalomov, who had contacts with Shanghai and whose compositions demonstrated Chinese elements, were testimonies to the impact of cultural contacts, and their works were a product of transnationalism.

Last but not least, the intricate relationship between migrant culture and that of the host state, and the resulting contestation, negotiation, synthesization, and hybridization, are not to be taken lightly. Unfortunately this is still an underdeveloped area of migration study. Because of this lack in current literature, our approach in this volume is from the perspective of cultural contact and contact zones and the notion of networks that link them.

Volume Importance and Chapter Summary

Our volume treads mostly uncharted territory in both its subject matter and research methodology. Interdisciplinary in nature, it incorporates musical, cultural, and diaspora studies into a social history of cosmopolitan Shanghai, bringing together fields of musicology, ethnomusicology, social history, and cultural and migration studies. It demonstrates how Russian émigré culture formed and operated in Shanghai, adding to knowledge about Russian émigrés musicians, many of whom are forgotten due to their émigré identity. In addition, it provides insight into how émigré cultures integrate, assimilate, oppose, challenge, and contribute to the adopted culture. Furthermore, it shows how Russian musicians and musical activities played an important role in shaping the dialogues between Chinese and Western music, thus shedding light on Russian influence on Western musical development in China that has been overlooked in current literature, especially in the West.

Our volume also takes the view that music is not merely about musical texts, compositions, and notes. It is also about musicians and performances delivered through various types of institutions, and it is about material objects such as concert advertisements, programs, and reviews, agencies that reveal identity and power negotiations. Even though our volume's subject matter is ethnomusicological, focusing on various forms of musical behaviors and practices across different communities in Shanghai, our research methodology is musicological, relying almost exclusively on archival sources. We have interpreted our sources in light of critical theories, thus rendering the study a sociocultural history of networked music institutions, musicians, compositions, and performances.

Most of all, our volume demonstrates the impact of cross-cultural encounters on both Russian and Chinese communities. It shows how Russian émigré composers' synthesis of Western and Chinese elements have become models and inspirations for the next generation of Chinese composers and have paved the way for the development of Chinese new music and Western intercultural music. This music would further flourish throughout Asia and other parts of the world after the second half of the twentieth century with the worldwide migration of soloists, composers, ensembles, media, and other musical objects. Shanghai thus served as a rare, early microcosm for the East-West interaction that has since occurred on a larger scale as a result of globalization.

Divided into three parts, the original research as well as the writing have been conducted primarily by each of the authors, Simo Mikkonen for the first part, Hon-Lun Yang for the second, and John Winzenburg for the third. We have then taken extra efforts to cross-read and rewrite collectively to ensure as best we can the volume's narrative and stylistic coherence.

The first part (chapters 1 and 2) focuses on the Russian community and its inner workings. Chapter 1 opens with an advertisement of musical activities at a Russian restaurant, which signals the complexity of Russian identity. The chapter discusses the sociocultural nature of Shanghai's Russian emigration. It explains who the Russian émigrés were, where they came from, what views they held regarding their motherland and their cultural heritage, what challenges they confronted in the process of displacement, how they met with the difficulties arising from emigration, and, finally, what happened to them with the founding of the PRC in 1949. The next chapter opens with a newspaper report of a Russian New Year's ball that begins the discussion about different forms of Russian musical activities. First, the chapter traces the activities of various Russian organizations that often seem to be related to the diaspora but were typically more than that. It shows that (1) these music organizations were quite diverse, and many of them were fairly short-lived, (2) musicians' attitudes fluctuated and whether one was cosmopolitan or diasporic is often difficult to define, and (3) even though these émigré music societies were meant to be diasporic, serving émigrés' needs, they were often of interest to non-Russians of Shanghai, and their musical activities became cosmopolitan in nature. Finally, the chapter argues that many of the musical activities of the Russian community served to reach out to other communities, which accounted for Shanghai's prosperous musical scene and cosmopolitan soundscape in the interwar period and introduced Shanghai to Western musical idioms, sometimes never before seen.

The second part (chapters 3 to 5) discusses Russian musical activities from the perspective of Shanghai's international community and Chinese community by focusing on two cultural pillars: the Shanghai Municipal Orchestra (SMO) and the National Conservatory of Music. Chapter 3 opens with Tcherepnin's commendation of the SMO, which employed many Russian musicians as players and soloists. While describing Russian musicians employed by the SMO, the chapter also reveals how unfairly they were often treated. Despite the occasional tension between SMO conductor Mario Paci and some of the Russian musicians, it argues that the availability of the Russian musicians and the music-loving Russian community were crucial for the success of the SMO, which in turn became a tool of power negotiation for the Russian community. Chapter 4 begins with a newspaper report of a special Russian concert of the SMO, which allows us to look into SMO's concert programs and unravel the contributions made by the Russian musicians as well as the economic motivation behind the Russian-inclined programming of the SMO.

Chapter 5 opens with an article about the Russian pedagogue Boris Zakharov and his two Chinese students, that leads into the exploration of Russian musicians' activities at the National Conservatory of Music. In addition to identifying Russian educators and their respective students, the chapter analyzes their relationships as reconstructed from Chinese musicians' memoirs and writings. Finally, it demonstrates the Russian musicians' profound impact on the development of Western music performance in China through tracing the accomplishments of Russian pedagogues' Chinese students. Special attention is given to the performances of these students with the SMO, which were often viewed by Chinese with a nationalistic sentiment, a sense of triumph, as the institution was once a colonial icon inaccessible to Chinese.

The third part of this volume (chapters 6 and 7) consists of two case studies of Russian émigré composers. It moves the focus from the émigré community and social constructions to individuals. This part reflects on the cultural and human contact in the process of migration and the ways individuals moved between different cultures in their creative works. Chapter 6 opens with a Chinese student's impression of Tcherepnin playing his Chinese-flavored compositions, treating Tcherepnin as an actor moving between different networks. The four sets of his piano compositions from 1934 to 1937, namely the *Piano Study on the Pentatonic Scale* (without opus) and op. 51, op. 52, and op. 53, are products of "translation," a result of Tcherepnin's treading outside the Russian network and forming connections with intelligentsia in the Chinese community. His Chinese connections in turn had consequential impacts on the future networks he was going to engage. He left his first wife and patron to be with the Chinese pianist Lee Hsien Ming, whom he met at the National Conservatory. This forced him into a new path in which his migratory Russian émigré identity faced new kinds of influences. Most importantly, his new Chinese networks gave him the opportunity to inspire Chinese students to search for a musical language that would create a synergy of Chinese and Western elements. This had a profound impact on Chinese musical development in the twentieth century.

Chapter 7 opens with an article on the SMO concert "Grand Chinese Evening," which introduced the Russian-Jewish émigré composer Aaron Avshalomov. In contrast to Tcherepnin, Avshalomov, who came from a very different background, engaged in different Shanghai networks for more than a decade. His experimentation in synthesizing Chinese and Western musical as well as dramatic elements in his works and his attempt to symphonicize Chinese music were unprecedented acts with profound implications. Through looking into some of his works that could, due to their innovation, be regarded as a different form of "translation," this chapter unravels the different networks surrounding them. Most of all, it assesses the implications of the composer's innovations for the developmental trajectory of contemporary Chinese music.

The volume closes with an epilogue. We first revisit music's role in diaspora by highlighting how music connected individuals and communities in Shanghai, thus proposing a new understanding of diaspora against the classic one. Then we reflect on the importance of our study's contribution to "relational musicology," not only in our volume's subject matter, but also to the collaborative approach we have adopted. Last we look into how politics in both the former USSR and the PRC had led to the "disappearance" of the Shanghai Russian émigrés in dominant discourse of Russian and Chinese music prior to the 1980s, and then how the study of Sino-Russian music relations is taking a new turn in recent years.

CHAPTER 1

Between Limbo and a Haven

THE RUSSIAN ÉMIGRÉ COMMUNITY IN SHANGHAI

It was January 13, 1928, in Shanghai's French Quarter. People were packing into a Russian restaurant named Кавказ (Kavkaz, Caucasus in English). Despite its Russian name, written in Cyrillic above the entrance, not everyone in line was Russian. French and English, at least, could be easily spotted. Even though it was not the last day of the year, it was a celebration of New Year according to the Julian calendar used by the Russian émigré community for religious and festive purposes.

That night, Caucasus was sold out, just like many other Russian restaurants in Shanghai. Newspaper reports indicated parties continuing deep into the night, with abundant artistic programs merged with luscious meals prepared by the finest Russian chefs in traditional style combined with European trends of the time. The artistic program was a combination of traditional Russian fare with gypsy choirs and patriotic songs joined with ballet performances and exotic dances. Finally, a foxtrot orchestra would continue with the most modern dance music available anywhere ("V 'Kavkaz'" 1928, 4).

In the beginning of the 1920s, Russians were a small minority in Shanghai, hardly worth mentioning among the many European nationalities populating the international areas of the vast city. After 1922, however, Russian refugees began to migrate to Shanghai, already forming an influential—and distinct—section of Shanghai's population by the late 1920s.

As the reports of the Russian New Year's celebrations in 1928 allude to, it had already become a staple in Shanghai's yearly party schedule. This Russian tradition, which included all kinds of extravaganzas such as artistic performances, music, and dance, was warmly embraced by Shanghai's upper social strata. Reports of Russian New Year's celebrations like the one above were published yearly, and they grew both in number and size every year throughout the late 1920s and 1930s.

These reports contain revealing features that give us hints about Russians in Shanghai. For example, the programs of these celebrations featured typical Russian musical genres that hardly existed outside Russian circles. Of these, one of the most popular types was gypsy music, which was regarded as much a Russian genre as it was gypsy. The music performed was a combination of traditional and composed tunes. The performers might be either formally educated or self-trained, and they were typically either ethnic Russians or Russian gypsies. Yet these traditions had appeal beyond the Russian community in Shanghai. Russian romances, Russian author songs, and other popular genres drew audiences from other Shanghai communities as well.

Such a mixing of traditions related directly to Russian identity. The program of the New Year's festivities featured genres popular in prerevolutionary Russia, reflecting Russians' desire to preserve older customs and tunes that were familiar to them. In this sense, nostalgia for an imagined Russia was an important feature for the Shanghai dwellers. But it was also typical to have foxtrot and jazz bands as part of these celebrations, suggesting that mixing different traditions was fundamental to the social landscape. The presence of the strong gypsy tradition (not to mention those of other cultures, like Ukrainian, Jewish, and other groups considered to be part of their community by Shanghai Russians) also underlines the difficulties in defining a precise Russian identity for this population.

This single New Year's celebration thus reflects wider questions about the Russian émigré community in Shanghai: Who were the Shanghai Russians, and where did they come from? What was the sociopolitical profile of this community? And how did the émigré mindset translate into new roles within cosmopolitan Shanghai? This chapter provides an overview of the Russians in interwar Shanghai. It describes the demographics of the émigré population and what social systems and political orientations they brought with them. It also examines how life outside of Russia resulted in new gender roles and participation in the Shanghai underworld before historical forces led to a dispersion of the Russian émigré community. By examining the overall profile of the Shanghai Russians, we can better understand the nature of Russian musical activities in the semicolony to be discussed in the chapters to follow.

Mobility and Mindset in Emigration

The mobility of artists in general was very much visible in Shanghai. While the 1920s were colored by brief visits and extended stays of numerous artists, from the end of the 1920s onward, Shanghai became a magnet for artists throughout East Asia. Artists not only visited Shanghai, but an increasing number of Russians decided to join the Russian and artistic communities of Shanghai.

The conditions in which Russians lived and in which they were forced to operate changed in Shanghai over several decades. These conditions were greatly influenced by the general course of developments in Shanghai and Asia, which impacted the influx of Russians to Shanghai in the 1920s and the 1930s and finally leading to the large-scale outflow after World War II.

Throughout the 1920s and the 1930s, many Russian artists kept moving back and forth particularly between Harbin and Shanghai, but also on tours throughout East Asia and India. There were also occasional announcements in Russian-language newspapers of artists who emigrated either to Europe, the United States, or Soviet Russia. Even though there were those who returned to the Soviet Union before 1945, in the run-up to World War II, the main direction of Russians was away from the Soviet Union, particularly from Harbin to Shanghai. In the 1920s, Harbin was the indisputable center of Russian influence in China, but from the 1920s onwards, Shanghai became the most important Russian center in the whole of East Asia. Apart from a few isolated exceptions, Shanghai Russians had been in different parts of Siberia at the time of the Revolution and therefore had been unable to move west when Bolsheviks took over Siberia. Thus they moved over the border to the closest Russian colony, which was Harbin.

It is difficult to gather information regarding how much the dispute between the Soviet Union and China over Manchuria, particularly the Sino-Soviet conflict of 1929,[1] increased the Russian influx from Harbin to Shanghai. But without question, the situation in Harbin gradually worsened in the eyes of many Russians. According to existing statistics, forty to one hundred Russians arrived daily, registering with the Russian Emigration Committee of Shanghai. Registering was not compulsory, but it helped in getting entitlements and identification documents needed for further travel. These statistics, however, must have been from the worst days, as the total number of arrivals to Shanghai rarely exceeded 2,000 a year. Yet the figure is still high. According to Victor Grosse, who headed the committee, in 1929–1931 a total of 5,106 Russians entered Shanghai and registered with the émigré committee he headed (Van 2008, 90).

But numbers had already been high before 1929, and they stayed high throughout the 1930s. With the Japanese invasion of Manchuria, partisan activities of the Chinese, and growing tension between Japan and the Soviet Union, Harbin kept leaking new Russian émigrés to Shanghai in the following years as well. In the summer of 1934 alone, 2,885 Russians and 292 Soviet citizens moved to Shanghai (Van 2008, 91). Individual conflicts, such as the one in 1929, do not appear to have led to huge yearly increases in movement from Harbin to Shanghai. Rather, the influx increased steadily, and in regards to artistic intelligentsia, it is relatively easy to see why they became concentrated in Shanghai.

The exact number of Russians residing in Shanghai is difficult to ascertain. The core problem is who to count as Russian. Some sources, like Simpson (1938,

156–157), only present statistics of Russian refugees, thus leaving out those that did not register as refugees. Furthermore, since Shanghai was divided into a French Concession, International Settlement, and Chinese administrations, there are not any coherent statistics. Yet when statistics from different sources (Ristaino 2001; Simpson 1938; Wang 1993) are put together, they show at least 2,500 Russians in 1922, and by 1930 the number was at least 13,000. These numbers do not include Jews, who at this point identified mostly as Russians. Whether someone was Russian or Jewish was for many an irrelevant question at the time. Thus many scholars have had problems identifying identities of individual Shanghai Russians (e.g., Goldstein 2015, 147). In 1932, the Russian Émigré Committee announced that there were 15,768 Russians in Shanghai. Yet most of the Jewish Russians did not register with the committee, and there were Russians and other nationalities that did not want to register with the committee. Thus the actual figure was notably higher. After 1932, with the situation in the Far East deteriorating with Japanese aggression, exact statistics are even harder to come by. The Soviets estimated (Ablova 2007, 152) that by 1936 the number of Russians would have been as high as 50,000, but this figure would have included Jews as well. The Soviets were interested in émigré communities since these were considered potentially hostile to the Soviet Union.

From the point of view of Russians, the Sino-Japanese conflicts in 1932 caused major changes, especially in Harbin. It is true that Shanghai also briefly became a theater of war, with Japan and China fighting for position in Shanghai. But it was the expansion of Japan in northeast China, where Harbin was located, that caused fundamental changes. It was reported in 1932 that lots of Russians were heading to Dairen (now known as Dalian and the former Russian city of Port Arthur) and Tsindao (Qingdao) on Japanese ships ("Dairen Maru" 1932, 6). In Shanghai, the changes were limited to Japanese being evacuated from Shanghai as part of the conflict, and thousands of soldiers were also moved away ("Tatsan pereshel k kitaitsam" 1932, 6). Even though the 1930s were the "golden era" for the Russians in Shanghai, it was also a decade when war news was common. In 1932 and 1937, Shanghai would become a theater of war between Japan and China. In the spring of 1932, Shanghai experienced a curfew, which severed the rich theater and concert life, since evenings, when performances took place, were off limits. The curfew was apparently repealed at the end of March, since it was announced that a coming Sunday would finally see the premier of the Russian Chamber Theatre's "Korol Veselitsia" ("Pervyi raz . . ." 1932, 4). When the war between China and Japan resumed on an extensive scale in the summer and autumn of 1937, conditions changed further. But it was only with the end of World War II that the position of Russians in Shanghai would be drastically altered. Before that, only a few Russians seriously considered moving to the Soviet Union.

Russian Demographics, Identity, and Ethnicity

Unlike the contemporary definition of Russian ethnicity, when we talk of Russians in Shanghai, we quite often bundle several different ethnicities together. These people were not ethnically homogeneous. Rather, they were made up of several different ethnic groups ranging from Poles and Finns that lived within the old Russian Empire to numerous minorities living in the area that now forms the Russian Federation. In exile, these people did not typically organize along ethnic lines, instead grouping as former subjects of the Russian Empire. The Russian language and the shared past as imperial subjects connected them. Therefore, when an evening of Czechoslovakian culture was held in 1930, for example, the Russian community considered it to be their own; just as any other Russian celebration, this evening was given wide publicity in the Russian-language media ("Chekho-slovtskii muzykal'no-literaturnyi chai" 1930, 3).[2]

Ethnic lines of division were generally not as distinct among this population as were political ones, particularly regarding attitudes toward the then new Soviet Union. Thus, even though Russian emigration to Shanghai included significant numbers of people from other ethnicities—especially Jewish, but also Ukrainian, Polish, and others—the authors of this book do not distinguish between these different groups unless the distinction is important to our research subject. The émigrés of that day did not emphasize ethnic differences, and neither did the local Chinese in Shanghai, who referred to these people collectively as Russians, despite their varying ethnicities. Even Jewish people were treated fairly equally as Russians until the exodus from Central Europe increased in the late 1930s and World War II brought Japanese policies closer to those of their German allies in the early 1940s. Thus, when speaking of Shanghai's Russian émigrés in broad terms, we refer to people of multiple ethnicities who were collectively associated with emigration from the Russian Empire, who spoke Russian, and whose primary reference group was Russian. For example, Aaron Avshalomov (protagonist of chapter 7) was Jewish, and Joseph Podushka (featured in chapter 3) was Polish but was nevertheless considered Russian when in Shanghai.

In some ways, the Russian identity was defined both by what people were (former Russian subjects) and what they were not. Russians were distinct from Shanghai's more powerful Western groups, namely the British, Americans, and French. Russians were regarded as different from Chinese and Japanese, but they were not considered to be equals with Shanghai's Western European elite. These latter groups were accustomed to their privileged status, and even though the colonial days of Shanghai had already started to wane when the Russian influx began, Europeans were still the elite who owned and ruled much of central Shanghai. Russians, however, were more diverse in socioeconomic status; some

Russians were wealthy but most were impoverished after losing most of their possessions as they escaped during and after the Russian Civil War.

Although many of the Russians arriving in Shanghai were educated, the traumatic experience of displacement, loss of homeland, and sudden poverty inevitably left its mark on many émigrés. An initial lack of networks and the continuing influx of new refugees led many Russians to be without work, and help was arranged for them by those who were still doing well. The elderly were reported to be in the direst situation. The Shanghai Russian media tried to remain optimistic, but it also realistically described the plight of some Shanghai Russians. In one such article, *Shanghai Zaria*, the main Russian newspaper, described an old man standing on a corner of the main street (Avenue Joffre), not begging (which was illegal) but trying to sell newspapers and flowers to get his daily bread ("Bez raboty" 1930, 3). The city had not been accustomed to seeing Western beggars before the arrival of Russians, but the sheer size and diversity of the Russian community brought new realities to the international areas of Shanghai.

The key problem for Russian émigrés in Shanghai was the language. Chinese was rarely spoken among Russian émigrés when they first arrived. Perhaps even more importantly, few émigrés spoke English, which was the main business language of Shanghai and the key to obtaining many jobs. French was the most common foreign language spoken by Russians, with German second (Ablova 2007, 84). German was of little use in Shanghai, but French helped some Russians to improve their lives and was among the main reasons that the majority of Russians settled in the French Concession. During the 1930s, more Russians would settle in the International Settlement and even in the Chinese-governed areas, but the heart of the Russian community would stay within the French Concession. Russians also established a number of their own newspapers and magazines that helped to promote a sense of community among Shanghai Russians. Most of these were printed in the French Concession.

Social Stratification

Alongside this demographic profile was a social system that both adhered to and shifted away from Russian social stratification that had existed before large-scale emigration took place. Particularly in the United States, as well as Central and Western Europe, many societies had already been changing before World War I. Industrialization, democratization, and urbanization had undermined the old order throughout those regions. In Russia, the change had proceeded much more slowly than in most parts of the West, and ancestry and rank thus still played big roles in the mindset of the Russian diaspora.

Many from the older generation of Russians in China stuck to old traditions and customs and declined to interact with those of lower ancestry and rank. This, however, was difficult to sustain given the new conditions faced in Shanghai. Some tried to maintain their own privileges by establishing organizations based on former elite class structures. In particular, certain army units adhered closely to their long-held military customs and previously established rank. This was reflected to some extent in Russian musical organizations that will be discussed in the following chapter.

The great majority of subjects of the defunct Russian Empire had been poor rural people who had never been outside their home villages. But these people were not a tangible part of the Russian emigration to Shanghai. The most privileged segment of Czarist Russian society—the wealthy members of the nobility—in most cases moved to Western Europe, Paris in particular. The lesser nobles and urban middle classes who were in Siberia when the Civil War began could not, in most cases, afford the trip to Europe via the Chinese ports, and the Trans-Siberian railroad connecting Asia with Europe was off limits. Instead, they were forced to start anew in Harbin, Shanghai, or some other city outside of Soviet Russia in the East. Typically, these Russians were urban professionals from the middle or upper classes. They were educated and had professions that had originally brought them to Siberia or East Asia. By virtue of upbringing, members of this class were versatile beyond their professional training alone. For this reason, many prominent Shanghai musicians emerged from the ranks of Russian émigrés, not because of a great supply of music professionals entering from Siberia, but rather because arts and music were so valued by the elite class in prerevolutionary Russia. Many people who had some other profession had also been educated in music; they had received extensive lessons in piano or some other instrument because this was considered a mark of civility. In the new context of life in exile, many turned this basic education into a profession.

Political Orientation and Assimilation

If Shanghai Russians were an ethnically and socially diverse lot, the same can be said about their political attitudes in the wake of the Revolution. Even as the Soviet regime tried to portray all Russian émigrés as White Russians whose only wish was to reinstate the monarchy and destroy the new Russia, this was far from reality. Russian traditions, new political realities, and the diasporic nature of the Shanghai Russian community were all on display in their attitudes toward the czar and his family. Those that supported restoration of czarist monarchy in Russia were called monarchists. Shanghai had quite a few people with military backgrounds and some nobility among them that were particularly prone to monarchist tendencies. On the other hand, the multicultural urban metropolis pushed many Russians in another direction.

Even though the monarchy raised mixed feelings, members of the czar's family were treated as celebrities irrespective of political attitudes. For monarchists, Kirill Vladimirovich, who had become the head of the Romanov house after the death of Czar Nicholas II, was the true Russian head of state after his position was legalized in London in 1924. In Shanghai, concerts were occasionally arranged to support the monarchist cause (e.g., "Patrioticheskii kontsert" 1936, 3). Yet monarchists were never in the majority among émigrés, contrary to Soviet claims. Furthermore, even monarchists had constant internal disputes over who was the rightful heir to the throne.

Outside of politics, members of the royal family were like movie stars for Russians, subject to idolization. This became obvious when Kira, daughter of Kirill, arrived in Shanghai in 1938, which was a cause for celebration throughout the Russian community. Her appeal was especially pronounced because she had just married the future pretender to the German throne, Prince Louis Ferdinand of Prussia, who accompanied Kira to Shanghai. The couple stayed at the Cathay Hotel, and their visit was widely reported in Russian-language newspapers. They were called "High Guests" and "Their Highnesses" in press reports, and Kira was also addressed as "Great Princess," following the royal tradition ("Vysokie gosti . . ." 1938, 5). Just as the Russian diaspora was united in its background as subjects of the Russian Empire, the czar's family linked it and transcended differences in political orientation or ideas about the future of Russia. In this way, obedience to the monarchy and adoration of the czar's family were two different things.

Although monarchists did not enjoy widespread popularity, they did manage to rally people behind Russian culture by emphasizing traditions. It could be said that they managed to capitalize on Russian history and culture and on the diasporic mindset of Shanghai Russians. Pushkin, in particular, was used as a rallying point. Yearly celebrations called the "Days of Russian Culture" reached Shanghai in 1925 and expanded from meager beginnings into a great festival by the 1930s. In 1933, Shanghai's Days of Russian Culture featured an official magazine, with its cover filled with emblems of the Russian Empire and Saint George's Order. Imperial heraldry was displayed with pictures of Orthodox churches and "Mother Russia" at the front of the magazine (*K dniu . . .* 1933). The use of imagery from the imperial era was common when trying to bring Russians together, but it was of limited use in the long term or for political purposes.

From a political perspective, a majority of Russians—while not outright monarchists—were united in their belief that Bolshevik rule in Russia was a temporary phase. This did not necessarily lead to political activity, however, and few Russians joined anti-Soviet political groups. But because of this belief, many of the numerous professional and intellectual groups that organized in the 1920s were thought of from the outset as temporary, and many merely waited for the time when they could return to the motherland. This attitude also led Russians to gather around tightly knit groups that made assimilation much harder. Such views, however, waned through the 1920s as Bolsheviks tenaciously maintained their grip on power.

The Shanghai Russian Orthodox Brotherhood's fifth anniversary celebration in the spring of 1928 reflected such changing sentiments. The brotherhood had set as its long-term aim the establishment of a Russian cultural and educational-charitable center in Shanghai. They wanted to establish a Russian cathedral, followed by a school and a hospital. The chairman of the brotherhood, D. I. Kazakov, challenged those who still believed that a return to Russia was imminent. Instead, he advocated measures that would help Russians take root in Shanghai. In Kazakov's opinion, Russians should start educating Chinese locals in Russian language and culture ("Russkii tsentr . . ." 1928, 2). This would ensure better survival of Russian culture and help émigrés assimilate to Shanghai. Russians also wanted to educate their own future generations. The First Russian School appeared as early as December 1921, when a member of the former Russian parliament, Aleksandr Nikolaevich Rusakov, arrived in Shanghai and established the school. He headed the school, at Broadway, Kunping Terrace, until his death on July 13, 1936 ("Konchina . . ." 1936, 9).

The politically important assimilation question continued to be relevant throughout the existence of the Russian community in Shanghai. Schooling, cathedrals, and medical facilities were seen as keys to this dilemma. Concern over Russian youth was constantly voiced, especially for those who were born in exile. The fear was that youth would be diverted away from Russian culture and even language. Therefore, some fiercely called for Russian schools, while others advocated participation in international schools. One of the advocates for internationalism, Boris Boguslavsky, had been accused of being unpatriotic. He in turn claimed that Russians had always dealt with foreign countries and cultures and that it was only natural for Russians to participate in French or English schools (Boguslavsky 1928, 5). Along with a school, two orthodox cathedrals were built. A hospital proved more difficult to come by even though there were a good number of high-profile Russian medical practitioners; Russians discussed the establishment of a medical cooperative as early as 1928 ("Otkliki . . ." 1928, 5). Many questions seemingly not related to political orientation were politicized by Russian émigrés, which often made it difficult to rally all Russians behind a common cause.

Russian Festivals and the Preservation of Heritage

The question of assimilation continuously divided Shanghai Russians, who placed high value in their heritage. Diasporic traits appeared even in those that assimilated, revealed in their choices of musical repertory, for example, and how they hung onto old Russian traditions. Russian émigrés who arrived in Shanghai in the early 1920s found themselves in an alien land without familiar features that would have helped them take root. They quickly formed different associations and organizations together with their countrymen, partly for social reasons but also for preserving their culture and traditions. Russians' yearning for their own culture, as manifested in the important role played by music, were visible within the Russian community of Shanghai early on. Already in 1923, A. P. Kriukov produced a series of Russian songbooks that spanned twelve volumes with twenty to thirty songs per book (Kriukov 1923). These songs were typically sung in the many gatherings and soirees held by Russian organizations in Shanghai. For many Russians, it was culture and arts that helped them to deal with their diaspora experiences and keep them in touch with their native land.

Slowly, Russians created their own spaces, both concrete and imagined, inside the metropolis. Growing Russian influence in Shanghai manifested itself in many ways. Just as the Chinese New Year became an important festival in San Francisco or New York, certain Russian festivals brought their own color to Shanghai of the 1920s and 1930s. In prerevolutionary Russia, Christian Orthodox traditions had played a notable role, and some of the Russian émigrés stuck hard to these traditions. Furthermore, as the Russian Orthodox Church followed the Julian calendar instead of the Gregorian one used by other Western countries, Russian festivities did not coincide with those of other Christians. Thus Russians celebrated Christmas, Easter, and many other holidays later than did the British, Americans, or French. All these had an effect on the wider international community of Shanghai, and music played a role in each of these as well.

Several of the Russian festivals that were at first celebrated only by Russian émigrés were eventually adopted as part of Shanghai's yearly calendar of festivities. Western New Year celebrations that had been important Shanghai social events before the Russians arrived were complemented by the celebration of the Russian New Year on the thirteenth of January. Shanghai had three or four major balls that took place every year and were celebrated by the entire international community of Shanghai. The Russian New Year had become one of these by the late 1920s. A report of the celebration at the Majestic Ballroom, one of the finest in Shanghai, listed numerous nationalities that were present at the ball in 1928. In addition to other European nationalities, there were Chinese celebrities present. Russians liked to compare the Russian New Year with the Chinese one, pointing out how people of other nationalities participated in their celebration too (Serbsky[3] 1928, 3; "Pod novyi god" 1928, 4).

Performers in celebrations for the Russian New Year in 1928 were all Russian, but this was the case with many non-Russian celebrations in Shanghai's Western communities. In non-Russian celebrations, however, Russian music and traditions were combined with classical Western entertainment and jazz ("Pod novyi god" 1928, 4). Balls like the one in Majestic, however, were only for the well-off Russians who could afford to pay the high prices. Other, much more affordable celebrations were arranged in restaurants and clubs popular among Russians, such as restaurant Kavkaz, where tuxedos were not required. One Russian-language newspaper in 1928 could list at least eight places with major celebrations for the Russian New Year ("V 'Kavkaz'" 1928, 4; "V Drugykh mestakh" 1928, 4).

But not everyone was happy about merging Russian traditions with those of Shanghai. Some Russians were worried that genuine Russian culture and old traditions would vanish in the process. One Russian woman, for example, fretted that Russian dances were completely forgotten. She complained that a Russian New Year celebration attended primarily by Russians featured mostly American foxtrots and waltzes ("O tantsakh" 1928, 5). This phenomenon speaks about changing customs and assimilation, but also about strong diaspora experience and the need to preserve Russia as émigrés remembered it. Thus, Russians were changing Shanghai, but at the same time, it necessitated that Russians adapted to local customs. One reason for Russian festivities becoming popular among other communities of Shanghai was the great amount of music and other performing arts featured in them. This was particularly salient with the Shanghai Municipal Orchestra (SMO), especially in connection with Easter, for which special Russian concerts became a staple (see chapter 4).

Reflecting the growing importance and perhaps the ability to negotiate, Russians managed to get concessions and understanding for their different customs. Viktor Grosse, the head of the Russian émigré community and chairman of the Bureau of Russian Affairs, approached Shanghai's Municipal Council with a query as early as in 1925, asking that Russians working for the council be granted a leave for January 7 and 14, which were Christmas Day and New Year's Day in the old Russian calendar. Later, a similar query was put forth by Grosse about Easter processions for May 2. Other Christians had celebrated Easter already four weeks earlier (SMA U-1-3-2859). Easter, Shrove Tuesday, and the beginning of Lent were traditional celebrations in the sense that Russian-language newspapers were filled with advertisements of traditional foodstuffs that were difficult to come by in Shanghai, like buckwheat flour, heavy sour cream (*smetana*), and caviar. Newspapers even had recipes for how to make traditional Easter pancakes (*blinis*) (Cover page 1928; on lent, see Advertisement 1928, 2; "Kak gotovit' bliny" 1928, 6).

New Gender Roles and Employment

Many Russians found jobs in foreign firms, factory work, and service work. Others decided to establish businesses. Yet the one sector in which Russians thrived was that of musical entertainment in Shanghai's numerous restaurants, movie theaters, cabarets, and night life. A Russian magazine, *Kabare*, which represented Russians working in the cabaret industry and restaurants, offers a glimpse to this side of Shanghai's Russian community. The header of the first issue complained that many Russians despised cabaret workers and declined to admit that a large share of Russians in Shanghai got their salaries from cabaret and trades related to it. According to the header, 1,200 women and 200 musicians were currently (in 1933) working full time, and 300 women were working part time in cabarets. It is difficult to say whether these figures included the so-called "dancing girls" (some of whom were prostitutes) and where the figures came from in the first place. Even so, the author emphasized that a majority of the salaries earned from cabaret eventually ended up in the pockets of Russian merchants and that therefore they should not loathe cabaret workers. The author was apparently defending the sizable group of Russian women who worked in Shanghai's night life, a sector that some within the Russian colony considered sinful and disgraceful ("Zhenshchina kabare . . ." 1933, 2).

The discussion about cabaret workers was connected with the changing image and role of women. The traditional idea that women should not work outside the home, which had been the prevailing idea among middle and upper classes in prerevolutionary Russia, was difficult to maintain in Shanghai. In exile, gender roles necessarily experienced some changes. Women's changing roles in the West had a more general impact as well. A picture of the L. Knizhe's Sports Academy published in a Russian magazine *Solntse* introduced women rowing, doing abdominal exercise, and training with a punching bag ("Damskii klass . . ." 1927, 4). Knizhe was an influential strongman and trainer within the Shanghai Russian community, and his gym displaying women was no small affair. Russian newspapers also featured advertisements of several Russian woman professionals, like Larissa Kocherzhinskaia, who was working as a dentist (Advertisement 1936, 4). Finally, advertisements in Russian newspapers and magazines would feature women doing different sports, smoking, and even drinking beer. But the area where the share of women was probably the biggest was music and cabaret, where Russian dancers were present in great numbers.

The status of women was also politicized among the Russian community, which is no surprise, as many other lesser issues became subject to political controversy. The patriotic and anticommunist newspaper *Russkyi Golos* wrote in 1939 about émigré women, emphasizing that while some women assimilated and took root in exile conditions, these were certainly in the minority. The wish of the author was that a majority of Russian women would move back to Russia as soon as it was free again. In addition to those who yearned to return to Russia, the article described others who would not adapt and were constantly angry at prevailing local conditions. Such women did not dream about a new Russia, but lingered in history. The author predicted that such women did not know how to calm down, were selfish, and would burn themselves out. According to the author, Russian women were generally stronger and more stable than men and should be better displayed in literature. They also took care of much of the education of future generations and could convey the necessary Russian patriotism to children. In general, the preservation of Russian culture for the future of a new Russia was an important task where women were seen as having a special role (Ol'chenko 1939, 4).

Even though Russian women seemed to see their situation gradually improve in comparison with men as they moved to Shanghai, there were also negative phenomena related to many of these developments. The independence of women was not always of their own choice but might have resulted from their husbands abandoning them, sometimes with children to raise while working in a foreign environment. Furthermore, the cabaret and restaurant industries, in particular, were not the most desirable working conditions, since they involved a lot of crime, exploitation, and wrongdoing, even though they also created opportunities for work for Russian women.

The End of Russian Shanghai

One remaining important question about Shanghai Russians is their eventual fate. After 1949, because of the Chinese civil war, Russian Shanghai ceased to exist. All remaining Russians were evacuated from Shanghai, but the decline of the Russian colony had begun earlier. Since this decline had a major influence both on the musical activities of Russians in the late 1940s and also on how the Russian influence is remembered (or forgotten) in Shanghai, it is important to take a look on the final years of Russian Shanghai before moving deeper into the musical activities of Shanghai Russians.

A majority of Shanghai Russians had long been wary of the Soviet Union and its aims. Soviet policies toward émigrés and anti-émigré propaganda did not help the situation, even though it was mostly directed against anti-Soviet political groups. Attitudes toward Japanese were more mixed, with anti-Soviet groups being the closest to Japanese, usually because they saw Japan as a counterforce to the Soviet Union in East Asia. Yet it was the increasing Soviet influence and communist threat that the Russian émigré community in Shanghai was most worried about in the 1930s. The Soviet consulate had existed in Shanghai throughout the 1920s, but the rise of fascism in Europe had its impact on Shanghai Russians as well, and it led to establishment of different fascist-leaning groups and parties. At the same time, Soviet activities in China and Shanghai increased.

Before World War II, few Russians in Shanghai had any plans—and even fewer realized them—to move to the Soviet Union. But this does not mean that there were none. When artists who had become popular among Russians in Asia were going back to the Soviet Union, it was always big news ("Teatralnaia Khronika" 1935, 15; "Khudozhestvennaia Khronika" 1935, 18). Based on the small amount of information that reached Harbin and Shanghai, *Evening Zaria*[4] reported that the fates of those who had returned to the Soviet Union had not been happy; they had little money or chance to make a decent living ("Neveselya dela" 1936, 4). Occasional news of people going back to the Soviet Union that surfaced during the 1930s was always controversial. The Russian media typically underlined the sad fates of those who returned, but information was difficult to get, and letters very rarely arrived. Some of those who returned in the 1930s were artists, and their return was discussed among those that stayed in Shanghai.[5] Not everyone was happy in Shanghai, either, with many missing their homeland, especially if they were not opposed to the Bolsheviks and they saw demand for their skills in Soviet Russia. Feelings of nostalgia and yearning might have played a role as well.

Especially from the mid-1930s, purges and Stalinist terror in the Soviet Union were directed particularly harshly toward "foreigners." This meant either people from nations considered suspicious, like Germans, Poles, or Finns who had been living in Soviet Russia, or those that had lived abroad at some point, like émigrés. Accusations directed against these groups usually named them as foreign spies, which could lead to decades-long camp sentences or outright execution. But this was something Shanghai Russians could only hear rumors about.

One of the foremost Shanghai Russian authors, Pavel Severny (1900–1981),[6] wrote a story in which he described the mentality among Russian émigrés, how especially in the spring Russian émigrés would yearn to go back to Russia but feared they would die in exile without a chance to see their motherland again. His story suggested that these sentiments were not typical among the youth, who had never actually seen Russia, or those who had left as children (Severny 1935a, 24). He continued along the same lines during Easter of 1935 by praising his motherland, which he considered to be the best in the world, and questioning their life in the huge city (Severny 1935b, 24). Severny, like many others, depicted the situation of Russian émigrés in terms of a controversial diaspora, speaking of Russian emigration as a singular entity, a people without a land who have lost their motherland forever. This, naturally, was not the case. There was always the choice of returning, a chance taken by many after 1945, Severny himself among them. But many more chose not to return, either because they lacked such nostalgic memories about Russia or because they were convinced that Bolshevik Russia was a place they did not want to live. They saw Shanghai as their new home. The war, however, changed everything.

Ablazhei (2007, 161–170) describes the Sovietization of the emigration in China after World War II. The change did not happen overnight but was gradual, increasing on a monthly basis. Not all the émigrés resisted this development. The Soviet strategy included establishing schools and providing support for organizing émigrés into associations, which either were or became pro-Soviet. Schools were established, for example, and were operated by societies of Soviet citizens. Other Soviet associations for sports and culture followed suit, and they expanded their activities in the latter part of the 1940s. Musicians and music were, likewise, used to propagate the benevolence of the Soviet government (Ablazhei 2007, 167–168).

This Soviet strategy aimed to repatriate all Russian émigrés from Shanghai back to the Soviet Union. Due to the postwar situation, it was a slow process and results could have been better, from the Soviet point of view, if they had been able to capitalize on the enthusiasm right after the war garnered by the Soviet victory over Nazi Germany. Repatriation only began in earnest, however, in the summer of 1947. On June 30, 1947, the timetable for the repatriation was finally announced in pro-Soviet newspapers *Novosti Dnia* and *Novaia Zhizn*. The same day, there was a meeting of 7,000 people in the local stadium attended by all major Soviet officials (Ablazhei 2007, 170). The first major boatload left Shanghai for the Soviet Union on the steamer *Ilich* on August 10, 1947. On board were 569 families, with 966 adults and 185 children under the age of sixteen, totaling 1,151. The *Ilich* picked up a second group of emigrants on September 5, this time 1,235 people in all, including 1,028 adults and 207 children. A third group was picked up on October 18 (1,105 people: 922/182), and a fourth embarked on November 8 with 746 people (635/129). A fifth group then left on November 30, 495 in all (414/81). In all, 4,750 people from 2,257 families, including 785 children, were taken back. From other cities, Tianjin, Beiping (Beijing), and Qingdao, there were 1,318 who returned. That 80 percent of the returning emigrants came from Shanghai shows that Shanghai was the center of the émigré community (Ablazhei 2007, 178). Harbin was a special case because Soviet troops were stationed there. Unlike in Shanghai, returning from there did not take place only on a voluntary basis.

Individual stories of Russian émigrés are difficult to come by, but figures of Russians returning to the Soviet Union indicate that a great majority of Shanghai Russians decided to move onward from Shanghai instead of returning to the Soviet Union. Among artists, however, there were more who decided to repatriate. It is difficult to follow the life stories even of persons who were staple names of Shanghai's artistic scene. Many of these people simply vanished sometime after the late 1940s. Many of them certainly continued their lives somewhere outside of Shanghai but not as the stars they used to be. Some of the most notable musicians in Shanghai, like cabaret singers Alexander Vertinsky and Vladimir Shushlin, whose life will be covered further in following chapters, eventually returned to the Soviet Union. Others, who were either anti-Soviet or who were otherwise uncertain about moving to the Soviet Union, decided to wait and see what would happen in China. Soon after Soviet repatriation efforts, the communists seized power, and by 1949 Russians had to leave. The problem for these Shanghai Russians was that initially no country was willing to accept more than a few, and only those who had family abroad or particularly desirable skills. The majority of émigrés had to stay in Shanghai until it was about to fall to the communists. At that point, the international community, through the United Nations, arranged for the evacuation of the remaining Russians. Most of those were transferred to the remote Philippine island of Tubabao, where they had to wait for up to two years before they found their destinations. Eventually, a majority of Shanghai Russians ended up on the west coast of the United States, but some had to make a detour of some years through countries of Latin America before migrating to the United States in the late 1950s and early 1960s. Those who had money had already emigrated to the United States or Australia earlier. Thus, from 1945 through 1949, Shanghai Russians were dispersed once again, with a smaller part returning to the Soviet Union and the rest re-emigrating by 1949 as the Chinese Communist Party took over Shanghai and mainland China. The United States, Australia, Canada, Israel, and several countries of Latin America became new host countries for these Russians. For this reason, their story is mostly forgotten.

Russian Shanghai shone for a quarter of a century. Russians were an important part of Shanghai's fabric, and, though they were active in many areas, the area where they left perhaps the most lasting mark was music. While this chapter has dealt with only the general societal fabric and organization of Russians in Shanghai, it is nonetheless important for understanding the Russian influence over Shanghai, as well as the Russian period in general, which has since been lost to us for numerous reasons. Many Russians were destitute when they arrived in Shanghai and hardly spoke any of the local languages. Building a life from scratch was a reality for most of them. Perhaps at least partly for these reasons, Russians clung to their traditions and customs, aiming to save what they could of the old (imagined) Russia. This was also reflected in their music making, in the choices they made when choosing repertory, and in which composers and pieces they would champion, not only among Russians, but with other Europeans and Chinese as well.

CHAPTER 2

Networking the Diaspora

MUSICAL ACTIVITIES OF THE RUSSIAN
COMMUNITY

An issue of the Russian-language artistic magazine *Phoenix* in mid-November 1935 featured an advertisement proclaiming the opening of the "salon of the Bohemians." The venue was Cafe Renaissance, at the bustling heart of the French Concession's Avenue Joffre, which was comparable in prosperity to Nanjing Road in the English-speaking International Settlement. The advertisement continued by announcing that the salon featured fine artists, musicians, poets, and journalists. There would be singing, melodeclamation,[1] and dancing. At midday there would be lunch, at five o'clock afternoon tea, and at eight o'clock "modern dinner." Throughout the day, there would be artists present, although it was not clarified if they would be performing. Finally, prices were promised to be "Bohemian," which was presumably a hint about affordable prices (Advertisement 1935a, 17).

By the 1930s, the formerly quiet French Concession had become a cultural center of the city, with different types of Russian establishments active there. The above advertisement also shows that Russians were providing entertainment in restaurants throughout the city, with Russian musicians and dancers performing from daylight deep into the night. But this advertisement of Bohemians was not a regular restaurant feature. While Cafe Renaissance was a business venture of its own, "Bohemians" was shorthand for a type of Russian club that brought together artists from different fields. Behind the often hilarious and even extravagant soirees was a deeper yearning of Russians to team up with like-minded people. This trend of establishing groups of artistic intelligentsia was typical for Shanghai Russian emigration. Organizations of different kinds were established and collapsed over the years. Some organizations, however, left their mark, and some persisted for years.

This small advertisement reflects a big change in the cultural scene of Shanghai from 1920 to 1935. The advertisement above featured an operation that Russians had inaugurated and that involved a number of Russian organizations, but which had already stretched beyond to reach non-Russians in increasing amounts. Musical life in Shanghai had become so rich and multifaceted that when Sergei Aksakov, the leading Shanghai music critic, theorist, and historian, tried to summarize a single musical season of 1934–1935 in the second volume of *Vrata*,[2] he deemed it difficult due to the sheer number of concerts, performances, and different groups. Aksakov himself was an émigré composer whose compositions were featured by the Shanghai Municipal Orchestra (SMO) a number of times, and he was also a professor at the National Conservatory. Aksakov ended up describing the musical life in Shanghai by dividing it into three main strands: the SMO, the many chamber concerts, and the National Conservatory of Music. He explained (1935, 242–243) that this left out operetta and numerous bands playing in theaters, clubs, and restaurants, which all deserved to be mentioned. While the SMO and the National Conservatory will be covered in later chapters, this chapter will focus on numerous other musical activities of the Russian community of Shanghai. Yet these activities were so extensive that the main aim is a general overview of Russian musical activities with some in-depth examples of important organizations established by the Russians in which music played an important role.

First, music had multiple roles within the Russian community. Music making was not only important among musicians and musical organizations, but also among other literary and artistic organizations. Not to be overlooked is that these organizations were quite diverse in orientation, some cosmopolitan in outlook whereas others nationalistic. One of the key dilemmas of Russian émigrés was to find a balance between the need to emphasize Russian national heritage, which was seen to be endangered because of the Bolshevik Revolution, and living in an international metropolis. Therefore, it is no wonder that Russian artistic organizations also wavered between these two tendencies, some emphasizing cosmopolitanism and the international nature of arts in general, and others focusing on the distinctly Russian heritage, introducing works that were often poorly known among non-Russian audiences but were very dear to Russian émigrés themselves. In music, this heritage typically began with Mikhail Glinka and emphasized the likes of Alexander Borodin and Nikolai Rimsky-Korsakov, but also included Piotr Tchaikovsky, Sergei Rachmaninov, and others who were less national romantic in style.

Second, music was considered crucial by many émigrés in maintaining Russian heritage, with efforts to educate the younger generation of Russians and to develop church and community choral performance serving to preserve culture. Such a phenomenon was a process of diaspora formation. The emigres' commitment to sustain their Russian identity and distinctiveness was, as suggested by Cohen (1997, 26), typical for diasporic communities.

Finally, this chapter concludes by presenting the case of Shanghai's first permanent opera company, which was established by Russian musicians. It was a venture that required not only enormous effort, but also a high concentration of artistic know-how and extensive multinational networks, underlining the long-term commitment of Russian émigré musicians to develop Shanghai's artistic scene.

Early Attempts to Connect Émigré Artists

Russian musical activities in many ways mirrored the growth of Shanghai's Russian community overall during the interwar period. In the early 1920s, when the number of Shanghai's Russian residents was enough only to arrange individual concerts, a few active Russians were already organizing musical activities beyond their individual livelihood. A case in point was the singer and teacher Petr Filippovich Selivanov, a graduate of the Saint Petersburg Conservatory. He established his own music school and gave lessons in singing, but he was also active in organizing the early Russian musical scene in Shanghai (Koliesnikova 1926, 220). His attempt to establish the Russian Organization of Music and Arts in 1920 was the first of many similar ones, even though it was unsuccessful and collapsed within a year ("Teatralnaia khronika" 1921, 29).

Rather than concentrating solely on music, artistic organizations of Russians in Shanghai typically brought together artists from different fields, even when their primary activity was arranging concerts. In his second attempt at establishing a musical organization, Selivanov was more successful. Here he cofounded the Literary-Artistic Association (LAO) with fellow singer E. P. Vladimirova-Burskaia, with the latter taking a more active role in LAO activities. The LAO was a relatively long-lasting establishment and arranged many events from the 1920s. Its particular aim was to present chamber concerts to the Shanghai public, and one exemplary concert took place on February 5, 1928. As was typically found in LAO programs, the concert introduced many Russian chamber works, particularly vocal music, including a number of arias from Russian operas but also from other classical European chamber repertoire. The small scale of the LAO organization is reflected by the fact that the February 5 concert venue was a small hall at the Officers' Club filled to capacity. Although the LAO lacked the means and connections to acquire greater halls, the concert was nonetheless considered a great success in press reviews, and it was hoped that such concerts would be repeated more often ("Kontsert LAO" 1928, 5).

Such chamber concerts were typical for the Russian community in the 1920s, when the number of Russian artists was still small. By comparison, in the 1930s several artistic organizations and establishments not only competed with each other, but also strove to build their audiences in general, booking the biggest venues Shanghai could offer. Even so, a key dilemma remained whether we examine Russian organizations of the 1920s or 1930s. Russian émigrés were seeking a balance between the need to emphasize Russian national heritage, which was seen as endangered because of the Bolshevik Revolution, and living in an international metropolis. The aforementioned concert by LAO can also been seen as an attempt to connect the Russian heritage, poorly known to other nationalities of Shanghai at the time, with mainstream classical music. Russians were eager to point out that Russian classical music was a direct descendant of European heritage.

Indeed, Shanghai Russians did not live in a vacuum, but interacted with the international community, which had established its own artistic organizations, some even before Russians had arrived in significant numbers. Internationally oriented Russians often sought shelter in such organizations, especially in the 1920s, when Russian organizations were either too volatile or could not offer the artistic environment people were seeking. One of the more important of these international organizations was the "Foreign Artistic Union of Musicians and Authors" (Russian acronym KhSML), usually called simply the Artistic Club, or Art Club. As an international association of artists, this group was also an important platform for Russians. The organization, founded in 1927 or 1928, was multiartistic in nature ("Deiateli iskusstva" 1928, 5), but it mainly emphasized the fine arts, arranging yearly exhibitions like the "Fourth Exhibition of Shanghai's Art Club," held in 1930. Exhibitions rarely occurred without Russian participants and were occasionally even dominated by Russian artists ("Deiateli iskusstva" 1928, 5). The Art Club came to feature a musical section and quickly started hosting concerts after the collapse of the Shanghai Musical Society, which had been active in the mid-1920s. For example, on May 6, 1930, a concert of works by Purcell, Schumann, Schubert, and Tchaikovsky's Violin Concerto was conducted by Mario Paci, the music director of the SMO. This was likely a special concert of the SMO that the Art Club was hosting. The concert itself, however, is interesting, as it included excerpts of Chinese opera performed in Chinese ("Kontsert shankaiskikh pevtsov" 1930, 4), which showcased compositions of very different musical traditions. While there is little further information about this concert, it suggests wider interest of Russians toward Chinese traditions. This concert preceded a major concert in 1933 hosted by the SMO and titled the "Grand Chinese Evening," which included experimental Chinese-Western works by the Russian-Jewish composer Aaron Avshalomov (see chapter 7). Unlike Russian associations that heavily emphasized Russian music, the musical section of the Art Club was not exclusively Russian, and it most definitely had a cosmopolitan outlook ("Kruzhok liubitelei" 1930, 3).

The preparatory committee for establishing a musical section of the Art Club illustrates the growing influence of Russians in international Shanghai. Of the seven members of the committee, three were Russian and one was the French national Charles Grosbois, who was a well-known friend of Russians and Russian culture ("Shanghai Art Club . . ." 1929, 256; "Muzykalnoe obiedinenie . . ." 1929, 4). Despite the musical section having a strong Russian representation, most artistic clubs established after 1929 usually had even stronger emphasis on Russian culture and were distinctly Russian in membership.

The existence of multiartistic and cosmopolitan organizations like the Art Club might have helped some of the more internationally oriented Russians, who were used to mingling with like-minded foreigners, to integrate into Shanghai society. One case in point was the pianist Boris Zakharov, who was in close collaboration with the SMO and contributed to Chinese pianism through his work at the National Conservatory. In fact, he eventually became an important bridge builder between the Russian community and other communities of Shanghai, and he seems to have been comfortable with Russians, other Europeans, and Chinese alike. He also served as a musical intermediary, performing Russian works for the international audience. Indeed, he became a local celebrity not only among Russians, but also among Shanghai's other communities. His arrival in Shanghai in 1929 was regarded as an important event, even though there were already several other notable pianists and piano pedagogues based in Shanghai. By that time, he was already a world-class pianist, having studied at the Saint Petersburg Conservatory together with Sergei Prokofiev and Nikolay Miaskovsky (Tassie 2014, 33–34; Robinson 1998, 38).

After Zakharov's arrival in Shanghai, he became associated with the Art Club and gave a lecture for it in late 1929. He also assumed major responsibility for the concerts arranged by the Art Club's musical section. The primary venue for the chamber music concerts was the American Women's Club on Bubbling Well Road ("Tretii kamernii kontsert" 1930, 5; "Kontsert Kardashevskikh" 1930, 4; "Uspekh S. S. Aksakova" 1930, 5). Programs of these concerts emphasized Russian music, but not exclusively. The significant presence of Russian music was likely due to the fact that the majority of musicians participating in the concerts were Russians. The chamber concert series soon became an undertaking on its own, growing out of the Art Club's auspices. A group of mostly Russian musicians led by Zakharov—like cellist Shevtsov and pianist Pribytkova, who along with the Jewish Italian violinist Arrigo Foa were all active at the National Conservatory—took over the chamber concert series. The concert held on May 18, 1932, was typical, featuring works of Handel and Haydn, with the rest consisting of works by Russian masters Mikhail Glinka, Alexander Dargomyzhsky, Modest Mussorgsky, and Sergei Rachmaninov ("Poslednyi kamernii kontsert" 1932, 4). Even though there were concerts with strictly Russian chamber music, most concerts featured at least some non-Russian works by prominent composers. At some point in the mid-1930s, the chamber concerts became unprofitable and abruptly ended. Other entities continued arranging chamber music concerts, but the original series organized by Zakharov and the Art Club was not revived. The Art Club itself faced the same fate. This organization seems to have disappeared in the mid-1930s, most likely because of the deteriorating situation in Asia that drove Europeans—excluding Russians—away from Shanghai.

The beginning of the 1930s was a time when the choice of employment for many Shanghai Russians was limited to working in an international organization or in one of the distinctively Russian organizations. The influx of Russian artists had made it possible for Russians to establish Russian institutions and in a way insulate themselves from other foreigners. Even Russian émigrés with international backgrounds, like Zakharov, had difficulties choosing between these two. From 1929 to 1931 he was a member of both international and distinctly Russian national organizations ("Organizatsia muzykalnogo obshchestva" 1929, 5). Eventually, many Russian artists followed the same course as Zakharov and tried to combine their love for Russian arts and culture with international orientation, preferring to deal with other Europeans and Chinese instead of insulating themselves. Toward the end of the 1930s, however, the rising tide of European and Chinese nationalism and the resulting outflow of foreigners from Shanghai would again force the Russian community toward nationalism. Russian emigres' orientation was like a pendulum, swinging between cosmopolitism and nationalism as a result of local and international events affecting Shanghai.

Figure 2.1 Piano Trio: Boris Zakharov, Arrigo Foa, and Innocent (Igor) Shevtsov (Shanghai Symphony Orchestra Archive)

Between Cosmopolitism and Nationalism

An organization by the name of KhLAM (meaning rubbish in Russian) became one of the best known in Shanghai in the 1930s. Its name was an abbreviation of the first letters of artists, authors, actors, and musicians in Russian, and it was modeled after the famous artistic cafe with a similar name that existed around 1918–1919 in Kiev. The association was also known as "the Bohemians" and its club was sometimes called Wednesday because it convened on Wednesdays.[3] As an organization, it was a manifestation of the dilemma between cosmopolitism and nationalism, and its aim was underlining art as a phenomenon that transcends borders and national definitions.

KhLAM is interesting as it consisted of the most prominent Russian artists of Shanghai (Van 2008, 99). Weekly gatherings of artists had preceded the formal establishment of KhLAM in the autumn of 1933, when it was registered with an English name, "Association of the Russian Writers, Artists, Actors and Musicians." KhLAM's board was completely Russian. It featured both men and women, though it was dominated by males: two of the foremost Shanghai Russian authors, A. V. Petrov (Polishinel') and M. Ts. Spurgot (Sir Maik), were original members. Most other leaders of KhLAM, however, were either actors, musicians, or both. Many were high-profile artists, some of whom worked in cabarets and operetta. There were Russian teachers from the National Conservatory, Russian Drama Theater, Russian Ballet, and Russian Operetta, and performing artists not associated with any establishment.[4]

KhLAM's eccentric Wednesday shows that took place almost every week, excluding a pause of about five months in summer, became popular and gathered a large audience of Russians and foreigners alike. KhLAM performed first at Cafe Kleinermann, then at the restaurant Omon, and finally adopting Cafe Renaissance as its venue for many years. But it still yearned for its own premises. There were discussions of establishing its own club with a working space, kitchen, and theater for 320 ("Godovoe sobranie KhLAMa" 1937, 4). Before signing a long-term contract for its own club at Cafe Renaissance,[5] KhLAM also held meetings at the Paramount and Canidrome, all major venues in which Russians worked.

KhLAM's bohemian appeal is emphasized by the fact that Alexander Vertinsky, one of the best-known Russian singers of the era, became one of its most active members quickly after his arrival in Shanghai in 1936. In the same year, Vertinsky was named "the first knight of the Shanghai bohemians" (Zhiganov 1936, 74–75).

Wednesday gatherings of KhLAM in the 1930s contained all kinds of performances, some scheduled and some improvised. Grotesque theater was advertised in 1936 as a new feature,[6] suggesting that Shanghai Russians closely followed European currents ("Vecher t. Ptitsynoi . . ." 1936, 5). Often, KhLAM would commit its evenings to talented young artists, giving them a chance to gain fame and possibly some extra income, as in the case of young ballerina Aleksandra Ganina, who performed with the organization in 1936 ("Ganina" 1936, 15). Of the several competing New Year's parties held annually in Shanghai, KhLAM's was considered the most popular among artists (Advertisement 1935b, 17). Bohemians, or khlamists, were mostly Russians, but there were foreigners among them, too, like singer Herta Sand and violinist Arrigo Foa, which underlined KhLAM's cosmopolitan outlook ("Teatr muzyka kino" 1936a, 14–15).

Even though KhLAM gathered high-profile artists, one of their primary aims was to bend the limits of high and low art. Their evenings at times featured Shanghai's foremost restaurant musicians, jazz in particular. Sergei Ermolaev's (Serge Ermoll) jazz band (which at the time served as the Paramount Theatre's orchestra) was among them (Picture 1935b, 15), as were violinist A. I. Bershadsky and pianist G. Ia. Rott, Shanghai's most wanted bandleaders of the 1930s. KhLAM mixed art forms with ease, which sometimes led to fruitful partnerships. Rott, for example, began to accompany Vertinsky during his concerts at the time ("Teatr Muzyka Kino" 1936b, 14.15). Typically, KhLAM's evening performances combined several different art forms ("Imeniny i vystavka . . ." 1936, 5). Often among the non-Russian audience was the aforementioned Charles Grosbois, who headed the French cultural operations in Shanghai. Grosbois served in various roles with the Alliance Francaise, French radio broadcasts, and the Foundation France Libre, and he held other prestigious positions in the French Concession ("Otkrytye vystavki . . ." 1936, 6). Russian celebrities like surgeon Sergei Voronov or Feodor Chaliapin were also entertained by KhLAM when they passed through ("Doktor Voronov" 1935, 13; "F. I. Shaliapin . . . (*Feniks*)" 1936, 14–15).

Many of the Russian artistic organizations in Shanghai were established to serve primarily Russian needs. In the case of KhLAM, however, the organization itself—even though KhLAM's audience was primarily Russian—was not patriotic in the sense that it focused simply on Russian issues, themes, or patrons. KhLAM's events frequently featured non-Russian visitors, not only other Europeans, but occasionally also Chinese performers. While it typically organized soirees, evening parties, rather than traditional concerts, there were sometimes bigger concert occasions. On Friday, April 16, 1937, for example, KhLAM organized a symphony concert with a Russian (Slutsky) and a Chinese (Vu Pa Chao [Zhao Meibo 赵梅伯]) as conductors. Henry Francis Parkes was mentioned as the music director, and he was essentially the third conductor for the concert. The appearance of the Chinese singer Marie Wong (Wang Wenyu 王文玉) was specially mentioned. The concert featured Tchaikovsky's *Slavonic March* (conducted by Slutsky), Mendelssohn's Symphony No. 4 (Italian) (Chao), Parkes' *Ballet Suite* (Parkes), and an aria from *La Traviata* (Slutsky). The final piece of the concert was Gershwin's *Rhapsody in Blue*, played by William Loescher and conducted by Parkes ("Simfonicheskii kontsert . . ." 1937, 2). Not to be overlooked is that Slutsky, Zhao Meibo, and Wang Wenyu would collaborate with the SMO on quite a number of occasions, particularly Slutsky, who later became one of the SMO conductors between 1943 and 1945, which testifies to the interconnectedness of the different networks and communities in Shanghai.

The Russian newspaper *Slovo* ("Simfonicheskii kontsert . . ." 1937, 2) paid special attention to the *Rhapsody in Blue*. Gershwin's work was new to Shanghai, and the score might have been introduced to the orchestra by Parkes, since he conducted it. Although the work was composed in 1924, it was written in a style not well-known among the Russian musicians. One Russian critique of the concert considered Gershwin's piece interesting but too difficult for the orchestra. Yet, the reviewer admitted, the orchestra consisted of young players, some instruments were missing, and they had only just begun to play together. All this probably played a role in the uneven performance ("Kontsert orchestra . . ." 1937, 2). Interestingly, Shanghai was not the first Chinese city to hear *Rhapsody in Blue*; the work had already been conducted by Aaron Avshalomov in Tianjin in 1930, shortly before he moved to Shanghai and gained recognition for his own experimental works. When it comes to KhLAM, however, choosing Gershwin's work illustrates Russian emigres' appetite for new and experimental initiatives. Even the SMO dared to perform the piece only in February 1941 with the Russian Jewish pianist Gregory Singer, Avshalomov's close collaborator, as the soloist (See SMO Concert Program 1941, February 23, in table 4.1). It is likely that Avshalomov, who was not part of KhLAM's networks, was involved in SMO's Gershwin performance but not with KhLAM's earlier one. Scores for the KhLAM's performance seem to have come from Parkes, again underlining KhLAM's networks beyond the Russian community.

Reaching Beyond Shanghai

Bringing Russian artists together was the primary objective of most Russian artistic organizations, including KhLAM. But many Russians also made attempts to reach beyond the artistic community of Shanghai. Harbin in the north was a natural destination for Shanghai Russians, and many artists traveled back and forth between the two cities. Tianjin was another center that had several thousand Russians, as well as Port Arthur (now Dalian) and certain Japanese cities. Many artists were contracted, either individually or as part of ensembles, for tours and performances around Asia, sometimes going as far as India but more often to Japan, Singapore, the Philippines, and Indonesia. Occasionally, Russians living in China would even travel to Europe or the United States, but more typically there were artists coming from these areas to perform in Shanghai.[7]

Connections to Europe and the United States, however, were not necessarily tied to traveling. Newspapers and magazines featured a lot of material about the proceedings in the Russian communities, particularly in Europe but also in the United States. Thus, Shanghai Russians acted in the spirit of diaspora, aiming at establishing connections with other Russian communities around the world, which accords with Cohen's (1997, 26) list of the defining features of a diaspora. Several artistic organizations indicated having foreign correspondents, which underlined their desire to be in touch with Russians elsewhere. Some of this work was practical, such as with the acquisition of scores and new works from different parts of the globe, and only partly related to maintaining Russian links. Certain centers, like Paris, were considered particularly valuable for the Russian émigré community. Shanghai's Russian Ballet, for one, emulated the success of Diaghilev's Ballets Russes, performing works introduced by Diaghilev, ranging from ballets composed by Stravinsky to De Falla's *Three-Cornered Hat* and many others. Paris was a natural direction as it had already become the center of the Russian artistic intelligentsia before the mass emigration, and this status was only inflated by the Revolution and civil war (see Raymond and Jones 2000, 23–30).

In creating extensive connections, Sergei Aksakov, one of the backbones of Shanghai's classical music scene, went the furthest. He strove to extend global Russian connections in the early 1930s through the Russian Musical Association Abroad (RMOZ). In one of his lengthy weekly columns in *Shanghai Zaria*'s afternoon issue committed to music ("Znaete-li Vy . . ." 1933, 4), Aksakov publicized how the RMOZ (established in Paris in 1931) had in less than a year gathered three thousand members. Aksakov established a Shanghai chapter of RMOZ, with membership costing five Shanghai dollars, a considerable sum at the time ("Rossiiskoe muzykalnoe . . ." 1933, 4). The chapter was said to arrange concerts, and one such concert did feature Russian composers such as Rachmaninov, Gretchaninov, and Nikolai Medtner. Performers were among the best in Shanghai, like Yeltsova, Shushlin, Shevtsov, Zakharov, and Foa ("Kontsert RMO" 1932, 5).

Both RMOZ and KhLAM strove to reach beyond Shanghai, but the aims of the two organizations' efforts diverged. Although RMOZ was aiming at building international connections, it was primarily diasporic rather than cosmopolitan in its objectives, connecting Russians in different locales and emphasizing the prevalence of Russian music over others. Its foremost pursuit was to connect

Russians everywhere around the world, rather than specifically linking Shanghai Russians with the outside world. Thus, whereas some of the Shanghai Russians were truly cosmopolitan, committed to arts regardless of where the art and artists came from, for many ethnicity or nationality played a major role. For them, Russian art and Russianness in art were the most important factors of their artistic pursuits.

National Orientation in the Arts

Most Russian artistic associations in Shanghai were distinctly literary societies, even though they included some artists and composers. A major difference between primarily musical and literary oriented associations was that literary associations were typically nationally oriented. Since this volume focuses on musical activities, it serves to mention the names of some of these literary associations that were important from the point of view of music. Ponedelnik (Monday) was perhaps the longest-lasting Russian artistic association consisting mostly of writers. Its meetings could gather more than a hundred participants, largely because of the artistic events they offered, although its membership was typically more limited. Although it was primarily a literary organization, Ponedelnik also arranged its own public literary-musical evenings (Shcherbakov 1931, 50). While Ponedelnik's focus was not music, even Boris Zakharov was a member in 1930, but after that he seems to have found a closer connection to other organizations.

Ponedelnik was one of the first large-scale artistic associations of Shanghai Russians, but its ideological platform was mixed. National tendencies were strong and its membership consisted exclusively of Russian-speaking émigrés. At the same time, however, many of its members were interested in East Asia, known then as the "Far East," even though in a Russo-centric way. One meeting, which had a typical program, included readings of new works by various members, but it also included Russian translations from a Chinese author, combined with a performance of Korean songs ("Zakrytie sezona" 1932, 4). It seems that many artists were more interested in Russian national art than Asian art since several artists left Ponedelnik in 1933 to establish their own organization (Severny 1935c, 15). Although the name of this new organization was Vostok (East), it consisted of nationally minded Russians ("Vrata" 1934, 191–195).

In comparison to Ponedelnik, however, Vostok arranged a musical section early on, as the composer Sergei Aksakov became its active member. The section aimed at arranging a series of evenings that would consist of two parts: the first introducing a (Russian) composer and the second featuring new music composed by Russians in the "Far East" ("Vrata" 1934, 191–195). One such event was organized for Alexander Gretchaninov to celebrate his seventieth anniversary (Aksakov 1935, 242–243). Even though Vostok's approach to peoples and the arts of Asia was colonialist and Russo-centric (or Eurocentric, as suggested by their use of the term "Far East"), it was no more Eurocentric than those of other Europeans at the time.

While in the beginning Vostok seems to have been distinctly a literary organization, Aksakov seems to have become an increasingly important figure in it. One picture of Vostok, in which it was called a "literary-artistic-musical association," featured Aksakov with other members of Vostok, including his wife, V. S. Aksakova (likely their daughter), the composer Tcherepnin, and others who were writers or artists (Picture 1935a, 18). Aksakov's increasing role in Vostok was certainly behind the increased focus on music, but it also affected the group's orientation. While Vostok's platform indicated attention to Chinese and other Eastern cultures, Aksakov seems to have been first and foremost a Russian composer who paid less attention to Chinese than did some of his colleagues in Vostok. Even so, when writing about the conservatory, he always made note of Chinese students and how they improved. He compared the situation in China to that of Russia in the eighteenth century, when primarily Italian music teachers started to educate Russians. He saw a similar future for China, where Russians were now helping Chinese to master Western classical music. Even though Chinese musicians had existed before the conservatory, Aksakov considered the conservatory as something that for the first time allowed Chinese students to receive proper education in music theory, aesthetics, and harmony (Aksakov 1933, 3). Aksakov thus considered the conservatory superior to anything else existing in China at the time. Compared to Avshalomov, Aksakov's approach was Western-centered and paternalistic, seeing Chinese as subjects needing training in Western classical music. Aksakov himself, however, did not show interest toward Chinese culture and traditions, and he seems to have seen Russian traditions and culture as superior to those of China, at least in the field of music.

Vostok later merged with another Russian organization in 1936, forming a new one called "Shatior" (meaning "umbrella"). Soon after its establishment with Aksakov as its key member, Shatior arranged an evening introducing Aksakov's new symphonic work at the Russian Social Union (ROS)[8] premises on 1053 Avenue Foch (now Yan'an Road) in the French Concession ("Vecher 'Shatra'" 1936, 5). Aksakov's ambition for introducing contemporary Russian music in Vostok continued with Shatior. The organization was small, but it had at least one notable guest in Alexander Tcherepnin, the Russian émigré pianist-composer. Tcherepnin's two visits to Shanghai were highly publicized, and the

Chinese community considered them to have made a significant impact on Chinese musical development, as will be discussed in greater detail in chapter 6. Tcherepnin was featured in Vostok's yearbook in 1934 ("Novoe obiedinenie 'Shatior'" 1935, 18), and he appeared as a guest at Shatior at the invitation of Aksakov three years later. In 1937, Tcherepnin played four of his pieces at a Shatior soiree. As typically occurred at Shatior's evening gatherings, the authors Shcherbakov, Shchegolev, and Slobodchikov also read their poems, thereby fulfilling the group's multiartistic objective ("Kompozitor A. N. Cherepnin . . ." 1937, 4).

Russian Musical-Educational Association

Artistic organizations mentioned so far have been societies that brought together like-minded Russian artists. But many Russians hoped for more musical opportunities for Russian youth. As pointed out by one Russian commentator in 1933, there were only ten Russian students studying at the National Conservatory, which was considered too few. The conservatory, which was modeled on the Saint Petersburg Conservatory, was staffed with a good number of Russian pedagogues whose primary teaching language was Russian. Yet the school was headed by Chinese and was not intended for Russians in the first place ("Shankhaiskaia konservatoriia . . ." 1933, 4), even though the Russian pedagogues played important roles in the early history of the National Conservatory. So some of the Russian émigrés yearned for institutions that would serve Russians rather than having Russians serve primarily other nationalities. This was linked to the desire to preserve Russian culture and traditions. Reasons for this ranged from outright patriotism to the fear for the future of Russian music because of the spreading of Russian intelligentsia around the world after the Russian Revolution. Russian youth were considered to be in a key position to preserve Russian culture for future generations.

Aside from the lack of proper professional music training for the young, some pedagogues viewed Shanghai, the metropolis that teemed with jazz, movies, and Hollywood influences, as threatening to the very existence of Russian culture. For this reason, three piano pedagogues—Zakharov, Zoya Pribytkova, and Aksakov—all teaching at the National Conservatory, established the Russian Musical-Educational Association.[9] Its stated aims were:

(1) to unite currently scattered musical forces;
(2) to establish an audience of Russian youth for which there would be lecture-concerts of Russian music that would acquaint them particularly with opera and the works of Glinka, Tchaikovsky, and Rimsky-Korsakov;

(3) to establish a symphony orchestra and opera group to play Russian music of great composers from Glinka to Stravinsky and Prokofiev;

(4) to open up a Russian conservatory in the future (Zhiganov 1936, 147).

The Russian Musical-Educational Association was involved in staging the first Russian opera in Shanghai in 1932, as discussed below. But it also worked toward strengthening Russian musical culture in Shanghai through education. A Russian conservatory remained a distant dream, but the First Russian Music School, established by the people active in the Russian Musical-Educational Association, began to advertise itself in January 1936. Zakharov, however, was apparently no longer involved in the undertaking.

The address of the school was 359 Rue Cardinal Mercier (currently South Maoming Road). The piano teachers of the school were listed as L. Zander-Zhitova, Boris Lazarev, and Zoya Pribytkova. The latter two also taught at the National Conservatory. Singing was taught by V. I. Yeltsova, and the violin teacher was J. Podushka, the viola principal of the SMO. Cello was taught by A. S. Estrin. There was also a special opera class headed by A. Iu. Slutsky. Theory and composition was taught by Slutsky and Aksakov, and, finally, music history was taught by Aksakov, who was a full-time professor at the conservatory as well. All the teachers were among the foremost musicians of Shanghai at the time. Unsurprisingly, all were also Russian. Teaching began on January 15, 1936 (Advertisement 1936b, 2; Advertisement 1936c, 3). Some of the teachers were busy with other endeavors: Pribytkova was constantly producing and directing plays at the Russian Drama Theater; Slutsky conducted orchestras, operettas, and operas; and Aksakov was active in several organizations and wrote for *Zaria*.

The first anniversary concert of the First Russian Music School was held in 1937, and its program suggests that Russian music played an important role in the school's curriculum. The concert was committed to the thirtieth anniversary of the death of composer Anton Arensky, and the program included a presentation on Arensky followed by a concert of his works. The concert featured a trio consisting of J. Podushka (violin), I. Shevtsov (cello), and L. Zander-Zhitova (piano). In the first part of the concert, B. M. Lazarev and A. Lvova performed as soloists on works for two pianos. V. I. Yeltsova also sang romances of Arensky. In addition to faculty appearances, there were also student performances. Choosing to celebrate Arensky, not a particularly well-known Russian composer, was apparently part of the school's objective of making Russian heritage better known ("Godovshchina 1 Russkoi . . ." 1937, 2). Indeed, in his preconcert presentation, Aksakov emphasized that it was "Russianness that creates sincerity, warmth, and soulfulness of [Arensky's] music." ("Kontsert 1-oi Russkoi . . ." 1937, 7). There is no indication of how the First Russian Musical School fared beyond this initial period, but it operated at least until the early 1940s, which demonstrates the serious attention given to maintaining Russian heritage through musical training.

Russian Choirs

Russian nationalistic traditions in music differed to some extent from those of other European countries. Choirs were particularly important, not only in dramatic works but also within the Russian Orthodox religion. Russian Orthodox churches needed a cappella music sung by a choir led by a conductor called a regent. Because of this sacred tradition, vocal music was more important to some Russians than was instrumental music. Through the church, choirs played an important role in Russian social and religious life, in addition to their artistic value. The Russian community valued its choir traditions, and several high-profile choirs existed inside Shanghai's Russian community. There were also choirs that nurtured connections with other European groups.

Furthermore, Russian folklore teemed with folk songs and their choir renderings. Russia had rich and locally varied folk traditions, and many patrons yearning for their Russian motherland loved the sound of Russian folk songs being performed by a choir, whether it was a Cossack choir, Ukrainian folklore choir, or Russian classical men's choir. Numerous Russian associations had their own choirs, but there were also a few semiprofessional choirs that operated for a time in the Shanghai music scene, such as the ones established by Piotr Mashin and Ivan Kolchin.

The first proper choir concert by Russians was held in December 1924 at Town Hall. It was led by Ukrainian-born Piotr Nikolayevich Mashin, who was then visiting from Harbin. Mashin was educated at the Kharkov Imperial Musical School, and from 1907 to 1924 he taught singing at the Harbin Commercial School. He was also among the establishers of Harbin's First Musical School in 1921. In 1925, Mashin moved to Shanghai, where he organized a choir for the Saint Nikolai Church, underlining the importance of the Russian Orthodox Church in Russian choir traditions; even secular and community choirs often had links to the church, and most choir conductors worked as regents in different churches.

Mashin can be credited for educating and bringing together a good pool of choir singers that made performing major choral works possible in Shanghai in the late 1920s and 1930s. Mashin's amateur choir circle drew at least half a hundred people. The first performance of the choir circle[10] took place with the SMO conducted by Paci on March 5, 1928, at Town Hall ("Khorovoi Kruzhok" 1928, 3). The program contained choir scenes from Glinka's opera *A Life for the Tsar* and Polovtsian Dances from Borodin's opera *Prince Igor*, both of which were extremely important works for Russians ("Russkii kontsert" 1928, 4). Such Russian concerts became more frequent after this initial display of Russian prowess.

Mashin also established his vocal studio, which displayed the same enthusiasm for Russian musical heritage as did his choir activities. When his studio gave a concert on June 9, 1929, at the American Women's Club, its program consisted of Rimsky-Korsakov, Gretchaninov, Tchaikovsky, and others, even though some of Mashin's students were of other European nationalities besides Russian ("Kontsert studii . . ." 1929, 6).

In addition to Russian culture, Mashin was a major proponent of Ukrainian culture, which was reflected in his choir activities. For example, on March 24, 1929, he organized a Ukrainian concert at a local business club titled "Ukrainian evening" to commemorate the Ukrainian national poet Taras Shevchenko. The concert boasted a big choir accompanied by soloists and dancers, and performers were clad in Ukrainian national costumes. The concert was followed with dances and the serving of Ukrainian food and drink ("Ukrainskii vecher" 1929, 5). Choir concerts featured perhaps the most vocally nationalist elements. Press articles and commentaries about choir concerts were often sentimental and emphasized traditions considered to be at risk due to life in exile.

The repertories of Mashin's concerts suggest that he combined his role as a regent with that of a representative of the Russian diaspora and guardian of Russian heritage. He tended to combine Ukrainian and Russian works, secular and spiritual, and classical repertory with a few folk songs. A sacred concert at one of the Russian churches on Sunday, April 8, 1928, for example, contained

Figure 2.2 Colonel Frizovsky's Russian-Ukrainian Choir in the late 1920s (Zhiganov 1936)

works of Tchaikovsky, Mussorgsky, and Alexander Arkhangelsky, which were considered staples of Russian spiritual repertory with a classical twist ("Dukhovnyi kontsert" 1928, 4). A Russian choir concert led by Mashin on February 26, 1929, in turn featured Tchaikovsky, Ippolitov-Ivanov, Arkhangelsky, and Russian folk songs. But these Russian works were combined with works by Brahms, Verdi, and Gounod, which were valued by the Russian audience but which also appealed to other European nationalities in Shanghai. Finally, this concert featured Ukrainian folk songs and dances in national costumes ("Kontsert russkoi kapelly" 1929, 3).[11]

While Mashin was a Russian nationalist, he understood that for choirs to be truly successful in Shanghai, other Europeans and even Chinese audiences needed to be taken into account. This was reflected in his concerts that featured popular non-Russian works.

The importance of a vibrant choir scene in Shanghai is underlined by the fact that several different organizations, like the SMO, the Shanghai Opera, and the Russian Operetta, came to use these choirs. The SMO frequently played works that required a choir, and numerous opera and operetta performances throughout the 1930s also required a substantial pool of singers. Thus when Mario Paci made an initiative for a Wagner anniversary concert that took place on May 28, 1933, it featured not only Russian soloists, but also a praised Russian choir led by Mashin. The next year, the SMO organized a grand concert with 70 musicians and 180 choir singers. J. S. Bach's B Minor Mass was performed in full length, with Russians forming the core of the choir (Zhiganov 1936, 148). In fact, these two were just a few of the collaborations between the SMO and the Russian choir. In this regard, Mashin's work was important not only in preserving cherished Russian traditions, but also in enriching Shanghai's cultural scene.

Figure 2.3 Choir conductor Piotr Mashin and his Tersky Cossack Choir (Zhiganov 1936)

Even after World War II, when cultural life faced considerable difficulties, choirs still played an important part in Russian cultural life. This time, however, Soviet influence could be seen in that choirs performed in celebrations of May Day and First Victory Day, a Soviet celebration commemorating the end of the war (Advertisement 1946, 4). Both events were a staple of Soviet festivals. It would seem, then, that despite political inclinations, the importance of choirs and singing for the Russian community was indeed significant. Choirs and choir music were something that transcended ideology and were important despite the political outlook of people. But this was also something the Soviet authorities had noticed, and music, as well as culture in more general terms, was used to soften the attitudes of people around the world toward the Soviet Union. Russian émigrés in Shanghai were no exception; Soviets willingly supported cultural activities in the Russian community of Shanghai in order to win the allegiance of Russian émigrés. The Soviet Union wanted to be seen as a place where Russian cultural traditions, choir music included, were alive and well. Indeed, many Shanghai Russian musicians responded to such overtures and eventually moved to the Soviet Union in the late 1940s.

The Shanghai Russian community's vibrant choir life and the culture of song nurtured a whole new generations of singers, which in turn contributed greatly to the musical life of Shanghai. Singers and choirs were needed in musical theater, cabarets, and operetta, all of which had been key features of Shanghai's night life since the 1920s. Yet the biggest enterprise of Shanghai's Russian community was the establishment of an opera company in the latter half of the 1930s.

Russian Opera in Shanghai

Shanghai Russians had a special relationship with opera. Even though there were different types of concerts, such as chamber, choral, and orchestral concerts of Russian music, many Russians still yearned to hear Russian operas. Opera was an important part of the elite Russian culture before the Russian Revolution, and it was almost impossible to hear such large-scale works outside Europe after the Revolution. Traveling troupes, like Adolf Carpi's "Grand Italian Opera," a troupe touring Asia and featuring Russian singers and dancers, occasionally visited Shanghai, but it performed Italian operas. Russian operas were not heard in Shanghai in the 1920s, even though many of the first Russian music teachers in Shanghai, such as Selivanov, were singers (Khisamutdinov 2010, 207). Others were typically educated for the opera stages as well, but could not find stages in Shanghai on which to perform.

In February 1932, Modest Mussorgsky's *Boris Godunov* became the first all-Russian opera production in Shanghai and a major event in all respects. The staging of the opera displayed the artistic prowess and potency of the Russian artistic community. The Russian Musical-Educational Association, which had mentioned staging of Russian operas in its program declaration, led the preparations for the opera (Zhiganov 1936, 147). Advertising of *Boris Godunov* began more than a month in advance, and there was a buzz surrounding the production throughout. The opera chosen was grand, but so was the cast. An orchestra of thirty was conducted by Slutsky and a choir of thirty-five was directed by seasoned choir conductor Piotr Mashin. V. I. Varlamov directed the opera, which took place at the prestigious Embassy Theatre. Singers consisted of the foremost Russian émigré artists, including Yeltsova, Krylova, Klarin, Blokhin, Kudrevatykh, and Shushlin (Advertisement 1932a, 2). Due to the production's popularity, it was repeated three months later at the Embassy on May 6, 1932 (Advertisement 1932b, 2).

A Shanghai Russian newspaper, *Novyi Put*, expressed gratitude for the Russian Musical-Educational Association for staging *Boris Godunov*. *Novyi Put* urged the "Russian colony" to support the association so that "Russian youth would not forget what it meant to be a Russian" ("V Muzykalno-prosvetitelnom obshchetve" 1932, 4). People experiencing unpleasant diaspora experiences seem to have found some comfort in the ability of the Russian community to stage a work that was considered to have a universal meaning for all Russians. Even organizations that had little interest in culture otherwise hailed the staging of the opera and supported it with patriotic statements. The widespread reporting of the event in the Russian press and the many Russian émigrés participating in the event indicates that even though these patriotic attitudes were not necessarily shared by the more cosmopolitan-oriented part of the Russian emigration, Russian heritage seems to have united Russians in Shanghai. Russian opera found support across the community even though the community was otherwise divided by numerous political and ideological issues.

Few scholars have written anything about Shanghai's Russian opera, even though a good deal of repertoire was performed in Shanghai in the 1930s, which eventually led to the establishment of a stable opera company in Shanghai. At the time, there were not many places that would have performed Russian classics on such an extensive scale. In émigrés' minds, the Soviet Union did not count, although many Russian classics were actually thriving there (Fairclough 2016). Paris, which was the center of Russian emigration, and Shanghai were among the few places outside the Soviet Union where Russian classics were regularly staged in the 1930s. Mussorgsky's *Boris Godunov* was followed by Dargomyzhsky's *Rusalka* and Tchaikovsky's *Eugene Onegin*, all of which were performed in 1932. From the first Russian opera performance onwards, Russians aimed at producing large-scale works rather than chamber operas. This made productions even more demanding and called for joint efforts of numerous artists and groups. But all the requisites already existed in the early 1930s: numerous Russian musicians were available, choirs had been established, and several ballet schools actively produced new dancers for the productions. Finally, the conductor of the orchestra, Alexander Slutsky, owned a library of opera scores, and thus all the necessary elements for staging operas existed ("Shankhaiskaia opera" 1937, 4).

The number of Russian associations and their short-lived nature points to the difficulties Russians encountered when trying to pull together. Yet the successful staging of *Boris Godunov* raised high hopes among Russians and prompted discussions about establishing a permanent opera house in Shanghai. It was concluded that the idea was interesting but would require Chinese input. This, it was stated, might be possible, since the project had drawn a large Chinese audience and much attention in the Chinese community ("Muzykalnye zametki" 1932, 4). The dream of an opera house was largely just that, a daydream. It did not materialize during the 1930s or at any time before Russian émigrés were forced to leave Shanghai. While a great many opera performances were staged by Shanghai Russians, it was completely another matter to actually found an opera house. Financial obstacles were formidable, and the lack of major financial investments prevented an opera house from ever materializing. Resource questions were also the reason why the first opera performances in 1932 did not immediately lead to the establishment of an opera company. Enthusiasm for operas did not disappear, but the tremendous efforts required for merely staging operas, never mind establishing an opera house, made it difficult to come up with a working group.

In Russian Shanghai, organizations changed, and certain individuals were often crucial for their functioning. In Shanghai, the operatic bass Vladimir Shushlin was a key figure in Shanghai's musical life generally, but he was also one of the most active organizers behind the Russian opera. In comparison with Zakharov, Shushlin's route to Shanghai, while it shared some features with Zakharov's path, was more typical for Russians. Shushlin was a talented singer whose performances were frequently praised and whose contribution to the early development of Chinese singers is considered crucial. After living in Harbin from 1924 to 1927, Shushlin toured Japan and the Philippines ("Shushlin" 1930, 5). In 1930, he spent some time in Shanghai and subsequently received numerous pleas to become a teacher there. Despite these requests, he decided to go back to Harbin once more for the summer ("Otiezd V. G. Shushlina" 1930, 4), but he stayed there only for that season. Whether the situation in Harbin was worse than he had recalled or the offer to teach in Shanghai was too tempting is not certain, but he decided to return to Shanghai in the autumn of 1930 and take a teaching position at the National Conservatory ("Shushlin" 1930, 5). He stayed in Shanghai for the next twenty-five years.[12]

In the spring of 1934, two years after the first Russian opera performances, it was announced that Shushlin had established a new opera ensemble. Before any full-scale operas would be performed, the group was told to perform excerpts and scenes from different operas, without staging or costumes. The group's first performance was at the Japanese Club on April 26, 1934. The opera selected was Gounod's *Faust*, performed without a choir and with a small orchestra. Other singers included Markov and Gravitskaya, both of whom would be participating in the later Shanghai Opera Company ("Opernii kollektiv . . ." 1934, 4). It was probably no coincidence that *Faust* was also the first opera that the Shanghai Opera Company performed in the autumn of 1937. In addition, for the sheer love of opera, Shushlin and other singing teachers tried to provide their students genuine opportunities to practice their stage skills while at the same time preparing the ground for a full-scale opera company.

Before an opera company came into existence, Shanghai had a Russian operetta, which provided an important testing ground for the future opera. Shanghai's Russian Operetta was formed from previously touring operetta troupes that had been traveling around Asia, and it employed a lot of Russians. Most of the traveling groups had used Harbin as their base. As Russian artists began moving to Shanghai, operetta performances became more frequent in Shanghai, with full seasons occurring in some years. By the mid-1930s, a permanent company called the Russian Operetta (Opera Comique in French and Russian Light Opera in English) came into existence.[13] While it mostly performed operettas—which were easier to stage, less serious, and lighter in musical content than full operas—the troupe proved its capabilities for serious works by performing Alexander Borodin's *Prince Igor* and Rimsky-Korsakov's *The Legend of the Invisible City*, both key Russian operas, in the spring of 1935. The conductor was one A. Labinsky ("Russkaia opera . . ." 1935, 4). It is possible that the visiting conductor brought the key elements, such as the set and costumes and the score with him, but without further sources this is difficult to ascertain. In 1935, however, the Russian Operetta was the only stable operatic company in Shanghai. There were other Russian dramatic groups, but they concentrated mainly on theater rather than opera or operettas. But the Russian Operetta proved wildly popular and its performances drew full houses throughout the season, which could be read as a sign that there was a potential audience to support a full season of opera performances. Thus far, there had been only occasional performances of single operas, and even though these performances drew full houses, it was a different thing to have a complete season of opera performances.

Finally, in the 1937–1938 season, the dream of Shanghai's opera enthusiasts was fulfilled as an ambitious opera company began its existence. Already before October 1937 there was talk of a new Shanghai Opera, and some of the best soloists from the Russian Operetta—baritone Georgi Kudinov and soprano Sofia

Zorich, to name two—were hired by the new opera company to bring some star power from a cultural institution that already had a committed audience (HIA, Kudinov 1-4-31a). Experienced opera artists and teachers Shushlin and Krylova were involved in the opera company's formation. Indeed, the Shanghai Opera gave vigorous performances throughout the season, making grandiose impressions and receiving great reviews. In the press, this was considered a courageous and risky effort, but it was also warmly welcomed. In general, the 1937–1938 season seems to have been successful. Slutsky was hired as the conductor, and Klarin, who had previously worked in the Drama Theater, was the producer (HIA, Kudinov 1-4-31b).

There was, however, a major setback for the opera company that was not of its own making. Right after the first performances of the company, the Chinese-Japanese war threatened to cut the season short. The Shanghai Opera Company's leadership remained defiant, announcing that "War or no War, Shanghai is going to have its own Grand Opera this season" (HIA, Kudinov 1-4-31b). Newspapers during the opera season, especially in the autumn, were filled with pictures of war and destruction. It was reported that even during some of the performances one could see bullets and shrapnel flying, and occasionally the sound of the orchestra was buried under the noise of heavy weaponry and bombs, especially during performances of *Faust* and *Boris Godunov*, when Shanghai was under siege ("Shankhaiskaia opera" 1937, 4). The Japanese invasion would greatly change Shanghai's power relations and drive non-Asians, Russians excluded, back to their native countries. In the long run, this exposed the fragile nature of Russian networks in Shanghai and their dependence on other nationalities, even though in autumn 1937 the Russian community seemed to be at the height of its artistic activities.

The opening production of the Shanghai Opera Company, which premiered on October 10, 1937, was a French classic, Charles Gounod's *Faust* ("Segodnia 'Faust'" 1937, 4; "Gounod's Faust . . ." 1937). The premiere had some technical deficiencies, and the stage was small for such a large-scale opera, but it was otherwise a success. The audience was reported to have a lot of foreigners and Chinese alike ("Na opere 'faust'" 1937, 4). Russian participation was obvious. The French, who were typically supportive of Russians, were also present. For example, Charles Grosbois and French consul Bodais both attended ("Eshcho o Fauste" 1937, 4). French support continued even though the next production was a Russian opera, Tchaikovsky's *Eugene Onegin* (HIA, Kudinov 1-4-32a). Choosing a French opera to start with illustrates how the Russian community depended on the French. Its base of operations was in the French Concession, and Shanghai's French elite were ardent supporters of the company.

Indeed, although the company was distinctly Russian, its repertory consisted mostly of international classics, like Georges Bizet's *Carmen*, which drew a full house on November 13, 1937 ("Anshlag na 'Karmen'" 1937, 6). *Carmen's* performances, too, coincided with the full-scale Japanese invasion of China. Thus, the editor of *Shanghai Zaria* could only wonder how the company could have reached such "fantastic and ever-improving performances" under such conditions ("Speshite zapastis . . ." 1937, 4). Apparently, the Russians committed themselves, regardless of the course of hostilities. Despite greater Shanghai being a theater of war, the company kept staging works in the center of the city. Thus, a week after *Carmen*, *Rigoletto* followed, as did many other works practically every week throughout the season. The choice of repertory seems to be a result of careful pondering, offering operas that were classics and were familiar to audiences from different European countries. But the extensive nature of Russian networks—and perhaps a certain degree of calculation—manifested in other connections as well.

The staging of *Rigoletto* raised special interest in the media because the production featured two Chinese singers in major roles alongside Russians, a case in point of the diaspora's ability to reach out beyond its own Russian-oriented networks. *Rigoletto* was said to be the first time Chinese performed Western opera in Shanghai, and thus it was historically significant in the development of Western music in China. Whether this was a show of solidarity for the Chinese plight at the time of war or an appearance scheduled well in advance cannot be ascertained. But the two young Chinese artists, Marie Wong (Wang Wenyu) 王文玉 and Sze Yi-Kwei (Si Yigui) 斯义桂, were given a lot of visibility in Shanghai's Russian media. They were particularly praised in the review of the premiere. Originally, Wong and Sze had been advertised in the cast for the first production of the season, *Faust* (HIA Kudinov, 1-4-31b), but this was apparently postponed until *Rigoletto*, which was mentioned as being the debut of both Chinese singers on any opera stage.

The audience of *Rigoletto* was said to include many other Europeans and Chinese in addition to Russians ("Uspekh 'Rigoletto'" 1937, 4). The appearance of Wong and Sze was indeed a rare occasion in an art form that until that point had been almost completely dominated by Westerners. Both Wong and Sze had Russian teachers, Wong studying with Krylova and Sze with Shushlin, a fact that was not missed by Russian newspapers. Both were praised and heralded as future Chinese stars based on their performance in the opera (Mishin 1937, 2). In this, it turns out, the reviewer was quite right.[14] It was also emphasized that this was the first time Chinese artists performed with Europeans in an Italian opera ("G. Kudinov—Rigoletto" 1937, 2). Wong's stage character and body language were considered to have been great. Rumors were already circulating in Shanghai that Wong would be invited for a tour of Italy, possibly Milan, the following spring ("Meri Wong—Dzhilda" 1937, 2).

Rigoletto was already the sixth opera production of the season. Ulianov, who had experience in Moscow after working there in the early 1920s, replaced Klarin as producer. During the season, each production was usually staged two or three times. In the case of *Rigoletto*, the dates were November 23, 25, and 27 (HIA, Kudinov 1-4-35a). Productions usually drew full houses. Indeed, *Carmen*'s premiere had such a large audience that program handouts ran out and some people had to stand. Some of the audience was apparently unfamiliar with opera behavior, at least as British commentators saw it. In the British press, the Russian habit of clapping at every possible occasion, even when sets were revealed, was deplored (HIA, Kudinov 1-4-33a). This, however, was a cultural clash more than anything else, with British audiences being more reserved in comparison with enthusiastic Russian audiences.

Soon Shanghai's opera scene came to feature a neat "Shanghai Opera" logo introduced around December 1937. At about the same time, the company received a new director in Helen Crosnier, a former Miss Shanghai (1931) and an opera lover who was said to be able to recite from memory parts of more than forty operas ("Shankhaiskaia opera . . ." 1937, 4). Crosnier was the daughter of Alexander Slutsky, who had formerly been the conductor of the Russian Operetta and now conducted the Shanghai Opera Company. The company took advantage of Crosnier's nomination and arranged a cocktail party for the media at the Park Hotel on December 17. She introduced three points that formed the credo of the company: (1) art would rule over commercial success, (2) the best local artistic forces would be used, and (3) the audience would be treated as guests at the performances. The press was also reminded of the challenges related to establishing an opera company and was asked for help in pressuring their readers to support the establishment of an opera house in Shanghai ("Shankhaiskaia opera . . ." 1937, 4).

At the same time that Crosnier started as the head, the company decided to move from the Canidrome to the Carlton Theater, which was considered to be good news. The last performance at the Canidrome was Jacques Offenbach's *The Tales of Hoffman*, played during the Christmas holidays (Advertisement 1937, 2). The Canidrome was said to be unpleasant for audience and cold for artists, and the stage was relatively small, making it difficult for large-scale performances. It was considered sheer heroism that the group had managed performances there. It was announced that the relocation to the Carlton would be completed by January 5, 1938, and that *La Juive* by Fromental Halévy would be performed on January 8. The Carlton had already seen large-scale performances like ballet, huge revues, and Italian opera and was thus considered fit for the Shanghai Opera. Selivanova continued as the choir director, Sokolsky as the ballet master, and Slutsky as conductor ("Shankhaiskaia opera pereshla . . ." 1937, 2).

While the Canidrome had been in the French Concession, the Carlton was in the International Settlement, which made the move a risky venture even though artistic conditions were better according to the review of the company's first performance—*La Juive*—in the Carlton. After all, the great majority of Russians lived in the French Concession. Concerns were voiced about going by bus to a different part of the city at a late hour. Russian artistic networks focused on the French Concession, and a step to the International Concession was possibly overstretching these connections and possibly threatening the future of the opera. Further complaints were that the hall was cold (it was winter) and, at the premiere, group scenes were still not as good as they could be (Vivas 1938, 5). Yet the house was full at the Carlton premiere, and the bus problem was solved by the opera administration, which hired special buses to take audience members back to their residences ("Segodnia—'Skazki Gofmana'" 1938, 2). Generally, the company received rave reviews for its performance despite initial difficulties. Shushlin, in his role as the cardinal, was mentioned as great as ever, but it was the new acquisition, Shemansky, hired from the Harbin Opera to perform at Shanghai, who stood out this time. In the review, the troupe was mentioned to have given an "absolutely fantastic performance." *La Juive*'s performances were followed by Rossini's *Barber of Seville* and the rerun of *Tales of Hoffman* ("'Zhidovka'..." 1938, 2).

Under Crosnier's leadership, opera performances went on with great ambition. The Shanghai Opera tackled Puccini's *Tosca*, Léo Delibes' *Lakmé*, and Giuseppe Verdi's *La Traviata*. Globally, Puccini's *Tosca* had been among the most frequently performed operas in the three decades leading up to its premiere in Shanghai on January 17, 1938. By that time, since its world premiere in 1904, *Tosca* was said to have seen 806 performances in 29 cities ("Floriia Toska" 1938, 2) and had thus become one of the most-beloved operas ever, with guaranteed success. But *Lakmé* and *La Traviata* were not any less successful. *Lakmé* was briefly reviewed, and its success was underlined by the fact that tickets were sold out in advance of its performance ("Lakme i Traviata" 1938, 2).

While the Shanghai Opera Company's repertory featured international operas, it was also careful to keep the dream of the Russian intelligentsia alive by performing key Russian operas as well. In addition to Mussorgsky's *Boris Godunov* and Tchaikovsky's *Eugene Onegin* that were performed in October 1937 ("Boris Godunov" 1937, 4; "Evgenii Onegin" 1937, 4), Glinka's *A Life for the Tsar* was performed in March 1938. This opera was considered to be the first Russian opera and perhaps the most patriotic and promonarchy in appearance. It was performed three times in Shanghai in the spring of 1938 ("K stoletiiu..." 1938, 1). The performance was said to have aroused great interest among the Russian audience because they had not had the chance to hear it for more than twenty years ("Zhizn za tsaria..." 1938, 3; Advertisement 1938, 2). The diasporic nature of the performance is seen in its monarchist libretto: the work was hardly performed in the Soviet Union until 1939, when the libretto was reintroduced and the title changed to *Ivan Susanin*. Thus the work symbolized the great Russian tradition that many Russian émigrés around the world wished to preserve.

The Shanghai Opera Company's following seasons were not as ambitious as the initial one. The company staged works in the 1938–1939 season, but the number of performances was notably smaller than in preceding years. That trend continued in 1939–1940 and in following seasons. The company did not completely disperse even during the war, which suggests that some kind of an agreement was reached with the Japanese. Performances continued up until 1945 at Lyceum Theatre (Zhao 2015, 243–294). This is in contrast with the Russian Operetta, which had started before the opera company and continued with success throughout the later 1930s and early 1940s. Then again, the Russian Operetta never left the French Concession and used Lyceum as its base of operations.

There is insufficient evidence to determine why the first, highly successful season was followed by a decline in the number of performances by the Shanghai Opera Company. The bold announcement about "art before commercialism" suggests that the opera's leadership was not fully up to task with the financial risks involved in the venture. Financial success would have required a lot of support from the business community, and nothing indicates that the opera's board had adequate connections to Shanghai's business elite for such success. Furthermore, war made it difficult for international businesses as well, even though Shanghai was spared the hardships of many other Chinese cities. Furthermore, a diminishing clientele, marked by Chinese fleeing toward China's interior and Europeans and Americans leaving Shanghai for security reasons, reduced the well-off circles that had made opera possible in the first place.

Shanghai as China's City of Western Culture

In the 1920s, Harbin stood as the center of Russian emigration in China and the center of Russian cultural activities. But by the end of the 1920s, the influx of Russian artists from Harbin to Shanghai accelerated, making Shanghai the Russian cultural center. Russian activities in the field of music were manifold. Music played an important role within the Russian community. It was an important part of different social and cultural events, with musicians typically providing the entertainment. But musical activities were themselves also an important form of social activity among Russians, and many organizations not related to arts and music had their choirs and bands consisting of nonprofessional musicians.

The potential importance of choirs in Shanghai's Russian community resulted in several choirs being established during the 1920s, even before the major influx of Russian émigré artists from Harbin to Shanghai. This in turn made it possible for the SMO to perform major works requiring extensive choirs and also made later operetta and opera performances possible.

By the early 1930s, the number of Russian artists in Shanghai increased to a point where they began to establish literary and artistic organizations. Music often played an important role in these organizations of the Russian intelligentsia, but the majority of their members were not musicians. Only certain smaller organizations, like the Russian Musical-Educational Association, were first and foremost musical establishments that served as gathering grounds exclusively for music professionals.

The artistic associations of Russian émigrés had different aims. Some were aimed at connecting Russians with artists of other nationalities both in and around Shanghai. More typically, however, Russian émigré organizations were inward-looking, nationalistic, and patriotic by nature and were primarily concerned with preserving Russianness and Russian art in alien conditions. Even Russians with a cosmopolitan orientation seem to have been particularly alarmed by the attitudes of the younger generation toward Russian musical heritage. They were worried that life outside Russia, in an urban metropolis abundant with foreign entertainment forms, would be catastrophic for the future of Russian art.

It is difficult to ascertain whether Russian artistic organizations succeeded in educating younger generations. Musical activities of the Russian émigrés, however, expanded on a yearly basis throughout the 1930s. Numerous concerts and performances introduced Russian musical heritage. Choral, symphonic, chamber, and finally even operatic works were staged by Shanghai Russians.

A climax of Russian musical activities in Shanghai was experienced in the autumn of 1937. At the time of the Japanese invasion of China, several Russian troupes were at the height of their creative activities. The Russian Operetta, the Shanghai Opera Company, the Russian Ballet, the Russian Drama Theater, and the Theatre of the Russian Social Union, as well as various choirs and nonprofessional groups, all operated at the same time. In addition to this, there were artistic societies, smaller performance establishments, and bands that were active at the time. A single week in the winter of 1937–1938 could include performances of the Shanghai Opera, the SMO, choirs, chamber music groups, operettas, drama theater groups, individual artists and bands, as well as ballet troupes, all of which involved Russian performers.

Even though Shanghai was a metropolis with cultural and artistic activities not related to Russians, the Russian influence cannot be overlooked. Many of the major Western art forms that Chinese performers have since adopted and have excelled at were first introduced by Shanghai Russians. The center of Russian activity was within the French Concession, but the Russian presence spread throughout Shanghai, with Russian artists performing and working within the International Concession and Hongkew area. As the Russians interacted with European, American, and Japanese communities of Shanghai, their involvement with the two major musical institutions in Shanghai, the SMO and National Conservatory, had a significant impact on Shanghai's musical scene. The Russian musicians would thereby leave an enduring mark on modern Chinese musical development.

CHAPTER 3

An Imperfect Musical Haven

RUSSIAN MUSICIANS AND THE SHANGHAI MUNICIPAL ORCHESTRA

As mentioned in the previous chapter, Shanghai had become a culturally vibrant community by the mid-1930s thanks to the arrival of many artistic and musical Russian émigrés. More than fifty musicians found permanent employment with one of the cultural pillars of the city, the Shanghai Municipal Orchestra (SMO), and a handful of others played with the orchestra as soloists. Shifting the focus away from the Russian community to the cultural pillar of the city, the SMO, this chapter examines Russian émigré musicians' lives as orchestral players in the ecosystem of the SMO by looking into musicians' contracts and the SMO's meeting minutes to shed light on this otherwise overlooked page of Russian émigré history.[1] The SMO, like other institutions in Shanghai at the time, was far from a haven of racial harmony and job stability. Indeed, as research data reveals, Russian players of the orchestra faced challenges not experienced by their colleagues. Due to their refugee status, they were vulnerable to discrimination and exploitation. A handful became the SMO's "replacement players" and "temporary players" on a long-term basis due to their lack of options. While some of the refugee musicians thrived in Shanghai, quite a few fell victim to gambling and alcohol.

The purpose of this chapter is first to provide glimpses of émigré musicians' lives by revealing their interactions with the SMO. Then it shows how they became pillars of the orchestra as section principals and soloists to argue that despite the unfair treatments these Russian émigré musicians experienced, they were indispensable to the SMO. In a way, just as the SMO director Mario Paci was responsible for the orchestra's reputation as the "Far East No 1,"[2] so were these Russian musicians, who made up more than 50 percent of the orchestra's players. An array of these musicians who often played as soloists helped to enrich the SMO's repertoire and render its concerts more appealing to the Shanghai audience. Most important of all, the presence of these Russian émigré musicians, as will be shown, helped Paci address the many challenges the SMO encountered, as they directly as well as indirectly contributed to the institution's survival.

The SMO

Established in 1879 as a public band, the SMO changed its name from the Municipal Band to the Municipal Orchestra and Band in 1922.[3] The public band's original function was to serve the settlers in the International Settlement, its expenditure supported by rates (taxes), and thus the band was a public institution of the Municipal Council overseen by a band committee with members from the community as well as the council. It played at ceremonial occasions and provided musical entertainment for the settlers. But as Shanghai grew to become a metropolis in the early twentieth century, the settlers had higher aspirations for their band, and they hired German conductor Rudolf Buck in 1907. Buck was thought to have bestowed the hope "to bring home to us dwellers in the Far East all the developments of music, the grand music of the past, the promising music of the present, and perhaps the perplexing music of the future."[4] Buck was successful in transforming the public band into a symphony orchestra. With additional musicians hired from Europe, he made the Municipal Band's Sunday concert a classical music showcase while keeping the "light music" repertoire for the Friday concert, thus creating two identities for the band.[5] As of 1912, the institution was already a mid-size orchestra with ten European and twenty-two Filipino musicians.[6]

But when Mario Paci was appointed as the Municipal Band's conductor in 1919, he had to start anew.[7] In 1917, as a result of the ratepayers' highly charged sentiments toward Buck and other German players because of World War I, the Municipal Council had to make the decision to revert the orchestra back to a band after the German musicians left.[8] Fortunately, it did not take Paci long to shape it up. The concert held on November 30, 1919, the second one of the season, already won the support of the local critic, who looked forward to "even better performances, when conductor and performers have worked longer together" ("The Sunday Concert" 1919, 709).[9]

Hiring Russian Musicians

Indeed, Paci did succeed in bringing the Shanghai audience good concerts. But he did not accomplish it through working together with its original group of players but instead through hiring temporary musicians. While Paci managed to cope with a shattered ensemble when he took up the conductorship in 1919, what he had in mind was an orchestra of the highest possible standard, which, when translated into practice, meant letting the less capable players go. In July 1920, he wrote to the council secretary to request that the clause "three months' notice" to be added to musicians' contracts for the following reasons: (1) to keep them diligent, (2) to give the conductor power to change and replace musicians, and (3) to get rid of players no longer giving satisfactory service.[10] His pleas must have fallen on deaf ears, and probably as a result of not getting support from the council, Paci adopted a different strategy: look for extra musicians from nearby areas or even locally as a way to strengthen his orchestra. The availability of Russian musicians was a godsend.

In November 1921, four extra Russian musicians were hired on temporary contracts.[11] But Paci was not too enthusiastic about these musicians, as he complained in his letter to the budget controller that they were not entirely reliable and were always nagging about being paid on time.[12] One of these musicians was the Russian violinist A. Brodsky. According to Paci's note, he was the only one willing to stay in the orchestra for the full season until the end of May. Probably as a result of desperate need for good players, Paci was willing to put up with Brodsky's holding an outside engagement at the same time so long as Brodsky took part in all daily rehearsals and the Sunday concerts at 5 p.m. and Friday tea concerts, but not for private services. Brodsky was offered a salary of Tls.120 per month,[13] which was even lower than the average salary of the Filipino musicians.[14] While he was not required to take part in private services, he also did not get the supplement of Tls.15 (SMA U1-3-286, [n.p.]).

The trumpeter F. Ponomariov (Ponomaroff) was another of Paci's early hires, whose experience with the SMO exemplifies the sad fate of refugees and displaced people.[15] Ponomariov went to see Paci in 1919 about the possibility of a position at the SMO. While performing in Shanghai with the Russian Opera in Harbin, he had heard about the SMO's reputation and its good salary and benefit package. Paci advised him to apply somewhere outside Shanghai such as Manila or Hong Kong, and he did. Later that year, when Paci needed a trumpet player, he asked Ponomariov to come to Shanghai for an audition.[16] Ponomariov did, but due to his health, was only offered a contract (called then an agreement) with probation for four months from January 27 to the end of May in 1920 at a salary of Tls.125, which would be raised to Tls.135, plus an additional Tls.15 for private services, after the probation.[17] Confident about what the SMO promised for his future, Ponomariov accepted the contract and resigned from the Russian Opera and moved to Shanghai from Harbin. As was pointed out in chapter 1, Shanghai Russians came from different routes, some from Russia and Siberia directly, others from Harbin. Ponomariov was one of the latter.

For orchestral musicians, a position with the SMO would be a dream job with a stable salary, medical benefits for a player and his family, and long paid leave every seven years, in addition to the superannuation fund at the end of service. But Ponomariov was not among the lucky musicians who received such generous treatment, as he failed the probation.[18] Even though Paci was not entirely happy with him, he kept him until a better player was available. Probably for that reason, Paci recommended a pay raise of Tls.15 at the time of Ponomariov's contract renewal, pointing out that Ponomariov had served under modest salary conditions and had not tried to take advantage of the fact that the trumpet was especially important during the summer open-air brass band concerts (SMA U1-3-097, 8 or 9).[19] Again in 1922, Ponomariov was offered a temporary contract for an indefinite period because of the illness of another trumpet player (SMA U1-3-097, 25). But he was soon dismissed in December 1923 shortly after the new trumpet player arrived, and there was no trace of him afterward.[20]

Many musicians shared the same fate as Ponomariov. Being on temporary contracts, they were excluded from the haven of the Municipal Council. A few such musicians were Ovchinnikov (Ovchinnikoff) (oboist, hired from Harbin for five months before the arrival of Griffiths from London, 1921), Khmelnitsky (Hmelnistsky) (pianist of the Moscow Trio, hired to play the harp for summer concerts in 1925), his wife L. Khmelnitsky (cellist hired in 1923), and N. S. Varfolomeyev (Varfolomeyeff) (cellist to replace Schiller on long leave in 1932).

Temporary Contracts

There is a general misconception about the pay mechanism of the SMO. It is assumed that all the employees of the SMO were paid equally well. For example, in Wang Zhicheng's monograph E'qiao yinyuejia zai Shanghai (Russian musicians in Shanghai, 2007), he stated that "[t]he monthly salary of musicians of the Municipal Orchestra was very high. The lowest pay of Russian musicians was $200 and with an annual increment that could go up to $450. For an annual average salary of $3,000, it was eight times the average income of a Chinese resident in Shanghai. Then they enjoyed the benefits of other municipal employees such as long paid leave, free medical care and subsidized travel" (Wang 2007, 27).[21]

It is true that SMO players' income was significantly higher than the average Chinese, but many of the Russian players were not hired as municipal employees. Not only that, but a significant number were hired on temporary contracts, some on a short term of only several months as replacements for musicians on long leave or as needed due to the termination of contracts or during summer months when the orchestra needed extra musicians to play concerts at public parks several times a week. As Paci himself admitted, "the question of temporary musicians' salaries is a very delicate and complicated one, on which the whole economic organization of the orchestra and band is based" (SMA U1-3-2574, 64 or 65).[22]

Indeed, this operation of temporary contracts, which took advantage of an excessive supply of refugee musicians, was a crucial mechanism to keep the wheels of the SMO turning. When the orchestra's budget tripled from Tls.56,677.91 in 1919 to Tls.154,117 in 1925,[23] the settlement's ratepayers as well as members of the Municipal Council were concerned. Paci was asked to reduce the orchestra's size and not to hire musicians from Europe, and there were many voices talking about cancelling the orchestra in 1925. Based on the reduced expenditure of the following few years,[24] it is obvious that Paci was advised to keep expenditures at bay.

As a result, Paci had to be watchful toward musicians' salaries, and so he insisted on rewarding them according to their "usefulness" to the orchestra. In this regard, Paci used musicians' temporary agreements to his benefit, offering such agreements to Russian musicians who needed jobs. He often put them on probation for a period before a substantive contract would be offered. While such a practice gave Paci more control over the orchestra's standards, as well as savings for the Municipal Council, it also harbored animosity between him and his players. The lack of job security often led these musicians to look for other opportunities.

For instance, the Russian harpist Mrs. A. Kunze was on temporary contract for seven years from 1920 to 1927. Even though she was rewarded reasonably well by 1925 at a salary of Tls.180 and then an additional sum of Tls.40 for transporting, hiring, and repairing the harp, she resigned in April 1927 to leave Shanghai. She explained in her resignation letter that it was partly for an urgent family matter and partly for the uncertainty of being a temporary musician (SMA U1-3-286, 153). Even though she inquired about returning to the SMO in August, she was offered a position on the old terms, which she refused (SMA U1-3-286, 161).

The double bass player M. Bakaleinikov (Bakaleinikoff)'s experience was another case in point. Hired in 1923 at age thirty-three and deemed by Paci as a good double bass player and "one of the best Shanghai pianists for jazz," he wrote the following in his resignation letter:

> In a certain way I am actually sorry to leave the orchestra, especially to discontinue working under your leadership, but to work under no agreement, or, as it is at present, under an agreement with three or four months' notice, it does not give me sufficient guarantee for myself and my family. That is why, having now found a position that ensures me a safer future, I hope that you will accept my resignation. (SMA U1-32068, 8–9)[25]

Incidents such as these show that there were job opportunities for émigré musicians in Shanghai beyond the SMO. The bands at various theaters, nightclubs, and even record companies such as the Pathé lured musicians away from the SMO. Other musical institutions such as the various Russian bands established in the 1920s also created job opportunities for Russian musicians. For example, a Russian Cadets' Band was established in 1923 led by F. D. Shut, and a twenty-five-strong French Municipal Brass Band was also founded in 1926 by the municipal authorities of the French Concession. There were rivalries between these bands, perhaps symptomatic of a general Anglo-French rivalry that existed in Shanghai. When the Race Club engaged the services of the Russian Cadets' Band instead of the Municipal Band in 1923, the SMO Council was so disappointed that it forbade members of the Municipal Band to direct the Cadets' Band (SMA U1-1-130).[26] In addition to these bands, the French Concession also had its own orchestra to rival the SMO. The Orchestra of the Alliance Française (French Concession), which consisted of thirty-five players, all of whom were Russian, was founded in 1933 by the oboist and conductor Vladimir Sarychev (Sarichev). Sarychev was also an oboist of the SMO from 1927 to 1945, after Paci brought him from Harbin (Wang 2007, 211).

In this regard, Paci's complaint in his note to the budget controller about these temporary musicians' unreliability, their passing up SMO engagements for higher-paying jobs at entertainment venues, and their demanding timely remuneration, had not taken into account the context of living as refugees. Even though many of these Russian musicians were properly trained in major Russian music schools and possessed great musical talents, they did not enjoy the same social and legal status in Shanghai as musicians in Europe did. They did not have passports and they could not travel freely. For the majority of them, making ends meet was their primary concern, so they lived frugally from paycheck to paycheck. But there is no doubt that being a player in the SMO did carry a sense of prestige, whereas musicians who played at nightclubs and cabarets were looked down upon by those engaged in the classical music scene. This can be seen in the concert pianist Boris Zakharov's response to his student's father playing at entertainment venues, to be discussed in chapter 5.

Musicians Fighting Back

Indeed, not every temporary musician was willing to accept Paci's unfavorable engagement terms. But whether they were able to find better alternatives often depended on their playing skills and marketability. A "dispute" between Paci and the Russian-Czech violinist J. Hayek, who came to Shanghai in 1920, illustrates the negotiation process between the player and the orchestra. In Paci's letter to Assistant Council Secretary McKee on March 13, 1922, he requested that Hayek be offered a definite agreement at a salary of Tls.165 per month plus

Tls.15 for private services. This offer was based on his musical skills and character and most of all on Hayek's willingness to learn the clarinet so he could play in the outdoor brass band concerts in the summer (SMA U1-3-286, [n.p.]).[27]

It is interesting to note that Paci's letter was written in the middle of the month for a contract that should have started a half a month earlier. According to Paci, it was Hayek who asked him for a definite contract in February. Aware that Hayek was playing for different theaters in Shanghai but given Hayek's temporary status with the SMO, Paci had no choice but to give Hayek what he asked if he wanted to keep him.[28] Paci was soon to find out on March 28, 1922, that despite what he had promised Hayek, the latter was auditioning for various positions including the Carlton Café, with which he also had signed a temporary contract. He had already played there on the evening of Saturday, March 25, which caused him to miss the March 26 SMO rehearsal and concert.[29] Paci was upset that Hayek did not honor their verbal agreement and his insistence that he had done nothing wrong. Paci wrote to McKee on March 30, 1922, to ask for Hayek's immediate dismissal as well as to levy a penalty on his salary, paying Hayek only as a temporary musician for the month of March as well as withdrawing part of his salary for his replacement. Paci thought that "his punishment will be to receive only about Tls.100 instead of the Tls.180 expected by him. The penalty is perhaps not as severe as his offence deserves" (SMA U1-3-286, [n.p.]).[30] What further angered Paci was that Hayek hired a lawyer to speak on his behalf, challenging Paci's termination of his contract without one month's notice as stipulated in the agreement (SMA U1-3-286, [n.p.]).[31] Not only that, Hayek returned to work on April 5, supposedly continuing until May 1, which Paci felt was "a terrible slap in the face" (SMA U1-3-286, [n.p.]).[32] In the end, Hayek won the battle over Paci and got his April salary without having to play at all.

What Hayek did was not honorable, but from a legal perspective he did nothing wrong. His acting against Paci and putting him in a difficult position, though, could be taken as a justifiable act toward his oppressor, an act of asserting his rights, an act on behalf of temporary musicians who were being exploited by Paci and whose rights were not protected by any regulations.

Another case in point was the trumpeter Phedorov (Fedoroff)-Kozmenko, who was once regarded by Paci as the only trumpet player around willing to take the rate of Tls.150 per month stipulated by the Finance Committee (SMA U1-3-863, 255).[33] In fact, Phedorov-Kozmenko had been playing for the SMO for several years prior to 1932, such as when the conductor of the S.V.C. (Shanghai Volunteer Corps) Band, W. Schroeter, was on long leave from June 1930 to February 1931 (SMA U1-3-863, [n.p]). But in 1932, Phedorov-Kozmenko refused Paci's offer to replace the Italian trumpeter Fiocchi on long leave. He put it simply: "[E]specially during the Summer Season I will certainly find a much better job and therefore I cannot bind myself to stay here until the end of August. The minimum pay I will accept is Tls.165" (letter dated April 13, 1932, SMA U1-3-863, 256). In the end, Paci had no choice but gave in to Phedorov-Kozmenko's demand (SMA U1-3-863, [n.p.]).[34]

As to how many temporary musicians served each year, it is impossible to calculate. A document pertinent to a dispute between the council and the musicians shows that there were nineteen of them in 1928. These temporary musicians were required to commit to playing a minimum of ten and a maximum of eleven concerts per month plus the necessary rehearsals for four months a year (SMA U1-3-2884, 105).[35] But according to Paci, they refused to sign such an agreement. Rather than soliciting each musician's view, Paci suggested a meeting, which was held on March 10, 1928. The meeting's outcome is not clear except that Paci was discouraged by the fact that the violinist Phedorov (Fedoroff) resigned to take a better position at the Carlton Theater for a monthly salary of $500 plus free medical benefits (SMA U1-3-2884, 119).[36] Due to Bakaleinikov's earlier resignation and now also losing Phedorov, who were also the only two who could play the piano, Paci wrote, "It must therefore be noted that from now on it's impossible to accept any private engagement for any group of musicians where the piano player is required" (SMA U1-3-2884, 119). This reveals that there were quite a number of Russian musicians who had classical training but still preferred to work at restaurants because of the pay. For instance, the pianist Leo Itkis and the violinist A. G. Bershadsky, though they were both virtuoso instrumentalists, chose to make their living as restaurant musicians.

Russian Musicians Replacing Filipinos

Even though Paci had in mind the players he would like to recruit for his orchestra, things did not always go his way. In a letter he sent to the hiring agent from Genova, Italy, in July 1925 while he was on his first long leave, he complained about not being able to hire a horn player in France or Italy "due to the bad news about China published in newspapers" (SMA U1-3-863, 204–205). Apparently, the horn player to be hired was to replace the Filipino musician J. Pintato, who had served the SMO since 1911 and whose contract terminated in 1925 (SMA-U1-3-863, 180).[37] In fact, most Filipino musicians' contracts were terminated after 1930. For example, when G. Alberto's contract ended in 1926 after fifteen years of service, he was offered a temporary contract on more or less the same terms as before, and in fact his salary in the new contract was Tls.170, an increase of Tls.15. But in just a few months, the assistant conductor de Kryger requested that his contract be canceled. At the time he was fifty years old and had served the SMO for sixteen years (SMA U1-3-863, 161–169).

That certain Filipino musicians were kept during the period suggests that Paci's act was probably not racially motivated. For instance, Paci's recommendations for F. Calibo and R. Santos were strong. In the case of Santos, he was recommended for a Form "B" agreement. Paci rated him as useful as he played both the viola and the cornet, "which are very rarely played by one man. It would be difficult to replace him therefore by a temporary musician" (SMA U1-3-863, 122–125), which would be needed in the summer months when the orchestra served as a band. Both Calibo and Santos continued to play for the SMO into the 1930s (SMA U1-3-863, 83 and 122–125, respectively).

Classified separately as "Manilamen," Filipino musicians served on contractual terms different from their European counterparts. Though they enjoyed the same benefits as other European musicians, such as free medical care and long leave, their salaries were significantly lower. The availability of an array of Russian players in Shanghai was thus a godsend for Paci as well as for the orchestra. Given that Paci had to operate the orchestra within the budget stipulated by the Municipal Council, taking advantage of the Russian musicians in the community and hiring them to replace the Filipino ones would seem a good option. For example, N. Kuznetsov (Kousnetzoff) was hired from June 29 to August 31, 1926, when F. Calibo returned to Manila for a vacation. While Calibo's salary was Tls.165 per month, his replacement's was only Tls.100, without medical benefits or uniform (SMA U1-3-863, 83). In another example, the hiring of the percussionist V. Osadchuk in 1928 was an answer to the irreplaceable Filipino player San Juan, whose contract was terminated. Even though his contract was terminated in 1927, he was regarded as the only kettle drum player in Shanghai at the time (SMA U1-3-863, 68), so he was offered a temporary engagement at a high salary of Tls.200 per month, Tls.60 higher than his original salary, to keep him for a few more months until the arrival of his replacement. After the arrival of Osadchuk on November 2, 1928, San Juan's contract was terminated on November 4 (SMA U1-3-863, 60–76).

The change in the SMO's demographics during Paci's tenure is revealed through a study of the players' names from 1919 to 1942. While the earlier lists did not include temporary musicians, the latter ones did. According to the lists, Filipino players were gradually replaced by Russian ones. For example, there were still twenty Filipino players in 1923 but only three by 1936, whereas the number of Russian players increased from one in 1920 to thirty-two in 1936 (see table 3.1).[38]

It is difficult to pinpoint the exact number of Russian musicians employed by the SMO over the years because (1) existing sources are not always reliable, (2) it is not easy to determine the nationality of the players from the name list, and (3) many of the players on temporary contracts were not included in the orchestra's list. For example, in a staff list of 1929, there were only twenty-three

Table 3.1 SMO musicians' national origins from 1919 to 1941

	European	Russian	Filipino	Others	Total
1919	7	0	21	0	28
1920	5	1	21	0	27
1921	5	1	21	0	27
1922	12	8	20	0	40
1923	14	11	20	0	45
1924	14	12	18	0	44
1925	13	12	18	0	43
1926	15	14	16	0	45
1927	14	21	12	0	47
1928	15	21	10	0	46
1929	16	22	8	0	46
1930	13	26	7	0	46
1931	13	25	6	0	44
1932	13	25	7	0	45
1933	12	28	5	0	45
1934	12	27	4	0	43
1935	11	28	4	0	43
1936	12	32	3	1 (Japanese)	48
1937	14	27	4	2 (Japanese)	47
1938	16	26	3	1 (Chinese) +1(Japanese)	47
1939	16	28	3	3 (Chinese) +1(Japanese)	51
1940	19	26	3	5 (Chinese) +1(Japanese)	55
1941	20	24	3	5 (Chinese) +1(Japanese)	53

Source: *North China Desk Hong List*

musicians under "agreement" (not counting Paci and de Kryger, the assistant conductor); nineteen were European and four were Filipino. Of the nineteen Europeans, nine were Russian. Players came and went. Some stayed for a long period, some for merely a few months, which makes it hard to trace who these players were. Existing sources such as agreements, payment records, musicians' lists for special occasions from different periods, and the listing of musicians in the *China Hong Desk List* and the *Shanghai Municipal Directory* provide clues to the musicians hired for the period of Paci's tenure from 1919 to 1942, and most of these Russian musicians stayed until the late 1940s. In a nutshell, there were more than fifty Russian musicians who served the SMO in a span of over twenty years (see table 3.2), and they generally accounted for 50 percent of the orchestra's players in the 1930s.

Table 3.2 Russian players in the SMO from 1919 to 1942

Andreyeff, G. 1937–42 (vc)	Milievsky, J. 1930–36 (vn)
Antopolsky, E. 1925, 1927–28 (vn)	Osadehuk, B. 1929–36 (perc)
Bakaleinikoff, M. 1925, 1927–28 (db/pf)	Pashevitch, G. A. 1941 (timp/perc)
Beloff, A. 1938–42 (db/tba)	Patkeeff, G. 1937–42 (trp)
Beriulin, P. 1930–42 (hp/pf)+	Pecheniuk, A. 1928–42 (fl/pic)
Brodsky, A. 1922–23 (vn)	Podushka, J. 1923–42 (va)+
Chernichenko, F. 1924–30 (trp)	Ponomaroff, F. 1923 (trp)
Chernikoff, V. 1927–36 (trb)	Prihodko, V. 1928–29
Daniloff, E. P. 1941 (bsn/db)	Riskin, M. 1935–42 (vn/sax)
Derenevsky, V. 1933–36	Sarichev, P. 1927–41 (ob)**
Dobrovolsky, V. 1936–42 (trp/cnt)+	Shevchook, Y/Z. 1923–42(trb/tba)+
Dramis, V. 1922–37 (cl)	Shevchuk, N. 1929–30 (trb/eup)
Dubroff, A. 1922	Shevtzoff, I. 1924–36 (vc)
Estrin, A. 1925	Shevtzoff, P. 1934–42 (vn/sax)
Feodoroff, Y. 1927–28 (vn)	Schiller, J. 1928–42 (vc)
Fedorov-Kozmenko, S.V. 1930 (trp)	Schvaikowsky, S. 1924–33 (ob/cor)
Froumson, F. 1933–41 (vn/va/cl)	Singer, G. 1936 (pf)
Gelvakoff, I. 1927–28, 1939, 1941–42 (timp/perc)**	Siroido, V. 1920–21 (vn)
	Slizikoff, P. 1937–39 (vn/sax)**
Gerasimuk, W. 1930	Spiridonoff, A. 1928–36 (fl)
Gershgorn, B. 1922–23 (va)	Stupel, I/J. 1926–42 (vc/perc)
Gerzovsky, R. 1928, 1930–42 (vn/va/ assistant concertmaster)+	Tchernikov-Ossovsky, Y. 1937–39, 1941– 42 (trb/tba)
Gorbachenko, A. 1934–36 (trp)	Teplitzky, L. 1930–36
Hajek, Y. 1922 (vn)	Tornapolsky, V. 1923–42 (vn/cl)
Jalvakoff, J. 1937–42 (timp/perc)	Ullstein, J. 1934–38 (vc)
Kout, J. 1927–36 (db)	Ullstein, T/R. 1939–40 (vn)**
Kunze, H. 1922–27 (hp)	Usiskin, B. L. 1934–42 (db)
Laudjil, J. 1922–27, 1941–42 (va)	Vernik, A. 1938–42 (cl)+
Livshits, M. 1928–42 (vn, 2nd vn principal)+	Vierkowsky, N. 1924 (fl)
	Vodrazka, F. 1938 (hr)
Maracheck, S. 1933–40 (vn/cl)**	Wadrasha, F. 1924
Maresek, R. 1933–40	Wadrashka, T. 1924–38 (hr)
Markitant, B. 1930–42 (db/tba)	Zelensky, F. A. 1940–41

Source: Listings of SMO personnel published in the *North China Desk Hong List* (1919–1941) biannually / Player List 1939, SMA U1-4-945 / Player List 1942, Shanghai Symphony Orchestra Archive

** Temporary musician listed in 1939 list

Same Work Different Pay

The Filipino musicians were not the only group who suffered from pay discrimination. Russian musicians, as a result of their refugee status, suffered the same fate during the early years of Paci's tenure. In 1926, the Municipal Council finally approved Paci's reorganization of the orchestra, financially rewarding musicians according to their roles in the orchestra, which Paci had proposed in 1923.[39] In the new pay-scale system, the orchestra formed a permanent nucleus of sixteen musicians—i.e., principals in the orchestra or someone considered to be "doing very important duties"—on Form "A" agreements and the rest on Form "B" agreements. The Form "C" agreement was for musicians engaged locally or from places near Shanghai on a temporary basis, that is, an "individual contract to suit each individual case and not to carry privileges of home leave, etc. as accorded to employees serving under 'A' and 'B' Form agreements." The "D" agreement was for "Manilamen," though those hired earlier would still be granted their original benefits.[40]

Rather than treating players all the same based on their skills and disregarding their ethnicity or origin, Paci appeared to favor Italian musicians, he himself being Italian. Perhaps not coincidentally, as evident in a memo he sent to the council in which he listed all the principal players on Form "A" agreements, two Italian musicians—the third French horn player G. Speroni and the first violinist in charge of clerical work, G. Lestuzzi—were also included even though they were not principals. What "important duties" they were required to do was not clearly stated. Of the players Paci proposed be on Form "A" agreements, all were hired from Europe, and none were Russian. The principal viola, cello, and double bass positions were listed as vacant, even though they had been filled by J. Podushka, I. Shevtsov (Shevtzoff), and Keut, respectively, all Russian but rated "unsatisfactory." The first trombone player, Z. Shevchook, was listed as on probation (SMA U1-3-2884, 55). Paci's argument was that these were good musicians but not good enough to be put on Form "A" agreements even though they were required to do the jobs of the principal players.[41]

It was in fact Paci's original plan to fill up the "vacancies" of this permanent nucleus with musicians from abroad, as he stated clearly in his proposal submitted to the council. "In case of vacancies amongst these fifteen members, the conductor should be authorized to recommend to fill up the vacant positions with men engaged from home, when it should be impossible to find them locally" (SMA U1-3-2884, 55). "Home" could easily be understood as Italy, where Paci originated, or simply Europe. Paci's plan nonetheless did not materialize due to a lack of support from the council. In the end, he still had to count on the Russian players, as they were the best available, which is evident in his request for another pay increase of Tls.30 for Podushka in 1931 for the following reasons: "(1) that the Council has for the last two years rejected my recommendation for the engagement of a First Viola-player from Home under definite agreement; (2) that I could on no condition miss a leader of the Violas and that Mr. Podushka is the only one available in Shanghai" (SMA U1-3-2031, 14).[42]

There is no doubt that Paci valued Podushka's service, but the latter was not treated fairly. Hired in 1923 on a temporary basis with a salary of Tls.165 even though he was considered a "first-class Viola and Violin player" (SMA U1-3-2031, 1),[43] no pay raise was accorded to him until 1927. As explained by Paci in his letter to the council secretary regarding Podushka's request for salary adjustment (SMA U1-3-2031, 6),[44] Podushka was not offered a Form "A" agreement because of his age (forty-nine years) and because Paci thought Podushka was not good enough. In Paci's letter, he reiterated that should another first viola be found from home or abroad and definitely engaged, Podushka would be allowed to serve as the second viola and then on a much reduced salary (SMA U1-3-2031, 6). Even in 1931, being the principal viola player for eight years, he was still on a Form "C" agreement, hired on temporary basis, his contract cancelable on a fortnight's notice (SMA U1-3-2031, 14). Perhaps as a result of his relatively senior age, Podushka did not fight back, but instead supplemented his earning with teaching. In a survey conducted by the SMO in 1940 on musicians' income, Podushka reportedly made Tls.250–300 monthly from giving lessons to supplement his SMO salary (SMA-U1-4-904, 76). As a matter of fact, he was the violin teacher of the famed Chinese composer Nie Er, discussed in chapter 5. Despite the unfair treatment Podushka received, he developed a good rapport with Paci, who valued his service exceptionally, as evident in a note Paci sent to the council about disciplinary measures for the second oboist S. Schvaikowsky in 1933. Paci stated in his memo, "I wish to remind the Council that with the exception of the leader of the Violas, Mr. J. Podushka (who has given very efficient service for more than nine years and who receives a monthly salary of Tls.215), no other temporary musician in the Orchestra receives a monthly salary higher than Tls.170."[45]

Podushka was not the only victim of Paci's discriminatory practices. The cellist I. Shevtsov, thirty years of age when he joined the SMO in 1923 as the principal cellist, was on a probation contract for several years. Though Paci was finally willing to give him a definite agreement in 1925, it was a Form "B" agreement only, thus his salary was only Tls.165 per month. In his contract renewal in 1928, even though he was recommended for the maximum pay raise accorded to the principal instrument players, he was still on a Form "B" agreement. Paci explained: "(a) [Shevtsov] does not wish to be bound by the clause added to Form "A" agreements regarding the possible Alteration of Allowances; (b) and that the Conductor might have the opportunity to replace him with a real first Cello Soloist (which would be very desirable to add interest to the programmes) and pass him to the second stand, which he might refuse."[46] Only in 1931 was Shevtsov finally offered a Form "A" agreement as "Cello Soloist" at a new salary of Tls.270. Paci explained that Shevtsov had improved after further studies in Europe and had good qualities as an employee (SMA U1-3-491, 19 or 50).[47] As will be discussed in the following chapter, Shevtsov was to become an important pedagogue at the National Conservatory of Music after he quit the SMO in 1936 (*North China Desk Hong List* 1936).

Other Russian players of principal instruments such as flutist A. Spiridonov (Spiridonoff) and timpanist V. Osadchuk also suffered the fate of being put on Form "B" agreements during their initial service with the SMO. Probably as a result of financial needs, both of them put forward a petition for compassionate allowances granted to married men in 1930 (SMA U1-3-1098, 13).[48] When they were first hired, they were engaged as "unmarried," on probation and on Form "B" agreements with no benefits to family members. But they were actually married, and they wanted to live decently on their pay. The petition was supported by Paci, who ironically had been the one that put them on unfavorable terms earlier. Had Paci not supported the two players' petitions, he would not have been able to keep them. Presumably as a result of these musicians' negotiations, Paci was forced to grant them Form "A" agreements in their next contract, as seen in Spiridonov's contract renewal in March 1931, at a higher salary of Tls.200 per month (SMA U1-3-1098, 14 or 26).[49]

A Life Falling Apart

Not every refugee musician thrived in adversity, not even in a haven like the SMO. Some were able to make the best of their adopted home, leading a modest but meaningful life, as Podushka and Shevtsov had done; but for some, living lives away from home, their belongings, properties, and sometimes even hopes and joys, the losses were just too painful to bear. While the community was said to be responsible for many of the crimes in the city, Russian refugees were plagued by alcoholism and gambling, and their suicide rate was high.[50] Oboist S. Schvaikowsky and trumpeter F. Chernichenko were two examples. The following account of Schvaikowsky's various disputes and interactions with the SMO allows glimpses into the life of a refugee musician who suffered from his own irresponsible behavior.

Schvaikowsky was hired in March 1924 from Harbin to replace Griffiths, an oboist hired from the UK in January 1921.[51] At the time, Schvaikowsky was thirty-one years old and married with one child. He was to serve a probationary period of six months on a monthly salary of Tls.165, plus an allowance of Tls.15. He would be offered a definite agreement afterward if his performance was satisfactory, and his travel expenses from Harbin to Shanghai would be covered by the Municipal Council.[52] Shortly after his arrival, he wrote to the council for a salary advance of Tls.180 to bring his family from Harbin to Shanghai and agreeing to pay it back to the council by deducting Tls.30 per month from his salary.[53] Paci was in support of the loan to help Schvaikowsky settle down as soon as possible, and the loan was guaranteed by Schevchook, a Russian and a permanent member of the orchestra, who was one of the few Russian players participating in the superannuation fund.

Schvaikowsky proved himself to be a very good oboist and English horn player. He was offered a definite agreement in January 1925, with his salary remaining the same but with the addition of a children's bonus as well as getting free medical benefits for himself and his family.[54] For his next contract, to begin in January 1928, he was given a raise of Tls.20. By then he was participating in the superannuation fund, entitled to a long leave (he took seven months off in 1929)[55] and the privilege of a passage allowance for him and his family to go back to his country if the orchestra were to be disbanded.[56] In the next contract he received in 1931, he got a raise of Tls.20, and due to the withdrawal of long leave benefits in the orchestra's restructuring, his actual monthly salary was Tls.240, inclusive of bonuses.[57]

But as would be revealed, Schvaikowsky's life was spiraling downward. In April 1932, he wrote to the council for a "special advance" of Tls.850 from his superannuation fund, claiming that his wife had been suffering from a "nervous disease" in the previous two years and was ordered by the doctor to go to Japan for climate treatment.[58] But as it turned out, it was Schvaikowsky himself who was in trouble, as was made evident in the warning letter Paci sent him on June 24 of the same year because of his absence from concerts two nights in a row on June 22 and 23. In the letter, Paci warned him of the possibility of contract termination if his behavior did not improve.[59] What Schvaikowsky suffered from was alcoholism, which was possibly linked to or compounded by his excessive debts.[60] In September 3, 1932, Paci wrote to the council secretary for Schvaikowsky's dismissal, explaining that "as a musician he is no longer efficient[,] and as a man now absolutely addicted to alcohol, he fails else [sic] to obey my orders as regards Rehearsals and Service" (SMA U1-3-2574, 52 or 53).

But there was disagreement between Paci and the council regarding how to dismiss Schvaikowsky properly. Paci thought what Schvaikowsky had done deserved immediate dismissal with forfeiture of all benefits. But Paci changed his mind in his letter to the secretary dated September 21, 1932, not wanting to deprive Schvaikowsky's wife and daughter of their livelihood. Instead, Paci recommended that Schvaikowsky terminate his contract himself, forfeiting all the benefits except the superannuation fund, which in Paci's mind should be used to pay off his debts and provide Schvaikowsky a new start. Then, regarding the hiring of Schvaikowsky as a temporary musician, Paci objected to the council paying him his original salary of Tls.240, though he would still like to retain Schvaikowsky's service until a replacement would be available (SMA U1-3-2574, 62 or 63). But the council thought paying Schvaikowsky Tls.170 as a temporary musician was taking advantage of his financial difficulty given that Schvaikowsky had been with the orchestra for a long time and his missing two concerts was his first offense.[61] In the end, the council ruled that Schvaikowsky could stay with his job on his original terms of service, but Tls.100 per month would be deducted from his salary to pay off his debts (SMA U1-3-2574, 121–122 or 122–123).

But Schvaikowsky did not take advantage of the second chance given to him and got into trouble again in just a few months. As reported by Paci to the council secretary on February 13, 1933, Schvaikowsky missed another rehearsal and was seen by a Chinese staff member taking an instrument away, presumably reported missing by another musician. But Schvaikowsky denied knowing anything about it. When he was asked to bring back his own instruments (the oboe and the English horn) the following day, he failed to do so and was not able to provide an explanation.[62] Given Schvaikowsky's record, Paci suspected that he had pawned the instruments, and he reported it to the police.[63] Paci wrote again to the council secretary and requested the immediate dismissal of Schvaikowsky.[64]

It was found out later that Schvaikowsky left the rehearsal to appear in the District Court with the permission of Assistant Conductor Arrigo Foa on February 11, 1933. He did not return to work because he thought by the time he was finished at the court the rehearsal would be over. He took the trumpet of Filipino musician R. Santos without asking so his friend could use it to play at the cabarets. He had intended to get Santos' permission but forgot. He denied knowing anything about the instrument when interrogated by Paci because he was very nervous at the time. Regarding why he did not bring the oboe and the English horn back when asked, he said the instruments were at the home of his friend, who was not there at the time. Despite the circumstances, Schvaikowsky did bring back the instruments the following day.[65]

The incident seems to be a case of poor judgment and miscommunication rather than an intentional criminal offense. But Paci was determined to get rid of Schvaikowsky despite petitions from Schvaikowsky's wife and his daughter,[66] which was accompanied by the signature of nineteen musicians, almost all Russians. Such a gesture of sympathy and support of a fellow musician whose suffering they probably understood revealed the solidarity of the Russian musicians in the SMO.[67]

In the end, the council's decision was to dismiss Schvaikowsky and have his superannuation fund forfeited, which seem a punishment too harsh for the crime. Naturally, Schvaikowsky had nobody but himself to blame. But he was in need of psychological help, which was not available to him. Could Paci and the council have been more sympathetic toward him were he not a Russian émigré and if the prejudice of Russian refugees being connected to the underworld and crimes of Shanghai had not existed? It is hard to know. But the council was not entirely heartless in that Schvaikowsky and his family were granted passage to Moscow via Harbin, as Schvaikowsky himself requested (SMA U1-3-2574, 151).[68] Rather than third-class passage as originally granted, the council accepted Schvaikowsky's request, with Paci's endorsement, to provide the family the amount for second-class passage, so they could travel third-class and keep the difference for the family's livelihood.[69]

After the termination of his contract on March 20, 1933, Schvaikowsky and his family left Shanghai for Harbin, where they waited for visas to enter the USSR for eight months, but to no avail. On December 21, 1933, Schvaikowsky wrote to the travel agent Thomas Cook & Sons requesting that it apply to the Municipal Council for rerouting their journey to Lithuania (city of Vilna), his home country, and the council did authorize the travel agent to arrange for such a trip. But the council soon learned that Schvaikowsky changed his mind about going home and wanted to come back to Shanghai to discuss in person with the council about passage money, which was naturally denied. In any case, the family returned to Shanghai, presumably totally broke since Schvaikowsky was unemployed in Harbin, as his wife related to the council in a letter written in February 1935. The family was in dire circumstances. According to his wife, she worked as a dressmaker, but her eyesight grew so weak that she was no longer able to continue, so they were "entirely without means for livelihood." Thus she would like the council to refund the money left over from their untraveled journey to "save me and my daughter from starvation and permit me to live until my position will improve."[70] What she got was a speedy but cold reply from the deputy secretary that "as ex-Musician Schvaikowsky did not avail himself of the Council's offer to defray part of the cost of his repatriation from Harbin to Vilna within the stipulated period, the offer was withdrawn. I also have to inform you with regret that the Council is unwilling to reopen this question or favorably to consider your application for a monetary payment in lieu of passage money."[71] This was the last trace of Schvaikowsky and his family, who like many of the refugees at the time or any time, simply disappeared into the past without a trace.

Schvaikowsky and his family were not alone in their misfortunes. As refugees, they had to struggle not just to make ends meet, but also to adapt to the new environment and new culture. There were many who turned to gambling and alcohol, and when all seemed too overwhelming, some simply chose to end their lives. But it is fair to say that musicians were the lucky group among the émigré community, as jobs were plentiful, even if that might mean playing at restaurants or cabarets, as discussed in chapter 1. Even though the SMO's salary levels lagged behind the rising living cost after the mid-1930s, musicians were able to make ends meet by taking up part-time jobs playing at restaurants and theaters or giving private music lessons, which, interestingly, changed China's musical soundscape, as will be examined further in the following chapters.

Russian Players' Contribution to the SMO

Most of all, what should not be forgotten are the contributions made by the Russian musicians, particularly the section principals, who also took up the role of soloists. Even though these players were not superstars like the visiting musical virtuosi such as Mischa Elman or Benno Moiseiwitsch, their serving as soloists for the SMO did provide programming varieties for the Shanghai audience, and concert attendance improved significantly whenever a soloist was added ("Advances Made" 1928, 5). In fact, Paci even made an open call to local musicians, vocalists, and instrumentalists to appear with the SMO in 1938, thereby confirming the importance of having a soloist in the concert program. Indeed, the principals of the SMO represented the best instrumentalists in Shanghai. The majority of these principals were Russian (broadly defined), which included C. J. van Heyst (bassoonist), Joseph Podushka (violist), E. Antapolsky (violinist), A. Spiridonov (flautist), V. Sarychev (oboist), V. Dramis (clarinetist), I. Shevtsov and J. Ullstein (cellists), and P. Biriulin (harpist and pianist), to name some of them (see table 3.3 for a listing of Russian soloists performed with the SMO).

Because of the presence of these musicians, the Shanghai audience was able to hear a larger repertoire of works, as solo instrumentalists were not always available in Shanghai. For instance, the cellist Shevtsov appeared many times with the SMO as a soloist. In addition to performing the standard cello concerto repertoire,[72] he also played some less usual works.[73] The harpist and pianist Biriulin also played a number of harp concertos with the SMO,[74] as did viola principal Podushka and the clarinet principal Dramis. The number of times they performed as soloists as listed in table 3.3 provides us glimpses into their importance in the orchestra. It is not to be forgotten that it was because of these principal players of the SMO that Paci was able to organize many chamber music concerts for Shanghai's audiences.[75]

Though Paci's relationship with the Russian musicians was complex, he did acknowledge his indebtedness to them in his 1942 interview with the Russian newspaper *Shanghai Zaria*, at a time when he was about to part with the orchestra, and the International Settlement and the Municipal Council were to be transferred to the Japanese government in Shanghai:

Table 3.3 Russian musicians who performed with the SMO as soloists

Abramovitch, A. (sop)
1932.05.01; 1932.07.16*

Aksakov, S. (pf/composer)
1933.03.12

Alpert-Rosanoff, I. (sop)
1925.04.05

Andreyeff, G. (vc)
1941.03.09; 1941.05.04; 1942.04.12

Antapolsky, E. (vn)
1924.11.02; 1927.03.27; 1927.06.05;
1927.06.25*

Avshalomov, Aaron (composer/
conductor)
1933.05.21; 1936.01.19; 1936.02.02;
1937.05.23; 1937.12.19; 1939.03.12;
1940.03.17; 1941.02.23; 1945.04.04;
1945.12.16; 1946.02.24;
1946.03.02+03; 09+10; 16+17;
1946.04.07; 1946.04.14; 1946.04.21;
1946.04.28

Bakaleinikoff, C. (vc)
1919.12.28

Baka-Leinikoff, M. (db)
1923.11.08; 1928.11.19+25

Baturina, Sophie (sop)
1930.01.05; 1930.03.30

Berschadsky, Raya (sop)
1935.11.17; 1936.05.17

Biriulin/Beriulin, Paul (hp/pf)
1928.11.30; 1929.01.21; 1929.01.29;
1929.04.28; 1929.05.19; 1929.11.03;
1930.01.12; 1930.03.23; 1930.04.06;
1930.05.18; 1930.10.26; 1931.02.01;
1931.03.18; 1931.11.08; 1932.01.24;
1933.12.10; 1934.02.14; 1934.03.11;
1934.08.04&15*; 1934.08.18*;
1934.10.09; 1934.11.14; 1934.12.02;
1935.02.12; 1935.03.19; 1936.10.25;
1936.12.13; 1937.03.21; 1937.10.17;
1937.12.05; 1938.01.23; 1939.04.23;
1939.05.21; 1939.12.03; 1944.01.09;
1944.06.04; 1944.10.15;
1944.12.02+03; 1944.12.10

Borisoff, Josef (vn)
1927.11.20; 1927.11.24

Bouskaya, Helene (sop)
1930.04.06

Bourskaya-Vladimiroff, E.P. (sop)
1928.12.28

Chehoff, V. T. (bas)
1938.07.21*

Chernieskaja, Vera (pf)
1926.10.10; 1927.05.27; 1929.12.01

Chumakova, Tamara (mez/sop)
1937.09.19; 1944.03.25+26;
1945.05.24–27; 06.02–03

Dobrovolsky, V. (trp/cnt)
1936.01.05; 1936.04.05; 1936.09.16*;
1936.09.26+29*; 1938.07.03*;
1938.08.07*; 1938.08.19*;
1938.08.23+24*; 1938.08.27*;
1938.09.03*; 1939.07.29*; 1939.08.02*;
1939.08.27*; 1944.07.29+30*;
1945.06.24

Dramis, V. (cl)
1921.03.13; 1921.11.20; 1921.12.04;
1922.01.26; 1922.03.30; 1922.04.13;
1923.01.25; 1923.03.22; 1923.05.03;
1923.05.31; 1924.02.28; 1924.05.01;
1925.01.11; 1925.10.18; 1925.10.25;
1926.12.12; 1927.05.01; 1927.05.08;
1927.06.05; 1927.11.13; 1927.12.18;
1928.11.19; 1928.11.25; 1929.01.29;
1929.04.28; 1929.05.12; 1929.05.26;
1929.08.05*; 1929.11.17; 1930.01.12;
1930.03.02; 1932.02.28; 1933.04.02;
1934.01.28; 1934.12.02; 1935.07.31*;
1936.01.05; 1936.02.09; 1936.12.06

Dukstulsky, Roman (vc)
1936.12.13; 1936.12.20

Eltzoff/Eltzova,Vera (mez)
1926.05.23; 1933.01.15; 1933.05.28

Fedoroff, I. (vn)
1927.10.16

Fidlon, Gregory (vn)
1929.10.27; 1938.01.16

Table 3.3 (Cont.)

Gerzovsky, Rudolf (vn/va)
1928.11.19+25; 1929.05.26;
1930.03.02; 1933.08.01*; 1934.11.18;
1938.05.15; 1939.12.30; 1940.05.21;
1944.06.04; 1944.10.15; 1944.11.12;
1944.12.10; 1945.01.14; 1945.05.27

Glebova, M. (sop)
1933.05.28

Gorbachenko, A. (trp)
1932.07.19*; 1932.07.29*; 1934.08.14*;
1934.10.14*

Gravitsky, I. (sop)
1928.05.13

Grigorieva-Hmelnitskaya, E. (sop)
1928.12.16; 1928.12.23; 1928.12.28

Hataieva, Euphalie (voc)
1922.11.23

Havsky, Vladimir (pf)
1937.02.07; 1938.05.22;
1938.07.12*;1939.01.29; 1939.02.26;
1940.05.21; 1940.05.26; 1940.08.10*;
1940.10.29; 1940.11.03

Hmelnitzky, A. (pf)
1923.12.09; 1923.12.20; 1925.02.19;
1925.04.09

Itkis, Leo (pf)
1933.12.03; 1936.01.05; 1936.04.05;
1937.01.31; 1937.09.19; 1937.10.31;
1938.02.20; 1938.10.23; 1938.12.18;
1941.01.12

Jarikova, E. (sop)
1933.05.28

Koodrevatik, N. (bas)
1937.03.26

Koudinoff/Kudinoff, George V. (bar)
1939.05.28; 1939.11.05;
1940.08.03*; 1945.03.[n.d.];
1945.05.12;1945.06.23+24

Krilova, Maria (alt)
1932.12.07; 1932.12.30; 1933.05.28;
1936.04.14

Kucejova, Sonia (sop)
1933.04.09; 1934.02.11; 1938.05.08;
1941.10.12

Lavrowa, M. (alt)
1934.02.25

Livshitz, M. (vn)
1928.11.25; 1930.03.02; 1930.04.06;
1930.04.13; 1931.01.11; 1932.02.28;
1932.05.08; 1933.01.08; 1933.01.22;
1934.01.14; 1934.11.11; 1935.02.12;
1935.05.26; 1936.12.06; 1938.02.27;
1938.05.15; 1939.03.12; 1939.05.14;
1940.04.14; 1941.03.09; 1941.05.04

Lvoff, Ada (pf)
1936.11.29; 1938.03.06; 1939.05.14;
1940.02.25; 1942.04.26; 1942.08.02*;
1943.05.02

Makarova, Z. (sop)
1938.02.06

Makoveeff, E. (bar)
1944.09.02+03*

Margolinsky/Margolinski, Henry
(pf/conductor)
1940.02.26; 1942.03.08; 1942.07.15*;
1942.08.09*; 1942.08.30*; 1944.12.23;
1946.01.27;
served as conductor in 1946 from
May till Dec

Markoff, Peter (ten)
1934.02.25; 1935.01.27; 1938.04.10;
1943.05.23; 1944.03.25+26; 1945.03.
[n.d.]; 1945.06.23+24

Markovska, Julia (sop)
1934.01.07; 1938.01.02; 1938.02.06

Masloff, Tamara (pf)
1928.11.30; 1929.01.29; 1929.03.24;
1929.05.14; 1930.05.04; 1931.03.08

Melashich, Vera (mez)
1933.05.28; 1936.11.01; 1937.12.12

Milikowskaja, Ada (pf)
1933.10.29

Milikowski, T. (pf)
1922.04.13

Miller, A. (sop)
1933.05.28

(Continues)

Table 3.3 (Cont.)

Moiseiwitch, Benno (pf)
1933.05.07; 1933.05.14; 1933.06.16

Moskalenko, B. (bas)
1945.03.[n.d.]; 1945.05.12

Muraveff, Y. (ten)
1944.09.02+03*; 1945.05.12;
1945.05.24–27;1945.06.02+03

Onderwyzer, D. (bar)
1922.01.08+10

Osadschuk/Osadchuk, V. (xly)
1929.01.29; 1929.10.29; 1931.03.18,
1932.08.10*; 1934.08.04+15*;
1934.10.24

Pavlovsky, Valentin (pf)
1936.10.02

Pecheniuk, A. (fl)
1927.05.01; 1927.05.08; 1930.03.02;
1935.01.27; 1936.01.05; 1938.03.27;
1938.08.07*; 1940.03.03; 1943.02.28

Piatigorsky, Gregor (vc)
1936.10.02

Podushka, Joseph (va)
1923.11.08; 1923.11.18; 1923.12.20;
1924.01.17; 1924.01.31; 1924.02.28;
1924.03.13; 1924.03.27; 1924.04.10;
1924.05.01; 1924.10.19; 1925.01.08;
1925.02.12; 1925.02.26; 1925.03.08;
1925.03.12; 1925.03.26; 1925.03.29;
1925.04.09; 1925.04.23; 1925.11.01;
1926.10.24; 1926.10.26; 1927.10.16;
1930.04.06; 1930.04.13; 1931.01.11;
1932.02.28; 1932.05.08; 1932.07.27*;
1933.01.08; 1933.01.22; 1933.02.26;
1934.01.14; 1934.11.11; 1934.11.18;
1935.02.24; 1935.05.26; 1935.12.01;
1936.11.22; 1936.12.06; 1937.01.17;
1938.02.27; 1938.03.06; 1938.03.20;
1938.05.15; 1939.01.22; 1939.03.12;
1939.04.30; 1939.05.14; 1940.03.31;
1940.04.14; 1940.05.21; 1941.03.09;
1941.05.04; 1944.04.08+09;
1944.06.04; 1944.10.08; 1944.10.15;
1944.11.12; 1944.12.10; 1945.01.14;
1946.10.25

Riskin, M. (vn/sax)
1934.06.28*; 1934.07.04*; 1944.12.24;
1945.05.27

Riskin, Raya (sop)
1936.11.15

Robitchek, Lisa (sop)
1939.04.02; 1939.10.29; 1939.12.24;
1942.03.08

Romaniuck, B. (ten)
1938.02.06

Russian Chorus/Choral Society
(Mashin, P./Kolchin, I.A.)
1924.12.21; 1927.06.05; 1928.04.01;
1929.12.29; 1931.12.27; 1932.12.30;
1933.04.14; 1933.05.28; 1936.04.14;
1937.03.26; 1940.03.24; 1941.04.13;
1941.04.27; 1944.03.25+26; 1945.03.
[n.d.]

Russian Male Vocal Ensemble (Kolchin,
I. A.)
1937.12.12; 1938.07.21*

Russian Opera/Russian Grand Opera)
(Muraveff, Y.)
1944.04.09; 1944.09.02+03*;
1944.11.17–19; 1945.01.19–21;
1945.05.24–27;1945.06.02+03

Saharova/Zakharova, Fausta (pf)
1935.04.14; 1936.03.15; 1939.05.28

Saricheff, V. (ob/ca/conductor)
1934.01.28; 1934.05.13; 1934.12.02;
1939.05.14; 1944.01.11+12+15+16;
1944.11.15+28; 1946.08.26+27;
1946.09.09+10

Schwaikowsky, S. (ob)
1925.04.09; 1927.11.13; 1930.01.12;
1932.02.28

Seidl-Margolinsky, Irene (sop)
1946.12.29

Selivanoff/Selivanov, P. (bas)
1920.02.24; 1923.12.20; 1925.12.17;
1927.10.16; 1933.04.14; 1934.02.25

Shemansky, A. L. (ten)
1931.02.22

Table 3.3 *(Cont.)*

Shevchook, Z. (trb/euph)
1925.02.26; 1929.01.29; 1929.08.28*;
1930.08.08*; 1930.08.20*; 1931.07.03*;
1932.07.25*; 1933.08.18*; 1933.08.30*;
1934.10.06*; 1935.06.16+21*;
1935.07.20+23*; 1935.08.15*;
1935.08.24+25*; 1939.08.06*

Shevtzoff, Innocent (vc)
1923.10.28; 1923.11.04; 1923.11.08;
1923.12.20; 1924.01.17; 1924.01.31;
1924.02.28; 1924.03.13; 1924.03.27;
1924.04.10; 1924.05.01; 1925.01.08;
1925.02.08; 1925.02.12; 1925.02.26;
1925.03.01; 1925.03.12; 1925.03.19;
1925.03.26; 1925.04.09; 1925.04.23;
1926.01.10; 1926.03.28; 1926.06.23*;
1926.08.07+14*;1926.11.07;
1927.06.25*;1927.10.16;
1927.11.27; 1928.03.06;
1928.06.09*;1928.11.19+25;
1929.01.14; 1929.10.20; 1930.01.12;
1930.01.19; 1930.02.16; 1930.03.02;
1930.03.23; 1930.04.06; 1930.04.13;
1930.06.24*; 1930.11.30; 1931.01.11;
1931.01.18; 1931.02.27; 1931.07.07*;
1931.11.01; 1932.02.21; 1932.07.02*;
1932.08.17*;1932.12.04; 1933.01.08;
1933.01.22; 1933.08.09*;
[1933.12.03]**; 1933.12.10; 1934.01.14;
1934.01.21; 1934.07.28*; 1934.10.24;
1934.11.11; 1935.02.12; 1935.03.19;
1935.05.26; 1943.12.12; 1944.03.11;
1944.06.04; 1944.10.08; 1944.10.15;
1944.11.12; 1944.12.10; 1944.12.24;
1945.01.14; 1945.05.05; 1945.05.27;
1946.01.13; 1946.10.25; 1947.05.11

Shushlin, Vladimir (bas)
1930.02.02; 1930.03.23; 1932.12.07;
1932.12.30; 1933.04.14; 1933.05.28;
1933.11.19; 1935.02.24; 1935.03.10;
1935.12.29; 1936.01.14; 1936.03.01;
1936.04.14; 1936.11.08; 1937.03.26;
1937.04.17; 1938.02.06; 1938.04.10;
1939.02.19; 1940.03.24; 1940.05.21;
1941.02.02; 1942.08.13*; 1945.12.22

Silinskaia, Elisabetta (sop)
1934.03.18

Singer, Gregory (pf/composer)
1933.03.05; 1934.01.21; 1936.01.19;
1936.02.02; 1936.03.08; 1937.05.23;
1937.11.07; 1939.03.12; 1940.12.01;
1941.02.23; 1943.03.28; 1946.02.10;
1946.03.09+10

Siroido, V. (vn)
1920.02.29; 1920.03.28; 1920.04.30;
1920.11.21; 1920.12.05; 1920.12.19;
1921.03.13; 1921.04.17; 1921.05.15

Slavianoff, N. (mez)
1929.03.24; 1931.10.25

Slobodskoy, A. (ten)
1933.05.28; 1935.12.01; 1936.04.14;
1936.10.18; 1937.03.26; 1937.04.17;
1937.05.30; 1937.12.12; 1938.02.06;
1938.12.11; 1940.03.10; 1940.03.24;
1940.05.10; 1941.04.13; 1941.04.27

Sloutsky, Alexander (conductor)
1928.10.21; 1933.01.15; 1933.06.29*;
1933.07.11*; 1933.07.20*; 1933.07.28*;
1933.08.04*; 1933.08.18+20*;
1933.08.30*; 1936.07.23*; 1936.08.07*;
1936.08.14*; 1936.08.16+18*;
1936.08.21*; 1937.01.15–17+23+24;
1940.05.24; 1941.01.30+02.01+02.02;
1943.01 to 1945.07 as principal
conductor 1946.09.15*; 1946.09.21*

Speransky, M. (bar)
1941.04.13; 1941.04.27;
1944.09.02+03*

Spielman, S. (vc)
1928.03.18; 1928.03.22

Spiridonoff, A. (fl)
1928.01.29; 1929.01.29; 1929.04.28;
1929.05.12; 1929.08.05*; 1929.10.29;
1929.11.17; 1930.03.02; 1930.08.16*;
1930.10.26; 1931.08.08*;1931.08.27*;
1932.02.28; 1932.07.06*;
1932.07.23*;1932.08.03*; 1934.10.09;
1934.10.28; 1934.12.02; 1935.01.27;
1935.07.31*;1936.04.10; 1936.04.19

(Continues)

Table 3.3 *(Cont.)*

Stupel, J. (vc)	1936.12.06; 1937.01.17; 1937.02.21;
1930.01.19	1937.10.17; 1937.10.24; 1937.11.07;
Tcherepnin, Alexandre (pf/composer)	1937.12.26; 1938.01.30; 1938.02.27;
1934.05.13; 1934.11.25	1938.03.20; 1938.04.03; 1938.05.15;
Tcherkasskaya, M. B. (sop)	1939.04.16; 1939.10.22; 1940.05.21
1921.04.17; 1922.01.22+24;	**Vedernikoff, Tolia (pf)**
1922.03.12+14	1935.03.31; 1935.06.02; 1935.07.27*
Tcherkassoff, I. (vn)	**Velikanoff, Victor (conductor)**
1920.12.05	1930.01.05; 1930.03.30
Tomaszewska, Wincia (pf)	**Vernick, Anton (cl)**
1935.02.12; 1935.02.17; 1936.03.08;	1938.02.13; 1938.03.20; 1938.05.15;
1939.01.15; 1940.10.20; 1941.05.25;	1938.07.20*; 1938.08.07*;1939.08.02*;
1942.03.29	1941.02.23; 1944.03.18
Tomsky/Tomskaya, Alla (alt)	**Vierkowsky, N. (fl)**
1925.12.13; 1928.04.01	1924.02.03; 1924.05.01
Troutneff-Samorukoff, S. (sop)	**Vinogradoff, Paul (pf)**
1920.11.28; 1922.02.09	1922.11.26+28
Ullstein, J. (vc)	**Wadrashka, T. (hr)**
1929.01.29; 1929.02.03; 1929.03.03;	1924.05.01;1931.08.13*
1929.04.21; 1929.04.28; 1929.05.12;	**Yanushevsky, L. (ten)**
1929.08.19*;1929.08.24*; 1929.12.08;	1944.09.02+03*
1930.01.19; 1930.12.07; 1931.01.25;	**Zakharoff, Boris (pf)**
1931.11.15; 1932.02.28; 1932.05.08;	1930.05.18; 1933.04.30; 1936.04.26;
1933.03.05; 1933.12.17; 1934.06.16*;	1940.05.21; 1941.05.04
1934.07.14*; 1934.10.28; 1934.12.02;	**Zorich, Sophie (sop)**
1935.07.31*; 1935.08.29*;1935.11.24;	1937.11.28; 1943.01.17; 1943.08.21*;
1936.03.08; 1936.05.10;	1944.03.25+26; 1944.09.02+03*;
1936.08.12*;1936.09.02*; 1936.10.25;	1945.05.12

* Open-air concert held in the summer
Information compiled from extant programs of the SMO at the Shanghai Symphony Archive

When I started the work in Shanghai, the orchestra consisted almost entirely of Russian musicians. Some of them worked with me from the first to the last day, today, i.e., twenty-three years. Music has an enormous meaning for the Russian soul. The Russians feel it spontaneously and ardently. I want to and I have to note that in the multinational Shanghai the audience in symphonic concerts has been mostly Russian. Living with Russians, being in touch with Russian musicians on a daily basis at work, I try to grasp the soul and heart of Russians and Russian music that our orchestra always performs with great enthusiasm. ("Maestro Pachi o svoei . . ." 1942, 5)

While Paci's remarks need to be taken with a grain of salt, there is no doubt that the Russian émigré musicians were important assets to Paci and Shanghai's cultural scene. In fact, the Russian community was crucial for the survival of the SMO. Despite the recognition Paci brought to the SMO, he also ran into many difficulties after 1925, which were aptly pointed out in a newspaper article titled "Advances Made By Municipal Orchestra Shown By Contrast with Cruder and Earlier Days" (1928, 5).[76] First of all, every year Paci had to face the possibility that the orchestra would disband, as its continuation was contingent upon the taxpayers' vote at the annual meeting held every April. Second, Paci was thought to have taken "a mistakingly [sic] optimistic view of the musical culture of a cosmopolitan crowd which 'en masse' has none." For example, the chamber music concerts that he started and for which he put in a considerable amount of effort were not well received or attended even though he tried to organize them on dates not to interfere with sports events. Third, though concert attendance improved significantly whenever a soloist was added, this was not always possible in Shanghai. Fourth, the popular music concerts were thought to be not well publicized, and sometimes not even well played, and the lack of soloists at these concerts was thought to be responsible for the lack of audience interest. Fifth, Paci was criticized for not understanding "his badly defined surroundings" when selecting his programming, such as by ignoring the nature of the Shanghai audience and having too much preference for Italian works. Last, Paci had to bear the burden of educating the public alone with his orchestra, as music critics who wrote for newspapers were usually not trained for such a profession.

In light of the challenges the SMO faced as of 1928, the growing Russian community and the arrival of Russian musicians were indeed crucial for the SMO's survival. The chamber music concerts, which were said to be not well received in 1928, were reported to be successful in the 1930–1931 season, particularly in the case of the quartets and the trios. It should not be overlooked that the players of these chamber music concerts were largely Russian musicians, sectional principals of the SMO as well as other renowned soloists residing in Shanghai at the time. As proclaimed by the Russian pianist Boris Zakharov, who played at many of these concerts, in an interview from 1931, "Last year all of the performers at the Chamber Music concerts, with the exception of one Italian, were Russians. The Russian colony enjoys these concerts immensely" (Lewis 1931, 13).[77]

Indeed, Russian musicians did not shy away from expressing their support of the SMO. They wrote frequently in both Russian and English-language newspapers about Shanghai's lack of cultural accomplishment despite its success as a metropolis. Zakharov was probably one of the most outspoken against the disbanding of the SMO. Shortly before the taxpayers' meeting in April 1934 to vote for the continuation of the SMO, he wrote to the *North-China Daily News* to plead for the taxpayers' support. He argued that the SMO's running on a budget deficit should not be the cause for its discontinuation, as the institution had created good rapport among music lovers of different national origins and was taken as the cultural parallel of Shanghai's economic prosperity ("The Orchestra" 1934, 2).

Right before the ratepayers' meeting in 1935 to decide on the continuation of the SMO, an article titled "A United Front to Protect the Symphony" appeared in *Shanghai Zaria*, in which five prominent Russian musicians—Zakharov, as well as the ballet director E. Elirov and three singers, A. Markov, A. Slobodskoy, and V. Shushlin—voiced their support for the SMO. They emphasized that the institution should remain under the auspices of the municipality rather than going into private hands. Elirov even used the Moscow Symphony Orchestra as an example to argue for the need for such an institution to be under state support, that is, being under the budget of the Bolshoi Theater and its rising to great success after heavy monetary investment from its sponsor ("Yedinym frontom" 1935, 5).

Russian musicians' support of the SMO and their taking a proactive role in defending Shanghai's most important musical institution was a symbol of the émigrés asserting their voice. Though they were politically voiceless as refugees, through music they were able to participate in the international network, playing the role of Shanghai's cultural advocate by defending the most prestigious cultural body in international Shanghai. Most of all, the disbanding of the SMO would have resulted in many Russian players' losing their jobs, and likewise the weekly concerts enjoyed by the Russian community. After all, going to a concert was not only a social event, but a utopian experience. The audience, through the imaginative space created by music, could have various emotional experiences, including transcendence. There is no doubt that music could bring out as well as provide comfort for the complex emotions of being dispersed outside of their homeland. The rhythms, the melodies, the scales, and the sonorities of familiar works, consumed with fellow countrymen as an experience of musical embodiment, would carry special meanings for Russian émigrés.

The presence of a large number of Russian émigré musicians in Shanghai changed the city's musical landscape, transforming it from a mercenary city to China's cultural hub with the emergence of Russian opera companies and ballet troupes, cabarets, jazz bands, and the many chamber and solo concerts organized by Russian musicians. As many Russian musicians and émigrés became ardent supporters of the SMO, Paci's programming had to take into account the taste of the Russian public, which resulted in his concerts' heavy emphasis on Russian works and soloists, which will be the focus of the next chapter.

CHAPTER 4

Sounding Russian in a Metropolis

RUSSIAN CONCERTS AND SOLOISTS OF THE SHANGHAI MUNICIPAL ORCHESTRA

THOSE who frequented the Shanghai Municipal Orchestra (SMO) concerts in the interwar period would have noticed the high proportion of Russian players in the orchestra. They would have also noticed the high proportion of Russian concert attendees in general and especially at the special Russian concerts held several times a year. The one held on May 1, 1932, at the Carlton Theater, the twenty-ninth symphony concert of the SMO's 1931–1932 season titled "Special Russian Popular Programme," was a case in point. Conducted by SMO music director Mario Paci, the concert program featured Russian favorites that spoke particularly to the Russian audience, including works of strong Russian color such as Arensky's overture to *A Dream on the Volga*, adaptions from Glazunov's "Song of the Volga Boatmen," and Russian folk songs made popular by Andreyev's Balalaika Ensemble. Naturally, the program also featured works of famous Russian composers, namely Tchaikovsky, Borodin, Mussorgsky, Dargomyzhsky, etc. Most of all, the concert was spiced up further by having the Russian soprano A. Abramovitch sing arias from Tchaikovsky's operas and other well-loved Russian melodies.

Such special Russian concerts were generally well attended, and this particular one was no exception. The phenomenal success of the concert was noted in Shanghai's English-language newspapers ("The Municipal Orchestra" 1932, 12; "Municipal Orchestra" 1932, 177), which speaks to the impact of such concerts beyond the Russian community.[1] One of the reviewers wrote that "most of Shanghai's Russian community who could still maintain musical inclinations after the day's festivities appeared to be present." The inclusion of a Russian soprano was seen as adding "that spice to the program which never fails to swell the number of what might be termed the extra-fan section of the Sunday night audiences," while the program was considered to have "made a strong appeal to those who have a leaning towards the peculiar quality of Russian music—that mixture of sadness and emotion with twinges of almost barbaric frenzy" ("Municipal Orchestra" 1932, 177).

The above was just one of the many "Special Russian Concerts" presented by the SMO to appeal to Russian residents in Shanghai. As already mentioned in the introduction, by the early 1930s the Russian community in Shanghai had grown to approximately twelve thousand residents. One Russian writer joked in 1930 that the eight thousand Russians living in the French Concession should cause the area to be renamed the Russian Concession (quoted in Wang 1993, 80). Like any other newly emerged refugee community, the Shanghai Russian community was unique and was plagued by an array of social problems such as unemployment, prostitution, crime, alcoholism, and high suicide rates, discussed in chapter 1. Professional musicians were the lucky group, as their skills were in demand. Some of them found employment with the SMO, as discussed in the previous chapter, and many others played at other musical institutions as well as entertainment venues. Both professional and amateur music making served the Russian community well, as these musical activities were vital for musicians not only to make a living but also to hold on to their social and cultural status. As this chapter shows, the Russian émigrés' love of classical music did have an impact on the ecosystem of the SMO and Shanghai's cultural scene. Thanks to the presence of a large Russian audience in Shanghai, many special Russian concerts and Russian works were introduced to the SMO concert repertoire. While providing information on these Russian concerts, Russian works performed, and Russian soloists who collaborated with the SMO, this chapter also explicates how such a "Russian" phenomenon of the SMO was intertwined with the Russian community. It argues that such a phenomenon was not only a result of the SMO's cosmopolitan ideal but was also an outcome of political economy for the SMO, as these well-attended concerts were important justifications for ratepayers to vote to continue the institution.

Russian Repertoire of the SMO

Special Russian concerts like the one mentioned above started to appear after 1921, which coincided with the incoming Russian émigrés to Shanghai after the October Revolution (see table 4.1 for listing of special Russian concerts of the SMO). Paci, after taking up the SMO conductorship in 1919, regularly organized concerts around composers of different nationalities, probably as a result of Shanghai's multinational demographics. For example, in the 1920–1921 season, there were concerts of Italian, French, and Russian composers, as well as concerts devoted to individual composers, namely Beethoven, Mozart, Mendelssohn, Wagner, and Tchaikovsky. Paci's predecessor had already established these

Table 4.1 Special Russian concerts of the SMO

1911.12.10	*Fifth Concert: Tchaikovsky Program—Professor Buck*
	1812 Overture / Orchestral Suite no.3, op.55: IV / Symphony no.6 in B minor, op.74 "Pathetique"
1912.04.07	*Twentieth Concert: Tchaikovsky Program—Professor Buck*
	1812 Overture / The Nutcracker / Symphony no.5 in E minor, op.64
1912–1919	*Missing Program*
1920.04.11	*Twentieth Concert: French and Russian Composers—Mario Paci*
	Lalo, Namouna: Prelude, Serenade, fête foraine // Debussy, L'enfant Prodigue: Air de Lia / Les Cloches and Mandolinez [Zalsman, M. (sop)] / Prélude à l'après-midi d'un faune // Borodin, In the Steppes of Central Asia // Scriabin, Reverie, op.24 // Rimsky-Korsakov, Russian Easter Overture, op.36
1920.04.30	*Twenty-Second Concert—Mario Paci*
	Tchaikovsky, Symphony no.6 in B minor, op.74 "Pathetique" / Violin Concerto in D major, op.35 [V. Siroido (vn)] // Rimsky-Korsakov, Capriccio Espagnol
1921.01.23	*Tenth Concert: Russian Composers—Mario Paci*
	Ippolitov-Ivanov, Esquisses Caucasiennes, op.10 // Tchaikovsky, Symphony no.6 in B minor, op.74 "Pathetique" // Rimsky-Korsakov, Capriccio Espagnol
1921.01.30	*Eleventh Concert: Tchaikovsky—Mario Paci*
	Symphony no.4 in F minor, op.36 / Symphony no.5 in E minor, op.64: III / Marche Slave, op.31
1921.05.01	*Twenty-Fourth Concert—A. de Kryger*
	Tchaikovsky, Symphony no.5 in E minor, op.64 / Rococo Variations, op.33 [Stupin, S. (vc)] / Piano Concerto no.1 in B flat minor, op.23: I [Gillersberg, I.(pf)] / Marche Slave, op.31
1921.12.18	*Eleventh Concert: Russian Composers—Mario Paci*
	Tchaikovsky, Symphony no.4 in F minor, op.36 // Borodin, In the Steppes of Central Asia // Rimsky-Korsakov, Capriccio Espagnol
1922.01.03	*Thirteenth Concert: Tchaikovsky—Mario Paci*
	Tchaikovsky, Symphony no.4 in F minor, op.36 / Capriccio Italiano / Marche Slave, op.31
1922.01.29+31	*Seventeenth Concert: Russian Composers—Mario Paci*
	Tchaikovsky, Symphony no.6 in B minor, op.74 "Pathetique" // Scriabin, Reverie, op.24 // Stravinsky, Chant des bateliers du Volga // Borodin, Prince Igor: Overture *(continues)*

Table 4.1 *(Cont.)*

1922.02.19+20	*Twentieth Concert: Tchaikovsky—Mario Paci*

Symphony no.5 in E minor, op.64 / Piano Concerto no.1 in B flat minor, op.23 [Pittard, S. de S. (pf)]

1922.10.22+24	*Third Concert: Russian Composers—Mario Paci*

Borodin, Prince Igor: Overture // Mussorgsky, Night on the Bare Mountain // Ippolitov-Ivanov, Esquisses Caucasiennes, op.10 // Glazunov, Chant du Menestrel, op.71 / Serenade Espagnole, op.20, no.2 // Rimsky-Korsakov, Capriccio Espagnol

1923.02.11	*Twenty-First Concert: Russian Composers—Mario Paci*

Balakirev, Overture on a Spanish March Theme // Rimsky-Korsakov, Scheherazade, op.35 // Ippolitov-Ivanov, Suite "Esquisses Caucasiennes": Dans la "Aoule," Cortege du Sardar // Rimsky-Korsakov, Russian Easter Overture, op.36

1923.02.25	*Twenty-Third Concert: Russian Composers—Mario Paci*

Borodin, Prince Igor: Overture // Tchaikovsky, Symphony no.4 in F minor, op.36 // Rimsky-Korsakov, Capriccio Espagnol

1923.03.25	*Twenty-Eighth Concert: Russian and French Modern Composers— Mario Paci*

Mussorgsky, Night on the Bare Mountain // Scriabin, Reverie, op.24 // Glazunov, Stenka Razin, symphonic poem // Liadov, The Enchanted Lake // D'Indy, Fantasy on French Folk Tunes, for oboe and orchestra, op.31 // Dukas, The Sorcerer's Apprentice // Faure, Suite "Masques et Bergamasques": Menuet, Gavotte // Chabrier, Bourree Fantastique

1923.12.20	*Third Chamber Music and Soloist Concert: Russian Composers— Mario Paci*

Arensky, Piano Trio no.1 in D minor, op.32 [Hmelnitzky, A. (pf); Foa, A. (vn); Shevtzoff, I. (vc)] // Tchaikovsky, The Night / Rachmaninov, Christ Is Risen / Gretchaninov, The Death / Morozoff, Apples (A Sketch of Russian Country Life) [Selivanov, P. (bas)] // Gretchaninov, String Quartet no.1 in G Major, op.2 [Foa, A. (vn1); Wegman, W. (vn2); Podushka, J. (va); Shevtzoff, I. (vc)]

1924.03.23	*Twenty-Fifth Concert: Russian Composers—A. Simziss-Brian*

Borodin, Prince Igor: Overture // Rimsky-Korsakov, Capriccio Espagnol // Tchaikovsky, Symphony no.5 in E minor, op.64

1924.04.13	*Twenty-Eighth Concert—Mario Paci*

Tchaikovsky, Symphony no.6 in B minor, op.74 "Pathetique" // Wieniawski, Legende, op.17 // Tchaikovsky, Capriccio Italiano

Table 4.1 *(Cont.)*

1924.05.31	*Thirty-Third and Last Concert: Russian Composers—A. de Kryger*
	Tchaikovsky, Symphony no.6 in B minor, op.74 "Pathetique" // Liadov, Kikimora // Rimsky-Korsakov, Capriccio Espagnol
1924.11.16	*Seventh Concert: Russian Composers—Mario Paci*
	Tchaikovsky, Symphony no.6 in B minor, op.74 "Pathetique" // Liadov, Eight Russian Folksongs for Orchestra, op.58 // Ippolitov-Ivanov, Esquisses Caucasiennes, op.10
1924.12.28	*Twelfth Concert: Russian Composers—Mario Paci*
	Mussorgsky, Night on the Bare Mountain // Liadov, The Enchanted Lake / Baba Yaga // Rimsky-Korsakov, Capriccio Espagnol // Borodin, In the Steppes of Central Asia // Tchaikovsky, 1812 Overture
1925.02.19	*Sixth Subscription Concert: Russian Composers—Arrigo Foa*
	Tchaikovsky, Symphony no.4 in F minor, op.36 / Piano Concerto no.1 in B flat minor, op.23 [Hmelnitzky, A. (pf)] // Glazunov, Stenka Razin, op.13
1925.03.15	*Twenty-Third Concert: Russian Composers—Arrigo Foa*
	Tchaikovsky, Symphony no.4 in F minor, op.36 // Scriabin, Reverie, op.24 // Stravinsky, The Firebird Suite // Tchaikovsky, Marche Slave, op.31
1927.10.16	*Second Concert: Tchaikovsky—Mario Paci*
	Marche Slave, op.31 / Eugene Onegin: Aria of Prince Gremin [Selivanov, P. (bas)] / String Quartet no.1 in D major, op.11 [Foa, A. (vn); Fedoroff, I. (vn); Podushka, J. (va); Shevtzoff, I. (vc)] / Iolanta: Aria of the King [Selivanov, P. (bas)] / Symphony no.6 in B minor, op.74 "Pathetique"
1928.04.01	*Twenty-Sixth Concert: Grand Russian Operatic Evening—Mario Paci*
	Glinka, A Life for the Tsar: Overture / Introduction Chorus [Russian Chorus Society, Mashin, P.] / Scene at the Monastery [RCS, Mashin; Tomskaya, A. (alt)] // Rimsky-Korsakov, Sadko: Vsyu noch zhdala ego ya ponaprasnu? (Lyubava) [Tomskaya (alt)] // Glinka, Ruslan and Ludmila: Overture / Ratmir's aria, recitative and waltz [Tomskaya (alt)] // Borodin, Prince Igor (excerpt)
1928.04.15	*Twenty-Seventh Concert: Grand Russian Program—Mario Paci*
	Rimsky-Korsakov, Russian Easter Overture, op.36 // Liadov, Eight Russian Folksongs for orchestra, op.58 // Tchaikovsky, Symphony no.6 in B minor, op.74 "Pathetique": II, III / The Nutcracker: Suite

(continues)

Table 4.1 *(Cont.)*

1928.10.21	**Third Concert: Russian Programme–Alexander Sloutsky**
	Glinka, Jota Aragonesa: Overture // Tchaikovsky, Symphony no.4 in F minor, op.36 // Rimsky-Korsakov, The Tale of Tsar Sultan: Suite / Le Cocq d'Or: Introduction and March
1929.05.05	**Twenty-Eighth Concert: Special Russian Programme—Mario Paci**
	Glinka, Ruslan and Ludmila: Overture // Tchaikovsky, Symphony no.6 in B minor, op.74 "Pathetique" // Rimsky-Korsakov, Russian Easter Overture, op.36
1930.01.05	**Thirteenth Concert—Victor Velikanoff**
	Glinka, Ruslan and Ludmila: Overture // Tchaikovsky, Symphony no.5 in E minor, op.64 / Cherevichki: Oxana's aria and Pique Dame: Lisa's aria [Baturina, S. (sop)] / Francesca da Rimini
1930.03.30	**Twenty-Fifth Concert—Victor Velikanoff**
	Glazunov, Salome: Introduction and Waltz // Liadov, The Enchanted Lake / Kikimora // Tchaikovsky, Romeo and Juliet Fantasy Overture // Mussorgsky, Khovanshchina: Introduction // Tchaikovsky, Cherevichki: Oxana's aria and Pique Dame: Lisa's aria [Baturina, S. (sop)] // Glinka, Jota Aragonesa: Capriccio Brillante
1930.04.27	**Twenty-Eighth Concert: Russian Composers—Arrigo Foa**
	Balakirev, Overture on a Spanish March Theme // Stravinsky, The Firebird Suite // Ippolitov-Ivanov, Esquisses Caucasiennes, op.10: Dans l'Aoule // Tchaikovsky, Swan Lake: Valse bluette // Rimsky-Korsakov, Russian Easter Overture, op.36
1931.01.11	**Thirteenth Concert: Tchaikovsky—Paci, Mario**
	Cherevichek: Overture / Symphony no.6 in B minor, op.74 "Pathetique" / String Quartet no.1 in D major, op.11 [Foa, A. (vn1); Livshitz, M. (vn2); Podushka, J. (va); Shevtzoff, I. (vc)]
1931.04.12	**Twenty-Fifth Concert: Special Russian Program—Mario Paci**
	Rimsky-Korsakov, Russian Easter Overture, op.36 // Liadov, Eight Russian Folksongs for orchestra, op.58 // Mussorgsky, Night on the Bare Mountain // Tchaikovsky, Symphony no.5 in E minor, op.64
1931.10.25	**Third Concert: Grand Russian Program—A. de Kryger**
	Glinka, Ruslan and Ludmila: Overture // Tchaikovsky, The Maid of Orleans: Jeanne d'Arc's Recitative and Aria [Slavianoff, N. (mez)] // Glazunov, Stenka Razin, op.13 // Liadov, The Enchanted Lake / Kikimora // Rimsky-Korsakov, Sadko: Lubava's Recitative and Aria / The Tsar's Bride: Lubasha's Recitative and Aria [Slavianoff (mez)] // Tchaikovsky, Francesca da Rimini

Table 4.1 (*Cont.*)

1932.01.10	*Fourteenth Concert: Russian Program—Mario Paci*
	Mussorgsky, Khovanshchina: Introduction // Tchaikovsky, Serenade for Strings, op.48 // Rimsky-Korsakov, The Tale of Tsar Sultan: Suite // Glazunov, Symphony no.4 in E flat, op.48
1932.04.24	*Twenty-Eighth Concert—Mario Paci* **
	Rameau, Air de Ballet "Dardanus" // Respighi, Choral and Passacaglia // Mozart, Piano Concerto no.20 in D minor, K.466 [Trachtenberg, D. (pf)] // Avshalomov, The Hutungs of Peipin / Ay How Gee Ching Nyien (Poem by Sung Tung Ying) / Shan You Chu Si [Chorus of Chinese Ladies (unspecified)] / The Soul of Kin Sei: Dance of Sai Hu
1932.05.01	*Twenty-Ninth Concert: Special Russian Popular Program—Mario Paci*
	Arensky, A Dream on the Volga: Overture // Borodin, Prince Igor: Chorus of Peasants // Tchaikovsky, Musical Picture "In the Church" // Glazunov, Song of the Volga Boatmen // Tchaikovsky, Pique Dame: Lisa's aria and Opritchnick: Natalie's Arioso [Abramovitch, A. (sop)] // Mussorgsky, Khovanshchina: Persian Dance // Tchaikovsky, String Quartet no.1 in D major, op.11: II. Andante cantabile // Andreieff, Balalaika // Gretchaninov, Lullaby and You loved me once [Abramovitch (sop)] // Dargomyzhsky, Fantasia on a Cossack Dance "Cosatschoque"
1932.11.20	*Fifth Concert: Special Russian Program—Mario Paci*
	Rimsky-Korsakov, The Maid of Pskov: Overture // Scriabin, Symphony no.1 in E major, op.26 // Tchaikovsky, String Quartet no.1 in D major, op.11: II. Andante cantabile // Borodin, Prince Igor: Chorus of Peasants // Stravinsky, The Firebird Suite
1932.12.11	*Eighth Concert: Special Wagner—Verdi—Tchaikovsky Program— Mario Paci*
	Wagner, Der fliegende Holländer: Overture / Die Meistersinger von Nürnberg: Walter's Prize Song / Tannhäuser: Wolfram's Eulogy of Love and Wolfram's Recitative and Air "O Star of Eve" [McCandliss, R.(bar)] / Tristan und Isolde: Prelude and Isolde's Liebestod // Verdi, Aida: Prelude // Tchaikovsky, Eugene Onegin: Aria [McCandliss (bar)] // Verdi, Otello: Iago's credo [McCandliss (bar)] // Tchaikovsky, Romeo and Juliet Fantasy Overture
1933.03.12	*Twentieth Concert—Mario Paci*
	Mussorgsky, Pictures at an Exhibition // Aksakov, S., Symphonic Ballade for piano and orchestra [Aksakov, S. (pf)] // Tchaikovsky, Symphony no.6 in B minor, op.74 "Pathetique" (*continues*)

Table 4.1 *(Cont.)*

1933.04.30	***Twenty-Sixth and Last Concert—Mario Paci***

Tchaikovsky, Francesca da Rimini // Rachmaninov, Piano Concerto no.2 in C minor, op.18 [Zakharoff, B. (pf)] // Scriabin, Reverie, op.24 // Liadov, Kikimora // Glazunov, Piano Concerto no.1 in F minor, op.82: I [Zakharoff (pf)] // Borodin, Prince Igor: Dances

1933.05.21	***Twenty-Ninth Concert: A Special Grand Chinese Evening—Mario Paci / Aaron Avshalomov *****

anon., Tai Tung [Cheng, Chung Wen (conductor); Chinese Orchestra] // anon., "A musical description of a battle" [Wei, Chung Loh (pi pa)] // Avshalomov, The Last Words of Tsin-Wen [Liu, C. F. (voc)] / The Hutungs of Peipin / The Soul of the Ch'in [Avshalomov, Aaron (conductor); International Arts Theatre Group of Shanghai]

1934.02.04	***Sixteenth Concert—Mario Paci***

Tchaikovsky, Francesca da Rimini / Symphony no.5 in E minor, op.64 / Orchestral Suite no.4 in G major, op.61 "Mozartiana"

1934.05.13	***Twenty-Ninth Concert: Russian Composer-Pianist Alexander Tcherepnin—Mario Paci****

Respighi, Suite "Gli Uccelli" // Tcherepnin, Piano Concerto no.2 in A minor, op.25 [Tcherepnin, A. (pf)] // Wagner, Tristan und Isolde: Prelude and Isolde's Liebestod [Saricheff, V. (fg)] / Die Meistersinger von Nürnberg: Prelude to Act III, Dance of the Apprentices, Hymn to Hans Sachs / Lohengrin: Prelude to Act III // Tcherepnin, Slavic Transcriptions, op.27 [Tcherepnin (pf)] // Grieg, Lyric Suite, op.54: I, II, III, IV

1934.05.20	***Thirteenth Concert—Emanuel Metter***

Tchaikovsky, Symphony no.4 in F minor, op.36 / Orchestral Suite no.3, op.55—IV // Scriabin, Reverie, op.24 // Glazunov, From the Middle Ages, op.79: Prelude / Valse de Concert

1934.11.25	***Sixth Concert: Alexander Tcherepnin—Mario Paci****

Mendelssohn, A Midsummer Night's Dream Overture, op.21 // Beethoven, Symphony no.5 in C minor, op.67 // Tcherepnin, Piano Concerto no.1 in F major, op.12 [Tcherepnin, A. (pf)] / The Wedding of Sobeide: Festmusik

1935.12.29	***Twelfth Concert: Popular Program, Tchaikovsky-Borodin—Arrigo Foa***

Tchaikovsky, Marche Slave, op.31 / Serenade for Strings, op.48: II, III / Eugene Onegin: Aria of Prince Gremin [Shushlin, V. (bas)] / Symphony no.5 in E minor, op.64: II / Symphony no.4 in F minor, op.36: III // Borodin, Prince Igor: Overture / Chorus of Peasants / Aria of Kontchak [Shushlin (bas)] / Dances

Table 4.1 *(Cont.)*

1936.01.19	*Fifteenth Concert—Mario Paci / Aaron Avshalomov***

Mozart, Le Nozze di Figaro: Overture // Beethoven, Symphony no.8 in F major, op.93 [conducted by Paci] // Avshalomov, Piano Concerto in G major [Singer, G. (pf)] / The Soul of the Ch'in: Sai Ho's Dance; Kinsei's Death [conducted by Avshalomov]

1936.11.15	**Sixth Concert: A Russian Program—Mario Paci**

Glinka, Ruslan and Ludmila: Overture / Recitative and Aria of Gorislova [Riskin, R. (sop)] // Borodin, In the Steppes of Central Asia // Dargomyzhsky, I am sad because I love you [Riskin (sop)] // Rimsky-Korsakov, Eastern Song: The Nightingale Enslaved by the Rose, op.2, no.2 [Riskin (sop)] // Liadov, Eight Russian Folksongs for orchestra, op.58 // Tchaikovsky, Symphony no.6 in B minor, op.74 "Pathetique"

1937.01.15–17 *+23+24*	*Le Ballet Russe: Scheherezade and Pavillion d'Armide—[Alexander Sloutsky]*

Rimsky-Korsakov, Scheherazade, op.35 // Tcherepnin, Pavillion d'Armide

1937.04.11	*Twenty-Fifth Concert—Mario Paci*

Tchaikovsky, Capriccio Italiano / Piano Concerto no.1 in B flat minor, op.23* [Schapiro, M. (pf)] / Symphony no.5 in E minor, op.64
*due to illness of first bassoon player, it was replaced with Chopin's Piano Concerto no.1 in E minor, op.11

1937.10.31	*Third Concert—Mario Paci*

Mussorgsky, Khovanshchina: Introduction // Borodin, In the Steppes of Central Asia // Rachmaninov, Rhapsody on Theme of Paganini, op.43 [Itkis, L. (pf)] // Tchaikovsky, Symphony no.6 in B minor, op.74 "Pathetique"

1937.12.12	*Ninth Concert: A Special Russian Program—Mario Paci / I. A. Kolchin*

Part I—Borodin, Prince Igor: Overture // Scriabin, Symphony no.1 in E, op.26 [Melashich, V. (mez); Slobodskoy, A. (ten); Chorus] // Part II—Mussorgsky, Tell me why, o maiden (Otchego, skazhi) [Slobodskoy (ten)] / At the Dear Father's Gate // Gretchaninov, Shall I then go out, shall I // Dubatoff, Alas! There was not just one path across the meadow // Napravnik, Quadrille on Russian Songs // anon., Accordion [Slobodskoy (ten)] // Part III—Russian Folk Song, Stormy Weather Gaily Rising / Hail thou mother Volga mine! / Along the River Volga / Heigh-ho! Volgar barge puller's shanty [Part II & III were performed by Russian Male Vocal Ensemble, organized and conducted by I. A. Kolchin; regens chori of St-Nicholas Orthodox Church] *(continues)*

Table 4.1 *(Cont.)*

1938.07.21	***Open-Air Concert—Mario Paci / Arrigo Foa / Wilfrid W. Sayer (Bandmaster)***

Part I—Borodin, Prince Igor: Overture // Glazunov, Valse de Concert // Tchaikovsky, The Nutcracker

Part II—Russian Male Vocal Ensemble (conducted by I. A. Kolchin): Rubinstein, Demon: The Dark Night // Galxovsky, The March of Welcome Vilna Academy // Glinka, The Night Review // anon., Songs / Valse [Chehoff, V.T. (bas)] / "Heigh-ho" (Volga barge pullers' shanty) / Russian Folk-Song [Chehoff, V.T. (bas)] / Accordion [Romaniuk, N. I with humming]

1938.11.13	***Sixth Concert—Mario Paci***

Mussorgsky, Night on the Bare Mountain // Tchaikovsky, Symphony no.6 in B minor, op.74 // Rimsky-Korsakov, Le Cocq d'Or: Suite

1939.01.29	***Fifteenth Concert—Arrigo Foa***

Balakirev, Overture on a Spanish March Theme // Rachmaninov, Piano Concerto no.2 in C minor, op.18 [Havsky, V. (pf)] // Tchaikovsky, Symphony no.4 in F minor, op.36

1939.07.06	***Open-Air Concert: Russian and Italian Composers***

Borodin, Prince Igor: Overture // Rimsky-Korsakov, Scheherazade, op.35: III only // Tchaikovsky, String Quartet no.1 in D major, op.11: II. / Symphony no.5 in E minor, op.64: III // Ippolitov-Ivanov, Suite "Esquisses Caucasiennes": Dans L'Aoule, Cortege du Sardar

1940.05.21	***First Performance; Tchaikovsky Festival; Chamber Music****

String Quartet in D major, op.11 [Foa, A. (vn1); Gerzovsky, R. (vn2); Podushka, J. (va); Winkler, E. (vc)] // Piano Variations in F major, op.19 [Havsky, V. (pf)] // Songs–The Night / I Bless the Forests / No! only he who thirsted . . . / In the midst of a clamorous ball / Don Juan's Serenade [Shushlin, V. (bas); Paci, M. (pf)] // Piano Trio in A minor, op.50 [Foa, A. (vn); Ullstein, P. (vc); Zakharoff, B. (pf)]

1940.05.24	***Second Performance; Tchaikovsky Festival; Grand Ballet "The Swan Lake"—Alexander Sloutsky****

Le Ballet Russe; Shevlugin (Prince); King, Audrey (Swan)

1940.05.26	***Third and Last Performance; Tchaikovsky Festival; "Symphony and Concertos"—Mario Paci****

Violin Concerto in D major, op.35 [Foa, A. (vn)] / Piano Concerto no. 1 in B flat minor, op.23 [Havsky, V. (pf)] / Symphony no.6 in B minor, op.74 "Pathetique"

Table 4.1 *(Cont.)*

1941.02.23	*Twentieth Concert—Mario Paci / Aaron Avshalomov*

Rieti, Concerto for Fl, Ob, Cl, Hr, fg, 2 Trp and Str [Girardello, E. (fl); Girardello, G. (ob); Vernick, A. (cl); Fortina, A. (fg); Bianchini, G. (hr)] // Honegger, Symphonic Movement "Pacific 231" // Gershwin, Rhapsody in Blue [Singer, G. (pf)] // Avshalomov, The Soul of the Ch'in: Kinsei's Death / Three Short Pieces for Erhu and Small Orchestra [Wei, Chung Loh (Er-hu)] / Piano Concerto in G major [Singer (pf)]

1941.12.14	*Tenth Concert: Tchaikovsky Program—Arrigo Foa*

Serenade for Strings, op.48 / Francesca da Rimini / Symphony no.4 in F minor, op.36

1942.05.24	*Thirty-Third Concert—Arrigo Foa*

Tchaikovsky, Romeo and Juliet Fantasy Overture // Liadov, Eight Russian Folksongs for Orchestra, op.58 // Rimsky-Korsakov, The Tale of Tsar Sultan: Suite // Tchaikovsky, Piano Concerto no.1 in B flat minor, op.23 [Woo, Lois (pf)]

1942.08.16	*Eighth Open-Air Concert: Tchaikovsky's Program—Arrigo Foa*

Romeo and Juliet Fantasy Overture / Symphony no.4 in F minor, op.36: II & III / The Nutcracker / The Swan Lake: Scene, Valse, Danse des Cygnes, Danse Hongroise-Czardas / Marche Slave, op.31

1943.01.17	*Thirteenth Concert—Alexander Sloutsky*

Glazunov, Symphony no.5 in B flat major, op.55 // Rimsky-Korsakov, The Legend of the Invisible City of Kitezh and the Maiden Fevroniya: Prelude, Intermezzo "Carnage at Keryenez" // Borodin, Prince Igor: Arioso of Yarsolava [Zorich, S. (sop)] // Yurashovsky, Trilby: Aria of Trilby [Zorich (sop)] // Rimsky-Korsakov, The Tsar's Bride: Aria of Marfa [Zorich (sop)] // Tchaikovsky, Capriccio Italiano

1943.03.21	*Twenty-Second Concert—Alexander Sloutsky*

Glazunov, Raymonda: Suite // Rimsky-Korsakov, Le Cocq d'Or: Suite // Tchaikovsky, Manfred Symphony, op.58

1943.03.31+ *04.01+02+04*	*Le Ballet Russe Presents Le Lac des Cygnes—Sloutsky, Alexander***

Tchaikovsky, Swan Lake [Shevlugin, F (choreo); Domracheff (scene); Bobinina (Swan); Svetlanoff (Prince)]   *(continues)*

Table 4.1 *(Cont.)*

1943.05.23	*Thirty-First Concert—Alexander Sloutsky*
	Tchaikovsky, Orchestral Suite no.3, op.55—IV / Eugene Onegin: Lensky's Aria [Markoff, P. (ten)] // Napravnik, Dubrovsky: Vladimir's Aria [Markoff (ten)] // Rimsky-Korsakov, May Night: Levko's song and Sadko: Song of Indian Guest [Markoff (ten)] // Kalinnikov, The Cedar and the Palm // Borodin, Symphony no.2 in B minor
1943.07.24	*Fourth Open-Air Concert: A Souvenir of Russian Composers—Alexander Sloutsky*
	Borodin, Prince Igor: Overture // Glinka, Waltz (unspecified) // Tchaikovsky, Swan Lake: Scene, Valse, Danse des Cygnes, Danse Hongroise-Czardas // Ippolitov-Ivanov, Suite "Esquisses Caucasiennes": Dans le Defile, Dans L'Aoule, Cortege du Sardar // Rimsky-Korsakov, The Snow Maiden: Procession, Dance at Buffoons // Tchaikovsky, Marche Slave, op.31
1943.08.21	*Seventh Open-Air Concert: An Evening of Russian Opera—Alexander Sloutsky*
	Rimsky-Korsakov, May Night: Overture // Mussorgsky, Khovanchtchina: Aria (unspecified) / Rachmaninov, Aleko: Aria (unspecified) [Roland, Victor (bar)] // Tchaikovsky, Eugene Onegin: Letter Scene [Zorich, Sophie (sop)] / Finale Scene [Zorich, S. (sop); Roland, V.(bar)] // Rimsky, Suite: The Tale of Tsar Sultan
1943.10.06–08	*Le Ballet Russe Presents Le Cocq d'Or—Alexander Sloutsky***
	Rimsky-Korsakov, Le Cocq d'Or [Sokolsky, N. (producer); Tourenin (Tsar); Masahide (Gvidon); Wiener (Aphrone)]
1943.11.28	*Second Concert—Alexander Sloutsky*
	Tchaikovsky, Fatum, op.77 / Violin Concerto in D major, op.35 [Adler, F. (vn)] / Symphony no.5 in E minor, op.64
1944.01.11+12 +15+16	*Le Ballet Russe Presents The Sleeping Beauty—V. Saricheff***
	Tchaikovsky, The Sleeping Beauty [Sokolsky, N. (producer); Shirovsky, M. (scene); Eliroff, Ed. (King); Kokoreva, M. (Queen); Bobinina, H. (Aurora); Shevlugin, L. (Desire)]
1944.02.06	*Twelfth Concert—Alexander Sloutsky*
	Rimsky-Korsakov, Fairy Tale, op.29 // Glazunov, From the Middle Ages, op.79: Prelude // Kalinnikov, Symphony no.1 in G minor

Table 4.1 *(Cont.)*

1944.03.25+26 *Nineteenth Concert—Alexander Sloutsky*

Rimsky-Korsakov, The Tale of Tsar Sultan: The Three Wonders of the Island in the Sea / The Tale of Tsar Sultan: Act II [Zorich, S. (sop); Markoff, P. (ten); Chumakova, T. (mez); Russian Chorus; Muravieff, V. (dir)] // Scriabin, Symphony no.1 in E, op.26 [Markoff (ten); Chumakova (mez); Russian Chorus; Muravieff (dir)]

1944.06.04 *Fourth and Last Chamber Music Concert***

Rimsky-Korsakov, Piano Quintet in B flat major [Girardello, E. (fl); Girardello, G. (ob), Biriulin, P. (pf); Fortina, A. (fg); Bianchini, G. (hr)] // Gretchaninov, Piano Trio no.1 in C minor, op.28 [Biriulin (pf); Foa, A. (vn); Shevtzoff, I. (vc)] // Borodin, String Quartet no.2 in D major [Foa (vn); Gerzovsky, R. (vn); Podushka, J. (va); Shevtzoff (vc)]

1944.06.15–17 *Petroushka: Shanghai Philharmonic Orchestra with Le Ballet Russe—Alexander Sloutsky***

Tchaikovsky, Romeo and Juliet Fantasy Overture // Glazunov, The Seasons // Stravinsky, Petroushka [Sokolsky, Nicolai (choreo)]

1944.11.05 *Fourth Concert—Arrigo Foa*

Liadov, The Enchanted Lake / Kikimora // Wieniawski, Violin Concerto no.2 in D minor, op.22 [Adler, F. (vn)] // Tchaikovsky, Symphony no.5 in E minor, op.64

1945.06.03 *Tenth Concert—Alexander Sloutsky*

Shostakovich, Golden Age: Suite // Glière, The Red Poppy: Dance of Russian Sailors "Jablotchko" // Stravinsky, Petroushka: Suite // Kalinnikov, Symphony no.1 in G minor

1945.12.22 *Grand Symphony Concert—Jonathan Sternberg*

Glinka, Ruslan and Ludmila: Overture // Tchaikovsky, Symphony no.4 in F minor, op.36 // Glinka, Ivan Susanin: Aria of Susanin / Tchaikovsky, Eugene Onegin: Aria of Prince Gemin / Borodin, Prince Igor: Aria of Kontchak [Shushlin, V. (bas)] // Tchaikovsky, 1812 Overture [with 681 AAF Band; USS *Estes* Band] works, as the purchasing of scores and parts was a budget item that required permission from the Municipal Council. Probably for the sake of variety, Paci gradually introduced other programming tactics to build his audience, such as introducing the chamber music and soloist concert series in 1923, the subscription concert in 1925, and the young people's concert in 1926.

A survey of SMO's entire run of concert programs shows that there were generally at least two special Russian concerts held annually, with programs that featured all Russian works as well as Russian soloists. Showcases of music of other nationalities, such as works of German, British, French, or Italian composers, were much less frequent, perhaps once a year or once every few years. Naturally, Russian composers' works were often featured along with other composers' works in regular concerts, and Russian soloists were showcased in many of the concerts, playing not only Russian works but also works of other composers. On average, around 40 percent of all the SMO concerts showcased certain Russian elements, be it the theme, repertoire, or soloist. There were years such as 1925, 1933, and from 1936 to 1938 that the percentage of Russian elements was even higher, at 50 to 60 percent. These statistics demonstrate the Russian-inclined programming of the SMO. Such an observation challenges the current literature's presumption that the SMO's concert programming leaned toward the standard repertoire of German works.[2]

It is also evident that Paci made an effort to make these Russian concerts relevant to the occasion and the Russian audience concerned. For example, the concert held on May 5, 1929, titled "Special Russian Programme on the Occasion of the Russian Easter," not only featured Russian works such as Glinka's overture to *Ruslan and Lyudmila* and Tchaikovsky's Symphony no. 6, but also included Rimsky-Korsakov's *Russian Easter Festival Overture*, subtitled "upon liturgical themes of the Russian Church." This was not only an SMO premiere but it also articulated the Russian Orthodox faith that must have meant something to the Russian audiences at the concert.

The Russian concert that featured the Russian soprano A. Abramovitch mentioned at the beginning of this chapter was held for the celebration of the Russian Easter festivities. Paci reportedly had to borrow scores from the Russian conductor A. U. Slutsky (Sloutsky), who was said to possess a large library of Russian music ("The Municipal Orchestra" 1932, 12). This suggests that the concert was specially organized for the Russian community and most of the works performed were not in the SMO's repertoire, even though they were popular in Russia. Aside from the two Tchaikovsky arias, the rest of the works in the program were Shanghai premieres. The concert was thought to be interesting not only to the Russians, "who will have the opportunity to hear again their own and old well-known tunes, but also for all other Shanghai music lovers, who will have the opportunity to hear them in Shanghai for the first time" ("The

Municipal Orchestra" 1932, 12). Interesting to note is how the critic tried to articulate the Russian qualities of the music—the use of the minor key and Russian folk song—a mixture of "sadness and emotion with twinges of almost barbaric frenzy" that he thought was attractive to a certain audience group ("The Municipal Orchestra" 1932, 12).

Russian works were not only performed in Russian concerts, but also alongside other non-Russian works in regular SMO concerts, and likewise many Russian soloists performed non-Russian works. Works of Tchaikovsky, probably the most popular Russian composer of all time, were featured in three different types of concerts: (1) concerts dedicated to him exclusively,[3] (2) concerts of all-Russian programs, and (3) regular SMO concerts alongside works of other non-Russian composers.

To be certain, Tchaikovsky was already familiar to the Shanghai audience prior to the influx of Russian émigrés. Though there are not enough early SMO programs extant to confirm it, concert reviews from 1909 suggest that Tchaikovsky's Symphony no. 6, *Pathétique*, was introduced to the band's repertoire, which made the settlers quite proud ("The Sunday Concerts" 1909a, 287; 1909b, 277; "The Past Musical Season" 1910, 422).[4] Indeed, Tchaikovsky's works were already regularly featured at the Municipal Band's concerts during Buck's tenure.[5] Likewise, they were also frequently featured at Paci's concerts (see table 4.2). In particular, Tchaikovsky's Symphony no. 4, no. 5, and no. 6, as well as the *Italian Capriccio* and *Slavonic March* were the most popular, repeated almost every season. Other works such as the *Rococo Variations*, suite from *The*

Table 4.2 Russian works performed by the SMO

Andreieff [?]	*Symphonic Ballade for Orchestra and Piano, op.27*
Balalaika	1933.03.12
1932.05.01	*Symphony no.1 in B minor, op.29*
Arensky, Anton	1937.04.25
A Dream on the Volga: Overture	**Alyabyev, Alexander**
1932.05.01; 1933.08.03*;	*Le Rossignol*
1944.07.22+23*	1928.12.23
Egyptian Nights	**Avshalomov, Aaron**
1933.08.03*	*A Stroll in an Ancient Garden*
Piano Trio no.1 in D minor, op.32	1937.05.23
1923.12.20; 1935.02.12	*Ay How Gee Ching Nyien*
Serenade	1932.04.24
1935.03.19	*Chinese Dance*
Aksakov, S.	1944.12.02+03
Piano Concerto in E minor, op.30	
1938.10.23	*(continues)*

Table 4.2 *(Cont.)*

In Distant Climb (Chinese Folk Song of Tsing-Hai, orchestrated by Avshalomov)
1946.04.28

Indian Dances (orchestrated by Avshalomov)
1939.08.26+31

Piano Concerto in G major
1936.01.19;1936.02.02;
1937.05.23;1941.02.23; 1946.03.09+10

Soul of Kin Sei [The Soul of the Ch'in]
1930.11.30; 1932.04.24;
1933.05.21;1936.01.19; 1941.02.23

Symphony no.1 in C Minor
1940.03.17

The Hutungs of Peipin
1932.04.24; 1933.05.21

The K'E Still Ripples to Its Banks
1937.05.23

The Last Words of Tsin-Wen
1933.05.21

Three Short Pieces for Erhu and Small Orchestra
1941.02.23

Shan You Chu Si [Wan Chee Szu I]
1932.04.24

Violin Concerto in D major
1938.01.16

Balakirev, Mily

Overture on a Spanish March Theme
1923.02.11; 1925.02.08; 1930.04.27;
1939.01.29

Tamara
1926.11.07

Borisoff, Josef

Humoresque Oriental
1927.11.24

Borodin, Alexander

In the Convent
1933.08.03*

In the Steppes of Central Asia
1920.01.11; 1920.04.11; 1921.12.18;
1923.01.21; 1923.06.09+16*;
1924.01.06; 1924.12.28;

1926.01.03; 1926.07.27*;1927.02.27;
1927.07.22+23*;1928.07.29*;
1929.08.19*;1930.07.19*;
1930.07.24*;1931.06.25*;
1932.06.18*;1932.07.31*;
1933.07.18*;1934.02.14; 1934.06.27*;
1935.03.22; 1935.08.29*;1935.11.08;
1936.11.15; 1937.10.31;
1938.08.11*;1939.07.15*; 1941.05.17;
1944.01.09; 1944.07.08+10*

Prince Igor
1922.01.29+31; 1922.10.22+24;
1923.02.25; 1923.03.18; 1923.05.13;
1924.01.13; 1924.03.23; 1925.12.06;
1926.04.18; 1926.06.19*;1926.12.05;
1927.07.27*;1927.11.06;
1928.04.01;1928.06.13*;
1928.07.29*;1928.08.22*; 1929.06.19*;
1929.08.03*; 1930.07.15*;
1930.07.26*; 1931.08.22*;
1931.08.29*; 1932.05.01; 1932.07.02*;
1932.07.09*;1932.08.17*; 1932.11.20;
1932.12.07; 1933.04.30; 1933.06.15*;
1933.07.04*;1933.07.29*; 1933.11.19;
1933.12.17; 1934.06.27+28*;
1934.07.12*;1934.07.28*;
1935.07.10*;1935.07.18*;
1935.07.27*;1935.08.28*; 1935.12.29;
1936.07.01*; 1936.08.29*;1937.03.21;
1937.12.12; 1938.07.21*;
1939.07.06*;1939.07.29*; 1942.01.11;
1942.06.18*; 1943.01.17; 1943.07.24*;
1943.09.03*;1945.05.05; 1945.12.22;
1946.02.17; 1946.03.16+17

String Quartet no.2 in D major
1922.03.30; 1922.12.28; 1924.01.31;
1944.06.04

Symphony no.2 in B minor
1935.01.13; 1937.11.28; 1943.05.23;
1946.04.07

Symphony no.3 in A minor
1923.05.13

Cui, César

Causerie, op.40, no.6
1936.04.26

Table 4.2 *(Cont.)*

Kaleidoscope, no.9, op.50: Orientale
1934.11.23

Dargomyzhsky, Alexander

Cherviak
1939.02.19

Cloudy Sky
1936.11.01

Fantasia on a Cossack Dance "Cosatschoque"
1932.05.01; 1934.06.23*

I am sad because I love you
1936.11.15

Melnik
1939.02.19

Russian Dance (unspecified)
1933.08.24*

Davidoff, Carl / Davydov, Karl

Kobza, Fantaisie upon Ukraine Themes for Chorus a cappella
1924.12.21

Dubatoff, [A.]

Alas! There was not just one path across the meadow [arranged from a Russian country song]
1937.12.12

Glazunov, Alexander

Chant du Menestrel, op.71
1919.12.28; 1922.10.22+24;
1928.03.22; 1932.05.15; 1933.08.09*

Christ Is Risen: Psalm of the Believers
1933.04.14

From the Middle Ages, op.79: Prelude
1934.05.20; 1944.02.06

Scene Dansante, op.81
1933.08.17*

Piano Concerto no.1 in F minor, op.82
1933.04.30

Raymonda: Suite
1933.08.17*;1943.03.21

Salome: Introduction and Waltz
1930.03.30

Scene de Ballet, op.52

1933.08.03*;1944.02.27

Serenade Espagnole, op.20, no.2
1922.10.22+24; 1923.10.28;
1923.11.04; 1932.05.15;
1932.07.02*;1932.08.17*;
1933.08.09*;1934.06.16*;
1934.07.14*;1935.08.25*; 1936.08.12*

Song of the Volga Boatmen
1932.05.01

Stenka Razin, Symphonic Poem
1923.03.25; 1925.02.19; 1926.05.23;
1929.01.21; 1931.10.25; 1936.03.29;
1942.01.04; 1942.07.09*; 1945.07.28*

Symphony no.4 in E flat major, op.48
1928.01.08; 1932.01.10; 1935.11.24;
1938.12.18; 1939.11.19; 1940.12.15;
1942.04.19

Symphony no.5 in B flat major, op.55
1943.01.17; 1944.04.15+16

The King of Jews
1933.04.14

The Seasons
1944.06.15-17

Theme and Variations in F sharp minor, op.72
1922.10.26

Une fête Slave, Symphonic Sketch
1923.03.18; 1925.01.25

Valse de Concert
1928.01.15; 1931.11.15; 1934.05.20;
1935.10.20; 1937.01.24; 1938.07.21*;
1940.10.29; 1942.08.02*; 1944.01.30;
1944.07.01+02*

Glière, Reinhold

The Red Poppy, op.70: Dance of Russian Sailors "Jablotchko"
1945.06.03; 1945.07.28*; 1946.09.21*

Glinka, Mikhail

A Life for the Tsar
1928.04.01; 1934.02.25

Ivan Susanin: Aria
1945.12.22

(continues)

Table 4.2 *(Cont.)*

Jota Aragonesa
1925.01.18; 1928.10.21; 1930.03.30

Komarinskaja: Fantasie
1931.07.07*;1934.07.19*

La revue de minuit
1930.03.23

Romance for bass and piano
1930.03.23

Romance for flute, viola and harp
1921.10.16

Ruslan and Ludmila
1926.08.04*;1926.08.10*;
1926.10.28; 1927.07.25*; 1928.04.01;
1929.05.05; 1929.07.31*;1930.01.05;
1930.07.17*;1931.08.13*; 1931.10.25;
1932.12.07; 1933.06.27*;1933.11.19;
1934.08.22*;1935.08.29*;
1935.08.31*;1936.11.15;
1938.08.13*;1940.05.05;
1943.02.07;1945.06.30+07.01;
1944.07.01+02*; 1945.12.22;
1946.04.28

The Night Review
1938.07.21*

Valse-Fantasie
1944.07.22+23*;1945.07.28*

Waltz (unspecified)
1933.07.20*; 1943.07.24*

Gretchaninov, Alexander

Berceuse
1929.11.16; 1940.01.21

Jadis tu m'as aimé
1940.01.21

Lullaby
1932.05.01

Piano Trio no.1 in C minor, op.28
1925.01.08; 1944.06.04

Shall I then go out, shall I
1937.12.12

String Quartet no.1 in G Major, op.2
1923.12.20; 1924.03.13

Symphony no. 2 in A Major, op. 27 "Pastoral"

1939.11.05

The Death
1923.12.20

The Steppes
1922.02.09

You loved me once
1932.05.01

Halvatch, [?]

"Russian Melodies"
1946.09.21*

Ilyinsky, Aleksandr

Noure et Anitra: Suite
1933.08.10*

Ippolitov-Ivanov, Mikhail

Esquisses Caucasiennes, op.10
1921.01.23; 1922.10.22+24; 1923.02.11;
1923.07.21*; 1924.11.16; 1926.01.03;
1926.07.27*;1927.01.09+11;
1927.07.25*;1927.08.31*; 1928.02.26;
1928.07.15*; 1928.08.25*;1929.07.31*;
1930.04.27; 1930.07.19*;
1930.07.24*;1931.08.22*; 1932.04.10;
1932.07.04*; 1932.08.22*;1933.07.06*;
1933.08.05*;1934.06.16*;
1934.07.25*;1935.03.22;
1935.08.31*;1936.08.15*;
1936.08.20*;1938.07.30*;
1939.07.06*;1939.07.18*;
1939.08.26+31*;1940.07.06*;
1941.05.17; 1942.09.06*;
1943.07.24*;1946.02.24; 1947.07.13*

An Oriental Scene
1934.11.23

Kalinnikov, Vasily

Le cèdre et le palmier
1930.02.09

Symphony no.1 in G minor
1929.10.13; 1930.01.26; 1931.10.18;
1931.12.20; 1932.08.27*;1933.08.12*;
1934.04.08; 1936.03.08; 1936.05.03;
1937.02.07; 1938.03.06; 1939.07.18*;
1940.01.21; 1941.01.19; 1942.02.22;
1942.08.02*; 1943.04.11; 1944.02.06;
1945.06.03; 1946.03.02+03

Table 4.2 (Cont.)

The Cedar and the Palm
1943.05.23

Kochetoff, [?]

Balalaika
1933.07.20*

Ladukhin, Nikolay

Dusk
1928.02.05

Liadov, Anatoli

Baba Yaga
1923.04.29; 1924.12.28; 1927.02.27

Danse de L'Amazone
1933.08.03*

Eight Russian Folksongs for Orchestra,
op.58
1923.03.18; 1923.04.19; 1924.11.16;
1926.03.28; 1927.12.11; 1928.04.15;
1931.04.12; 1934.04.22; 1936.05.17;
1936.11.15; 1941.04.06; 1942.05.24;
1947.05.11

Kikimora
1923.04.22; 1923.06.09+16*;
1924.05.31; 1926.03.21; 1929.03.17;
1929.08.10*; 1930.03.30; 1931.10.25;
1933.04.30; 1933.11.19; 1939.11.05;
1944.11.05

The Enchanted Lake
1923.03.25; 1923.04.29; 1924.12.28;
1926.03.21; 1929.03.17; 1930.03.30;
1931.10.25; 1933.11.19; 1939.11.05;
1941.04.06; 1944.11.05

Une Tabatiere a musique
1922.03.30; 1924.01.31; 1926.11.25;
1927.10.26; 1928.01.29; 1929.01.29;
1933.07.29*

Mistowski, Alfred

Aria
1929.10.13

Morozoff, [?]

Apples [A Sketch of Russian country life]
1923.12.20

Moszkowski, Moritz

Boadbdil

1933.06.15*; 1933.07.06*; 1934.06.07*;
1934.06.20*

Serenade
1921.05.08; 1928.06.30*;
1928.07.29*;1928.10.26;
1929.06.26*;1930.06.24*;
1930.08.02*;1931.06.09*;
1932.08.27*;1933.06.27*;
1933.07.28*;1933.08.04*;
1935.08.07*;1935.08.28*;
1936.08.22*;1936.09.17*;
1938.06.29*;1938.09.01*;
1939.07.11*;1944.08.19+20*

Spanish Dance(s)
1930.07.23*;1930.08.25*;
1931.07.20*;1932.06.17*;
1933.08.29*;1934.07.28*;
1934.08.02*;1935.08.07*;
1936.08.21*;1936.09.05*;
1939.08.02+06*

Mussorgsky, Modest

At the Dear Father's Gate
1937.12.12

Ballada (Foreign one)
1944.12.23 (vocal recital of Chen
Ko-Sin, Margolinski piano)

Bloha (Song of the Fiea)
1944.12.23 (vocal recital of Chen
Ko-Sin, Margolinski piano)

Boris Godunov
1930.02.02

Fair at Sorotchinsk
1946.09.21*

Gopak
1946.09.21*

Jesus Navine
1931.03.18

Khovanshchina
1930.03.30; 1932.01.10;
1932.05.01; 1933.01.15; 1934.02.25;
1936.11.01; 1937.04.04; 1937.10.31;
1939.07.01*;1942.06.30*;
1943.08.21*;1944.03.11

(continues)

Table 4.2 *(Cont.)*

Ba Dnyeprye (On the River Dnejepar)
1944.12.23 (vocal recital of CHEN
Ko-Sin, Margolinski piano)

Night on the Bare Mountain
1922.10.22+24; 1923.03.25;
1924.12.28; 1925.03.29; 1926.03.21;
1928.02.01; 1929.01.21; 1931.04.12;
1934.04.29; 1936.10.25; 1938.11.13;
1940.12.15; 1942.08.09*;1943.12.12;
1946.03.16+17

Pictures at an Exhibition
1926.01.10; 1926.11.07; 1929.05.26;
1933.03.12; 1936.02.09; 1936.12.20;
1942.01.11; 1943.02.28; 1944.02.13

*Russian Songs: Trepak, Soroka,
S'Kookloi, Hopak*
1922.11.23

Savishna (Love Song of an Idiot)
1944.12.23 (vocal recital of Chen
Ko-Sin, Margolinski piano))

Sorochintsy Fair: Hopak
1926.05.23

Tell me why, o maiden (Otchego, skazhi)
1937.12.12

The Seminarist
1939.02.19

The Song of the Flea
1939.02.19; 1946.09.09+10

Napravnik, Eduard

Dubrovsky: Vladimir's Aria
1943.05.23

Quadrille on Russian Songs
1937.12.12

Peterlayko, [?]

God Is Risen
1933.04.14

Prokofiev, Sergei

*Gavotte, op. 12, no. 2 [dedicated to
Zakharov]*
1936.04.26

Rachmaninov, Sergei

Aleko: Aria
1939.11.05; 1943.08.21*; 1945.07.28*

Christ Is Risen
1923.12.20

15 Romances, op.26: 15. All Things Past
1936.11.01

Humoresque, op.10, no. 5
1935.07.27*

In the Silent Night, op.4, no.3
1946.11.29+12.01

Life
1926.05.23

Melodie, op.3, no.3
1941.05.04

Piano Concerto no.2 in C minor, op.18
1933.04.30; 1933.05.14; 1935.05.05;
1936.04.26; 1939.01.29; 1939.02.26;
1940.10.29

Piano Concerto no.3 in D minor, op.30
1933.12.03; 1937.01.31

Prelude (unspecified)
1927.11.20; 1939.06.01+04*

Prelude in G minor, op.3, no.5
1933.08.03*;1936.08.16+18*

Prelude in C sharp minor, op.3, no.2
1926.01.03; 1926.06.23*; 1927.02.27;
1929.07.15*; 1930.02.16; 1931.05.24;
1931.06.16*; 1931.06.27*; 1933.08.03*;
1942.09.06*; 1944.08.12+14*

Rhapsody on Theme of Paganini, op.43
1937.09.19; 1937.10.31

These Glorious Nights
1922.02.09

Rebikov, Vladimir

Love Song
1933.07.11*

The Christmas Tree: Suite
1929.12.29

Valse
1933.07.11*

Retschnukoff, [?]

*Serenade Espagnole (Russian song with
piano accompaniment)*
1930.03.23

Table 4.2 (Cont.)

Rimsky-Korsakov, Nicolai

Capriccio Espagnol
1920.04.30; 1921.01.23; 1921.12.18;
1922.10.22+24; 1923.02.25;
1924.01.06; 1924.03.23; 1924.05.31;
1924.12.28; 1925.10.25; 1926.12.19;
1928.12.09; 1930.02.02; 1930.11.23;
1934.04.08; 1934.07.07*;
1934.08.04*;1935.08.03*;
1935.08.10*;1935.12.01;
1936.08.26*;1936.09.12*;
1937.04.16; 1937.04.18; 1937.09.19;
1939.07.15*; 1940.03.31;
1940.07.13*; 1941.03.23; 1942.02.01;
1942.07.19*;1944.08.12+14*;
1945.11.25; 1946.04.14

Chanson Hindoue
1927.01.27

Eastern Song: The Nightingale Enslaved by the Rose, op.2, no.2
1936.11.15

Fairy Tale, op.29
1944.02.06

Flight of the Bumblebee
1936.12.13; 1940.08.24*

Le Cocq d'Or
1927.11.20; 1928.10.21; 1938.11.13;
1943.03.21; 1943.10.06-08

May Night
1943.05.23; 1943.08.21*

Piano Quintet in B flat major
1944.06.04

Russian Easter Overture, op.36
1920.04.11; 1923.02.11; 1925.01.18;
1926.05.02; 1928.04.15; 1929.05.05;
1930.04.27; 1931.04.12; 1933.04.14;
1935.04.28; 1937.05.02; 1938.04.24;
1942.04.05; 1943.04.25; 1946.04.21

Sadko
1928.04.01; 1929.10.20; 1931.10.25;
1934.07.01*; 1934.07.24*;1934.07.28*;
1934.08.12*;1934.08.26+28*;
1934.10.13*;1935.07.09*;
1936.08.14*;1936.09.27*;

1938.08.30*;1938.09.04*; 1939.11.05;
1943.05.23

Scheherazade, op.35
1922.04.23+25; 1923.02.11;
1923.05.24; 1924.10.26; 1925.11.15;
1927.01.16+18; 1927.10.09; 1929.02.03;
1929.08.03*; 1929.08.24*; 1929.12.15;
1930.08.16*; 1930.12.14; 1932.08.13*;
1932.10.30; 1933.08.01*; 1934.02.18;
1934.07.14*; 1934.12.16; 1936.04.19;
1937.01.15-17+23+24; 1938.02.27;
1939.07.06*; 1940.03.03; 1940.11.17;
1942.02.28; 1942.03.22; 1943.05.09;
1944.05.06+07; 1946.01.13

The Legend of the Invisible City of Kitezh and the Maiden Fevroniya
1943.01.17

The Maid of Pskov
1932.11.20

The Prophet
1933.04.14

The Snow Maiden
1929.03.24; 1933.01.15; 1934.02.25;
1943.07.24*

The Tale of Tsar Sultan
1928.10.21; 1930.11.09; 1932.01.10;
1932.07.06*; 1932.08.03*;1933.07.29*;
1934.03.11; 1934.07.28*; 1936.10.11;
1937.02.07; 1938.05.22; 1940.05.10;
1941.04.06; 1942.05.24; 1942.12.13;
1943.08.21*; 1944.03.25+26

The Tsar's Bride
1931.10.25; 1934.02.25; 1943.01.17

Wind Quintet in B flat major: Andante
1925.10.25

Rubinstein, Anton

Demon
1938.07.21*;1945.07.28*

Piano Concerto no.4 in D minor, op.70: I
1912.03.31

Toréador et Andalouse
1911.12.03; 1912.03.31
1933.07.11*; 1944.12.02+03

(continues)

Table 4.2 *(Cont.)*

Scriabin, Alexander

Nocturne, op.9, no.2
1922.12.07

Piano Concerto in F sharp minor, op.20
1938.10.30

Reverie, op.24
1920.04.11; 1922.01.29+31;
1923.03.25; 1925.03.15; 1927.06.12;
1929.03.03; 1929.07.15*;1933.04.30;
1934.05.20; 1940.01.21;
1944.04.22+23; 1946.03.16+17

Symphony no.1 in E, op.26
1931.03.08; 1932.11.20; 1937.12.12;
1944.03.25+26

Shostakovich, Dmitri

Golden Age: Suite
1945.06.03

Piano Concerto no.1, op.35
1936.01.05; 1936.04.05; 1945.06.24

Singer, Gregory

Preludio, Fuga e Allegro
1939.03.12

Spendiarov, Aleksandr

Esquisses de Crimee
1933.08.03*

Stravinsky, Igor

Le sacre du printemps
1933.11.12

Petroushka
1944.06.15-17; 1945.06.03

The Firebird Suite
1923.03.29; 1925.03.15; 1929.03.03;
1929.12.08; 1930.04.27;
1930.10.19; 1932.11.20; 1933.03.19;
1935.04.07; 1937.01.17; 1938.03.27;
1939.12.10; 1940.12.22; 1943.01.31;
1944.05.13+14;1945.03.[n.d.];
1945.12.09; 1946.01.06

The Volga Boatmen Song
1922.01.29+31;1924.03.30; 1926.11.25;
1942.08.02*

Tchaikovsky, Peter Ilyich

1812 Overture

1911.12.10; 1912.04.07; 1924.12.28;
1931.05.31; 1933.08.31*;1935.08.31*;
1940.05.10; 1945.06.24; 1945.12.22;
1946.09.21*; 1946.11.28

Capriccio Italiano
1921.03.20; 1922.01.03; 1922.11.12+14;
1923.05.27; 1923.06.30*;1923.07.07*;
1923.07.16*;1924.04.13; 1926.03.28;
1926.11.14; 1927.06.28*;1927.07.09*;
1928.01.22; 1928.07.18*;
1928.08.11*;1928.09.01*;
1929.07.22*;1931.08.29*;
1932.07.23*;1932.08.13*;
1932.09.10*;1933.07.22*;
1934.06.20*;1935.07.10*;
1935.07.18*;1935.08.28*; 1937.04.11;
1938.08.13*; 1938.08.20*;1938.09.15*;
1939.08.27*;1940.08.03*;
1942.07.15*;1943.01.17; 1944.03.11;
1945.08.12*; 1946.02.03

Chanson Sans Paroles, op.2
1930.08.13+15*; 1931.07.01*;
1932.06.28*;1934.08.10*; 1934.08.31*

Charodeika (The Enchantress): Aria
1935.05.12

Cherevichki
1930.01.05; 1930.03.30; 1931.01.11

Don Juan's Serenade
1940.05.21

Eugene Onegin
1911.11.26; 1927.10.16; 1932.12.11;
1935.03.10; 1928.07.16*;1928.08.20*;
1929.07.15*;1931.06.16*;
1931.07.14*;1933.07.06*;
1934.07.01*;1934.07.18*;
1934.08.24*;1934.10.13*;
1935.07.16*;1935.12.29;
1936.07.23*;1938.08.25*;
1942.08.13*;1943.05.23;
1943.08.21*;1945.04.04; (collaborated
with Shushlin's Academy of Music)
1945.12.22

Fatum, op.77
1943.11.28

Table 4.2 *(Cont.)*

Francesca da Rimini
  1924.10.26; 1928.02.05; 1930.01.05;
  1931.10.25; 1933.04.30; 1934.02.04;
  1939.11.05; 1941.05.11; 1941.12.14;
  1943.04.18

I Bless the Forests
  1940.05.21

In the midst of a clamorous ball
  1940.05.21

Intermezzo (unspecified)
  1932.08.25*

Iolanta: Aria
  1927.10.16; 1935.03.10

Legend
  1931.12.27

Manfred Symphony, op.58
  1943.03.21

Marche Slave, op.31
  1921.01.30; 1921.05.01; 1922.01.03;
  1925.03.15; 1926.03.21; 1926.07.27*;
  1927.04.24; 1927.07.20*;
  1927.08.26+29*; 1927.10.16;
  1928.08.11*; 1928.08.29*; 1929.07.20*;
  1930.08.09*; 1931.08.06*; 1931.08.15*;
  1932.07.25*; 1933.08.12*; 1934.08.04*;
  1935.08.07*; 1935.08.23*; 1935.12.29;
  1936.02.13; 1936.07.29+30*;
  1936.09.17*; 1938.07.16*; 1939.08.01*;
  1940.07.20*; 1942.04.07; 1942.08.16*;
  1943.07.24*; 1946.01.20

Mazurka (unspecified)
  1929.02.26

Musical Picture "In the Church"
  1932.05.01

No! Only he who thirsted . . .
  1940.05.21

None but a lonely heart
  1912.01.21;1940.08.03*;
  1943.02.07;1946.11.29+12.01

Opritchnik: Arioso
  1932.05.01

*Orchestral Suite no.1 in D minor, op.43:
IV*
  1926.12.23; 1928.08.11*

Orchestral Suite no.3, op.55: IV
  1911.12.10; 1933.01.15; 1934.05.20;
  1943.05.23

*Orchestral Suite no.4 in G major, op.61
"Mozartiana"*
  1934.02.04

Petite Suite
  1935.08.16*; 1936.08.07*; 1936.08.14*

*Piano Concerto no.1 in B flat minor,
op.23*
  1921.05.01; 1922.02.19+20;
  1925.02.19; 1931.11.08; 1933.06.16;
  1933.11.05; 1938.12.18; 1940.05.26;
  1942.05.24; 1943.03.14

Piano Trio in A minor, op.50
  1940.05.21

Piano Variations in F major, op.19
  1940.05.21

Pique Dame: Aria
  1930.01.05; 1930.03.30; 1931.02.22;
  1932.05.01; 1933.01.15; 1935.11.17;
  1939.11.05; 1940.08.03*; 1945.07.28*

Polka
  1929.02.26

Rococo Variations, op.33
  1921.05.01; 1928.03.18; 1929.02.03;
  1936.12.20

Romance no.5
  1933.07.27*

Romeo and Juliet Fantasy Overture
  1929.01.14; 1930.03.30; 1930.10.19;
  1931.03.08; 1932.02.14; 1932.08.20*;
  1932.12.11; 1933.10.29; 1935.04.14;
  1935.11.17; 1937.05.16; 1937.09.19;
  1939.01.22; 1942.05.24;
  1942.08.16*;1944.06.15-17;
  1945.07.28*;1946.02.03

Serenade for Strings, op.48
  1930.10.26; 1932.01.10; 1932.11.06;
  1934.10.28; 1935.03.19; 1935.12.29;
  1936.09.05*;1936.11.29; 1941.12.14;
  1944.05.13+14

(continues)

Table 4.2 *(Cont.)*

Six Romances, op.73
1923.12.20; 1930.03.23; 1933.02.19;
1940.05.21

String Quartet no.1 in D major, op.11
1923.01.11; 1923.03.22; 1924.03.13;
1927.10.16; 1931.01.11; 1932.05.01;
1932.11.20; 1934.04.15;
1934.07.07+12*;1935.03.10;
1935.08.03*;1935.08.10*; 1935.11.17;
1939.07.06*; 1940.05.21; 1941.05.17;
1946.04.28; 1946.09.15*

Symphony no.4 in F minor, op.36
1921.01.30; 1921.12.18; 1922.01.03;
1923.02.25; 1925.02.19; 1925.03.15;
1926.02.14; 1926.05.16; 1927.11.13;
1928.10.21; 1930.08.09*;1930.11.30;
1932.07.11*;1932.12.04;
1933.08.05*;1934.05.20; 1934.12.30;
1935.12.29; 1936.03.29; 1937.01.10;
1938.01.09; 1938.07.30*;
1939.01.29; 1939.07.11*;
1939.07.28*;1939.07.30*; 1940.10.27;
1941.12.14; 1942.08.16*;1943.02.21;
1944.04.29+30; 1945.12.22

Symphony no.5 in E minor, op.64
1912.02.18; 1912.04.07; 1921.01.30;
1921.05.01; 1922.02.19+20;
1923.05.27; 1923.12.09; 1924.03.23;
1925.10.11; 1926.02.21; 1926.05.09;
1927.04.24; 1927.05.01; 1927.08.27*;
1928.02.19; 1928.08.11*;
1928.08.22*;1929.02.10; 1930.01.05;
1930.07.08*; 1931.04.12; 1933.02.05;
1933.07.25*;1934.02.04; 1935.04.14;
1935.12.29; 1936.04.10; 1936.07.01*;
1937.03.24; 1937.04.11; 1937.05.02;
1938.01.30; 1938.09.10*;1938.10.09;
1939.07.06*; 1940.04.21;
1941.01.30+02.01+02.02; 1942.02.01;
1942.08.09*; 1942.11.17; 1943.11.28;
1944.11.05; 1945.12.16; 1946.11.24

Symphony no.6 in B minor, op.74
"Pathetique"
1911.12.10; 1919.12.21; 1920.04.30;
1921.01.23; 1922.01.29+31;
1923.04.05; 1924.04.13;

1924.05.31; 1924.11.16; 1926.01.17;
1926.10.10; 1927.07.20*; 1927.10.16;
1928.04.15; 1928.08.11*;1929.05.05;
1929.07.29*;1929.12.22;
1930.07.24*;1931.01.11; 1932.05.29;
1932.08.27*; 1933.03.12; 1933.07.25*;
1934.03.02; 1934.06.09*;
1934.08.18*;1935.03.10; 1935.11.17;
1936.09.12*; 1936.11.15; 1937.10.31;
1938.11.13; 1939.11.26; 1940.05.26;
1941.01.26; 1941.12.28; 1942.07.19*;
1943.02.07; 1944.01.02; 1945.05.20;
1946.01.20

*The Maid of Orleans: Jeanne d'Arc's Rec-
itative and Aria*
1931.10.25

The Nutcracker
1911.12.03; 1912.02.18; 1912.04.07;
1921.05.08; 1925.10.04; 1926.03.14;
1926.07.21*;1926.08.10*;
1927.07.20*;1927.08.17*;
1927.12.18; 1928.02.29; 1928.04.15;
1928.06.16*; 1928.08.11*;1929.02.26;
1929.06.19*;1929.07.31*;
1929.08.31*;1930.07.01*;
1930.08.23*;1931.06.23*;
1932.06.29*;1932.08.10*;
1933.07.15*;1934.07.25*; 1934.11.14;
1935.04.30; 1935.11.08; 1936.05.17;
1936.08.15*;1938.07.21*;
1939.07.22*;1940.06.29*;
1940.08.24*;1942.05.03; 1942.08.16*;
1944.07.22+23*; 1944.12.14-17;
1945.12.23

The Seasons, op.37
1922.04.13; 1928.06.30*;
1928.08.11*;1928.09.01*;
1929.06.29*;1930.07.05*;
1932.07.25*;1936.09.10*; 1938.09.10*

The Sleeping Beauty
1933.08.10*; 1935.02.12;
1944.01.11+12+15+16;
1944.08.19+20*; 1946.09.09+10

The Sun Is Sinking Low
1922.02.09

Table 4.2 *(Cont.)*

The Swan Lake 1930.04.27; 1932.08.27*; 1934.06.09*; 1940.05.24; 1942.08.16*; 1943.03.31+ 1943.04.01+02+04; 1943.07.24*; 1946.02.17; 1944.07.01+02*;1945.04 [n.d.]; 1946.02.17 *Valse (unspecified)* 1932.07.23*; 1936.07.08*; 1936.07.30* *Violin Concerto in D major, op.35* 1920.03.28; 1920.04.30; 1927.11.20; 1937.03.24; 1940.05.26; 1943.11.28; 1946.10.26 *The Queen of Spades, op.68* 1926.11.25	**Tcherepnin, Alexander** *Piano Concerto no.1 in F major, op.12* 1934.11.25 *Piano Concerto no.2 in A minor, op.25* 1934.05.13 *Slavic Transcriptions, op.27* 1934.05.13 *The Wedding of Sobeide: Festmusik* 1934.11.25 **Tcherepnin, Nikolai** *Pavillion d'Armide* 1937.01.15-17+23+24; 1943.05.[n.d.] **Yurashovsky, Alexander Ivanovich** *Trilby: Aria of Trilby* 1943.01.17

* Open-air concert held in the summer

Nutcracker, and the Piano Concerto and Violin Concerto were part of the repertoire. The *1812 Overture*, though it had been played in 1913, was only brought back in the twelfth concert of 1924 (on December 28) as the last piece to mark the end of the year as well as the beginning of the new one, and the piece was not played again until 1945. His *Manfred Symphony* was only played once in 1943, but his overtures such as *Francesca da Rimini* and *Romeo and Juliet* were repeated many times.

Over the years, the SMO managed to build an extensive repertoire of Russian works that other contemporary orchestras would not have played so often or at all.[6] For instance, works of Glinka and Dargomyzhsky, the Mighty Handful (Balakirev, Borodin, Cui, Mussorgsky, and Rimsky-Korsakov), Alexander Glazunov, Vasily Kalinnikov, Anatoli Lyadov, and Rachmaninov were in the SMO's repertoire and received many repeated performances. The works of lesser-known composers such as Alexander Alyabyev, Iosif Borisov, Karl Davydov, Reinhold Glière, Alexander Gretchaninov, Mikhail Ippolitov-Ivanov, and Alexander Yurashovsky also received one or two performances. Worth noting is the introduction of works of Stravinsky and Shostakovich. Stravinsky's *The Firebird Suite* was first introduced in 1923,[7] but a review from 1930 still regarded it as "a well-known subject of controversy" ("The Municipal Orchestra" 1930, 12), even though it was repeated many times subsequently.[8] Shostakovich's Piano Concerto no. 1 was first introduced in 1936, with Leo Itkis as the soloist.[9]

Composing Diaspora

Of all the SMO Russian concerts, those that featured works of contemporary émigré composers who had connections with Shanghai—Alexander Tcherepnin, Aaron Avshalomov, and Sergei Aksakov—were the most endearing to the Shanghai Russian community and thus the most interesting to unravel. While concerts of Tcherepnin and Avshalomov will be discussed in later chapters, this one will introduce those of Aksakov. Comparing the three of them, Tcherepnin was more a visiting émigré composer than a local one, whereas Avshalomov had an additional identity of also being Jewish and had better networks with the Chinese and international communities, which made him less bound to the Russian community. Though Aksakov's works did not endure the test of time and were probably less interesting than those of Tcherepnin and Avshalomov, when compared to these two he played a much bigger role in the Russian community as the émigrés' cultural and musical spokesman. He was the key figure in a number of artistic clubs and the editor of the music column of the Russian newspaper *Shanghai Zaria*, as pointed out in chapter 2. But due to Tcherepnin's and Avshalomov's connections with the Chinese community, they are better remembered than Aksakov, particularly in Chinese-language literature. The following excerpt from an article in *Shanghai Zaria* shortly before the premiere of Aksakov's *Symphonic Ballade for Piano and Orchestra* (op. 27) on March 12, 1933, reveals the importance of such an event for the Russian émigrés:

> Besides his undeniable musical abilities, tomorrow's performance of the "Symphonic Ballad" of S. S. Aksakov has a special significance and meaning for Russian Shanghai. In the presence of cosmopolitan Shanghai that is cultured, that is full of the love for music and the presence of different types of music, a piece by a Russian emigrant composer will be performed. Not only will this be an important day in the life of composer Aksakov, this day should also be written in the history of Russian Shanghai and in general in the history of Russians abroad. The latter have nowadays nothing except our talent, abilities, energy, and our brilliant cultural past. Especially in the world of musical art, we can say this without risk of getting reproaches for any kind of exaggeration or boasting. The history of Russian music includes such names as Glinka, Dargomyzhsky, Mussorgsky, Tchaikovsky, Rimsky-Korsakov, Skryabin, Ippolitov-Ivanov, Glazunov, and Gretchaninov, which are known throughout the world, celebrated and fully appreciated. ("Simfonicheskaya ballada" 1933a, 3)

Aksakov was regarded as the representative of Russian culture. That his work was performed in an all-Russian program concert that also included

Mussorgsky's *Pictures at an Exhibition* and Tchaikovsky's Symphony no. 6 (SMO Concert Program 1933, March 12) rendered him the successor of the great Russian musical tradition. Composed in 1932, Aksakov's *Symphonic Ballade*, set in five variations, was regarded as being in the "Russian style." One of these variations was written in the form of a piano cadenza played by Aksakov himself. The variations were based on a theme in Mixolydian, the old Russian church mode, which was used throughout the entire piece whenever possible ("Simfonicheskaya ballada" 1933a, 3). Though there is no extant score to examine, one assumes the work might show some parallels to Glinka's *Kamarinskaya*.[10]

The contents of the piece demonstrated Aksakov's affinity for absolute music. Although attaching no nationalistic sentiments to his piece programmatically, Aksakov emphasized his musical style be a direct descendant of the new Russian school headed by Rimsky-Korsakov, Aksakov himself being a student of Rimsky-Korsakov's student A. Gretchaninov and his friend S. Lyapunov. For Aksakov, Rimsky-Korsakov was the cornerstone in the development of Russian music ("Simfonicheskaya ballada" 1933b, 13). In this regard, Asakov's composing was both diasporic as well as cosmopolitan. His works, while continuing the great Russian tradition, were also "universal" in the sense that they were not nationalistic toward a particular nation. Nonetheless, the continuation of the great tradition of Russian music that was "known throughout the world," the music of the so-called New Russian School represented by the Russian Five, including Rimsky-Korsakov, as opposed to the old Saint Petersburg school of Tchaikovsky, had long been associated with musical nationalism rather than with cosmopolitanism. In a way, Aksakov's musical aesthetics and his attempt to articulate the great tradition of Russian musical nationalism through the cosmopolitan approach of the Hanslick school mirrored his cosmopolitan-diasporic stance. While he was active in Shanghai's international musical scene as a composer and pedagogue, he was also committed to preserving Russian cultural heritage, as evident in his writings in *Shanghai Zaria*.[11]

Aside from his *Symphonic Ballade*, Aksakov's Symphony no. 1 in B minor was performed on April 25, 1937, by the SMO, and his Piano Concerto in E minor premiered on October 23, 1938, with Leo Itkis as soloist. In fact, by the late 1930s, his role as an "émigré composer" as well as a local Shanghai composer was well established. His new symphony was reported to have raised great interest in Shanghai musical circles ("Novaia Russkaia Simfoniia" 1936, 6). When his Piano Concerto was premiered, it caused a small controversy. A review of the work in the *North-China Daily News* criticized it for lacking originality, but the review was refuted by an array of concertgoers of the international community, all speaking in defense of Aksakov's continuing with the style of Tchaikovsky and Glazunov.[12] In one note, the author tried to comfort Aksakov, stating that Tchaikovsky's works were considered "dull" during the composer's lifetime, and reiterating that the audience really loved Aksakov's work ("Local Concerto: A Critic Criticized" 1938, 203). The author of another note wrote that "we should always welcome a new composer, as, to my mind at any rate, his efforts come as a stimulating change from the constant hearing of the works of old masters" ("Composer Congratulated" 1938, 203). All the support Aksakov received from Shanghai's international audience, while not necessarily an accurate measurement of his work's artistic merit, no doubt indicated that he had been included into Shanghai's international community. In that regard, music served to transcend the boundaries of diaspora.

Performing Russianness

Paci, though often criticized for favoring Italian works,[13] supported émigré composers' endeavors, which was probably related to his awareness of the Russian community's propensity for music that reminded them of their cultural heritage. In return, it was a good opportunity to bring in new repertoire in addition to showcasing renowned soloists. Most of all, a full-house concert meant increased revenue for the Municipal Council, which was often necessary to offset the less well-attended concerts. Based on SMO's statistics, from 1933 to 1939 the number of people who attended the special Russian concerts accounted for 54 percent of all concert attendees. In 1933, the number of people was 70 percent and the income was 71 percent of the total income of that year; in 1937, the number was 64 percent and the income 58 percent (Wang Yanli 2010, 38).

The "Special Russian Operatic Concert" held on April 1, 1928, that featured the renowned Russian contralto Alla Tomskaya and enhanced by the Russian Choral Society, was a case in point to show the popularity of such a concert. The concert program was all Russian. Part 1 consisted of three fragments from Glinka's opera *The Life for the Tsar*, part 2 consisted of recitatives and arias from Rimsky-Korsakov's *Sadko*, followed by two more numbers from Glinka's *Ruslan and Lyudmila*, and part 3 contained selections from Borodin's *Prince Igor* sung by the Russian Choir with orchestra (SMO Concert Program).

The economic motivation for such an event is readily evident in Paci's letter to the council secretary (SMA U1-3-235-1300, 169), which is reproduced as follows:

> To the Secretary, S.M.C.
> SHANGHAI.
> RE PROPOSAL OF SPECIAL RUSSIAN CONCERT:
>
> I beg herewith to be authorized to arrange for Sunday, April 1st, at 9.15 p.m., a "Special Russian Operatic Concert" with the collaboration of the

professional singer, well known in Shanghai, Madame Alla Tomskaya, and the Russian Choral Society (42 voices) under the leadership of Mr. Mashin.

I have been rehearsing and preparing this concert for the last two months, and I am certain of its success for two principal reasons: Firstly, because this concert will be in the meantime a jubilee concert of Mme. Tomskaya who is very popular, especially amongst the Russian Community, and secondly, because choral performances are generally very much appreciated.

I do not think, however, that, although the programme is very interesting, we should make of this concert an extra Symphony Concert at $3, -. 2.-, 1.- entrance fees. I beg therefore to recommend that entrance fees for this concert be fixed (as we did for the Operatic Concert on Sunday, March 4th) to $2.- and $1.- for the main hall, and 60 cents for the gallery, with booking at Moutrie's.

At this time there will be not only the soloists to be paid, but also the choral society, I beg to recommend that a percentage of 30 percent from the gross receipts be paid as a total fee, both for the soloists and the choral society.

Wishing to start as soon as possible the necessary advertising for this concert, I beg urgently to be granted the Council's official authorization.

Mario Paci
The Conductor

From the above note, it is clear that the popularity of Tomskaya and the choral performance was the main motivation for the concert. Tomskaya, who had come from Harbin and was to leave for France in the following year ("Proshchalnyi kontsert A. M. Tomskoi" 1929, 5), was regarded as "one of the best known teachers in the East of the 'Belcanto' method of singing, and has sung in Russian Opera in Russia with Chaliapin and Sobinov, and in Italian Opera in Petrograd with Cavalieri and Armondi" ("Capacity House" 1928, 4). As anticipated, the concert was a full-house event. Given that the Carlton Theater was a venue with 750 seats, the gross revenue would be around $1,000 or more. So even after deducting the basic costs of running the concert as well as paying the performers' fees that were fixed at 30 percent, there would still be a reasonable profit of several hundred dollars for the SMO.

Such a concert, particularly with the performance of the Russian Choral Society under the leadership of Mashin, whose important role in the Russian community has been discussed in chapter 2, must have provided Shanghai's international audiences a "novel" experience of colorful Russian music. It also had layers of meanings for the Russian community. The old guards of Imperial

Russia who were then in Shanghai were said to be there to hear music from home. In addition to the performance, there was also a ceremony of reading tributes to Mme. Tomskaya from her students as well as from the Russian community ("Capacity House" 1928, 4). In fact, Tomskaya was a professor at the newly established National Conservatory of Music, though for a short period of less than two years, so it is safe to assume her students included both Russians and Chinese as well as students of other national origins. In that regard, the concert was not just a performance anymore. Instead it became a performative, a utopian space as well as a ritual for the Russian community. The former was for émigrés to experience a sonic homecoming, whereas the latter was a ceremony to affirm the continuation of the Russian heritage. The connection of musical experience to the notion of utopia is not an innovative idea. One of music's powers is its capacity to take the listener to "a world not yet reachable at present," being an agent to fulfill "the longing for transcendence" (quote from Hans Heinrich Eggebrecht in Music 2008, 665). The cultural historian Richard Dyer also suggests that any form of entertainment is utopian insofar as it provides "temporary answers to the inadequacies of the society" (2002, 25). In this regard, the Russian music played by the SMO must have been extremely special for the Russian audience in Shanghai, providing them a moment of transcendence, a moment to forget the losses they had endured, a moment to feel at home with their motherland. It is no wonder that Russian émigrés would not miss such an event if they could afford to go.[14] The concert ticket, which cost one or two dollars, was not cheap, but it was certainly affordable for those who had employment. A musician at the SMO was paid between $165 and $215 a month while white bread cost about $0.60 a pound and a private music lesson around $10.

Russian Vocalists

Tomskaya and Abramovitch were just two of the many Russian vocalists who performed with the SMO. When compared to the concert programs of other symphony orchestras, the SMO's stood out in the number of operatic and choral programs it presented, thanks to the presence of many Russian operatic singers and accomplished vocalists in Shanghai at the time. As one writer wrote, "the sad fate of Russia has proved an artistic boon to Shanghai in respect of the fine voices it has, from time to time, brought to our doors" ("A Wagner Opera in Shanghai" 1922, 281). Indeed, the Russian emigration brought hundreds of professionally trained Russian vocalists to Shanghai, some of whom had been leading vocalists of renowned opera houses in Russia (two hundred vocalists listed in Wang 2007, 340–375). These vocalists helped contribute to the Shanghai operatic scene as described in chapter 2. Some of these vocalists, particularly the leading ones, were often invited by Paci to perform with the SMO, singing a wide range of works, including Camille Saint-Saëns's *Samson et Dalilah*, Smetana's *The Bartered Bride*, Dvořák's *Rusalka*, and Richard Strauss' songs, as well as Puccini's *Manon Lescaut, Tosca,* and *Madame Butterfly,* to name but a few.

Whether by their own insistence or upon the request of Paci, some of these vocalists performed an array of Russian works, particularly at concerts in celebration of Christmas and Easter. For instance, in the May 26, 1926, concert, the mezzo-soprano Vera Yeltsova, in addition to singing the "Habañera" from Bizet's *Carmen,* also sang a selection of songs by Rachmaninov, Mussorgsky, and Glazunov (SMO Concert Program). Yeltsova was a graduate of the Saint Petersburg Conservatory who moved to Harbin in 1923 and then to Shanghai in 1931. Apparently she was invited to perform with the SMO in 1926 while she was still in Harbin. She was one of those émigré musicians who thrived in their new habitat. Not only was she a prominent singer in various Russian opera productions in Shanghai, she also had her own private vocal school (Wang 2007, 347–348). The renowned bass Vladimir Shushlin, who arrived Shanghai in 1929, was another success story in Shanghai.[15] He collaborated regularly with the SMO. For example, the concert held on December 29, 1935, again featured an all-Russian program with Vladimir Shushlin as the soloist, singing arias from Tchaikovsky's *Eugene Onegin* and Borodin's *Prince Igor* (SMO Concert Program). The concert on November 15, 1936, also a Russian program, featured the Russian soprano Raya Riskin, who sang an array of arias from works of Glinka, Dargomyzhsky, Rimsky-Korsakov, and Lyadov. Another impressive Russian opera concert was held on December 12, 1937 (SMO Concert Program). The mezzo-soprano Vera Melashich and the tenor A. Slobodskoy sang an entire concert of Russian folk songs in arrangements by Mussorgsky, Gretchaninov, Dubatov, and Mapravnik, as well as songs inspired by the river Volga (SMO Concert Program).

Interesting to note is the number of Russian soloists singing famous operatic excerpts of composers from other nations, particularly those of Wagner, which must have been a treat for the Shanghai audience as a whole. Due to the technical demand of Wagner's vocal parts, such a repertoire was not frequently performed in Asia, then as well as now. That Wagner was already not a novelty to Shanghai's audience in the interwar period testifies to the SMO conductors' cosmopolitan ideal as well as their efforts to keep the orchestra's repertoire on par with its European counterparts. In 1908, Buck introduced Wagner's music to his concert program to commemorate the twenty-fifth anniversary of the composer's death ("Wagner Concert" 1908, 612). At the time, such an event attracted a lot of attention from the international community ("Richard Wagner" 1908, 593).[16] For Shanghai's Public Band to be able to play Wagner was a sign of Shanghai settlers' cultural accomplishment. It proved that even in faraway Asia, Shanghailanders could still have a piece of culture from home. When Wagner's music was performed in 1920, it was, however, received "in a matter of fact" manner, with the critic paying more attention to the performance rather than to the composition (see for example "Operatic Concert at Town Hall" 1920, 552), which suggests that Wagner was no longer a novelty to Shanghai. In the 1920 concert, the renowned Russian bass Petr Selivanov, chairman of the Russian Artists in Shanghai, sang "Wotan's Farewell" and "Magic Fire" from *Die Walküre*.[17] Sharing the concert with him was the soprano L. Isenman, who sang Elizabeth's air from Act III of *Tannhäuser*. Both of their performances were warmly received. In 1921, the soprano M. B. Tcherkasskaya, a former prima donna of the Imperial Theater Petrograd and La Scala, sang Brünnhilde's aria "Ho jo to ho!" from *Die Walküre* (SMO Concert Program). In the following year, Tcherkasskaya banded with Isenman and Heidenstam to sing a concert of Verdi's and Wagner's arias, testifying to the popularity of these operatic concerts.[18]

Vladimir Shushlin, mentioned above regarding his appearance at special Russian concerts, also appeared in many Wagner concerts of the SMO. The special concert held on May 28, 1933, is worth noting, as it showcased an array of Russian singers, namely A. Slobodskoy and Vladimir Shushlin as soloists, and V. Eltzova, M. Glebova, E. Zharikova, M. Krylova, and V. Melashich as five of the eight valkyries (SMO Concert Program). In 1938, a special Wagner concert was held on February 6 that featured soprano Yulia Markovska, tenor A. Slobodskoy, and Shushlin singing excerpts from *Lohengrin*, *Die Walküre*, and *Die Meistersinger von Nürnberg*, while the concert opened with the Prelude from *Lohengrin* and ended with the Overture from *Tannhäuser* (SMO Concert Program). Though the 1938 concert was a full house, the critic's review was lukewarm, perhaps as a result of Slobodskoy's having a cold that affected his performance ("Wagner Played by Orchestra" 1938, 5). That Wagner's works were reported to have been sung in three languages, German, English, and Russian, was worth pondering. While this could be read as a sign of Shanghai's cosmopolitanism, one must not overlook the pragmatism behind the SMO's attempt to appeal to both the anglophone and russophone audiences, who were both important to Paci despite the work's original language.

Russian Soloists

Shanghai was indeed the hub of a great many talented Russian musicians, both vocalists and instrumentalists. They can be classified into four categories: (1) world-renowned Russian soloists on tour to Shanghai, (2) locally renowned

Russian musicians appearing as soloists, (3) Russian players of the SMO appearing as soloists, and (4) Russian students of renowned Russian pedagogues.

A roster of world-renowned Russian soloists who visited Shanghai during the first half of the twentieth century included Mischa Elman, Efrem Zimbalist, Jascha Heifetz, Benno Moiseiwitsch, Alexander Tcherepnin, Feodor Chaliapin, Gregor Piatigorsky, etc. (Wang 2007, 176–192). Concerts of Russian musicians held special meanings to the Russian community in Shanghai, as these musicians were seen as heroes and their successes a source of pride among the émigrés. A case in point was the visit of Russian bass Chaliapin in January 1936. The event was highly anticipated, as demonstrated by the voluminous press coverage and welcoming gestures. A huge group met him at the pier with a banner even though he was just passing through Shanghai on his way to give a concert in Japan ("Segodnia pribyvaet F. I. Shalyapin" 1936; F. I. Shalyapin v Shankhae, 1936). As mentioned in a *Shanghai Zaria* article, Chaliapin's visit was deemed "the great event in the life of the Russian colony. . . . We have to realize that we happen to be contemporaries of a genius and will have the pleasure to see and hear someone that will create legends in 40–50 years. . . . Now we can imagine ourselves in a place of the distant contemporaries of living geniuses" (Aksakov 1936, 10).

Not all the top-notch émigré Russian soloists appeared with the SMO. For example, Chaliapin, who performed in Shanghai twice in 1936, did not cooperate with the SMO, and he thought that Shanghai's lacking a suitable venue for opera performance was unconscionable given the city's economic prosperity ("F. I. Shalyapin v Shankhae" 1936 (*Slovo*), 6). But some—such as Elman, Zimbalist, and Moiseiwitsch, to name but a few—did perform with the SMO to great success. These internationally renowned Russian émigré musicians' concerts were organized by the impresario Awsay Strok, who for example was behind Tcherepnin's China tour discussed in chapter 6 and who tended to organize these tours on a profit-sharing basis, though the terms applied were usually case by case. Take for instance the pianist Benno Moiseiwitch, who appeared in two special concerts on May 7 and 14, 1933, and who was engaged on the condition that the first one thousand dollars of the gross receipt be paid to the Municipal Council and the excess of the receipt then be apportioned 80 percent to the soloist and 20 percent to the council. In general, soloists took a 70 percent share of the receipt after deducting the gross expenditure by the council. But Moiseiwitch's popularity among the Shanghai audience, particularly the Russian one, gave him extra bargaining power. Based on Paci's estimation, the full seating capacity of the Grand Theater of 2,050 seats would generate a gross receipt of $5,550. Aside from the $1,000 deduction for the gross income, there would still be an additional profit of close to $1,000 for the SMO, which meant a very handsome return for the council, even after the soloist received 80 percent of the profit.[19]

Soloists of Moiseiwitch's caliber were often hard to come by, thus it was the local talents that the SMO counted on. In that regard, the Shanghai community was indebted to the Russian émigrés for the many talented musicians residing in the city. For example, the renowned pianist Boris Zakharov, who decided to settle in Shanghai in 1929,[20] not only performed at many of SMO's chamber music concerts, which was covered briefly in chapter 2, but also played concertos with the SMO.[21] The concert held on April 30, 1933, at the Carlton Theater in honor of the twentieth anniversary of his musical career (after he graduated from the Saint Petersburg Conservatory) was regarded by the music critic of the *North-China Daily News* as "one of the most memorable ovations ever accorded an artist in this hall" ("Final Concert in Carlton" 1933, 12). In a way, it was just one of those Russian Easter concerts that featured all Russian works, with Zakharov playing Rachmaninov's Piano Concerto no. 2. His playing was hailed as a "striking illustration of his gift for evoking full and resonant tone without a trace of exaggeration ("Final Concert in Carlton" 1933, 12). Perhaps of all Zakharov's contributions (and likewise Shushlin's), he should be remembered for introducing Paci to a number of his best students, Russian as well as Chinese, and providing them the chance to shine on the stage with the SMO. In so doing, he paved the way for the musical career of a number of Chinese pianists, who were to develop Chinese pianism in the second half of the twentieth century, which will be discussed in greater length in the following chapter.

Aside from Zakharov, there were a number of Russian pianists who performed with the SMO, among them T. Milikowski, Vera Chernieskaja, Tamara Maslov, Wincia Tomaszewska, Tolya Vedernikov (Tolia Vedernikoff), Leo Itkis, Vladimir Havsky, Ada Lvov, Ada Milikovskaya, and Fausta Sakharova, and Grigory Zinger (Gregory Singer) (see table 3.3 in the previous chapter for a list of Russian soloists who collaborated with the SMO). While Singer will be discussed in connection with Avshalomov's compositions in chapter 7, it is worthwhile to briefly visit the career of two child prodigies, Tolya Vedernikov and Vladimir Havsky, both born in China and both starting their careers with the SMO at a young age. Their rise to stardom in Shanghai was revealing of the émigrés' new life in their adopted country and community. That these young musicians had the opportunity to share the stage with the SMO also showed the intricate relationship between the institution and the émigré community and how they relied on each other for their own gains. While the SMO helped build these young musicians' reputations, they in turn stirred up the audiences' curiosity about the wonder-child phenomenon, a curiosity that brought audiences to the SMO concerts.

Young Pianists the Hope of Future

Tolya Vedernikov, born in 1920, was from Harbin, and he was not yet fifteen when he played with the SMO in 1935.[22] His concert on March 31, 1935, in which he played Grieg's Piano Concerto in A minor, Chopin's Nocturne in C minor and Franz Liszt's *St. François d'Assise: la prédication aux oiseaux*, was a huge success. Before his Shanghai debut, the following appeared in *Shanghai Zaria*: "It is a rare occasion that in difficult emigrant conditions such a young Russian talent grows up. But Tolya Vedernikov, against all odds, was born, raised and blossomed in full bloom of musical talent in emigration. So, who if not us, Russians, should take care of this great and bright gift?" ("Tolya Vedernikov budet" 1935, 5). As it turned out, such a plea was not necessary as the Lyceum Theater was totally packed and many had to be turned away. The audience received Vedernikov's performance with utmost enthusiasm: "the hall plunged into chaos of applauses and 'bravo' and 'encore' shouts that would not seem to have stopped had Paci not gestured a halt" (descriptions of the concert in "Blestiaschii triumf" 1935, 5). While the critic of *China Press* wrote a raving review about the concert ("Young Pianist Wins" 1935, 8), the Russian critic from *Zaria* hailed the performance a "triumph." Even the harshest and reserved locals were said to have "showed rare enthusiasm to the young Russian talent" ("Blestiashchii triumf" 1935, 5).

Vedernikov played again on June 2, 1935, in which he performed Beethoven's Piano Concerto no. 5 and Liszt's Hungarian Fantasy and Hungarian Rhapsody no. 2 (SMO Concert Program). Due to the great appeal of his performance, it was recommended that he be re-engaged for SMO's summer concert, "to give impulse to the public to patronize the orchestral concert during the rest of the season."[23] His concert at Jessfield Park, just like his other two concerts, was reported to have attracted more than 1,300 ("Boy Pianist" 1935, 3). Though there was mention of his hope to study in the United States in the following year ("Young Russian Pianist" 1936, 16), he actually returned to the Soviet Union with his family in 1936 to study at the Moscow Conservatory. His parents were said to be repressed, his father shot and his mother sent to prison for eight years in 1937, but the boy did turn out to enjoy a certain degree of success as pianist in the USSR. Particularly remembered was his premiere of some of Shostakovich's piano works. He passed away in 1993.[24]

The success of Vedernikov must have provided hope for those émigré children learning the piano. His path was soon followed by Vladimir Havsky, who was three years younger. Havsky was the son of Sergei and Mary Havsky and was born in Manchuria on February 16, 1923 ("Russian Pianist to Present Concert" 1942, 1). He was reported to have come from an old Russian family; his father, although a graduate of one of the most exclusive law schools in Saint

Petersburg, had to resort to music to earn his living ("In the Russian Colony" 1939, 21). His father relocated to Siberia after the Revolution, where he met his wife. They moved onto China, arriving in Beijing in 1926, and then went to Hankow (Hankou) in 1929. Vladimir left for Shanghai in 1934 and was later joined by his parents, who were still in Shanghai in 1942 ("Russian Pianist to Present Concert" 1942, 1).

Havsky's debut concert on February 7, 1937, with the SMO featured Beethoven's Piano Concerto no. 3, at a time when he was not yet fourteen years old. Paci wrote to the council secretary on February 8 requesting that $50 be awarded to Havsky, as the concert receipt was only $434 and the soloist received a mere $17 after deduction for the cost of expenditure, even though the concert was a great success. Paci wrote, "The boy's musical talent is very remarkable, and he deserves every encouragement and help. He is the son of a modest musician in Hankow, and has been sent here to have an opportunity to study and I'm informed Prof. Zakharoff teaches him gratis" (SMA U1-4-041-828, 35). In fact, Havsky had appeared in a solo concert of Zakharov's students in 1936.[25]

It is interesting to note that Zakharov wrote to the editor of the *North-China Daily News* on November 26, 1939, to clarify an advertisement for the Jessfield Club featuring a pianist by the name of S. Havsky, who turned out to be Vladimir's father, just shortly after Havsky's successful recital at the Lyceum on November 21. Zakharov emphasized that his student, who was then sixteen, was studying at the Thomas Hanbury School for Boys and his father would not capitalize on his son's fame. This suggests a divide in perception toward classical and popular music in Shanghai ("Young Pianist" 1939, 17), the former perceived by some as a high art whereas the latter merely a form of entertainment.

Like many émigré families, Havsky was needy, and Paci, seeing his talents and motivation to succeed, was eager to help whenever he could. For example, for Havsky's performance at the Tchaikovsky Festival in 1940 (to be discussed below), he advised the council to award Havsky $200 as "the young and popular Pianist, whose financial conditions are not very prosperous, I would recommend that instead of a 'souvenir' a fee should be paid to him."[26] By 1940, Havsky must have become a household name in Shanghai's music scene. He played Saint-Saëns's Piano Concerto no. 2 on May 22, 1938, and Rachmaninov's Piano Concerto no. 2 on January 29, 1939, which was repeated on February 26, all at packed halls and receiving rave reviews (SMO Concert Program). When asked during an interview, Havsky indicated that he wanted to be a composer and be able to write down the music that came to his head, and his greatest desire was to meet Rachmaninov and play for him ("In the Russian Colony" 1939, 21). It is uncertain if he ever had a chance to do so, but he did leave Shanghai for the United States after his farewell concert with the SMO on October 29, 1940. He started the concert with Chopin's Piano Concerto no. 2 and ended it with

Rachmaninov's Piano Concerto no. 2, with a handful of solo works in between. The concert was described as sensational, and tickets sold out far in advance. The critic of the *North-China Herald* was pleased with Havsky's rendition of Rachmaninov and praised his extreme speed and delicacy in playing the encore piece, but he thought that Havsky's taking the harder path of serious study would no doubt bring him to higher grounds. "[H]ere is a very gifted musician and personality; we hope that all the study, environment and comparisons of wider horizons to which he is going, will have the effect of turning him into a really great performer" ("Vladimir Havsky's Farewell Concert" 1940, 219).

What happened to Vladimir Havsky after he left Shanghai, and did he turn out to be a great pianist? These questions are beyond the scope of this chapter. Nonetheless, it is known that during his early years in the United States, he maintained an active concert profile with many engagements ("Russian Pianist to Present Concert" 1942, 1). Later he studied with Rudolf Serkin and Nadia Boulanger.[27] But he seems to have given up the career of a dazzling concert pianist and instead joined the music faculty at Bennington College.[28] He was active in his community as a pianist and conductor and gave his final concert with the Ossining Choral Society in 1987 at age sixty-four, after twenty-two years of being its director (Sherman 1987). He passed away on October 12, 2009, in New York, which he had taken as his permanent home, like many other Russian émigrés.[29]

1940: Two Special Events

The year 1940 was not only an important year in Vladimir Havsky's life, but it was also an important year for Paci and the SMO, as well as the Russian community. In Paci's report on the activities of the SMO, he regarded it as one of the most successful years in the orchestra's history. While newly featured works were well received, two-thirds of its concerts were full-house events despite the increase in ticket prices. Two programs highlighted by Paci in the report were especially connected to the Russian community.

One was the special vocal program for Easter Sunday that performed fragments of Wagner's *Parsifal* and Beethoven's Symphony no. 9. Described as "a most impressive concert" that can be seen as a testimony to Shanghai's cosmopolitanism, it showcased a combined force of 150 instrumentalists and singers, including four soloists—soprano R. Fullam, alto M. Stewart, tenor A. Slobodskoy, and bass V. Shushlin—as well as choir members from the Shanghai Choral Society, Shanghai Songsters, and a group of professional Russian singers led by Kolchin ("The Easter Sunday Concert 1940, 2).[30] Tickets were sold out early on and some two hundred people had to be turned away. Such large-scale choral concerts could be traced back to P. Selivanov's 1935 proposal to add a Russian choir onto the SMO's permanent structure and to include choral performance in its regular concerts. The request was turned down by the Municipal Council.[31] In fact, the 1940 concert found precedence in the April 1936 concert that premiered Dvořák's *Stabat Mater* and Beethoven's Symphony no. 9, a concert that probably played a role in saving the SMO from discontinuation.[32]

The other special event of 1940 was the Tchaikovsky Festival celebrating the composer's centenary with three performances: a chamber music concert on May 21, the ballet *Swan Lake* on May 24, and the symphony concert on May 26 (SMO Concert Program). Four Russian musicians were invited to be soloists, namely the pianist Zakharov, cellist J. Ullstein, bass Shushlin, and the boy pianist Havsky, and four SMO members were highlighted in Tchaikovsky's op. 11 quartet. The symphony concert featured Tchaikovsky's Violin Concerto, played by Foa, the concertmaster of the SMO, and the First Piano Concerto, played by Havsky. While neither the chamber music concert nor the symphony concert was "novel" to the Shanghai audience, the main attraction was the production of *Swan Lake* by the Russian Ballet, accompanied by the SMO but conducted by the Russian conductor Slutsky, whose activities were covered briefly in chapter 2. A gross income of $11,000 was estimated if all the performances were full houses, which they were indeed. After deducting all the expenditures, estimated to be $6,200, including $5,000 for producing the ballet as well as the cost to hire nine additional players to strengthen the string section, the remainder was still "in favor of the Municipal Orchestra," as Paci worded in his proposal to the council.[33] Indeed, as mentioned in Paci's 1941 report, the Tchaikovsky Festival was "one of the greatest artistic and financial successes of the Orchestra," which testified to the cultural impact of the Russian community ("Successful Year" 1941, 334).

Worth noting is how Paci pitched his proposal to the council in April 1940. First, he regarded the celebration of Tchaikovsky's centenary as a worldwide event that Shanghai should celebrate, with the SMO taking the lead. Second, he regarded the "universality" of Tchaikovsky's music as a "guarantee of the great success of such a musical enterprise" and suggested that the popularity of Tchaikovsky's music would draw audiences from different communities of Shanghai. In his program planning, he did aspire to show the best and also the most familiar repertoire of the master that entailed both chamber and symphonic works. He thought it a pity not to be able to produce a Tchaikovsky opera for Shanghai, which was out of his domain as explained in chapter 2, thus he suggested going for the ballet as an alternative (SMA U1-4-913, 127–130).

In fact, the SMO's collaboration with the Russian Ballet, the performance of *Swan Lake* on May 24, 1940, was one of the three productions of the company. But, as agreed upon, no announcement or advertisement was allowed on the part of the Russian Ballet for the other two performances until after the Tchaikovsky celebration (SMA U1-4-913, 127–130). Then, since the Russian Ballet had prepared to produce *Swan Lake* for its 1939 season ("In the Russian Colony" 1938, 454), collaborating with the SMO was as much a matter of convenience as a "win-win" endeavor for both institutions. Since the SMO was hired at a cost of $600 to play at the other two performances, it reduced what the company charged the SMO from $4,500 to $3,900, even though musicians' parts had to be copied at an additional $425, and the cost of renting and decorating the theater added another $575. But in the end, all the extra efforts paid off, not only artistically and financially but also sociopolitically. After all, as pointed out in the "In the Russian Colony" article above, "the purchasing power of the Russian colony is steadily rising. Russians form a large percentage of cinema audiences. They supported the Russian Theater, Operetta and even the Ballet. Large numbers throng to the Municipal Orchestra Concerts. Without them several of these enterprises would never be able to cover overhead expenses and would rapidly pass out of existence" (1938, 454).

So Paci's Tchaikovsky Festival did not just pay tribute to the master but also to the Russian community to the extent that an article in Russian by Aksakov was included in the festival program. Aksakov defended Tchaikovsky's Russianness at length but at the same time placed him in the group of world-class geniuses, presumably the masters of Western music. The Russian community indeed took the festival quite seriously. The chair of the Russian Emigrants Committee, Ch. Metzler, wrote to the chairman of the Municipal Council's Orchestra and Band Committee shortly after the concert and stated, "The International Community in Shanghai has paid conclusive tribute to our Greatest Composer and we, Russian Emigres, highly appreciate this good will of the Cosmopolitan Community of Shanghai" (SMA U1-4-913, 72).

The Tchaikovsky Festival was just one of the many concerts in which the Russian community collaborated with the SMO, an institution of Shanghai's international community. It reveals the interconnectedness and interdependence of these communities, which was perhaps just temporary. In a way, it is not too far-fetched to see the festival as an agent to foster connections that allowed the joining of Russian soloists, musicians, the Russian Ballet, Mario Paci, the SMO, and the musicians of other nationalities in the name of Tchaikovsky, a Russian composer who transcended the boundaries of Russian music. Most of all, it is not to be forgotten that such events did not just serve the Russian community but also the other communities of Shanghai. Despite the ephemerality of such events, the effect they had on the Russian community and the international community is not to be understated.

CHAPTER 5

Foundations of New Chinese Music

RUSSIAN PEDAGOGUES AND CHINESE STUDENTS

T<small>HE</small> following article, "Professor B. S. Zakharov and his Prize-Winners: Historic Graduates of the National Conservatory," which also showcased a photograph, appeared in Shanghai's Russian newspaper *Shanghai Zaria* on July 7, 1933:

> Our photograph shows the celebrated Professor B. S. Zakharov with his two prize-winning students from the National Conservatory of Music, Miss Li and Mr. Chiu, brother of the popular lawyer Mr. Franklin Chiu. Under the supervision of Prof. B. S. Zakharov, Mr. Chiu and Miss Li studied for three years, completing a course of the highest musical education following the programs/syllabuses of major European conservatories. Students graduating from the National Conservatory course under the supervision of experienced professors will have completed courses in instrumentation, history of music, theory of piano playing, harmony, aesthetics, and other subjects. On completion of the course, the National Conservatory awards a diploma certified by the central government, equal to that given by other major conservatories. It is of particular importance that Mr. Chiu and Miss Li are the first in Chinese history to have completed a course of the highest level in European classical music in China by graduating from the National Conservatory with Honors. It gives us particular pleasure to note that this most important fact of cultural significance is linked closely to the name of the talented Russian pedagogue and outstanding pianist Boris S. Zakharov. ("B. S. Zakharov i laureaty . . ." 1933, 6)[1]

The three protagonists featured in the article were the Russian pianist Boris Zakharov and his two Chinese students, Lee Hsien Ming (Li Xianmin) 李献敏 and Qiu Fusheng 裘复生, two of the three graduates of the National

Conservatory of Music in 1933. Lee, one of Zakharov's star students and future wife of the Russian émigré composer Alexander Tcherepnin, graduated from the undergraduate course majoring in piano performance, whereas Qiu graduated with a diploma in piano performance.[2] The third graduate of that year was Yu Yixuan 喻宜萱, a vocal student of Slavianova from 1929 to 1932. Even though Yu's major was music education, her vocal talent was so great that she was to become a renowned soprano in the People's Republic of China (PRC).[3] All three graduates were among the best students of the conservatory at the time. Both Lee and Qiu were scholarship winners of 1931, and they were to further their study abroad.[4]

Known in Chinese then as the *Guoli yinyue yuan* and now the Shanghai Conservatory of Music,[5] the National Conservatory is regarded as the vanguard of Western music in China (see for instance Enomoto 2003 and Li 2010).[6] Even though there were only three graduates from the conservatory in 1933, the number was to increase significantly in the coming years, just as the number of Russian pedagogues who were to join the conservatory after 1929. The purpose of this chapter, aside from tracing the careers of the Russian pedagogues and their students in the conservatory, will look into their relationships. It argues that the Russian pedagogues at the National Conservatory laid the foundation for the development of Western music in China, as many of these Russian pedagogues' students were to become leading musicians in the PRC.

The Conservatory: A Symbol of Chinese Modernity

As pointed out in an earlier article (Yang 2012), the National Conservatory symbolized a Western and forward-looking China. The institution's two founders—Cai Yuanpei 蔡元培 (1868–1940) and Xiao Youmei (Hsiao Yiu-Mei) 蕭友梅 (1884–1940)—were advocates of Western ideas and practices, regarding them as a necessary means to liberate the nation from outdated customs and traditions after the May Fourth Movement.[7] Cai believed that the study of art—as opposed to the study of religion—was part of the struggle against feudalism and oppression and that an arts education including the study of music should be available for all.[8] For him and some of his contemporaries, Western music represented a more advanced stage of human evolution, with a wealth of repertoire and theoretical foundation that should be promoted on Chinese soil.[9]

It was Xiao Youmei who aspired to establish a professional music institute in China after studying abroad.[10] He first studied music theory and composition at the Leipzig Conservatory and then studied conducting at the Sternsche Konservatorium in Berlin. He received a doctorate degree in musicology from Leipzig University before he returned to China in 1919.[11] In 1920, he founded the music department of Beijing Women's Normal University (Beijing nuzi shifan daxue). Two years later, Cai Yuanpei appointed him as the head of Beijing University's Music Research Institute (Beida yinyue yanjiusuo).

Xiao Youmei was a determined advocate of "New Music"—*xin yinyue*—Western-format-based music practiced in China and by Chinese composers, just like the new literature of the May Fourth Movement, which were both seen as replacing "feudalism" with "modernity" (Mittler 1997, 25).[12] As pointed out in the recruitment advertisement of the conservatory in Shanghai's *Shen Bao* on September 1, 1927, "[the objective of] the national government to found a music institute in Shanghai is on the one hand to introduce music of the world and on the other to systematize Chinese music so as to reach *datong* (meaning a single form of music), through which to nourish our people's sense of beauty, harmony and [their love] of arts" ("Guoli yinyue yuan zhaosheng" 1927, 2).

Despite limited financial support from the government,[13] that the institution was a "national" endeavor made it a symbol of nation building. Paradoxical as it might seem from a Western viewpoint, this act was commensurate with the May Fourth Movement's definition of nationalism, which stressed the adoption of radical—from a Chinese perspective—Western ideas, such as democracy, Western science, and even music for the good (i.e., the modernization) of China. While Western music was taken as "the music of the world," the National Conservatory aspired to cultivate a "New Chinese Music" that would be a synthesis of traditional Chinese and Western classical music. Evident from the conservatory's concert programs, many students did not only learn to play one or several Western instruments but also a Chinese instrument, in addition to taking both theoretical courses on Western and Chinese music (see for instance the curriculum listed in *Xiaoshe luocheng jinian kan* 1935, 56–64).

The success of the National Conservatory was partly due to its location. Xiao Youmei's decision to have it in Shanghai was deemed by many as visionary. Shanghai was after all the most populous city in China and contained a community of approximately sixty thousand foreigners by the early 1930s.[14] Shanghai's prosperous Western music scene afforded the conservatory access to the city's many residing Russian musicians, many of whom were well trained and even world-class performers, not to mention an environment for students to attend as well as give performances.

Xiao Youmei visited Shanghai in October 1927 and attended three concerts of the Shanghai Municipal Orchestra (SMO) on October 9, 16, and 23, the many concerts of which were covered in the previous chapter. After the concerts, he wrote a review in which he lamented the Chinese government's unwillingness to establish a state-funded symphony orchestra. His earlier plan was to form one by having the Russian conductor Geschkowitsch of Harbin's Russian Opera bring twenty players from his orchestra to add to the small ensemble Xiao had founded at Beijing University's Music Research Institute, but this did not materialize. While China had no orchestra of its own, Xiao was surprised to learn about the municipal-funded SMO. Very impressed by concerts he attended, he thought:

> Since there are so many opportunities to appreciate music, and in sight of the national government's interest in establishing a music conservatory, I have suggested it to be placed in Shanghai. Those who study music need the environment so they can have a better understanding of the music, particularly important for those learning new music. Now that the Government College has made the decision to launch a conservatory and is in the process of recruitment, it is really a moment to celebrate. Therefore, I very much would encourage comrades who want to study music to attend the SMO concerts frequently. If one is only willing to attend concerts organized by our government, it is not going to materialize in at least two to three decades. (Xiao 1928, 211–213)

The Russian Pedagogues

When the National Conservatory was first started in 1927, there were only eighteen faculty and staff members in total. In the faculty-staff list, three of the four non-Chinese professors were Russian: a Mrs. Levitin teaching piano, a Mr. Antapolsky and a Mr. Lestuzzi teaching the violin, both playing for the SMO as temporary musicians, and a Mr. Maltzev in charge of aural training.[15] In the following year, there were some changes in personnel. Of the aforementioned four, only Levitin stayed, and the school was joined by the Jewish Italian violinist Arrigo Foa and the Russian cellist I. Shevtsov. The former was the concertmaster and the latter the principal cello of the SMO. Aural training was taken up by the Hungarian musician L. Walker. The renowned vocalist Alla Tomskaya (listed as Tomsky), whose farewell concert is discussed in the previous chapter, was also on the list.[16]

The year 1929 was a special one for the National Conservatory. It experienced an administrative setback when the education ordinance recently introduced by the government required the conservatory to be downgraded from a university level institution to a technical college. This resulted in curriculum restructuring and the shortening of study years for the programs offered (Luo and Qian 2013, 32).[17] But it was also in this year that the conservatory welcomed a number of its most committed faculty members, both Chinese and Western, who were to become its pillars and who contributed to educating a great number of China's key musical figures to be.[18] Despite the institution's changed status, the number of faculty and staff members increased to twenty-nine, with seven of the nine non-Chinese faculty members being Russian. Foa, Levitin, and Shevtsov continued and were joined by Boris Zakharov, Sergei Aksakov, and the flutist Spiridonov, as well as three female pedagogues, pianists Pribytkova and Valesby and the vocalist Slavianova. Aside from Foa and Valesby, the rest were Russian.[19]

This above list of Russian pedagogues was enlarged in the coming years by the violinists M. Livshits and R. V. Gerzovsky, the flutist Aleksandr Pecheniuk, the oboist and conductor Vladimir Sarychev, the clarinettist Anton Vernik, the trumpeter V. Dobrovolsky, the pianists Boris Lazarev, G. Margolinskii (Margolinsky), V. Kostavich, V. A. Chernetskaia (Chernieskaja), and F. Sakharova, and the singers E. Levitina, Vladimir Shushlin (Schuschlin), M. Krylova, Petr Selivanov, Elena Selivanova, and I. G. Gravitskaia.[20]

Of these pedagogues, some taught for a long period, whereas a handful stayed for only a short time. Almost half the full-time and a third of the part-time teachers were Russian (figures provided in *Xiaoshe lecheng jinian kan* 1935, 84–89). There is no doubt that these pedagogues' teaching and experiences in music performance were an important factor that accounted for the conservatory's success.

The first sign of success was the rapid increase in student enrollment. Only 23 students were admitted in 1927, but by 1933 there were close to 150 students registered, not to mention the many who had been turned away because they did not meet the entrance requirements. Interesting to note is the rapid growth of the number of students studying the piano and voice. Based on enrollment statistics of 1932, there were 60 students studying the piano, 25 studying voice, 20 violin, and fewer than 10 each on Chinese music, theory and composition, or other orchestral instruments. Above all, the success of the conservatory was measured by international recognition such as reports of student activities in Shanghai's foreign-language newspapers.[21]

The conservatory's organization and curriculum were gradually shaped to be on par with conservatories in the West. It consisted of five departments: Theory and Composition, Keyboard (which was originally just piano), Orchestra (which was originally just violin, cello, and other orchestral instruments), Voice, and Chinese Music.[22] Of these five departments, the three performance departments—keyboard, orchestra, and voice—were highly recognized and were led by Russian pedagogues. Students from different parts of China and who had limited knowledge of Western music were thought to have performed miracles under the hands of their Chinese and Western pedagogues, as testified by the annual student concerts in which Russian teachers and their students played an important role.

Another sign of the conservatory's success was that students easily found employment after graduation, and some even just after studying a few semesters (Fu 1935, 26). For instance, Ding Shande, a student of Zakharov, whose concert is mentioned in the introductory chapter of this volume, was hired to teach at Tianjin Women's Normal University right after his graduation in 1935 at a salary of $240 (Zhao 1994, 6).[23] In addition to attracting Chinese students, the conservatory also enrolled a good number of Western students.[24]

Zakharov: The Founder of Chinese Pianism

Of all the Russian pedagogues at the conservatory, two deserve extra attention, even though the rest should still be remembered. One is the pianist Boris Zakharov, the other the vocalist Vladimir Shushlin. The former taught from 1929 to 1943, the latter from 1930 to 1956 (Luo 2010, 66–68), and they left an indelible mark on China's music development in the twentieth century and were remembered fondly by their students.

Boris Zakharov (1887–1943) is largely forgotten outside the PRC, but he is hailed there as "founder" and "father" of Chinese pianism (see Wang Yamin 2013), and his name gets a mention in almost all writings pertinent to the early history of piano playing in China.[25] He was the teacher of the first generation of renowned Chinese pianists that included Lee Hsien Ming 李献敏 (also Li Xianmin) (1915–1991), Qiu Fusheng 裘复生 (no information), Li Cuizhen 李翠贞 (1910–1966), Fan Jisen 范继森 (1917–1968), Wu Leyi 吴乐懿 (also Lois Woo) (1919–2006), Yi Kaiji 易开基 (1912–1995), Wu Yizhou 巫一舟 (1913–1997), and Xia Guoqiong 夏国琼 (Mary Hsia) (1916–2012). He also taught composers such as He Luting 贺绿汀 (1903–1999) (though for only a short period), Ding Shande 丁善德 (1911–1995), and Jiang Dingxian 江定仙 (1912–2000).

Most of these musicians played an important role in the musical development of China in the second half of the twentieth century. To name just the most accomplished, He Luting was made the president of the Shanghai Conservatory, the successor of the National Conservatory in 1949. Jiang Dingxian became the vice president of the Central Conservatory in 1961. Fan Jisen served as the head of the Shanghai Conservatory's Piano Department from 1954 until his death in 1968 during the Cultural Revolution. Wu Leyi also served as the head of the Piano Department of the Shanghai Conservatory from 1979 to 1989.

Zakharov graduated from the Saint Petersburg Conservatory in 1913. He was a student of Anna Esipova ("Prof. Zakharoff at Carlton" 1933, 18), who also taught Prokofiev and Heinrich Neuhaus. In fact, Zakharov was a childhood friend of Prokofiev, and Prokofiev made references to him and his family in his diaries (see Philips 2006). His classmate Neuhaus was the author of the highly regarded volume *The Art of Piano Playing* and one of the most prominent piano pedagogues of the former USSR as the teacher of famed pianists such as Sviatoslav Richter and Emil Gilels. At the Saint Petersburg Conservatory, Zakharov also studied composition with Rimsky-Korsakov and Liadov and was chosen to perform at the fiftieth anniversary celebration. After completing a year of study in Vienna with Godowsky, Zakharov returned to his alma mater to teach until he left Saint Petersburg in 1922, first for Terioki, a border town in Finland, and then to settle in Paris with his wife's family.[26] His wife was the famous Russian violinist Cecilia Hansen, a pupil of Leopold Auer, and they had a daughter.[27] It was during their concert tour to Asia in 1928 that Zakharov decided to settle in Shanghai a year later.[28]

As mentioned in the newspaper article "Prof. Zakharoff at Carlton" (1933, 18), the appeal of Shanghai was that it was like a virgin field and that it afforded opportunities for teaching a rising generation of foreign and Chinese musicians. Zakharov was approached by Xiao Youmei, and although initially reticent, he accepted Xiao's offer after three visits from Xiao and an offer of a handsome salary.[29] He was appointed the head of the Piano Department in October 1929.[30]

Another reason for Zakharov to call Shanghai home was his strained relationship with his wife. They had been on tour for almost ten years prior to 1929, and apparently Hansen was more successful as a concert violinist than was Zakharov, who was relegated to being her accompanist.[31] Zakharov also came across a number of his old friends in Shanghai (Xu 2009, 40). Though it is not clear exactly who Zakharov met, many Russian émigrés in Shanghai in 1929 were musicians, and more than a handful were graduates of the Saint Petersburg Conservatory, among them the conductor Slutsky, the oboist Sarychev, the harpist and pianist Biriulin, and the vocalist Eltzova, to name but a few (see Wang 2007 for information of these musicians).

Shortly after settling in Shanghai, Zakharov quickly became a prominent musical figure in the city's musical scene. Some of his activities have been mentioned in the previous chapters. For example, Zakharov was the key figure in the Art Club, and under its auspices regular chamber music concerts were organized, with Zakharov on the piano and his colleagues Igor (also Innocent) Shevtsov on the cello and Arrigo Foa on the violin, as discussed in chapter 2. He also performed with the SMO a number of times, invariably to rave reviews, as mentioned in chapter 4.

But it was in teaching that he found the most satisfaction. Though he was originally skeptical about the performance standard of the conservatory's Chinese students, he was pleasantly surprised by their motivation and dedication, which converted him into a dedicated pedagogue, one comparable to the well-respected Chinese pedagogues such as Xiao Youmei and Huang Zi. It is interesting to note that he appeared in many of the early photos of the conservatory, always sitting next to Xiao Youmei, which shows not only his highly revered status, but also his commitment to students' activities. Indeed, his students remembered that he was always present at their performances to give them support as well as helpful and constructive feedback.

Such was exactly how Wu Leyi, Zakharov's most successful student, remembered him. She began her study with Zakharov in 1934 when she was only fifteen. In just a few years, she became a rising star of Shanghai's musical scene, giving her debut concerto performance with the SMO in 1937, discussed in the later part of this chapter. She was to become a leading musical figure of the PRC as a renowned piano professor at the Shanghai Conservatory. She wrote the following about Zakharov in her autobiography:

> Zakharov was very strict. He prized talent above all else, and thus cared about students with talent irrespective of their specialization. He even gave free lessons to those who could not afford to pay. At his students' recitals, he was so concerned that he always paced at the backstage, smoking and eating chocolate. He took care of everything himself, including checking the piano, the stool, and even the lighting. Before every performance, he would ask me what color of a dress to wear and reminded me when to be at the venue. He even cared what I ate at breakfast. Everything that needed to be thought of, he did. After the concert, he would comfort me and say, "you can have fun tomorrow, but have to practise the day after." He was such a great teacher. He taught me not only music, but also how to walk onto the stage and how to be a performer. He devoted himself to his students and very often gave them extra lessons on Sunday to help them. (Wu 1994, 222–223)

Ding Shande also remembered Zakharov being very strict. But it is obvious that Zakharov's demand on his students was accompanied by dedication and care, as he expected them to do their best. Ding entered the conservatory as a *pipa* (plucked lute) major, but was assigned to Zakharov because Xiao Youmei saw the talent in him. When he started to study with Zakharov in 1929, he had only studied the piano for a short time. Zakharov originally only accepted advanced students, but made miraculous strides with Ding, pushing him to reach a professional level after six years of study. Here is how Ding remembered this:

> I studied with Zakharov for six years. It was not easy being his student. . . .
> In lessons when I did not play correctly or according to his wishes, [I was] yelled at, my neck pinched, my shoulder punched, or my head was slapped.
> . . . I know he did this out of good. I hated myself for not being better.
> When I played well, he showed his approval with hugs and embraces. I

then would be delighted. When I played at school concerts, he was always there and sought me out afterwards. When I did well, he praised me, and when I did poorly, he criticized me. I had deep respect for him, and I did not want to disappoint him . . . it was because of this teacher's dedication that I received a first-class diploma in piano performance after six years of studying with him, and became the first person in this country to give a public piano recital. (Ding 1982, 4)

Zakharov was proud of Ding's accomplishments.[32] He told his Chinese colleague Wei Hanzhang 韦瀚章 that he was impressed by Ding's progress, which was a result of Ding's dedication and hard work (Dai 1991, 7).[33]

Zakharov's greatest contribution to the conservatory was to have established a well-structured curriculum by introducing a rich repertoire of works of varying difficulties to students of different levels (Bian 1996, 18). A sampling of the jury repertoire of one of his students, Wu Yizhou, provides glimpses into Zakharov's curriculum structure, teaching philosophy, and expectations. In Wu Yizhou's elementary level piano jury held in January 1932, he played Czerny's op. 299, no. 18; Bach's Invention, no. 12; and Gliere's *Aux Champs*. In his intermediate jury held two years later, he played Czerny's op. 740, no. 26; Bach's C minor Fugue; and Haydn's Variations. Then in his final jury for his teaching certificate in education in June 1936, he played scales and arpeggios, and then Bach's Prelude and Fugue, no. 2; Czerny's op. 740, no. 15; Chopin's Nocturne B-flat minor; Arensky's Etude F-sharp major; and Beethoven's Sonata in A-flat major. A year later, he played the first movement of Bach's Italian Concerto and Liszt's Hungarian Rhapsody no. 11, probably for a performance certificate, which was the same repertoire that Lee Hsien Ming did after finishing the undergraduate program (Qian 2013a, 224).

To summarize, a student at the conservatory would be expected to do the following: (1) scales and etudes, (2) polyphonic works of Bach and Handel, and (3) masterpieces of the piano repertoire, namely works of Bach, Beethoven, Schumann, and Chopin, as well as Russian composers. It was important to set up a piano curriculum that was on par with those in Western conservatories. Such a process was indeed a milestone in the development of pianism in China. As piano playing was a new musical practice only recently introduced to China in the early twentieth century, the rigorous standard established at the conservatory was crucial for the recognized success of the first generation of Chinese pianists. In turn, their success was crucial for the indigenization of piano playing as a "local" art form that could be embraced by Chinese youngsters.

Furthermore, the works Wu Yizhou played at various concerts also reveal Zakharov's teaching philosophy: students must learn a wide range of repertoire. None of Wu's jury pieces was repeated at the concerts even though the two were sometimes just one or two months apart (Qian 2013a, 224). In addition to the works mentioned above, Wu played works of Handel, Beethoven, Schumann, and Chopin (Qian 2013a, 224).

It was no wonder, as Ding Shande recalled, that soon after Zakharov began teaching at the conservatory, students were introduced to a large repertoire of piano classics, including many concertos they had never heard before (Ding 1982, 4; Wei 1982, 62). Doing this enabled Zakharov to raise the performance standard of his own students as well as those of others, as all students at the conservatory were aware of what they were expected to accomplish within a particular time frame. So they all worked very hard, particularly those assigned to Zakharov's class, as they all valued the opportunity to be taught by such a renowned pedagogue.

According to Wu Leyi, Zakharov did not just teach well, but he also knew the quality of the students and the type of learners they were. Most of all, he knew how to lead them on the path of piano performance. For those who were not suitable for performance, he also knew how to teach them to succeed (Xu 2006, 41).

In fact, Wu Yizhou was an example of Zakharov's success as a pedagogue. Unlike Lee Hsien Ming or Qiu Fusheng mentioned at the beginning of this chapter, Wu Yizhou was not a natural performer nor was he an award-winning student. Like Ding, he started the piano late and had to start at the elementary level. But due to his dedication and hard work in the seven years that he studied with Zakharov, he became an excellent piano professor at the Wuhan Conservatory of Music. Presumably, that was the same case with Fan Jisen and Yi Kaiji: the former became the head of the piano department of the Shanghai Conservatory and the latter that of the Central Conservatory.

Another student of Zakharov was the composer Jiang Dingxian, whose works will be discussed in chapter 6 in connection with Tcherepnin. Jiang studied piano as an elective student, and he remembered how his teacher tried to guide him to become a good accompanist, knowing his strength in interpretation and sightreading (Jiang 1994, 297).[34] Zakharov's extreme dedication to his teaching and students is evident in that even when Jiang served as an accompanist to other students' performances, Zakharov would still be there to coach him (Jiang 1994, 297; Liao 2001, 90). The opportunities to play with singers, violinists, and cellists were regarded by Jiang as "[having] expanded his musical vision, so he was able to become familiar with the characteristics of different instruments" (Jiang 1994, 297), which must have been useful for his composition career.

Zakharov was remembered for not putting too much emphasis on helping students to acquire playing techniques. Lee Hsien Ming recalled that Zakharov seldom discussed how to use the fingers or the proper position of the hands and wrists, preferring instead to claim that "if you are musical, you can play with your palm facing up!" (Kreader 1984, 19).

Even though Zakharov was considered "serious" and "distant" by some, he was a kind man with a good heart (see Wu 1994; Jiang 1994). For example, Jiang remembered how Zakharov corrected his rhythmic mistakes in playing Chopin's Mazurka by dancing the Polish steps to him (Jiang 1994, 297). Wu Leyi recalled how Zakharov took her to a Russian clinic and ordered the needed operation for appendicitis before her father even arrived at the hospital. Zakharov was said to have told him, "Your daughter is going to give concerts in the future. When venues are booked, advertisements are made, and tickets are sold, but she gets sick and miss the concert, would it be a bigger loss?" (Xu 2009, 39).

Zakharov was not good only to Wu Leyi. He cared about all his students who were talented. In 1937, because of the outbreak of the war, some of the students did not receive their remittances in time to be registered properly. Zakharov, who saw them roaming around campus without going to class, took them to the registry and asked the office to let them register first so they could have lessons. He volunteered to be the guarantor for their fees. He even paid for their living expenses until they got their remittance (Xu 2009, 39).

Most of those who had studied with Zakharov held him in high regard, and many of his students and friends paid tribute to him at his funeral in January 1943 at Shanghai's Russian Orthodox Church (Luo 2001, 99).[35] Most of all, he is not forgotten even today and is regarded as a key figure in bringing Russian pianism to Chinese soil (Wang Yanli 2011, 113).

Shushlin: The Father of *Bel Canto* in China

The impact of Vladimir Shushlin (1894–1978) on the development of vocalism in the PRC was as profound as Zakharov's influence on Chinese pianism. Several of his students also became leading vocalists in the PRC. It is no wonder that even He Luting, one of the renowned composers and prominent musical figures in the PRC, regarded him as the founder of China's vocal education (quoted in Zhang 2010a, 16). Shushlin's importance lies in the fact that he produced a good number of the first generation of great Chinese vocalists, as well as professional vocal pedagogues, by introducing *bel canto* singing to China (Cheng 2007, 50). The list of his renowned Chinese students is even longer than that of Zakharov. It includes sopranos such as Huang Youkui 黃友葵 (also Eva Hwang) (1908–1990), Lang Yuxiu 郎毓秀 (also Pansy Long) (1918–2012), Tang Rongmei 唐榮枚 (1918–2014), and Gao Zhilan 高芝蘭 (Kao Chih-Lan) (1922–2013), basses Sze Yi-Kwei 斯義桂 (Si Yigui) (1915–1994) and Wen Kezheng 溫可錚 (1929–2007), and a number of the PRC's leading vocal pedagogues, including Man Fumin 滿福民 (1903–1985), Shen Xiang 沈湘 (1921–1993), Yang Shusheng 杨树声 (1918–2002), and Li Zhishu 李志曙 (1916–1994). Through these vocalists, Western vocal techniques were further developed, as demonstrated by the emergence of many world-class Chinese vocalists in the late twentieth and early twenty-first century.

Shushlin was a child prodigy with an exceptionally beautiful voice and had his debut at age eight. He entered the Saint Petersburg Music School at age fifteen to major in violin and minor in piano. At nineteen, he entered the Saint Petersburg Conservatory to study singing and opera (see Liu and Liu 2002, 42). A year prior to his graduation in 1919, he was already engaged by the prestigious Mariinsky Opera, where he sometimes sang in the "B" cast alongside the world-renowned bass Chaliapin (Zhang 2010a, 16), whose visit to Shanghai was mentioned briefly in the previous chapter. In 1924, Shushlin visited Harbin with a Soviet performing troupe and decided to stay when the troupe dissolved. The following year, he joined the Harbin Opera and the Glazunov Music Academy. The Harbin Opera had an active performing schedule both in the city and beyond, touring in Japan in 1927 and Java and Manila in 1929, not to mention performing in Shanghai (Liu and Liu 2002, 42). In 1930, Shushlin was featured as a soloist in two SMO concerts. On the one held on February 2, he sang a scene from *Boris Godunov*, and on other, held on March 23, he sang Wolfram's arias from Wagner's *Tannhäuser* and a selection of Russian songs accompanied on the piano by Beriulin (SMO Concert Program). Many other concerts in which he was featured have been discussed in the previous chapter. Xiao Youmei was present at the concert and was so impressed by Shushlin's performance that he paid him a visit afterward, as he had done a year before with Zakharov, to invite Shushlin to join the conservatory (Liao 1998, 95).[36] Shushlin accepted the invitation and became a part of the conservatory in the fall of 1930.[37]

Shushlin was remembered fondly for his teaching as well as his down-to-earth personality. For instance, he was said to always come to school ahead of his teaching to get ready. While waiting for his students, he liked to chat with his colleagues and even shared his telephone conversations with them (Liao 1998, 95). He was also remembered to have a liking for Chinese culture, such as signing his name in both Chinese and Russian using a Chinese calligraphy pen and preferring Chinese beer to Western beer. Shushlin's former wife was overtly jealous, to the point of disturbing his teaching. His second marriage, to his student Zhou Muxi 周慕西, was a happy one, and Zhou followed Shushlin back to the Soviet Union in 1956 (Liao 1998, 95; Liu 2006, 112). Shushlin, probably one of the luckiest of the repatriated émigrés, perhaps as a result of his knowing Shostakovich and being highly regarded in the PRC, got a position at the Moscow Conservatory, where he taught until his retirement in 1974. Shushlin's love of Chinese culture was most evident in his including Chinese works in his concerts. He was the first Western singer to sing Chinese songs (Liao 1998, 95). At a concert held at the conservatory, he sang Xiao Youmei's "Wen" 问 (Ask), and at another concert he sang Zhao Yuanren's 赵元任 "Jiao wo ruhe bu xiang ta?" 教我如何不想他? (How could I not think about him?) (Liao 1998, 94–96).

According to Shushlin's student Wen Kezheng, who studied with him from 1946 to 1956 and who had a close relationship with his teacher, Shushlin's teaching was straightforward, passing onto his students the proper Italian *bel canto* vocal techniques of finding the right position for the voice, using diaphragm support in voice production, and delivering the right tones through "mask singing" to create resonance in the upper part of the body (Cheng 2007, 50; Liu 2006, 111).

Not only was Shushlin able to explain these basic techniques clearly, as one of his students, Lang Yuxiu, remembered (Qian and Zhang 2011, 48), he was good at demonstrating these techniques himself to show students what he meant. This was particularly essential when language fell short on both ends. When in the right mood and with the right company, as remembered by Wen Kezheng, Shushlin would even sing happily along with students in his lessons (Cheng 2007, 52). Most of all, Shushlin introduced students to a great repertoire of operatic works and guided them into singing challenging operatic arias (see for instance Qian and Zhang 2011; "Gao Zhilan . . ." 2003; Cheng 2007). Students in his class tended to have more beautiful voices and progressed much faster than those in studios of other vocal teachers, as remembered by both Lang Yuxiu and Gao Zhilan (Qian and Zhang 2011, 48; "Gao Zhilan . . ." 2003). As a result, his students had more opportunities to perform publicly, be it at SMO concerts or operatic performances produced by the Russian operatic companies, which will be discussed later in this chapter.

Other Russian Pedagogues

While Shushlin's name is a staple in numerous articles pertinent to the development of Western singing in China, the contributions of other Russian pedagogues should not be overlooked, even though their affiliations with the conservatory may not have been as long as Zakharov's or Shushlin's nor did they produce as many top-notch students as these two. But their dedication to their students was equally remarkable.

Two vocalists' teachings in particular were fondly remembered by their students. One was the mezzo-soprano N. Slavianova, who taught at the conservatory from 1929 to 1932. A graduate of the Saint Petersburg Conservatory, Slavianova was a student of the famed coloratura Nataliya Iretskaya (1845–1922), who was a student of Pauline Viardot. She had performed at the Harbin opera for two seasons before settling in Shanghai, where she acquired a glowing reputation for both the operatic repertoire and Russian romances. Her student Yu Yixuan (1909–2008), one of the first three graduates of the conservatory mentioned earlier, who became a leading soprano of the country as well as the vice president of the Central Conservatory from 1961 to 1984, spoke fondly of her teacher in her memoir (2004, 11–12). Yu regarded Slavianova as a dedicated pedagogue as well as a high-caliber performer. In those three years Yu studied with her, she taught Yu all the basics in vocal techniques as well as a large repertoire of art songs and arias. In addition to the twice weekly lessons, Slavianova often gave extra lessons to Yu free of charge. In Yu's words, "those three years of teaching [from my instructor] had a great impact on the course of my life and my artistic aspiration. Her teaching and passionate demonstrations will never be forgotten" (12).

Another vocal pedagogue, M. G. Krylova, also left a mark on her students even though her teaching at the conservatory was short-lived.[38] A contralto, Krylova was once a principal singer of the Mariinsky Opera. She relocated to Shanghai in 1929 from Harbin, where she had been an active performer and pedagogue (Wang 2007, 353). She probably taught at the conservatory in 1936, but for some reason stopped.[39] Mentioned in Yang Shusheng's (1991) long article about her teaching, she taught the revered anti-Japanese song composer Zheng Lucheng 郑律城, Cai Shaoxu 蔡绍序, Lao Jingxian 劳景贤, Liu Zhenhan 刘振汉, and Hong Daqi 洪达琦, as well as himself. Yang, who also studied with Shushlin in the early 1950s, though not an accomplished performer, turned out to be a great pedagogue and theorist of vocal pedagogy. He was hailed for introducing *bel canto* to China's northwest region as the founder of the vocal department of the Northwest Normal University (Wang Xiaoping 2013, 53). In his article, Yang expressed a deep sense of yearning and gratitude for Krylova. He described in detail what Krylova had taught him in his first lesson and the other vocal techniques he had learned from her, such as how to breathe and how to sing with soft and hard "attack," and he recalled how Krylova used different tricks to make certain vocal techniques easy to grasp. For example, when she taught breathing, she would ask students to blow a glass-and-paper-wrapped comb to learn how to regulate the breath, to sing while bending down or slanting sideways, and to practice breathing while singing different intervals (50–53). He wrote:

> She taught me a lot of Handel's repertoire as well as other baritone arias from different operas. She also played recordings of these works, particularly those of Titta Ruffo. She very much concentrated on our vocal techniques. . . . Her attitude was very intimate, but she was demanding. Once I did not produce the "r" sound correctly; she worked on me on just that sound for more than six minutes until I sang it correctly. . . . Her life in Shanghai was a lonely one and she supported herself through teaching. . . .

Her love and passion, she gave them all to her Chinese students. She took pride and found satisfaction in our accomplishments. . . . Her untimely death saddened us. Her students would always miss her. (Yang 1991, 54)

Overshadowed by the accomplishments of the piano and vocal pedagogues, the cellist Igor (also known as Innocent) Shevtsov's long career at the conservatory is not to be overlooked. A graduate of the Saint Petersburg Conservatory like Zakharov, Shevtsov came to Shanghai in 1923 to serve as the principal cellist of the SMO, and in 1928 he also became a faculty member of the conservatory, where he taught until he returned to the Soviet Union in the early 1950s. When he first joined the conservatory, there were only a few cello players. In three years' time, the level of cello playing had improved enough that he was able to introduce an advanced class. He became head of the orchestra department in July 1937 and three months later became assistant conductor of the Conservatory Orchestra, a small ensemble of twenty players. Aside from students of the conservatory, it also included five nonconservatory players as well as Pecheniuk, the trumpet teacher, to make the voice parts complete (Luo and Qian 2013, 111). Though modest by today's standards, the ensemble did provide students the opportunity to make music together, not to mention that it was an important step toward the development of symphonic culture in China. Before the formation of the orchestra, Shevtsov had already conducted a string ensemble, giving string students an opportunity to play together. The formation of such an ensemble was deemed groundbreaking in contemporary Chinese music history, as it provided hope for Chinese composers who aspired to write music for such an ensemble. After all, to have the SMO perform the works of Chinese composers was impractical due to Paci's preference for masterpieces. Even though Shevtsov did not produce any stars like Zakharov and Shushlin had, he introduced cello playing to the conservatory students, and many chose cello as their minor instrument, which probably had to do with the quality of his teaching and his caring attitude.

Shevtsov's commitment to teaching is most evident in the number of cello teaching manuals he prepared for his students. His *Datiqin jiaokeshu* (Cello textbook) has become the standard textbook for aspiring Chinese cellists and is still in use today. He also composed or arranged a number of cello pieces, which have become a staple repertoire of Chinese cellists at the conservatory.[40] One of the pieces, *Pipa zhi sheng* (The sound of *pipa*), which alludes to "Chinese style," was probably a response to Alexander Tcherepnin's visit to the conservatory and Tcherepnin's challenge to Chinese composers to write music with Chinese characteristics, discussed in the following chapter.[41]

Li Delun, one of Shevtsov's students who later became the conductor of the Central Philharmonic, regarded Shevtsov as particularly sympathetic toward his students. Unlike some other faculty members at the conservatory, he was able to adjust his teaching to suit students' abilities. Li also recalled how Shevtsov was rare among teachers at the conservatory in that he would invite students to have coffee with him and, like Dobrovolsky, had copied a great deal of music for those who could not afford to purchase it (Luo 2001, 99). In fact, Dobrovolsky taught a number of China's renowned trumpet players, including Huang Yijun 黄贻钧 (1915–1995), Xia Zhijiu, and Zhu Qidong.[42]

While some pedagogues were remembered fondly by their students, one in particular stood out as receiving no mention at all. It was Sergei Aksakov, a graduate of the Moscow Conservatory, who immigrated to Harbin after the October Revolution in 1917 and to Shanghai in 1928 (Liu and Liu 2002, 380). Aksakov's involvement in musical activities in the Russian community and his compositions featured by the SMO have been discussed in chapters 2 and 4. A number of his students became prominent musical figures in the PRC. For instance, the music theorist and composer Lü Ji 吕骥 (1909–2002) went on to become the vice president of the Central Conservatory of Music in Beijing from 1949 to 1957 and chairman of the Chinese Musicians Association from 1953 to 1975.[43] Another was the composer Xiang Yu 向隅 (1912–1968), who became the vice president of the Shanghai Conservatory in 1949. Xiang was one of the composers of the socialist classic, the opera *The White-Haired Girl* (Baimao nü 白毛女) (1945). The composer Nie Er 聂耳 (1912–1935), one of the iconic figures of Chinese communist composers, although not a student of the conservatory, also received private piano and composition lessons from Aksakov from the summer of 1934 to April 1935 (Nie 1985, 147).[44] But it seems all these students studied only briefly with Aksakov due to unanticipated circumstances, personal, political, financial, or even ideological. Lü Ji, who was admitted to the conservatory in 1930 after three attempts, left in 1932 to join a leftist drama company (Guan 1994, 13). Xiang Yu, who entered the conservatory in 1932, quit two years later to support his newly formed family (Zhu 1994, 282). Although they did not finish at the conservatory, they went on to be influential musical figures of the radical left in the PRC, which perhaps explains their emphasizing politics over musical knowledge and skills in contrast with those who properly graduated from the conservatory, such as He Luting, Ding Shande, and Wu Leyi.

Tensions and Rivalries

Not every student at the conservatory had fond memories of the Russian pedagogues. Yi Kaiji 易开基 (1912–1995), a student of Zakharov who entered the conservatory in 1934 and later became senior professor of piano at the Central Conservatory (1950–1985), recalled a less amicable student-teacher relationship.

Although not singling out Zakharov, his experience led him to the belief that China needed to have its own conservatory-trained Chinese piano teachers. He wrote:

> The National Conservatory's performing sections were largely staffed at the time by foreign teachers of Russian origin who fled the October Revolution. They were really good. There is no doubt that they made a huge contribution to the development of our country's music education. But they were inevitably tainted by [the evils of] colonialism. A few of them discriminated against Chinese students, [were] very bad tempered, frequently yelled at students, [and] even threw their music scores out of the window. On the other hand, the same teacher treated foreign students differently. This difference in treatment left a deep scar on my youthful memory. I knew I started piano too late and it would not be possible to be a performer. I therefore decided to be a professional piano teacher. I even had a dream of opening my own school and staffing it with Chinese teachers so that we would not have to put up with foreigners. (Ying 1994, 329)

It would be difficult to discern if such special treatment for foreign students was a result of racial privilege or simply a matter of different dynamics because there was no language barrier between the student and teacher. It could also be that those non-Chinese students were seen as better because they were better equipped musically due to their background. Two of Zakharov's Western students, F. Sakharova and H. Gore, were prize winners and among the best piano students at the conservatory, but so were his Chinese students (Luo and Qian 2013, 121–125). Sakharova joined the teaching faculty after she graduated. Besides, Russian pedagogues were notorious for their bad temper and impulsiveness elsewhere where race was not an issue. This is not to deny Yi Kaiji's personal experience. After all, Shanghai was a city rife with racism and discrimination. Many Chinese then carried with them a collective memory of being oppressed by foreigners. Indeed, Chinese had been looked down upon by settlers as racially different and unequal (Bickers 1998, 184), and they were barred from most social clubs and sports venues. SMO Town Hall concerts were not open to Chinese until 1925 and public parks until 1928.

As at any music school, there were tensions at the conservatory that were played out at different levels and among different peoples, students and teachers alike. For example, the increasing number of non-Chinese applicants was at one point causing concern. Thus, starting in 1932, the quota allocated to non-Chinese students was set at 10 percent, and starting in 1935 only two non-Chinese students were allowed for each department to prevent excessive enrollment of

Western students, of which the majority were Russians, particularly in the study of the piano (*Xiaoshe luocheng jinian kan* 1935, 12).

Renowned pedagogues such as Zakharov and Shushlin tended to have the best, or at least better, students, which could be a source of collegial conflict. Krylova, who was so much missed by Yang Shusheng, taught at the conservatory in 1934 when Zhou Shu'an was on leave. When Zhou returned, Krylova was not rehired. But she was so much liked by some of her students, such as Cai Shaoxu and Tang Rongmei, that they left the conservatory to study privately with her (Wang 1994, 64).

The seemingly amicable relations between the Russian pedagogues and their Chinese students could in part be explained by the fact that the majority of Russians living in Shanghai did not fall into the category of "most other foreigners in China." They were refugees whose financial position was on a par with or worse than many Chinese, and they were certainly also looked down upon by settlers of other national origins. This alone may have promoted more of a sense of kinship between Russians and Chinese than among those of other nationalities and the Chinese, although some Russians would still no doubt have perceived themselves as white Europeans and therefore racially superior to their Chinese neighbors. That the majority of Russians lived in the French Concession, where nationalities mixed on a more equal basis than in certain other parts of the city, may also have been a factor in promoting amicable relations between the Russian pedagogues and their Chinese students.[45] Their shared love of music must have played a part in lessening the racial tensions in the institution.

Western Concerts and Chinese Musicians

Music performances such as concerts are generally seen as an effective way to promote racial harmony, then as well as now, even though its actual benefit is not easy to substantiate. Probably not for the sake of improving racial harmony but for the sake of exposing their students to a larger repertoire and different qualities of performances, Russian pedagogues were steadfast about the benefits of music students attending and playing at concerts. For example, Nie Er wrote in his diary about his violin teacher, SMO's principal viola Podushka, inviting him to attend concerts (December 26, 1931, reprinted in Nie 1985, 342–343).[46] At the SMO concert he attended, he noted the presence of a sizeable Chinese audience and a couple of Chinese students following the music with a full score (January 3, 1932, reprinted in Nie 1985, 345–346).[47] Podushka in fact taught many Chinese violinists. One of his most accomplished was Wang Renyi 王人藝 (also Wang Jenji, 1912–1985), who played Wieniawski's Violin Concerto no. 2 in D major with the SMO on October 20, 1935.

Li Delun mentioned in his memoir that he attended many of the SMO concerts, particularly the free rehearsals that took place on Saturday morning. He remembered dearly the first SMO concert he ever attended, which included the solo passage from Rimsky-Korsakov's "The Flight of the Bumblebee" played by the clarinettist Anton Vernik, who was also a pedagogue at the conservatory. According to Li, Vernik was the teacher of the best clarinettists of his time; the English horn solo passage from Dvořák's New World Symphony played by Vladimir Sarychev and Grieg's Piano Concerto by Wu Leyi both left a deep impression on him (Luo 2001, 100).[48]

Starting in 1930, the conservatory began to run its own concert series that entailed an annual student concert, a graduation concert, and a faculty concert, as well as other concerts of special occasions. There was a Concert Committee to oversee the administration and programming of these different types of concerts, and Russian pedagogues took part in the committee. For example, Zakharov (head of keyboard) and Selivanova (choral and voice training teacher) were members of the committee in 1935 (*Xiaoshe luocheng jinian kan*, 27).

The historic first student concert on May 26, 1930, was held at the American Women's Club (see program reprint in Luo and Qian 2013, 52). Of the nineteen programs, twelve were performed by students of Russian pedagogues, affirming the important role they played in developing the first generation of Chinese performers. Students of Aksakov, Levitin, Pribytkova, Zakharov, Gerzovsky, Shevtsov, Slavianova, and Spiridonov were on the program, and naturally students of other non-Russian faculty members. While piano and vocal works made up about two-thirds of the program, there was a cello solo by a K. Kluge as well as a cello quartet that played A. Kuznetsov's "Au Berceau," all under the tutelage of Shevtsov.[49] Piano students who took part in the performance were K. C. Hsia (Xia Guoqiong, also Mary Hsia) and F. S. Chiu (Qiu Fusheng) of Levitin, as well as F. Sakharova of Pribytkova—these three were to become Zakharov's students—and his three students, namely C. C. Li (Li Cuizhen), H. M. Li (Lee Hsien Ming), and M. C. Pao (Bao Mingjie) 鲍明洁, took part in the program. It is difficult to say how the programs were formulated, but they show a good balance of instrumentation, adequately allowing students of different teachers a chance to shine.

Aside from student concerts, the conservatory also hosted jury concerts and graduation concerts. The first graduation concert on June 22, 1933, held at the hall of the YMCA, was mentioned at the opening of this chapter. Ding Shande's concert from 1935 that was reported in *Shanghai Zaria* that opened this volume made another record in Chinese music history. His recital program bore the hallmarks of Zakharov's curricula structure: performers playing an all-period and well-balanced repertoire of works of contrasting style (see program reprint in Luo and Qian 2013, 95). It included Beethoven's Sonata op. 27, no. 2 (the

Moonlight), Debussy's *Arabesque* no. 1, Weber's *Invitation to the Dance*, Chopin's Etude (op. 10, no. 9) and *Polonaise* (op. 53), He Luting's *Lullaby* and the *Buffalo Boy's Flute*, Liszt's *Hungarian Rhapsody* no. 6, and Alexander Tcherepnin's Two Bagatelles.

Ding's playing his classmate He Luting's *Lullaby* and the *Buffalo Boy's Flute* and Alexander Tcherepnin's pieces marked another milestone in Chinese music development in the twentieth century, which will be further discussed in the following chapter. These concerts not only provided experience for students specializing in performance, but they also served as a music appreciation venue for the music-loving public in Shanghai. Perhaps as important as establishing the concert practice at the conservatory, it was these Russian pedagogues' musical network that was most valuable to conservatory students, as these musicians were able to provide their students opportunity to perform in public. The exposure they gained was crucial for their career advancement. Some really talented ones even had the opportunity to play with the SMO. As Wu Leyi recounted in an interview:

> We got an advantage back then—the opportunity to play with the SMO, which was under the Italian maestro Mario Paci. Zakharov and Paci were good friends. Paci was himself a good pianist. But his musical interpretation and taste were quite different from that of Zakharov, but they got along well. Zakharov often played concertos with Paci conducting. He also recommended his students to Paci. It was like an exam. If the performance went well, there were further collaborations. If not, there was no second chance. (Zhao 1996, 4)

Indeed, Wu Leyi was one who shone on the stage of the SMO thanks to Zakharov's close rapport with Paci and the SMO.[50] Wu Leyi's performance with the SMO no doubt helped her launch a brilliant career in piano performance. At her debut with the SMO on November 21, 1937, Wu played Grieg's Piano Concerto (SMO Concert Program). Her performance must have been very well received as she was asked to play again at the Grand Benefit Concert sponsored by the International Red Cross at the Metropol Theater on December 8 of the same year. The concert showcased Chinese-flavored works that included Avshalomov's ballet *The Soul of the Chin* and two Chinese pieces, the *pipa* solo *Downfall of Chu* and the ensemble piece *Moonlight of Chingyang* in the first half, and the Grieg Piano Concerto, followed by Brahms's Hungarian Rhapsody No. 1 in the second half, played by Wu ("Grand Benefit Concert" 1937, 421). The year 1940 was a triumphant one for Wu. She played in three concerts only a few months apart, and in the following few years she played repeatedly with the SMO, covering almost all major repertoire of the piano concerto literature.[51] Her collaboration with the SMO stopped after Zakharov's death in 1943. Devastated by the untimely death of her beloved teacher, she went through a crisis, but she was able to rise above it and further her study in France. As it turned out, she became one of the most prominent pianists in the first two decades of the PRC. Most important of all, she made a great contribution to Chinese piano playing through her teaching at the Shanghai Conservatory of Music.

In addition to Wu Leyi, other conservatory students, if they were up to Paci's standard, got opportunities to perform with the SMO. For instance, in a special SMO concert featuring the Shanghai Choral Society held on December 11 and 22, 1935, Shushlin's student Hu Ren appeared as one of the three soloists. Hu also shared the stage with Shushlin's nonconservatory student, the soprano Eva Hwang, at the Chinese premier of Haydn's *Creation* on January 14, 1936. This was another "first" for Shanghai, as there was no lack of Western singers in the city at the time. Probably as a result of the concert's success, both Hu and Hwang appeared again with the SMO in March of the same year. Other students of Shushlin that appeared with the SMO included the bass Si Yigui (Sze Yi-Kwei) and the sopranos Lang Yuxiu, Gao Zhilan, and Ellie Mao. While these Chinese musicians performed regularly in Shanghai during this period, they were to become leading Chinese vocalists. Of them all, Si Yigui was probably the most accomplished. He was to become a renowned bass and then a faculty member of the Eastman School of Music. As mentioned in chapter 2, together with Wang Wenyu, they were featured in *Rigoletto* produced by the Shanghai Opera Company (also known as the Russian Opera) in 1937, being the first Chinese to appear in the production of Western opera in China.

A Concert Network of Links

One other SMO concert from 1937 pertinent to the Russian émigré composer Aaron Avshalomov, the focus of chapter 7, illustrates the intricacy of the "concert network," how it as a nonhuman actor contributed to bringing human actors from different communities together,[52] solidifying the interconnectedness of the SMO, Russian musicians, and their Chinese students. Held on May 23, 1937, the concert featured Arrigo Foa conducting Beethoven's *Egmont* Overture and Symphony no. 7. In the second half, Avshalomov conducted three of his pieces, including *A Stroll in an Ancient Garden*, *The K'E Still Ripples to Its Banks*, and Piano Concerto in G major (SMO Concert Program). Although Avshalomov's connection with the National Conservatory was thin, probably because the scope of his works was generally beyond the capacity of the young institution, he invited one of Shushlin's students, Lang Yuxiu (Pansy Long), to sing the solo part of *The K'E Still Ripples to Its Banks*. To mark the special event, Lang's father invited Shushlin, Avshalomov, Mei Lanfang, and various others to celebrate at his home, an event that was captured in a photo that still hung in Lang Yuxiu's home in her late years (Qian and Zhang 2011, 50), and the event was publicized in the local newspaper ("Singer and Composer" 1937, 4).

Interestingly, Lang Yuxiu was chosen not because she excelled in *bel canto* singing, which she did quite well, but because she had taken Peking Opera vocal lessons with the Peking Opera star Mei Lanfang (Qian and Zhang 2011, 50). *The K'E Still Ripples to Its Banks* had been performed before with other soloists. Avshalomov's using a singer trained in both *bel canto* and Chinese operatic singing and having Lang dressed in a Peking Opera outfit to sing with the Western symphony orchestra was symbolic of what he saw as the future direction of Chinese music. While his attempt can be deemed as realizing the *datong* aspiration articulated in the National Conservatory's first recruitment advertisement, it anticipated the approaches attempted by contemporary Chinese composers in the twentieth and twenty-first centuries.

Thanks to the proper training provided by the Russian pedagogues and their network within Shanghai's international musical scene, Chinese students such as Wu Leyi, Hu Ren, Si Yigui, Gao Zhilan, and Lang Yuxiu had the opportunity to shine on a larger stage than they otherwise would have. The recognition they received from Shanghai's international community was taken by many Chinese as a national achievement, that is, *"weiguo zhengguang,"* meaning "to bring glory to the country."[53] To be musically on par with the West was one of the many reforms China aspired to, and thus the success of these Chinese musicians carried significant implications for the trajectory of Chinese music development in the twentieth century. Training performers of Western music was not the only goal of the National Conservatory. Its founder and president Xiao Youmei's aspiration was to nurture a new generation of Chinese composers who would be able to produce a new form of Chinese music that synthesized Chinese and Western cultural and musical elements. Interestingly, it is through the endeavors of two Russian émigré composers—Alexander Tcherepnin and Aaron Avshalomov— that such composition models were demonstrated to the budding Chinese composers, which are the focus of the rest of this volume.

CHAPTER 6

From "Folk Cure" to Catharsis

ALEXANDER TCHEREPNIN AND NEW CHINESE PIANO MUSIC

The minute I heard this piece, I thought I was in a dream. I looked at him as if he were a transcendent Chinese musician who had lived many centuries ahead of us. He has transfigured a simple Chinese tune into a kind of ever-changing and overwhelming divine power. When I came back to consciousness, I began to believe what Tcherepnin believes—that China will have many musicians like him in a short time.

—Chen Ziran, cited in Chang Chi-Jen, "Alexander Tcherepnin: His Influence on Modern Chinese Music"

WHEN music student Chen Ziran 陈自然 heard Alexander Tcherepnin perform his new piano work "Hommage à la Chine" at a masterclass in Nanjing in 1936, he was struck by the unusual sonority that blended traditional Chinese and modern Western styles on the keyboard. The efforts in music reform highlighted in chapter 5 of this volume were spearheaded in Shanghai and extended to other major Chinese cities, such as the then capital Nanjing and Beiping,[1] and Tcherepnin interacted with music students in all three locales. Tcherepnin had come to Asia in search of folk materials that could be adapted to his compositions, but Chen's reaction evinces an unforeseen effect that Tcherepnin had on the musicians he encountered as a performer, pedagogue, composer, and inspirational figure.

Chen Ziran speaks of transfiguration in Tcherepnin's music. The following chapters describe the pursuit of transfiguration in the cross-cultural explorations of two Russian composers who worked in semicolonial Shanghai. This chapter traces the interaction between Alexander Tcherepnin and Chinese musicians like Chen, as well as the impact he had on modern Chinese piano compositions during his involvement there from 1934 to 1937. The next chapter discusses the symphonic and theatrical works of Shanghai-based Russian-Jewish composer Aaron Avshalomov and his long series of collaborations with Chinese artists. Both composers played important roles in China's early path to musical modernity, when the nation first encountered Western forms on a large scale while maintaining ties to its own traditions. A comparative case study reveals how the networks the composers created with Chinese and foreign artists were driven by the necessity of migration in times of political crisis, how diasporic culture impacted their lives and creative endeavors, and how they, in turn, had a lasting impact on their host country.

I describe Tcherepnin's networks in China as they relate to his key activities and compositions from that period. Network formation involves bridging new or previously divided entities, be they conceptual, physical, or social. In the following discussion, I summarize Tcherepnin's migrational path from his upbringing in Russia to his exploring new cross-cultural artistic approaches in China. I then examine the professional networks that were vital to his teaching, performance, study, and publishing in Shanghai and Beiping. I also consider how his marital transition during this period became a key factor in his Asian endeavors.

Tracing Tcherepnin's Asian sojourn reveals that he crossed cultural boundaries outside of the Russian diaspora, especially in relation to educational institutions. While he received privileged access to China's artistic and educational elite due his status as a world-class soloist, a descendant of the Russian master-composer lineage, and a high-society debutant by marriage, he was compelled by personal agony brought on by displacement, an insatiable artistic exploration of mixing musical languages across cultures, and an inherent inferiority-superiority complex that he believed Russia and China shared historically vis-à-vis the West. His cross-cultural endeavors, coming from an apparently elite position, at times ran the risk of appearing to represent a prescriptive, if not condescending mindset, especially when compared to the circumstances surrounding fellow composer Avshalomov. Both composers endured the personal and professional trials of migrational life that were common to numerous Russian émigrés in Shanghai, but their involvement with specific sets of groups and individuals resulted in very different pathways. Whereas Avshalomov spent his final decades in relative obscurity in the United States, Tcherepnin experienced a vital breakthrough in life and was able to find greater personal and professional success after leaving China.

From Russian Exile to "Eurasian" in China

Tcherepnin is highly regarded among composers of the twentieth century for his output of piano, chamber, concerto, orchestral, and staged works.[2] He gained international standing from the 1920s as his works were performed, reviewed, and published. Two high-profile compositions were the ballet *Ajanta's Frescoes*, written for the ballerina Anna Pavlova in 1923, and his Symphony no. 1, op. 42, which stirred controversy with a second movement scored only for percussion. His compositional language found appeal for a unique combination of freshness, piquant modernism, and an indefinable connection to the Russian musical heritage.

Tcherepnin had "invented" his own compositional approach based on a "nine-step scale" as the harmonic foundation of his early works and a theory of "interpoint" that drove his musical texture.[3] In the 1930s, he sought less academic approaches that drew upon folk traditions of Asia, and from 1950 onward, according to Guy Wuellner, "Tcherepnin turned his attention to the exploration of new forms and textures" (1974, 18). His career was further boosted by the fact that he was an exceptional concert pianist. Tcherepnin's performance tours enabled him to showcase his own compositions, while his seemingly effortless mastery of the keyboard inspired a sense of awe that would not be lost on the Asian music students he later encountered. He was thus in the rare position of standing on two musical legs—compositional creativity and piano virtuosity—that fed each other's success.

Tcherepnin's musical development was closely tied to his migration, which overlapped with and diverged from the experience of other Russian musical émigrés. Tcherepnin and his parents joined the scores of Russians who scattered across the globe in the aftermath of the Russian Revolution. But Tcherepnin would more accurately be described as a "guest émigré" of Shanghai in view of the relatively short duration he stayed there in comparison to the other Russians discussed in this volume. As it was for many Russians, the outcome of the Revolution was neither certain nor sudden when they left Russia in 1918, so what at first was interpreted as temporary displacement would turn into a continuous life on the move for many. Tcherepnin, who initially resisted leaving behind his motherland, came to epitomize such a migratory life. From his childhood and adolescence growing up in Saint Petersburg, Russia, he would take up residence of various sorts in Georgia, France, the United States, Japan, China, Belgium, and England. His music and leisure travel would take him to numerous other places. He has thus recently been characterized by biographer Benjamin Folkman as a Russian "citizen of the world" (Folkman 2008, 105).

His wanderings offered Tcherepnin unexpected opportunities both within and without Russian musical communities. Raised among the Saint Petersburg elite at the turn of the century, Tcherepnin emanated from the lineage of Russian music masters. His father was the famous composer and conductor Nikolai Tcherepnin (1873–1945), who had studied with Rimsky-Korsakov, conducted at the Imperial Opera and on tour with Diaghilev's Russian Ballet, and taught at the Saint Petersburg Conservatory. Tcherepnin thus grew up in the company of Glazunov, Cui, Stravinsky, Prokofiev, and the full circle of musicians emanating from the generation of Tchaikovsky and the "Mighty Handful." To other Russian musicians in Shanghai, Tcherepnin's close connection to this lineage and international fame would be seen as a significant, albeit short-lived boost to maintaining the musical tradition of the motherland. Fortunes changed for many of the artistic elite, as Bolshevik victories drove numerous Russians abroad. For Tcherepnin, exile turned into a prolonged search for identity ever linked to a single point of origin. Moving outward, he would continuously absorb influences from various traditions in the manner of an insatiable cosmopolitan. But coming from a Russian music tradition that had only found its voice in relation to European classical music in the late nineteenth century, he was persistently drawn back to his homeland within his own mind. Rooted in this manner, according to Folkman, "as a Russian in exile, Tcherepnin thought it particularly important to understand what it meant to be Russian" (Folkman 2013, 18).

Tcherepnin kept a base in Paris until his first 1934 tour to Asia, and he maintained close ties to the city throughout his life.[4] After the professional strides Tcherepnin made in France during the 1920s, he began to study the history of ancient Russia. From this study, he formed his own "Eurasian" theory about Russian culture that had resulted from the historical merging of Mongols and Russians in the aftermath of the Mongolian Empire. Tcherepnin concluded that Russia is both European and Asian, with "an inferiority complex due to the superiority of Western culture, in relation to the East she feels an equal. . . . To a Russian the East is not exotic; it is familiar, a part of the Russian nature" (Tcherepnin 1934b, 17).

By the early 1930s, Tcherepnin had laid the ideological and practical groundwork for exploring non-Western musical languages, believing himself to identify as much with Asians as with Europeans. He also feared stagnation at the hands of an overly formulaic compositional style and began to seek a new "cure" via inspiration from folk music, not yet "blemished" by Western classical development (Wuellner 1974, 12 and 39). When he was approached with the opportunity to visit Asia for part of a 1934 world tour, he saw the possibilities for discovering a new musical and personal identity. This identity search framed the types of networks he would form in China as well as the nature of his musical activities.

Tcherepnin was part of the Russian music community in interwar Shanghai for only brief periods, but he merits special attention alongside Avshalomov because of the great impact Chinese culture had on his creativity and the possible approaches to piano composition that he, in turn, suggested to a new generation of Chinese composers. His work in China was carried out in conjunction with projects that involved Japan and other parts of China over three years, from April 1934 until March 1937. During that time, he spent a total of twenty-two months in Asia during two separate visits. Of those twenty-two months, he spent eleven and a half months in China (divided into four visits) and eleven months in Japan. Table 6.1 provides a chronological listing of Tcherepnin's China and Japan sojourns.[5] From this table, it is clear that Tcherepnin (1) was continuously on the move, (2) spent a maximum of four months in China at any one time, and (3) split his Asian stays between Shanghai, Beiping, and Japan. His work in each location developed over brief time spans and with Tcherepnin constantly keeping an eye on other locales.

The terms of Tcherepnin's Asian visits are important for distinguishing between his real and perceived musical accomplishments.[6] Tcherepnin's China path began with performance. He was also a composer of all types of music, but he focused almost solely on piano music in China. This was in large part due to his extraordinary piano skills, which in turn ignited and perpetuated his wider musical reputation.[7] An array of newspaper accounts from China and Japan testify to his power. A review of one of Tcherepnin's first recitals in China, for example, exclaimed that the pianist "left one with the impression of something

Table 6.1 Alexander Tcherepnin's China and Japan sojourns

Date	Country	Duration (Months)	City
1934—April	Japan	Transit	Yokohama (Apr 6), Tokyo
1934—April	China	3	Shanghai (Apr 10), Beiping (May 23)
1934—July	Japan	4	Kobe (July 8), Myanoshita, et al.
1934—November	China	3	Shanghai (Nov 5), Beiping
1935—February	Japan	1	Nagasaki (Feb 7), Tokyo, et al.
1935—March	USA (& Europe)	13	San Francisco (Mar 13), et al.
1936—April	Japan	1	Tokyo (Apr 16) et al.
1936—May	China	1.5	Shanghai (May 22), Nanjing and Beiping (June 7), Shanghai (July)
1936—July	Japan	4	Tokyo (July 11), et al.
1936—November	China	4	Mukden (Nov 16), Beiping (Nov 17), Shanghai (Dec), Beiping (Feb 18), Nanjing-Shanghai (Mar 9–10)
1937—March	Japan	Transit	Yokohama (Mar 16)
1937—March	USA (& Europe)		Seattle (Mar 27)

Note: The above dates mark approximate arrival points (or earliest indicated) in the countries listed, rather than departure dates; time for boat travel should be taken into account when considering length of sojourn.

Source: Folkman (2008); PSF (Alexander Tcherepnin Autobiography); LPW (1923–1946); Wuellner (1974); and newspaper coverage.

terrific, elemental and barbaric having been let loose. One was literally shattered with sound and came away strung up to breaking point by the ecstasy of the force and vigour of his execution" ("Composer's Recital Given Here" 1934, n. p.). More so than his Russian master lineage, every facet of Tcherepnin's interaction with musicians in China must take his performance prowess into account. Put another way, without the respect he commanded due to his piano artistry, Alexander Tcherepnin may not have been in a position to interact with so many prominent Russian and Chinese musicians. This was less a matter of colonial mindset that was endemic to Shanghai power relations than a timely sensationalism that occurred just as urban Chinese were making a first incursion into Western classical music. World-renowned soloists were expected to move on to other countries after their Shanghai solo engagements, but Tcherepnin chose to stay on, which added immediate impact in crossing the colonial power boundary. Table 6.2 lists at least twenty recitals, chamber concerts, and concerto performances Tcherepnin gave at different venues for various audiences in China.[8] It also underscores how rapidly he widened the geographical scope through which he viewed China in comparison to other Russians who experienced little beyond Shanghai. His range of musical activities in Asia would expand with similar speed and effect as he made contact with current and future leaders in various regions.

Tcherepnin in Shanghai: The Russian Community and National Conservatory

The foundation for Tcherepnin's China work was laid by a few key relationships that he established in Shanghai and Beiping. In both cases, he made initial contact with prominent Russians even as he gained access to main educational institutions and administrators, as well as performance opportunities. Tcherepnin was brought to Asia by the Russian-Jewish impresario Awsay Strok, who initially arranged Tcherepnin's professional engagements in China and Japan.[9] The China visit was to have been just one stop on a world tour, which Strok managed in conjunction with other international agents.[10] But Tcherepnin changed his plans almost immediately after his boat docked in Shanghai. Strok had wired ahead to Shanghai when Tcherepnin was en route from Japan. The result was that upon arrival on April 10, Tcherepnin was met at the steamer by a group of reporters who interviewed him and followed his undertakings throughout his China visits. Labeled as "one of the world's foremost contemporary composers and pianists" ("Young Composer in Shanghai" 1934, 10), Tcherepnin was not prepared for the sudden media attention, and he soon found himself adored by

Table 6.2 Alexander Tcherepnin's main China performances, 1934–1937

Date	Location
1934, April 27	Shanghai, American Women's Club
1934, May 4	Shanghai, National Conservatory
1934, May 10	Shanghai, "Vostok" Russian Association
1934, May 13	Shanghai, Shanghai Municipal Orchestra (Grand Theatre)
1934, May 17	Shanghai, YWCA (Afternoon Children's Concert)
1934, May 17	Shanghai, University of Shanghai (Baptist)
1934, May 29	Beiping, Women's College of Arts and Sciences
1934, June 1	Tianjin, Astor House Hotel
1934, June 4	Beiping, Grand Hotel de Pekin
1934, June 19	Beiping, Yenching University
1934, June 27	Beiping, Women's College of Arts and Sciences
1934, November 23	Shanghai, "Vostok" Russian Association
1934, November 25	Shanghai, Shanghai Municipal Orchestra (Lyceum Theatre)
1935, January 19	Beiping, Women's College of Arts and Sciences
1935, January 27	Beiping, Beiping Governmental Radio Concert
1935, January 29	Beiping, Grand Hotel de Pekin
1936, June 4	Nanjing, Nanjing Literary Society
1936, June 5	Nanjing, Nanjing University
1936, June 5	Nanjing, Nanjing Radio
1936, June 12	Beiping, Women's College of Arts and Sciences
1936, November 28	Beiping, Women's College of Arts and Sciences
1937, March 1	Beiping, Grand Hotel de Pekin
1937, March 9	Nanjing, Ginling College
1937, March 10	Nanjing, National broadcast on Central Broadcast Station
1937, March 11	Shanghai, McTyre School

Source: Folkman (2008); PSF (Alexander Tcherepnin Autobiography); LPW (1923–1946); and Chinese, English, and Russian newspaper coverage.

young Chinese music students as he discovered his own pronounced cultural interest in China.

He determined to extend his China visit when he took a romantic interest in a young conservatory student Lee Hsien Ming (Li Xianmin) 李献敏, whom he met soon after arriving in Shanghai.[11] His relationship with Strok then grew strained as he canceled his engagements outside of China and Japan. The two later made amends in Japan, but tension again erupted when Tcherepnin accepted a recording engagement with Victor records in Tokyo. As a result, Tcherepnin's later Japan performances in 1936–1937 were arranged by local managers. Despite these problems, it was Strok's commercial interests across Asia that provided a framework for Tcherepnin to embark on the tour and to remain in the region.

Tcherepnin did not typically confine himelf to Russian émigré communities when living in Europe, Asia, or North America. Before going to Shanghai, he was not even aware of the large number of Russians there. Soon after his arrival, however, Tcherepnin met an old friend of his father, the pianist and National Conservatory teacher Boris Zakharov. It was through Zakharov that Tcherepnin first channeled into the Russian music community. The two would collaborate with Zakharov's Russian colleagues on various occasions in the coming years.[12] Tcherepnin's first Shanghai appearance, as planned by Strok, was to have been with the Shanghai Municipal Orchestra in mid-May, but Zakharov approached Tcherepnin to perform a series of chamber concerts before that. Strok consented, and Zakharov thereby facilitated Tcherepnin's first three performances in Shanghai at the American Women's Club, the National Conservatory, and the "Vostok" Russian Association discussed in chapter 2, where he also collaborated with other National Conservatory professors, including Russians Igor Shevtsov, Sergei Aksakov, and Boris Lazarev, as well as Italian-Jewish violinist Arrigo Foa.[13] At the May Vostok concert, Tcherepnin spoke to the audience about Russian music development and its indirect connection to Chinese music ("Vecher A. N. Cherepnina v 'Vostoke'" 1934, 9). He performed for Vostok again in November 1934, at which time he performed the Russian opera *The Marriage*, originally written in part by Mussorgsky and completed by Tcherepnin.[14]

Shortly after the first Vostok performance, Tcherepnin gave the first of two 1934 concerts with the SMO, which had a high percentage of Russian players in the 1930s.[15] Both performances took place in front of significant audiences at major Shanghai venues.[16] At the May concert, Tcherepnin performed as soloist for his Piano Concerto no. 2, op. 25, and in November, he played his Concerto no. 1, op. 12.[17] As in these concerts, Tcherepnin performed mostly his own, earlier repertoire on programs from April through June 1934. The modernist musical language of his compositions challenged the ears of Chinese and Western audiences alike. Still, reviews of his Women's Club, Vostok, and SMO concerts helped spread Tcherepnin's name into the Shanghai music community. The reviews indicated that most listeners found favor with his works in spite of its new language on account of Tcherepnin's enlivening keyboard interpretation.[18] Their praise for his composition and performance techniques gave Tcherepnin an aura of indisputable authority. The intrinsic prestige Tcherepnin gained from these early performances enhanced his ability to initiate other projects as he established new contacts in the Chinese community.

Zakharov, Strok, and Russian players provided Tcherepnin a first footing into China, but the conduit for connecting with Chinese musicians came through another wave of contacts in Xiao Youmei (Hsiao Yiu-Mei) 萧友梅 and

Huang Zi 黄自 at the National Conservatory in Shanghai.[19] Xiao and Huang were respected pedagogues and administrators whose vision was instrumental in creating an educational infrastructure for China's first generation of Western music students. Before coming to Asia, Tcherepnin received a call in New York from Chao Mei-Pa (Zhao Meibo) 赵梅伯, who would serve as National Conservatory voice faculty member and had learned of the pending China tour from the press. Chao gave Tcherepnin an introduction to National Conservatory director Xiao Youmei (PSF).[20] As conservatory head, Xiao was instrumental in enabling Tcherepnin's most significant work in China, noted below. In February 1935, Xiao hosted a reception for Tcherepnin and named him an honorary professor of the conservatory. Xiao and the conservatory thereby benefited from Tcherepnin's prestige, affiliation, and mentoring when the institution was in its infancy. In turn, they gave Tcherepnin an institutional base from which he could launch his multifaceted projects. This mutually convenient "transaction" was not initiated by Tcherepnin, but rather by a young conservatory seizing upon the opportunity of his visit to better establish itself as part of a larger effort to gain national and international credibility.

Huang Zi was concurrently a composer, professor, and dean of studies at the conservatory. He helped Tcherepnin gain knowledge of Chinese folk music by helping him learn folk songs and facilitating contacts with Chinese musicians. As a member of the Piano Works Competition panel (below), it was Huang who announced the results of the contest in 1934. Students like He Luting 贺绿汀, Liu Xuean 刘雪庵, and Ding Shande 丁善德 also came into contact with Tcherepnin through Huang, which helped them achieve prominence. Huang Zi also gained insight from Tcherepnin, though Huang's compositional style was more conservative, and he advocated Tcherepnin's approach to Chinese-styled composition. He published one article in *Nong Bao* in October 1934 mirroring Tcherepnin's view that China could learn from the Russian experience, avoiding all-out Westernization but using Western music as a tool to mix with Chinese forms in order to create national music (Huang 1934). Together, Xiao, Huang, and other faculty members readily included Tcherepnin as an active member of the conservatory curriculum at various points during his time in China because he offered a rare combination of skills, prestige, and vision that no other musician in Shanghai possessed at the time.

Piano Works Competition

Tcherepnin sensed the need to incentivize conservatory students to go beyond mere adoption of the mainstream Western canon, and he was in a unique position to facilitate strategies that could benefit them. The most noteworthy endeavor was the Piano Works Competition that he sponsored in 1934. Tcherepnin had come to China primarily to perform and collect folk materials. His focus quickly changed, however, in response to what he viewed as a dangerously excessive, clichéd pursuit of Classic- and Romantic-style Western models by Chinese music students. As a Russian, Tcherepnin could caution China against following the path he believed his own motherland had taken in excessive imitation of the West. He thereby devised schemes to compel Chinese composers and performers to merge traditions and explore "oriental" sounds in the conviction "that perfected European instruments can serve to express any national idiom" (Folkman 2008, 171).

Obvious to this outlook is the notion that the process through which European instruments had become standardized over centuries of adaptation to concert hall performance—where projectional strength, range, regulated tuning, and timbral blend are the preferred aesthetic—represented an advancement toward modernity.[21] Russia had abandoned its indigenous instruments en route to becoming a Western classical music power but still maintained a sense of "Russianness" by incorporating other musical features. Why should China not do the same? Tcherepnin shared this cultural preference with Avshalomov, whose "symphonization" of Chinese music will be discussed in the following chapter. It should be noted that the seemingly benevolent intentions by both composers perpetuated, to some degree, paternalistic notions of cultural superiority they were intended to dissolve. While neither Tcherepnin nor Avshalomov should be regarded as high-handed colonialists, both appointed themselves as China's big brothers in the hope of helping it emerge from its inferiority complex vis-à-vis the West.

As he left Shanghai for Beiping on May 21, 1934, Tcherepnin wrote a letter to Xiao Youmei asking Xiao "to undertake the organization of a competition having as object the production of national Chinese music. A prize of $100 Mexican[22] would be offered for the best piano piece written by a Chinese composer and of national character, the duration of the piece not to exceed five minutes" (Tcherepnin 1934a). Xiao published the letter in English along with an extensive introductory article on Tcherepnin in Chinese, as well as an official competition announcement in the conservatory journal *Yinyue zazhi* (Xiao 1934). The Piano Works Competition results were announced in the same journal later that year, as well as at the November 1934 anniversary concert of the National Conservatory's founding.

The publicity and course of the competition had major ramifications for Tcherepnin and competition participants alike. The competition yielded eleven score submissions from Chinese composers, which were evaluated by a five-member jury that included Xiao Youmei, Tcherepnin, Huang Zi, Zakharov, and Aksakov. They selected the *Buffalo Boy's Flute* by He Luting as the First Prize winner. The jury decided to give four additional second prizes, with another $100 added to be split between the four. He's short work found appeal because of the way it blended Chinese idioms with Western practices. Receiving the First Prize immediately transformed his life and inspired other Chinese composers to envisage new possibilities. As the war with Japan escalated after Tcherepnin's departure, He utilized his skills in the new style to write film music that helped martial resistance sentiment among the Chinese populace. After 1949, He became a leading figure in the music community of the People's Republic of China, including eventual director of the Shanghai Conservatory, which was the successor to the National Conservatory, until he was demonized as "a prize winner of the competition sponsored by a White Russian" during the Cultural Revolution. He was later rehabilitated (Chang 1986, 143). He's competition piece has long been recognized for being the first significant Chinese folk-style piano work, placing He among the venerated early generation of modern Chinese musicians.

The motivation to combine Chinese and Western languages into a new compositional style was especially high around the time of Tcherepnin's visit because of the increasing threat of war with occupying Japanese forces. Using Western techniques as a means to produce new music with recognizably Chinese styles was not merely a matter of identity or aesthetics, as Tcherepnin was concerned with. It also became a means to national and political survival in the war years. Tcherepnin did not become as closely involved in partisan or national politics as Avshalomov did, but many of the Shanghai students that Tcherepnin worked with became increasingly active in the anti-Japanese movement during the 1930s. In addition to He Luting, this included fellow Piano Works Competition winners Chen Tianhe 陈田鹤 and Jiang Dingxian 江定仙, as well as other National Conservatory students, such as Tan Xiaolin 谭小麟, Liao Fushu 廖辅叔, and Liu Xuean 刘雪庵. Liu Xuean was especially prolific as a songwriter. As honorary professor of the National Conservatory, Tcherepnin gave special supervision to Liu and helped promote and publish his work internationally.

Jiang Dingxian, who is listed among Zakharov's students in chapter 5, was a Second Prize recipient of the Piano Works Competition. After the competition, Jiang realized the significant issues facing Chinese music that the event helped magnify. Especially in the case of *Buffalo Boy's Flute*, which used contrapuntal techniques, it raised a question of whether counterpoint was the most suitable expression for Chinese composers to express traditional idioms. For Jiang, the outcome was clear. "It wasn't that we shouldn't allow harmony or counterpoint," he concluded. "On the contrary, by enthusiastically embracing the two art forms and leading us toward harmony and counterpoint, we were able to open new ground in the folk style" (Jiang 1982, 5).

He Luting and the other prize winners thus became part of a concerted effort with Tcherepnin, partly by direct interaction with him and partly through their continued, expanding work, which had been validated by the competition. Tcherepnin did not expect masterworks from such an early generation, but he saw from the positive results that with encouragement, China's young composers were capable of combining Chinese and Western musical languages in the creation of their own works. The competition not only further motivated Chinese music students, it symbolically further elevated national music forms in the public mind to a more equal footing with Western classical forms. It is still recognized for its groundbreaking significance, especially in the development of modern Chinese piano music. This recognition was underscored at a 2013 commemorative conference held by the Shanghai Conservatory in Tcherepnin's honor. In assessing its enduring historical value, the premise of Tcherepnin's positive role as competition initiator to a strong degree counteracts the cultural privilege from which he approached it.

Composition and Pedagogical Publications

Tcherepnin demonstrated more marked cultural ambivalence in the new set of piano compositions and pedagogical materials he published collaboratively with the National Conservatory. During his China sojourns, Tcherepnin undertook intensive, albeit brief, study of Chinese musical and dramatic forms as he absorbed all he could about arts, culture, and history. The main purpose was to explore new folk sources for his compositions. Early in his journey, he heard Chinese instruments being performed and became fascinated with those that made the deepest impression on him. As a result, even as he upheld the models of Western instrumentation, he undertook elementary study of the *pipa* (plucked lute) and learned basic Chinese notation systems. He also frequented Chinese theater and shadow and puppet plays, and during his China excursions he made notes of temple and ritual music. As he befriended Chinese musicians (see below), he discussed the fundamentals of musical-theatrical forms to familiarize himself with performance contexts, myths and legends, scales, rhythms, colors, textures, idioms, and basic melodic structures.

These efforts bore immediate results in his output of Chinese-related compositions. Commentators have identified approximately fifteen Tcherepnin opus numbers, in varying lengths and containing individual and multiple pieces, that adopt manifold types of Chinese influences. Of these, the piano works written between 1934 and 1937—the *Piano Study on the Pentatonic Scale* (without opus) and op. 51, 52, and 53—are most relevant because they are the immediate outcome of his interaction with Chinese musicians.[23]

This set of piano works was written for pedagogical, creative, performance, and ideological purposes in one. In Tcherepnin's mind, they filled one part of a self-prescribed mission to cultivate, propagate, and interpret new Chinese piano music according to the historical experience of Russia. Tcherepnin intended to steer Chinese students (1) away from Western diatonic-chromatic (heptatonic) approaches that had developed in Europe through the seventeenth, eighteenth, and nineteenth centuries and (2) toward learning Chinese pentatonic-based formulae wedded to a twentieth-century Western language. The latter approach was founded upon the following assumptions:

- The anhemitonic pentatonic scale is the predominant cultural marker for Chinese music
- Pentatonicism in a modern context functions as both melodic and harmonic foundations
- As the harmonic foundation, pentatonicism acts as a pivot between Chinese and Western features, simultaneously allowing for
  - Folk-style melodies and rhythms as a continued Chinese cultural marker
  - Triadic and nontriadic/dissonant chords using scale tones
  - New contexts for dissonance and chromatic motion when nonscale tones are added
  - Nonfunctional or limited functional harmony, especially in the absence of built-in leading tones, tonic-dominant polarity, conventional bass motion, and voice leading
    - New contexts for Chinese and Western textures, including inventive counterpoint, homophony/homorhythms, and heterophony.

These assumptions are significant because they account for one major approach that developed in twentieth-century Chinese composition, namely, the heightened use of pentatonic-based folk features, rather than (1) compositions more imitative of Western Classical-Romantic styles (as was common through the midcentury) and (2) more modernist, postmodernist, or avante-garde explorations that arose after the Cultural Revolution. Tcherepnin's influence on Chinese musicians should be neither exaggerated nor discounted. He was not responsible for setting the course of modern Chinese music, but by virtue of ideological intent, international stature, and empirical propagation via publication, his network assumed meaning that no other musician could claim at the time.

Tcherepnin wrote the *Piano Study* in China and Japan in 1934 and early 1935 as a methodological approach to mastering basic pentatonic techniques. It is divided into five parts for this purpose:

- Part I introduces exercises for elementary fingering in different pentatonic positions and adding simple yet progressive two-hand studies to develop and reinforce these, all creatively using folk-style melodies like those used in He Luting's work.
- Part II covers preparatory exercises and scales in all the pentatonic keys progressing by the circle of fifths (half using sharps and half using flats).
- Part III is a set of twelve short pieces that reinforce methods covered in an advanced-beginner level, some of them stylized and some actual folk songs.
- Part IV covers preparatory exercises and arpeggios.
- Part V concludes the *Piano Study* with the concert piece "Hommage à la Chine" (Homage to China) requiring advanced-level virtuosity.

"Hommage" garners special attention because it was the first piece Tcherepnin wrote adapting a Chinese idiom. It is dedicated to his second wife, Lee Hsien Ming, and represents the "discovery" of his newfound love for her and for China. It is important in the Chinese repertoire because it was one of the first examples of a solo Western instrumental work that imitates the idiom of a Chinese instrument, the four-stringed *pipa*.[24] In "Hommage," Tcherepnin transferred basic *pipa* techniques, such as strummed chords and different manners of rapidly repeating notes, to the piano. Musically, it is also noteworthy because of Tcherepnin's style of combining traditional concepts with modern compositional language. The piece was regularly included in Tcherepnin's performances in Asia, Europe, and North America from 1935. It made a deep impression on Chinese listeners like Chen Ziran as mentioned above, who had not heard piano music composed and played in this way.

The *Piano Study* was published by the Commercial Press of Shanghai, in conjunction with the National Conservatory and with Xiao Youmei as intermediary, in 1935. For several years, it was adopted into the national curriculum. The book gained legitimacy in part from its preface written by Xiao Youmei, who explained the rationale behind Tcherepnin's system. A close look at Xiao's careful word selection, however, reveals that Xiao did not necessarily endorse the method. Rather, he states that "Mr. Tcherepnin *believes* that folk scales must not die out. Nowadays the popular piano textbooks are all based on the Western heptatonic scale. *Tcherepnin believes* that if Chinese piano students can use the pentatonic scale as a foundation from the beginning of their studies, they will more easily grasp it. Therefore, he has made this book and *requested that it be edited for inclusion* in this conservatory's collection and published by the Commercial Press" (Xiao 1935).[25] Xiao's wording suggests that the degree to which he supported Tcherepnin's approach was indeed limited, in contrast to the zeal with which Xiao had invited Tcherepnin to join conservatory activities and had endorsed the Piano Works Competition.

Tcherepnin persisted in his efforts, however, expanding the *Piano Study* materials into more pedagogical and performance works in opuses 51–53. Most of the short pieces from Parts I and III were reorganized and published by Heugel (Paris) in 1935 as his *Etude du Piano sur la Gamme Pentatonique*, op. 51, nos. 1–3. The third set of op. 51 consists of the twelve pieces from Part III, retitled the *Chinese Bagatelles*.

The *Five Concert Studies* make up op. 52, including "Hommage" and four additional works in contrasting styles and themes, but of a similarly advanced difficulty level. They were composed at various places between 1934 and 1936 and first performed as a complete set by the composer in Tokyo in 1936. They were published by Edition Schott the same year. Together, the works may be regarded as an early model for a high standard of Chinese piano composition. Like "Hommage," they subjectively draw upon elements of Chinese music, theater, and culture, but on the same pentatonic principles listed above. Tcherepnin scored "Shadow Play" and "Punch and Judy" along themes of popular Chinese shadow and puppet theater forms. In "The Lute," the piano imitates gestures from the Chinese *guqin* (plucked zither), and in "Chant," it draws inspiration from Buddhist ritual singing and accompanying music.

Tcherepnin also developed the preparatory exercises, scales, and arpeggios from the *Piano Study* into a more comprehensive set of *Technical Studies for Pianoforte on the Five Note [Pentatonic] Scale*, op. 53. It was published by C. F. Peters in 1936, with a preface, edits, and fingering by Tcherepnin's former Paris teacher Isidore Philipp. Its forty-one pages comprise a full array of preparatory exercises, scales, double notes, arpeggios, chords, and octaves in all pentatonic keys and modes.

To what degree were these materials embraced by Chinese piano students? There is little to suggest that the pedagogical portion of the opuses gained widespread usage.[26] From the standpoint of methodology, they offered a practical, comprehensive approach to learning pentatonic techniques on the piano. Despite Tcherepnin's convictions, however, they contradicted a reality of China's changing cultural climate that he did not recognize: Chinese students of Western music were uplifted by Tcherepnin's symbolic support for their tradition, but they *also wanted* to learn the piano music of Schumann, Chopin, and Schubert. Voice faculty member Chao Mei-Pa politely questioned Tcherepnin in a 1937 *Tien Hsia Monthly* essay, published in English:

> In the field of composition, suppose we should follow Tcherepnin's idea, shall we be satisfied with a harmony based upon the pentatonic scale with modulations? . . . [W]ill counterpoint without harmony satisfy us? . . . [He]

did not agree with our blind acceptance of Western ideas; but how far can his study help? Mr. Tcherepnin forgets that in working the Pentatonic Scale Study, he has Bach, and others behind him, and possesses their technique. . . . Will it be possible, on the other hand, for Chinese who have not had any training in the Western technique of writing, to create an equally important science by themselves, which will have a different effect but will possess the beauties and strength of all Western music? Or will it be possible for those who are trained in European schools to cast away what they have learnt, and recreate new ones? (Chao 1937, 283–284)

Chao revealed the limitations of Tcherepnin's approach. The "heavy weight of a classical repertoire" that burdened Tcherepnin personally was seen by many young Chinese as emancipation from the weight of their own tradition. Chao's response intimates that Tcherepnin was possibly projecting his own worldview on to Chinese music. Tcherepnin's position was based on subjective, rather than objective, assumptions: (1) that novelty and modernism are inherently more valuable than pre-twentieth-century Western repertoire; (2) that the European classical tradition is intrinsically contaminated, while other traditions remain "pure"; and (3) that he himself is justified in diagnosing and remedying China's cultural dilemma without fully accounting for its historical causes. While Chao recognized Tcherepnin's creative accomplishments, the Russian's ideological perspective did not fully resonate with China's reality. Did this constitute a colonial mindset repackaged via celebrity appeal?

If so, the latter seemed to carry more weight than the former. It must be recalled that the systemic propagation of Western music in the first half of the twentieth century was designed to counteract the very colonial oppression that had necessitated it in the first place. Political-artistic paradox was, therefore, inescapable. At the same time, in the process of discovery, Chinese of Xiao Youmei's, Chao Mei-Pa's, and Huang Zi's generation discovered that, power relations aside, Western classical music held gratifying aesthetic appeal across cultural boundaries. Artistically, Tcherepnin represented the virtuosity and musical lineage to which they and their students aspired, even as broader nationalistic threats, such as China's tensions with Japan, lessened the importance of "art for art's sake" in the eyes of political radicals, some of whom both Tcherepnin and Avshalomov interacted with. Culturally and politically, with Czarist Russia a fading memory and so many Russians themselves struggling for a livelihood in Shanghai, the chauvinism that may have emanated from Tcherepnin's approach was likely to be viewed as relatively mild.

In this respect, the students whose careers were bolstered by Tcherepnin did not seem to pay great attention to the pedagogical materials. Indeed, they remained devoted to Tcherepnin long after he left China. At a 1982 commemorative concert of Tcherepnin's works held by the Shanghai Conservatory, He Luting observed that Tcherepnin "exerted extreme effort in performing and promoting Chinese works around the world, while he wrote many of his own compositions in the Chinese style. Chinese musicians will forever remember and respect him" (He 1982, 1).

Enchantment in Beiping and Publishing in Japan

Shanghai was the center of new musical activity in China, but Strok had also scheduled performances for Tcherepnin in the northern cities of Beiping and nearby Tianjin. Tcherepnin and his wife found Beiping appealing for its temples, traditional culture, and history as the ancient capital. Tcherepnin also had a musical link via his aunt Camille (K. A.) Horvath, wife of former White Russian general Dmitri Horvath and voice teacher at the Beiping University Women's College Music Department. As Zakharov helped Tcherepnin set up in Shanghai, Mrs. Horvath did so in Beiping. The Horvath family assisted Tcherepnin with communication as well, given the language barriers he encountered. Tcherepnin and his wife spent a great deal of time traveling and socializing with the Horvaths, connecting him to both the Chinese present and the Russian past. But the Russian musicians were less numerous and active in Beiping. Tcherepnin's links to the émigré community there were thus limited compared to those in Shanghai.

Partly through Camille and partly through Xiao Youmei, Tcherepnin came into contact with Beiping University Women's College Music Department head Yang Zhongzi 杨仲子 (C. T. Yan). Tcherepnin recorded, "Before my leaving Shanghai, [Xiao Youmei] presented me with a fan on one side of which he wrote a [poem] and a dedication to me in beautiful Chinese characters. He advised me to bring this fan to his good friend Yang . . . thus introducing me to him and to ask him to fill in for me the other side of the fan" (PSF).[27]

Yang became Tcherepnin's greatest champion in Beiping, helping him establish a wider network for activities, primarily with music departments at Yenching University and Beiping Normal University. But the main activities were at Beiping University, where Tcherepnin performed more concerts than at any other single venue in China and where he included young Chinese musicians of varying abilities on his own programs. Tcherepnin enthusiastically shared the concert stage with students and faculty performers in order to stimulate greater creativity in mixing musical traditions, which is further testament to his underlying motivations. Yang acted as go-between and even English interpreter for Tcherepnin and musicians like Lao Zhicheng 老志诚, and he provided program notes in Chinese—an unusual practice for Western concerts at that time—for

Tcherepnin's January 29, 1936, "Farewell" concert. He also helped facilitate Tcherepnin's intensive study of Chinese music with experts in Chinese music.

In one main example, Tcherepnin undertook months of *pipa* lessons with Beiping University instructor Cao Anhe 曹安和, who taught several Chinese instruments. Through those lessons, Tcherepnin received a primer course in notation, technique, stylistic features, idiomatic practices, and related cultural background. Rather than seeking to become a virtuoso himself, Tcherepnin was able to work through (with the aid of Horvath's son as interpreter) basic details that he quickly turned into creative inspiration on the piano. Both "Hommage" and no. 7 from the *Chinese Bagatelles* mimic the *pipa* techniques from the lessons he learned from Cao. In these works and the wider sets in which they appeared, observes Frederick Lau, Tcherepnin turned his network into musical artifact, as he "pioneered the style of modern Chinese piano pieces" (Lau 2008, 97).

The new works also gained credence from Tcherepnin's associations with the elite of the Chinese opera world. Like Avshalomov, Tcherepnin befriended the renowned Peking Opera master Mei Lanfang 梅兰芳 and spent a great deal of time with him, especially in Beiping. Through Mei, Tcherepnin also formed a close relationship with Mei's manager Qi Rushan 齐如山, who was himself a celebrated playwright and Peking Opera scholar. Tcherepnin was able to discuss operatic and theatrical forms with these two at length, and he engaged in formal study with Qi (Tianshu Wang 1999, 43–44). In addition to the other various instrumentalists, performers, and teachers Tcherepnin met and learned from, he was able to draw materials from different areas of Chinese music that could serve as themes for the piano works listed above, as well as for songs, dramatic works, and instrumental compositions after he left China.

Tcherepnin also promoted the Piano Works Competition winners in his ongoing travels. First, he incorporated *Buffalo Boy's Flute* and Second Prize winner *Shepherd's Pastime* by Lao Zhicheng into his Beiping concerts beginning in January 1935. He also began performing Chinese piano works during concerts in Japan, Europe, and North America and continued to do so in the years that followed.[28] It was at the Beiping University concerts that both Tcherepnin's new works and the other new piano pieces he championed first gained attention with the Chinese press, as described in one *Dagongbao* report:

From this concert, Chinese people are already focused on the future of Chinese music. Especially from this type of effort to promote national music, our musical future must not only concentrate on all areas of Chinese music. At the same time, it must focus on using Western techniques in order to improve today's Chinese music. And Chinese ethnic colors and melodies must be used to create a new Chinese music for the future.

Obviously, this has already been shown to us at this concert. (Huo 1935, 15)

Compared to the earlier Shanghai concerts of 1934, which featured Tcherepnin's older works, and where press coverage was generally relegated to the non-Chinese press, the Beiping performances assumed groundbreaking significance. The Chinese media coverage given to these Beiping concerts surpassed the actual scope of concert attendance there, creating an expanded web of readers who may never have seen Tcherepnin or heard his performances.[29]

As noted in table 6.1 above, Tcherepnin was on the move between China and Japan as much as he was within China. Part of this was due to his performance and teaching schedule in both countries. Additionally, Tcherepnin created an innovative publishing enterprise that linked China to Japan, as well as Asia to the West. During his first year in Asia, he looked into possible publishing channels and eventually decided to establish his own Ryuginsha publishing firm in Tokyo.[30] Over the next several years, Ryuginsha published at least thirty-nine new works in several languages (Chinese, Japanese, English, and Russian) by Chinese and Japanese composers.[31] The Chinese portion of the collection included piano and vocal repertoire by He Luting, Lao Zhicheng, and Liu Xuean. Tcherepnin also arranged for distribution of these scores and others by Chinese composers in Beiping and Shanghai (Commercial Press, Inc.), New York (Shawnee Press Inc.), Tokyo (Ryuginsha), Vienna (Universal Edition), and Paris (À la Flute de Pan).

Working between China and Japan, Tcherepnin formed a particularly close mentoring relationship with Jiang Wenye.[32] Jiang Wenye 江文也 was born in Japanese-administered Taiwan in 1910 and received his training in Japan (under the Japanese name Ko Bunya). Tcherepnin met Jiang Wenye when he was in Japan and was especially impressed by Jiang's compositions. Tcherepnin offered him close guidance on new works, which were published by Ryuginsha and by other publishers abroad. Jiang Wenye surprised Tcherepnin by following him to Beiping in 1936 in order to research Chinese music. It was only then that Tcherepnin learned that Jiang was Chinese rather than Japanese. Initially, Jiang had been grouped with Japanese composers as Koh (known in Japanese as Ko) Bunya during Tcherepnin's Japan recitals and in the Ryuginsha collection. But Tcherepnin later grouped him with Chinese composers during performances, and he performed Jiang's Bagatelles for national broadcast on Chinese radio in 1937. The experience helped Jiang to focus more on his Chinese heritage in both his musical and personal identities, and he eventually moved to China after Tcherepnin had left.[33]

The extent to which Tcherepnin promoted the young Asian composers is telling. Tcherepnin's China network in many ways was linked to the Japan network, yet he was aware of cultural distinctions between Chinese and Japanese musicians. Increasingly frustrated by Japanese military aggression in China, Tcherepnin was careful to maintain an unbiased approach and to avoid public discussion of the political situation. But he resolved not to perform in Japanese-occupied areas of China, and he dedicated his November 28, 1936, Beiping concert for the benefit of Chinese soldiers resisting the Japanese. Tcherepnin's fondness for China can be seen in the way he described current Chinese music affairs in *The Music Quarterly* and *Musical Courier* (see Tcherepnin 1934b and 1935). But he maintained marked dedication to Japanese composers as well, some of whom followed him as he traveled between China and Japan.[34] The relationship between these two groups of composers merits further research, especially given the increasing tensions through the 1930s.[35]

Love, Marriage, and Catharsis

The balancing of Tcherepnin's work in China and Japan had more deeply personal underpinnings, which extended beyond Asia to Europe and North America. His identification with China and Japan as a Russian "Eurasian" had its roots during young adulthood, when Tcherepnin was learning about other facts of life. Eventually, the entire scope of his work in Asia became subsumed by his marital relations.

In the 1920s, Tcherepnin had met American Louisine Peters Weekes in Monte Carlo and married her in 1926 after she divorced from her first marriage.[36] Louisine came from an extraordinarily wealthy New York family and was fourteen years older than Tcherepnin. In addition to love, Louisine offered him unfathomable prospects for travel, wealth, and a maternal type of emotional support, which eventually enwrapped Tcherepnin in a new lifestyle that he found both irresistible and distasteful. According to his autobiography, Tcherepnin experienced deep misgivings even before he married Louisine (PSF). Through the years, he harbored growing feelings of alienation and discontent over his financial dependence on Louisine and their lack of common social and artistic interests.[37]

The years of their marriage directly preceded and overlapped with Tcherepnin's visits to Asia. His engagement with Chinese musicians cannot be discussed without considering Louisine's impact on his life and career. Surprisingly, her role has been almost completely overlooked in the related English and Chinese literature. For decades, only scant mention, if any, was made of her presence: Louisine appears in some of Tcherepnin's China press photos with little or no identification; Chinese- and English-language news reports of the day rarely mention even her presence at his events; and she is—astonishingly—ignored in most Tcherepnin biographical accounts, until Folkman's more recent coverage.[38] She is also conspicuously absent from Tcherepnin's earlier autobiographical accounts.[39]

Recent release of Louisine's diaries from 1923 to 1946 at Harvard University, along with Tcherepnin Society work and Paul Sacher Foundation materials, provides valuable insight into Tcherepnin's China and Japan years. In over a thousand diary slides, it becomes apparent that in spite of Tcherepnin's stated doubts, his first marriage enabled and enhanced his activities in China. In France, he was a penniless, displaced Russian artist turned international music figure trying to support his underemployed parents. Louisine was a high-society American divorcee nearly a generation his senior. The couple met and married in Monte Carlo, initially communicating in French, and later in mixed French and English. They traveled the world together, with Tcherepnin himself looking ever more the aristocrat in their collective photos.

Directly relevant to this chapter is that it was Louisine who enabled much of Tcherepnin's interaction with Chinese musicians. Despite his ambivalence, she offered him staunch support before his China visit, including payment for full-orchestra rehearsals of his First Symphony and dedicated attendance at his concerts. Louisine also shared Tcherepnin's passion for world travel. She accompanied him to most of his China events, and much of his discovery of Chinese culture occurred during excursions with her. Due to their different circumstances, the couple had a "50–50 agreement," in which "half the time he would devote to the travel and concertizing necessary for his career, the other half he would reserve for her, sharing her [New York] home and accompanying her to the fashionable and expensive vacation resorts frequented by those of her social set" (Folkman 2008, 164). Under this agreement, Tcherepnin was not certain that Louisine would allow him a prolonged world tour in 1934. But she gave her consent, without which Tcherepnin may never have visited China.[40]

Most importantly, she provided substantial, continuous financial support to Tcherepnin and his family, even after they had divorced and Tcherepnin had started a new family with Ming Tcherepnin.[41] Tcherepnin, though successful on the world stage, did not have a stable income—partly due to the marital obligations—and did not attain financial independence until the 1940s, especially when he and Ming assumed positions at DePaul University in Chicago in 1949. Louisine's financial support had important ramifications for Tcherepnin's China work. First, the money that Tcherepnin awarded to winner He Luting for the 1934 Piano Works Competition at least indirectly emanated from Louisine, since it was she who fully controlled the couple's overall finances and he was completely dependent on her.[42] Louisine was also a benefactor for the Ryuginsha publishing project that promoted works by Chinese and Japanese composers.

Internal documents from the SMO also reveal that Tcherepnin gave his first SMO performance in May 1934 for no fee, though he was aware that the performance would gain attention and provide further opportunities. For the second SMO concert in November of that year, Tcherepnin arranged for the "maximum fee" available so that he could donate it to a local university "as a contribution to a special fund for the study and development of Western Musical Culture amongst young Chinese" (SMA U1-4-259). These generous arrangements were possible, it was noted, because Tcherepnin was known to be "financially well off," an allusion to Louisine's wealth that testifies to Tcherepnin's partial reliance on her for his generosity to Chinese students (SMA U1-4-259).

Social differences, however, had severely constricted Tcherepnin's personal development. His sudden attraction to National Conservatory student Lee Hsien Ming when he met her after his first SMO concert in 1934 coincided with long-held doubts about his marriage. The unanticipated celebrity effect that Tcherepnin experienced when he was greeted by the press off the boat in Shanghai exacerbated a generational issue for Tcherepnin. Whereas he had been attracted to Louisine's beauty when they first met in 1926, the age difference with Louisine was becoming visibly pronounced. This was not lost upon the young Chinese, some of whom called her "Tcherepnin's old mama" or "Grandma" and commented that he looked around twenty and closer in age to Louisine's daughter, who was also with them in China.[43]

Ming, in contrast, was a gifted, intelligent, first-generation conservatory standout. She later recalled how Tcherepnin's interest in China deepened from the moment they first met. "My teacher [Zakharov] introduced Alexander Tcherepnin to me. . . . He saw me, and I thought that maybe it was love at first sight, and I didn't know it. . . . At the same time, he loved Chinese music. He loved the Chinese civilization, . . . so he thought that he wanted to stay for some time" (Lee 1984). Beyond natural attraction, Ming quickly came to represent a new opportunity in Tcherepnin's life: with her, he could engage in a more conventional relationship and focused professional life, and she could readily fit into a full-time society of musicians that he longed for (Folkman 2008, 170–176).

Some of Tcherepnin's activities were designed solely to impress Ming. The *Five Concert Studies*, op. 52, written between 1934 and 1936, began soon after the composer first met Ming. "As he was on his way to play at Shanghai University, his thoughts of the young lady took musical form as he jotted down the beginning of a piece that later was to become Hommage à la Chine—a piece whose 'inner content,' as he wrote, was the birth of his love for Lee Hsien Ming" (2008, 171). When Tcherepnin returned to North America after his first Asian visit, "the gifted pianist . . . Miss Lee Hsien Ming" was among the Chinese musical phenomena he described in his *Musical Quarterly* article (Tcherepnin 1935, 396).

Later in the same article he surreptitiously expressed his love for Ming by featuring her five-year-old brother in a photo and lauding him as "China's youngest composer." Ming was also a main reason for Tcherepnin's canceling his ongoing world tour so that he could return to China in November 1934 to spend the winter in China. But Ming had received a scholarship to study in Brussels and, to his disappointment, left Shanghai as Tcherepnin continued his music work there.

Tcherepnin spent the next four years in emotional tumult. He managed to see Ming multiple times in Europe before breaking off his first marriage, but he first informed Louisine of his feelings for Ming already in July 1935 (LPW 1923–1946).[44] From that time until late 1938, Tcherepnin was conflicted, trying to manage his relationship with Louisine and all the while growing closer to Ming. His condition worsened after he tried to leave Louisine in September 1937, relocating to Brussels to be with Ming, to the point where Louisine feared he was "mentally sick" by March 1938 (LPW 1923–1946).[45] The emotional strain appears to have abated over the following year, as Tcherepnin eventually informed Louisine that he and Ming were expecting a child (LPW 1923–1946).[46]

The tense personal and international circumstances surrounding this period shed some light on the extent of Tcherepnin's anxiety. According to Louisine, they were not granted the right to divorce until November 1938 (LPW 1923–1946).[47] But conflicting and uncertain reports of Tcherepnin's official wedding date with Ming emerge in the literature.[48] According to Chang Chi-Jen, to whom Ming confided while he wrote his doctoral dissertation, "in the late summer of 1937, Tcherepnin and Lee Hsien Ming were married in Paris" (Chang 1986, 93). In a footnote, Chang adds, "Mme. Tcherepnin told this writer that their wedding was a very simple one. They were married in late summer, 1937" (1986, 93).[49] Certain American news features on Tcherepnin and Ming also list 1937 as the marriage date.[50] Tcherepnin biographer Enrico Arias claims, however, "In the spring of 1938, Tcherepnin married Lee Hsien Ming" (1989, 15). Louisine herself wrote on August 22, 1939, that she had received her divorce papers and that she supposed that Tcherepnin was "probably remarried by this time" (LPW 1923–1946). The exact course of events during this pivotal period, while not fully clear, paralleled increasing wartime tensions in Europe and Asia, all of which affected Tcherepnin's professional endeavors.[51]

Regardless of the circumstances, Louisine chose to be supportive of the Tcherepnins and remained a friend of the family. Louisine also helped the Tcherepnins in the transition to their new life. At that time, Tcherepnin and Ming had meager finances, and Louisine continued to send Tcherepnin money during and after World War II. This occurred despite the deep pain Louisine expressed in her diaries over losing Tcherepnin to Ming (LPW 1923–1946).[52] To underscore the emotional sacrifice involved, Louisine met the new Tcherepnin family in 1946. Louisine mentions meeting Ming, who had been ill with tuberculosis, in her diary, with some disbelief: "Ming T, so pathetic & thin wants me to take [their son] Peter if anything happens to her" (LPW 1923–1946).[53] Ming eventually lived a long, fruitful life until her death in 1991, and by all accounts, she, Tcherepnin, and the family enjoyed great happiness and success. Louisine, for her part, took an interest in their children for some time (Folkman 2008, 181), and her continuous support of Tcherepnin played some part in his transition to a new life.

Tcherepnin never returned to China after 1937, but he and Ming together maintained a Chinese network in the West. For example, they have been credited with giving support to Chinese musicians, such as composer Ding Shande and soprano Zhou Xiaoyan 周小燕, in Europe. In Ding Shande's case, in addition to his performance of Tcherepnin's pieces in the 1930s as mentioned in the introduction and chapter 5 of this volume, when Ding came to Paris in late 1947, Tcherepnin's introduction letter helped Ding gain immediate acceptance to composition professor Tony Aubin's Paris Conservatory studio.

In Zhou Xiaoyan's case, Tcherepnin introduced Zhou and her younger brother Zhou Tianyou to a school in Paris in 1938 and took them to the entrance exam, offered them instruction to prepare for the exam, and gave them piano/theory lessons. Tcherepnin encouraged Zhou when she met school difficulties. As well, he and Ming frequently hosted them, took them to concerts, and helped improve their musical quality (Zhou 1982, 114). Both Tcherepnins collaborated with Zhou after the war in Paris and London cultural concerts as well as the 1947 Prague Music Spring and the opera/cantata *Pan Keou*.

With the above events in mind, it becomes clear that Tcherepnin found roots in China well before he embarked for Asia and continued to engage with Chinese music and musicians most directly until 1939 and indirectly in the following years. In retrospect, Ming proved to be both a love match and a cure for Tcherepnin beyond compositional inspiration. She was a breakthrough figure in Tcherepnin's life, as much as the 1930s were a cathartic, if not isolated, period for him. Ming validated his identity as an artist in ways that were impossible with Louisine. Ming did not just support his work externally, but understood it more deeply and could partner with him in family building, musical matters, and the promotion of modern Chinese music. With her, he eventually made his way to financial independence and fatherhood, and he would always have a tie to China, even as the immediacy of his experience there later faded. After Tcherepnin's death in 1977, Ming and the Tcherepnin Society sponsored a competition for violin-cello works in 1982 in the manner of the original 1934 competition, in which Xu Shuya's 许舒亚 Violin Concerto was the winner. Like the earlier generation of composers that Tcherepnin encountered, Xu has since become a successful composer and served as president of the Shanghai Conservatory from 2009 to 2014.

Tcherepnin's undertakings in China and Asia, then, were not merely an exercise in professional development. For him, China was a pivotal point in his migratory life, and the extended networks of Chinese, Russian, Japanese, and international communities, along with his two cross-cultural marriages, defined the scope of his musical activities. He briefly contributed to China's musical development on a limited but significant scale from the conflicted perspective of a Russian migrant celebrity in deep personal and social crisis: aspiring to cross-cultural composition but where Chinese forms were appropriated into the Western palette; initiating activities that offered Chinese musicians opportunities for advancement but where certain ideological underpinnings were harnessed by degrees of cultural chauvinism; and seeking deeper immersion into the Chinese and international artist community, even as he remained tempted by the privilege of high society.

His interaction with individuals, groups, and institutions in Asia had a cathartic effect on him in all these aspects. His exploration of his Eurasian self was interrupted by exigencies of World War II and his newfound responsibilities as a husband and father. In many ways, however, they found resolution in his new life with Ming. Continued migration after 1937 meant that his China-Japan years faded into one stage of Tcherepnin's continuous personal and professional development. But they were an important step toward his long-term process of self-definition, self-understanding, and self-actualization. This volume highlights the extreme difficulty Russian émigré musicians experienced under forced migration. Many, such as Aaron Avshalomov in the following chapter, were not able to find such fulfilling resolution.

CHAPTER 7

Partnering with the Shanghai Arts Community

AARON AVSHALOMOV AND SYMPHONIC-THEATRICAL EXPERIMENTATION

The [Grand Chinese Evening] performance of the Municipal Orchestra on the 21st of May [1933] was dedicated to Chinese music. Or it was at least the first attempt to completely pull together, if not merge, the Chinese melody into European harmony. It turned into an event that will not be forgotten in the history of Shanghai or the musical development of China. The huge Grand Theatre was absolutely filled with spectators from the upper echelons of society. The heads of the foreign settlements were present, as well as the Chinese aristocracy, in numbers that we have not seen before.

— L. Arnoldov, "O kitaiskoi muzyke" (On Chinese music)

INNOVATIVE though he was in the realm of piano music, Alexander Tcherepnin was not the first Russian to wed Chinese and Western music in the 1930s. The Russian-Jewish composer Aaron Avshalomov had already pursued his own vision for combining Chinese and Western musical languages for nearly a decade. His experiments in crossover composition gained attention in China well before Tcherepnin's Asian tour of 1934. Avshalomov's opera *Kuan Yin* was performed in Beiping in 1925, and his symphonic suite *The Soul of the Chin* was performed by the SMO in 1930.[1] But it was the above-mentioned "Grand Chinese Evening" described by Arnoldov in the Russian-language newspaper *Shanghai Zaria* in 1933 that was the milestone in modern Chinese music.

The event was hosted by the SMO as part of a four-concert series to initiate its move to the rebuilt Grand Theatre at the end of its 1932–1933 concert season. Nearly two thousand spectators attended the concert, which was described by the Shanghai Municipal Council Press Information Office as "a special performance dedicated to old and modern Chinese music and dances" (SMA U1-4-370). The program, discussed in detail below, featured Chinese instrumental performances by the *Datong yuehui* (Great Unity Music Society) orchestra, followed by new vocal, orchestral, and theatrical works on Chinese themes composed by Aaron Avshalomov. The concert was performed by the SMO in collaboration with Chinese soloists, dancers, and producers of the International Arts Theatre Group of Shanghai, which was made up of both Chinese and non-Chinese members. It was the first time that the Western orchestra, Chinese instrumental ensemble, and international ballet committee collaborated in a single event, and Avshalomov was the unlikely common link through which all the participants were connected.

The Grand Chinese Evening characterized Avshalomov's life and the networks he formed in Shanghai from 1931 to 1947. Like Tcherepnin, Avshalomov crossed cultural boundaries in Shanghai's music community in unique ways. Avshalomov's distinct background, migratory path, and thirty-year China sojourn, however, led him in different personal and professional directions. Tcherepnin focused on developing a Chinese piano repertoire and pedagogical approach via the top administrators and faculty that welcomed him at Shanghai and Beiping educational institutions. He was able to form this network quickly due to his Saint Petersburg lineage and his star quality as an internationally renowned composer-pianist.

In this chapter, I discuss how Avshalomov, in contrast, developed an uncommon set of professional collaborations over the course of many years, which resulted in seminal experiments in Chinese-Western symphonic-theatrical works. I first review Avshalomov's background and development of symphonic and musical-dramatic forms. I then describe how he partnered with individuals and organizations in the Shanghai arts community in an unprecedented series of more than fifty performances that highlighted his experimental works. Finally, I appraise Avshalomov's China sojourn in relation to that of Tcherepnin. Unlike Tcherepnin, who stimulated new Chinese piano developments as an "honorary" foreigner, Avshalomov furthered China's symphonic-theatrical reform as a localized non-Chinese participant. Both composers experienced personal crises and catharses relating to their China years, but they found different resolutions in the aftermath of World War II. Their combined impact on modern Chinese music is thus viewed within the context of the twentieth-century Russian diaspora experience, as well as the specific circumstances of interwar Shanghai.

Background and Musical Language: Straddling Borders

Like Tcherepnin and the many Russians who scattered across the globe in the twentieth century, Avshalomov followed an extraordinary migratory path.[2] Avshalomov's experience in exile was defined by a continuous, multilayered search: for statehood, means of survival, meaning and livelihood, new identities, personal relationships in foreign surroundings, and a new Chinese musical language reflective of his transcultural upbringing.

Avshalomov grew up in Nikolayevsk-on-Amur and Khabarovsk, Siberia, among mixed Russian-Chinese-Japanese communities. He was raised in a Jewish fish merchant family, where he was placed in the daily care of a Japanese nurse and Chinese factotum. These surroundings provided him with regular exposure to Chinese folk music and theater and Japanese folk songs. He also studied the Western violin and began conducting groups as a teenager. He spent short periods in Europe before the outbreak of World War I, which included music study in Zurich. Avshalomov had briefly enlisted in the Russian army but was released due to illness. He left Russia in 1914, before the Revolution, at the urging of his family and spent the next fifteen years split between various locales in China and the United States. He married his first wife Esther in San Francisco in 1916, and while scores of Russians fled their country after the 1917 Revolution, Avshalomov actually planned to move back there in excitement but had to abort those plans due to visa issues. Instead, he turned his focus to China, where he began years of researching folk music in earnest. During this formative time, he developed his ideas for composing mixed Chinese and Western forms and was able to gain experience in performing his works as director, producer, and conductor.

For Avshalomov, the move to Shanghai in 1931 was one of opportunity rather than refuge. Before Shanghai, he had experienced a period of growing personal and professional anxiety in Tianjin, where his musical activities and compositional ideas both developed. He had also felt confined by his family life and job circumstances outside of music. He left his first wife Esther and son Jacob in Tianjin for a Russian widow (Tatiana Sokolova, whom he eventually married in the late 1930s) in order to "pursue music only or perish" (Avshalomov 2001, 64). Shanghai's world-class orchestra, plenitude of trained Russian and Western musicians, and numerous Chinese artists offered him an appealing environment for advancing his creative projects. After his arrival, he was appointed to the new position of librarian of the Shanghai Municipal Library. This position did not place him in the middle of the musical establishment with the Russian pedagogues and the SMO, but it brought him a stable salary until his later dismissal during the Japanese occupation, and it offered certain connections in the city government and contact with numerous visitors from abroad. In addition, the job's working hours were flexible, which allowed him to compose at night and direct rehearsals of his various works at midday.

He thereby gained a steady platform for cultivating musical compositions and artist networks over a prolonged period. The Japanese occupation of Shanghai during World War II presented extreme hardships for Chinese and foreigners alike, but Avshalomov managed to continue his composition and performance work amidst the most difficult years from 1942, albeit slowly and without employment. The sudden success of his musical drama *The Great Wall* and his appointment as interim conductor of the SMO just after the war in late 1945 placed him atop the Shanghai musical world for a brief time. But he had long been eyeing opportunities to promote his Chinese works in the United States, and his heightened status made him vulnerable within China's intensifying civil war. He thus left China for the United States in 1947 without his second wife Tatiana and never returned. Avshalomov's Shanghai sojourn would prove to be the professional highlight of his life, however, for he was unable to gain the artistic foothold that he sought in the United States. Nor did he fully acclimate to American society. He spent his final years in abject poverty and relative depression in Manhattan without seeing his musical dramas come to fruition there.

As is reflective of his migration, Avshalomov might best be described as a Russian-Chinese-American composer. Tcherepnin's contributions to Chinese piano music were tangible, but China was a fleeting phase of his life. Avshalomov was likely the only non-Chinese composer to demonstrate lifelong devotion to modern Chinese music development (even in the United States) and to integrate himself as a bona fide participant in the Chinese and foreign arts communities. I have written elsewhere of the profound impact of his compositions, including (1) the subjective blending of Chinese and Western musical languages within politicized hybrid genres, (2) the elevation of the Chinese musical tradition as an equally valid artistic subject position in counterpoint to the predominant Western paradigm, (3) the historical precedence Avshalomov's works displayed in presaging later twentieth-century developments in Chinese music, and (4) *symphonicization* as a central feature to represent the musical strengthening of Chinese nationhood.[3]

These achievements were due to several important factors. First, his upbringing and moderate formal training in composition actually freed him to explore and galvanize an eclectic language of Western, Chinese, and Asian features. Second, the prolonged period of traditional music study and partnership with Chinese music experts enabled him to achieve relative depth of incorporating Chinese materials in his works.[4] Third, he engaged in genres that gained social validation due to their monumentality and cultural relevance, including both symphonic and theatrical forms with Chinese themes. Fourth, he was able to test, premiere, revise, and repeatedly perform his works with the prestigious SMO (often with him conducting), in partnership with key Chinese artists of interwar Shanghai and the early People's Republic of China (PRC). And fifth, these projects had both immediate, individual impact as well as a cumulative effect derived from a continuous series of performances when viewed over seventeen years, which was unmatched during that period.

Avshalomov's musical language was individual. Tcherepnin had built his international reputation by "inventing" a new harmonic and textural formula as an outgrowth of his elite, learned Saint Petersburg heritage. Avshalomov, in contrast, learned only the elements of composition and orchestration, beyond which he was left to his own creative devices. Much of this was based on his childhood, cross-cultural socialization, and ongoing study of music that stimulated him as he lived in various Chinese locales. But even his application of Western practices was selective, more a result of his own study rather than from tutelage. Through years of experience, he developed his skills at interweaving the Asian and Western languages. The general characteristics of his style may be summarized as follows:

- Musical crossover: He sought to modernize Chinese music via musical language that was fundamentally and eclectically Western, with Chinese themes forming structural foundations.
- Harmony: He deeply embedded the Chinese (anhemitonic) pentatonic scale as part of the harmonic-melodic foundation. But this was frequently mixed with other harmonic elements, including late Romantic (via heavy chromaticism and pitch substitution), modernist and non-Chinese "exotic" (whole tone scales and Greek modes), and hemitonic Japanese pentatonic scales for dramatic effect.
- Melody: He employed genuine or accurately stylized Chinese melodies, but often with thick layers of multiple, composed countermelodies.
- Instrumentation and orchestration: He used orchestral instruments to mimic Chinese colors and was likely the first to blend Chinese and Western instruments within the large Western orchestra.
- Experimentation in dramatic forms: He consciously explored radical reform options for Chinese theater via innovative Chinese-Western crossover in direct collaboration with Chinese theatrical reformers.

The most demonstrable impact of Avshalomov's experimentation lies in his symphonic output, including symphonic poems, concertos, symphonies, symphonic suites, and orchestral songs, as well as dramatic works (opera, pantomime-ballet, and musical-drama) with symphony orchestra. Numerous Chinese composers, musicians, artists, and historians have acknowledged the profound impact of Avshalomov's exploration on Shanghai-based contemporaries, students, and future musical leaders.[5] One reason was the dramatic *symphonicization* of Chinese themes that pervaded all of his major works. On one hand, he incorporated Chinese melodies, rhythms, tone colors, idioms, geographical locations, myths and legends, and poetry into his orchestral genres, which was a completely new phenomenon to Shanghai. From the period in the 1920s, controversy had emerged between those advocating all-out Westernization versus others who doubted that Chinese music could be played on Western instruments. Avshalomov adopted his own position, not advocating complete Westernization but believing "in the vast beauty and unique style of Chinese folk melodies, which were suitable for being played in the masterworks for Western instruments. . . . Chinese symphonic music would be absolutely able to attain a respectable position in the global music realm" (Jiang 1983, 40–41). Of equal significance was his symphonicization of Chinese theatrical works, in conjunction with a palette of cross-cultural, musical-theatrical elements, which together served as a major precedent for China's ongoing theatrical reform.

The simultaneous symphonic depiction of dramatic action occurring on stage was revolutionary in the context of China's theatrical traditions. To Avshalomov, it was the central cohesive feature that drove his entire output of dramatic repertoire, around which entire works were designed. But China's theatrical reform also involved decisions regarding plot and characterization, text, vocal delivery, scenery and lighting, costumes and makeup, dance and gesticulation, instrumentation, and other musical attributes. I have discussed the crossover musical-theatrical elements at play in Avshalomov's most prominent work *The Great Wall* in relation to later *yangbanxi* "model dramas" of the Cultural Revolution.[6] Table 7.1 outlines Avshalomov's general approach to these elements in all his main Shanghai dramatic works, including *The Soul of the Chin* (1925), *Incense Shadows/Dream of Wei Lien* (1935), *Buddha and the 5 Planetary Deities* (1941), *The Great Wall* (1943–45), and *Phoenix* (1944).

Another reason for Avshalomov's impact was the unparalleled exposure his works attained in Shanghai's combined Chinese and foreign communities over seventeen years. Most of the works were of monumental proportion and took years to conceive, compose, organize, and rehearse. New works would not be expected to receive regular, multiple performances in the manner of those that were part of an orchestral or theatrical canon. But as table 7.2 indicates, Avshalomov succeeded in gaining repeated performances—more than fifty in total—in a long series of high-profile productions. It should be noted that most of the performance dates for *The Great Wall* in 1945–1946 included two performances (afternoon and evening) each day. That production alone ran for more than thirty performances in Shanghai and Nanjing.

This lengthy list only begins to reveal the magnitude of Avshalomov's achievement. Full scores, parts, and piano reductions totaling hundreds of pages for each work needed to be produced at a time when copy machines and digitization did not exist. According to Qin Pengzhang 秦鹏章, who was acquainted with Avshalomov through Shen Zhibai 沈知白, Avshalomov handwrote these scores by himself (with some assistance from his son Jacob, Shen Zhibai, and others) (Jiang et al. 1994, 476). Most of the works were for the large SMO, which

Table 7.1 Musical-theatrical elements in Avshalomov's Shanghai dramatic works

Plot & characterization	Adapted from Chinese myths and folktales
	"Heroic tragedy-triumphs"
	Individual and expanded choral characterization
Sung text	Mandarin/Vocalize
Spoken text	Mixture of spoken and declaimed Chinese
Solo singing	Limited "arias" and Chinese folk tunes
Choral singing	Western antiphonal/canon/polyphonic
	Expanded role
Scenery & lighting	Modern/Western theater
Costumes & makeup	Chinese operatic/theatrical costumes
	Chinese operatic/nonoperatic makeup varies by production
Dance	Combined stylized Chinese operatic poses, Chinese folk dance, and Western choreography
Gestures	Mixed Chinese operatic gestures with Western pantomime
Musical dramatization	Symphonic—composed music drives all dramatic aspects
	Programmatic—mood music: incidental, melodrama, film music
Instrumentation	Full Western symphony orchestra
	Frequent inclusion of Chinese percussion
	Sometimes "mimicking" Chinese instruments
	Continuous accompaniment
Musical texture	Western homophony/polyphony; counterpoint
Melodic materials	Composed, Chinese motive-based, some folk tunes
Harmony	Western late Romantic & early modernist
	Heavily chromatic and dissonant
	Pentatonic/modal foundation

may have been relatively open to performing experimental works on Chinese themes by a Russian composer because of the large Russian community and presence of Russian orchestral musicians in Shanghai. The full orchestra itself required numerous rehearsals, and the dramatic productions only increased in scale, from *The Soul of the Chin*, which required just a handful of stage performers but a larger production crew, to *The Great Wall*, which included a cast alone of more than fifty members. All dramatic productions involved financing and months-long musical rehearsals, staging, choreography, set and lighting design and construction, costume production, ticketing, and publicity.

Table 7.2 Avshalomov's main Shanghai performances.

Date	Work	Location
1930, November 30	The Soul of the Chin (Symphonic Suite) (Entitled Soul of Kin Sei)	Shanghai, Grand, SMO
1932, April 24	In Hutungs of Peking (Beiping Hutungs— Symphonic Poem)	Shanghai, Carlton, SMO
1933, May 21	The Soul of the Chin (Ballet)	Shanghai, Grand, SMO/ International Arts Theatre
1933, May 21	The Last Words of Tsin Wen (Orchestral Song)	Shanghai, Grand, SMO, Liu Jingfang
1933, May 21	In Hutungs of Peking (Beiping Hutungs— Symphonic Poem)	Shanghai, Grand, SMO
1935, March 13–14	Incense Shadows (Dream of Wei Lien—Ballet)	Shanghai, Carlton, SMO/ International Arts Theatre
1935, March 13–14	The K'e Ripples to Its Banks (Orchestral Song)	Shanghai, Carlton, SMO
1935, March 13–14	In Hutungs of Peking (Beiping Hutungs— Symphonic Poem)	Shanghai, Carlton, SMO
1936, January 19	The Soul of the Chin: Sai Ho's Dance & Kinsei's Death	Shanghai, Lyceum, SMO
1936, January 19	In Hutungs of Peking (Beiping Hutungs— Symphonic Poem)	Shanghai, Lyceum, SMO
1936, January 19	Piano Concerto in G	Shanghai, Lyceum, SMO/ Singer, Chinese Orchestra
1936, February 2	Piano Concerto in G	Shanghai, Lyceum, SMO/ Singer
1936, December 15–16	The Dream of Wei Lien (Incense Shadows—Ballet)	Shanghai, Metropol, SMO/ International Arts Theatre
1936, December 15–16	The K'e Ripples to Its Banks (Orchestral Song)	Shanghai, Metropol, SMO/ Mrs. T. F. Waung

Table 7.2 *(Cont.)*

Date	Work	Location
1937, May 23	Piano Concerto in G	Shanghai, Lyceum, SMO/ Singer
1937, May 23	The K'e Ripples to Its Banks (Orchestral Song)	Shanghai, Lyceum, SMO/ Pansy Long
1937, May 23	A Stroll in an Ancient Garden (Sketch for Chamber Orchestra)	Shanghai, Lyceum, SMO
1937, December 8	The Soul of the Chin (Ballet)	Metropol, SMO
1938, January 16	Violin Concerto	Shanghai, Lyceum, SMO/ Gregory Fidlon
1939, August 26	Indian Dances	Shanghai, Jessfield Park, SMO/Devi
1939, August 31	Indian Dances	Shanghai, French Park, SMO/Devi
1940, March 17	Symphony no. 1 in C Minor	Shanghai, Lyceum, SMO
1941, February 23	The Soul of the Chin: Kinsei's Death	Shanghai, Lyceum, SMO
1941, February 23	Piano Concerto in G	Shanghai, Lyceum, SMO/ Singer
1941, February 23	3 Short Pieces for Erhu and Orchestra 1. On the River K'e 2. Dancing in a Twilight 3. Nocturne	Shanghai, Lyceum, SMO/ Wei Zhongle
1941, June 16, 18	Incense Shadows (Dream of Wei Lien—Ballet)	Shanghai, Lyceum, SMO/Chinese Ballet Association
1942, June 12–14	Buddha and the 5 Planetary Deities (Ballet)	Shanghai, Lyceum, SMO/Chinese Ballet Association
1942, June 12–14	Indian Dances	Shanghai, Lyceum, SMO/Chinese Ballet Association
1942, December 17–18	The Dream of Wei Lien (Incense Shadows—Ballet)	Shanghai, Grand, SMO/ Chinese Ballet Association

(continues)

Table 7.2 *(Cont.)*

Date	Work	Location
1945, Nov. 25, 29, 30	The Great Wall (Music Drama)	Shanghai, Lyceum, Chinese Ballet and Music-Drama Association
1945, December 1–2	The Great Wall (Music Drama)	Shanghai, Lyceum, Chinese Ballet and Music-Drama Association
1946, March 9–10	Piano Concerto in G	Shanghai, Lyceum, SMO/ Singer
1946, March 27–28	The Great Wall (Music Drama)	Shanghai, Lyceum, Chinese Ballet and Music-Drama Association
1946, November 6– (Multiple dates)	The Great Wall (Music Drama)	Nanjing, Lizhishe Auditorium, Chinese Dance Drama Co.
1946, November 6– (Multiple dates)	The Soul of the Chin (Ballet) Buddha and the 5 Planetary Deities (Ballet)	Nanjing, Lizhishe Auditorium, Chinese Dance Drama Co.
1946, December 5–12 (Two per day)	The Great Wall (Music Drama)	Shanghai, Nanking, Chinese Dance Drama Co.
1946, May 27	Phoenix (Symphonic-Vocal Ballet)	Shanghai, Avshalomov Residence

Source: Aaron Avshalomov scores; Jacob Avshalomov 2001; Archival holdings; Chinese, English, and Russian newspaper and journal coverage.

Collaborative Networks and Experimental Works in Shanghai

Avshalomov could not realize these performances in isolation, but he was not greeted by reporters off the boat as Tcherepnin was. Tcherepnin's international reputation and background opened up his Asian networks, which immediately facilitated his China activities. Avshalomov, as a relatively unknown composer in 1931, needed to build a multifaceted network step by step, convincing the SMO of his compositional worthiness, finding sponsorship, and forging ties with Chinese and foreign artists. He lacked a single "gateway" for deepening his artistic ties. While he interacted with a number of Russians, most of his professional networks relied on those outside of the Shanghai Russian and Jewish communities.[7] From the time he left his home just 1,500 kilometers to the north, he eclectically and comfortably acquainted himself with those of varying nationalities in order to build his personal and professional life.

Throughout his Shanghai years, Avshalomov engaged with artists who would assume important positions in the PRC after 1949. From 1931 to 1947, a general trend is observable in Avshalomov's collaborative networks: with an ever-present tie to the SMO as a continuous underlay, (1) he developed strong ties to the Shanghai international community while interacting with Chinese artists of various pursuasions (leftist, official, reformist, and traditional) in the early to mid-1930s, (2) he became more closely aligned with Soviet and underground Chinese Communist Party (CCP) members from the late 1930s to late 1945, and (3) his final two years in Shanghai were marked by a sudden swing toward American-backed, governmental-KMT sponsorship. Arriving in Shanghai in October 1931, Avshalomov immediately targeted symphonic opportunities. He completed his symphonic poem the *Beiping Hutungs*, discussed below, during the second half of 1931 based on his life and music study in the northern city in the early 1920s.[8] By April of 1932, it was premiered by the SMO and quickly found favor among audiences in China and North America.[9]

Also in 1932, Avshalomov began conducting and orchestrating for the Chinese arm of Pathé Records, where he came into regular contact with new Chinese composers in the film and recording industry. Via Ren Guang 任光, who wrote the title track to the film *Fisherman's Song*, Avshalomov met and mentored important left-wing composers such as Nie Er 聂耳, He Luting 贺绿汀, Lü Ji 吕骥, and Xian Xinghai 冼星海, as well as film artists An E 安娥, Sun Shiyi 孙师毅, and Ouyang Yuqian 欧阳予倩. He also met musicians like Peking Opera star Mei Lanfang 梅兰芳, future theorist and pedagogue Shen Zhibai, and Chinese instrumentalist Wei Zhongle 卫仲乐, with whom he formed close collaborations for the duration of his Shanghai life. Mei Lanfang himself was working to reform Chinese opera, and he either directed or provided guidance to Avshalomov on his main dramatic works. According to Jiang Chunfang 姜椿芳, Shen Zhibai and Avshalomov were nearly inseparable for fifteen years (Jiang et al. 1994, 330–333). Shen assisted and advised Avshalomov in every aspect relating to the Chinese content of his works. Wei Zhongle provided additional expertise on Chinese instrumental forms and contacts with other Chinese instrumentalists, and he was the featured performer in several of Avshalomov's works. Together with Avshalomov, Shen and Wei formed a Chinese Music Study Society and facilitated contact with other Chinese music societies, such as the *Datong yuehui*. To the Chinese musicians, Avshalomov possessed rare skills in theory, orchestration, and conducting at a time when China's nascent music, film, and recording industry needed mentorship and development in orchestral music. And his multifaceted experimentation stimulated Chinese composers and reformers to seek their own creative paths.

For Avshalomov, his Shanghai networks and musical experimentation thus became mutually dependent: his prolific stream of large-scale, innovative Chinese-Western works allowed him to partner with the prestigious SMO and newly formed artistic groups, while his deepening, expansive network gave him unique opportunities for enacting his experiments. At the same time, Avshalomov utilized his conducting skills to execute his esoteric musical language, which would have required unpalatable amounts of work for other conductors learning his larger works anew.[10] Working from the ground up, he relied on versatility and a prolific creative vision, which resulted in an unusually extensive network. In the following section, I outline Avshalomov's main projects from 1933 to 1947 as a framework for discussion of his compositions and the Shanghai network of groups and individuals that made them possible.

The Grand Chinese Evening

The reopening of Shanghai's Grand Theatre mentioned at the beginning of this chapter provided the impetus for the Grand Chinese Evening as part of a series of SMO concerts in May 1933. The concert was new and unique, even by contemporary standards. The first part featured the *Datong yuehui* orchestra performing three movements rearranged from its 1929 suite *Dongfang dayue* (Grand music of the East). It was followed by *Datong* member and *pipa* (plucked lute) virtuoso Wei Zhongle performing *Shimian maifu* (Ambush on all sides). *Datong* was a thirty-member amateur orchestra of Chinese plucked and bowed strings, winds, and percussion. It was founded by Zheng Jinwen 郑觐文 and was an important organization for continuing traditional Chinese music through historical research and reforming Chinese instrumental construction and practices. Avshalomov believed that Chinese music could best be modernized by using Western instruments to add color, harmony, and texture to older forms. But he cooperated with *Datong* and its members on this and future occasions as part of an ongoing, collective exploration of new avenues for Chinese musical modernity.

The SMO then performed two of Avshalomov's works. The first was the poem for Western orchestra and soprano "The Last Words of Tsin-Wen," sung in Chinese by soloist Liu Jingfang 刘经方. It was followed by *Beiping Hutungs*. Aided by written descriptive notes, *Hutungs* enacts aural events that Avshalomov had frequently encountered when living in Beiping in the 1920s. The eleven-minute work is scored for a large orchestra, aided by a battery of Western and Chinese percussion. As recounted by arts critic Fu Lei 傅雷 in a lengthy, praiseworthy concert review, Avshalomov "depicts the special mood of a full day in the ancient city. He utilizes the most popular melodies from Peking Opera to represent the singing calls of vendors like cobblers, barbers, and florists who advertise their trades. Even more directly, he uses the blowing and beating gestures of the Chinese suona [trumpet] and knobbed cymbals to paint the image of a funeral procession" (Fu 1933, 4). *Hutungs* is one of the earliest scores to feature programmatic depictions of Chinese sounds and musical gestures in the Western orchestral medium. It gained unusually high exposure in the 1930s and 1940s. In Shanghai, the SMO performed it on multiple occasions and recorded it in 1937.[11]

The second half of the concert featured the staged premiere of Avshalomov's Chinese pantomime-ballet *The Soul of the Chin* by the SMO and a cast of Chinese dancers under the direction of the composer and Mei Lanfang. As described elsewhere, the ballet "was an experimental stage adaptation in five episodes of a Chinese story that forewent the typically sung medium of Chinese opera in favor of visual effects, dance, gestured characterization, costuming, and scenery, all set against an orchestral-musical backdrop and aided by a written program that explained the story to the audience" (Winzenburg 2012, 65). Written in 1926, the work shows similar approaches to mixing musical traditions as those found in *Hutungs*. Its greatest innovation lies in its theatrical approach.

The work was produced by the International Arts Theatre Group of Shanghai (IAT), which was made up of both Chinese and non-Chinese members. It was not, however, a primarily Russian-formed organization. The cast was all Chinese, including *Tianyi yingpian gongsi* (Unique Film Production Co.) star Yuan Meiyun 袁美云, and both Mei Lanfang and Shen Zhibai were directly involved in the dramatization.[12] In addition to its symphonic orchestration, *The Soul of the Chin* was experimental for its substitution of two Chinese operatic features: it brought in modern Western scenery and lighting for greater realism in place of Chinese operatic symbolism,[13] and it substituted symphonic mime for operatic singing with the orchestra providing descriptive music. Still present were the stylistic dancing, gestures, costumes and decorations, and makeup from Chinese opera.

To fifteen-year-old Yuan Meiyun, who was trained in Chinese theater, and the seven male dancers from the Ellis Kadoorie School, this was the first time they had performed in such a production with the orchestra. They reportedly encountered difficulties adjusting to the new context in their early rehearsals. For example, Yuan adapted a scarf dance from classical Chinese theater in her performance as the Spirit of the Lake (Sai Ho). According to the *China Press*, "she has never danced with a foreign orchestra before and finds the difference between the orchestra of the Chinese theater and the foreign theater very great. In the former, according to Yuan . . . , a dancer controls the music—determining the tempo and tone—by carefully studied gestures which are understood by the musicians. Dancing with the foreign orchestra means that she must follow a certain definite time [including the uncommon triple meter], and at first she found this difficult" ("Yuan Mei-yuan" 1933, 5). But the dancers reportedly adjusted in a matter of weeks. The result, in the eyes of viewers like Fu Lei, was "a harmonious form of Chinese-Western opera" (Fu 1933, 4).

The production marked a beginning for collaboration among Chinese and foreign stage artists during the 1930s. The IAT was instituted by a conglomerate of prominent Chinese and foreign theater enthusiasts for the purpose of promoting dramatic arts across all national boundaries within the unique environment of Shanghai. The Soul of the Chin served as its pilot project, and the IAT sponsored the entire Grand Chinese Evening as its inaugural event. According to Jacob Avshalomov, "[Aaron's] compositions began to attract the attention and support of members of 'society'. Mrs. Bernardine Szold-Fritz, [Chinese dancer] Averil Tong and the American writer, Vanya Oakes sparked the formation of the [IAT]" (Avshalomov 2001, 72). On May 20, the China Press announced its long list of "distinguished patrons," including top representatives from the Bank of China and other financial institutions, journals, government ministries, academic institutions, and the National Conservatory of Music, as well as prominent Shanghai-based artists and arts patrons ("Chinese Pantomime-Ballet" 1933, 12).

A large number of foreign sponsors and general committee members were also listed, as well as an international publicity and production team. The assemblage of VIPs and the political-financial weight they carried ensured that the Grand Chinese Evening lived up to its title in both programming and audience attendance. The concert proved to be a great financial success for the SMO and IAT alike.[14] For the IAT, beyond covering the $2,500 in production expenses and payment to performers, it was able to make an additional $1,000 that funded its operations, other productions, and a move into a new space in 1935 (SMA U1-4-376). The IAT credited Avshalomov's production as the source of this success.

As a major event, the Grand Chinese Evening earned Avshalomov significant press attention and helped galvanize arts connections. Commentator and arts critic Fu Lei, for example, seized on his review of the event to issue a manifesto for Chinese cultural reform, calling it "of especially great significance. This concert is extremely important for the future of Chinese music and Chinese theatre—a soulful enlightenment" (Fu 1933, 4). Such was the effect on Fu Lei that he became a staunch supporter of Avshalomov in the ensuing years. The two became part of a wider network of Chinese writers and artists who discussed, experimented with, and produced works relating to China's theatrical reform.

Incense Shadows (The Dream of Wei Lien)

The Grand Chinese Evening proved to Avshalomov the importance of maintaining a network of organizations like those that participated in the event. Had he been primarily interested in solo piano music, as was Tcherepnin, his networking challenges would have been less acute. But given his specific interest in symphonic-dramatic forms, continued collaboration with the SMO after the two major successes of 1932–1933 would be vital as long as he stayed in China. The performances in table 7.2 (above) show that he achieved great success in this respect. His partnering with Chinese instrumentalists and groups like *Datong* also provided him with a resource for performers and experts in traditional Chinese music, while he stimulated them with new ideas for reform.

The most daunting challenge came on the theatrical end. As a production thirty minutes in length with a stage cast of just eight, *The Soul of the Chin* was relatively modest. Nonetheless, it required a massive organization with significant financial backing and sponsorship from the upper echelon of Shanghai's Chinese and foreign communities. He was able to secure this in the IAT through the mid-1930s by first gaining support from a handful of well-connected artist-enthusiasts like Fritz, Tong, and Oakes, who could muster wider support and media attention.

After the Grand Chinese Evening, he attained the firm backing of the IAT for his next pantomime-ballet *Incense Shadows (The Dream of Wei Lien)*,[15] first performed by a cast of twenty-two Chinese dancers and the SMO in March 1935. The three-scene story was written and directed by Vanya Oakes, who had also provided the English libretto for the Grand Chinese Evening ballet two years earlier. It was reported to be "the logical sequel of [*The Soul of the Chin*,] a further step towards another branch of the modern dance which, briefly, discards the idea of pure grace for virility, power, and pictured movements" ("'Incense Shadows' An Experiment" 1935, 14). Robert Stuart described the plot to Western readers of the *Musical Times* in 1937 after viewing a December 1936 performance:

> The first scene depicts the temple of Kuan Yin, the thousand-armed goddess of mercy. Before her image comes the maiden Wei Lien to worship, and to ask for guidance in her choice of suitors. The second scene is presumably part of a dream induced by the goddess. The maiden falls into the power of the denizens of a very realistic Buddhistic Hell. One of her lovers, a wealthy and conceited youth, comes to rescue her, but is defeated and led into captivity by the devils. His impecunious but scholarly rival routs the fiends and leads Wei Lien away in triumph. The last scene depicts a dream garden, in which Wei Lien and the triumphant lover feast. (Stuart 1937, 144)

Incense Shadows demonstrated a rare model for cross-cultural productions, achieving a number of advances over *The Soul of the Chin*. As Yuan Likang 袁励康, who became a close associate of Avshalomov, observed at a 1941 rerun of

Incense Shadows and recounted in the 1990s, not only did Avshalomov develop his skills in his orchestral scoring of dramatic action, gestures, and Chinese themes, he actually produced a drama that was "fully driven by musical development. Each character and scene has its own specific music" (Jiang et al. 1994, 461). The 1935 production also achieved great spectacle in terms of the stage scenery, created by the Russian Makary Domrachev and his students of the National Institute of the Arts in Hangzhou, as well as fantastic lighting effects and breathtaking costume design. The collaboration of Oakes, the SMO with Paci conducting, and prominent choreographer Yang Yulou 杨玉楼 added to the professionalism of the performance. The combined musical and dramatic effects were mesmerizing, prompting viewers like the young Nie Er to write, "after watching the third act, I thought: 'perhaps this is the right path for improving Chinese opera'" (Nie 1935).[16]

The production signaled an even wider web of collaboration for Avshalomov. As explained by his son Jacob, however, the public impact of the March 1935 premiere was limited:

> Knud Jordan, old friend and patron, came to Shanghai from Peking, having been promoted to Head of Chinese Customs. He financed a production of the just completed *Incense Shadows*. Rehearsals were held in a warehouse. The gifted young Russian-Jewish pianist and composer, Gregory Singer (Grischa) came on the scene and began his sterling service as rehearsal pianist, which would continue for a decade. . . . Alla Grigorievna, Russian critic, assisted in the promotion. . . . Press notices were good, but the house was half empty, and the show was a financial failure. Jordan, undaunted, "was very pleased and did not regret the loss of money." (Avshalomov 2001, 72)[17]

The IAT remained equally undaunted. Encouraged by the artistic success of the work, it expanded its activities in 1935–1936 to include various theatrical productions, lectures, workshops, and public debates on social issues of the day. It also developed its committee organization, with Avshalomov being elected to the IAT general committee on March 23, 1936. It then reproduced *Incense Shadows* over two nights in December 1936 under the revised title *The Dream of Wei Lien*. These performances again enjoyed good artistic acclaim, but audiences were small.[18] The experimental success, however, prompted IAT supporters to seek performance of the work in New York via Columbia Artists in the belief that it would appeal to American audiences. Columbia sent a representative to Shanghai in June 1937 to preview the work. After receiving confirmation of Columbia's interest, Avshalomov tried unsuccessfully for several years to arrange the tour.[19]

The Shanghai arts environment that had bred international collaboration in the IAT, however, quickly deteriorated due to the approaching war with Japan. While the core IAT committee could initially ensure smooth execution of their performances without undue political wrangling, such ease was a fleeting mirage within Shanghai's inherently unequal and unstable political setting. Under its semicolonial structure before and shortly after World War I, one avenue to gain leverage with Chinese financial and political leaders was through influential foreign business leaders. But the increasing threat from Japan and eventual occupation prompted many foreigners like Bernardine Szold-Fritz to leave China.[20] The circumstances that enabled the IAT's establishment and operation were thus short-lived, and it vanished from the Shanghai arts scene in 1937.

For the next several years, Avshalomov struggled to find sponsorship. He had received some support from family members in the United States, but when that was no longer available, he had to expend all of his own resources to keep rehearsals going. He also experienced artistic and financial difficulties with the choreographer and dancers. For his future dramatic performances of *Incense Shadows*, Avshalomov formed a new dance company and shifted toward Chinese-sponsored collaborations in partnership with the SMO. The June 1941 and December 1942 performances were produced by the Chinese Ballet Association (CBA) with new artistic direction from Shanghai artists Chen Tsong (Chen Zhong) 陈钟 and Cui Yanfang 崔艳芳, as well as new cast members.

The CBA structure was not elaborate like the IAT's had been. As the war ensued, news reports became increasingly terse, publications were restricted, and organized cultural activities were heavily curtailed. Press reports for Avshalomov's wartime productions offered only vague descriptions with names of only a few leading figures. Avshalomov's communication with Jacob was completely cut off during that time, and his recollective notes from the 1960s are not yet publicly available. Avshalomov's collaboration with the CBA, however, reflected his increasingly close working relationship with Chen Tsong. The CBA produced all of Avshalomov's 1941–1942 dance works, including both runs of *Incense Shadows*, *Buddha and the 5 Planetary Deities*, and the *Indian Dances*. Chen then served in the key role as Avshalomov's assistant director and choreographer for *The Great Wall* in 1945–1946. Avshalomov had such great confidence in him that he considered taking Chen along to the United States to set up a *Great Wall* company there if he was unable to take an entire cast from Shanghai.

Piano Concerto in G, on Chinese Themes and Rhythms

Avshalomov formed another important partnership from the first *Incense Shadows* production with the aforementioned Russian pianist Grigory (Gregory) Singer.[21] Born to a Russian-Jewish family in Harbin in 1913,[22] he came to

Shanghai in the mid-1930s and gained attention there for his excellent piano and musical skills. During the 1930s, he studied piano with Mario Paci and Boris Lazarev, who taught at the National Conservatory, and he worked at the Pathé recording studio as a pianist and conductor between 1935 and 1941. He reportedly worked for the Soviet radio in Shanghai from 1941 and spent time teaching at the National Conservatory in 1945–1946 before moving to the Soviet Union.

Singer first began working closely with Avshalomov as a rehearsal pianist and coach for *Incense Shadows*. He continued in this indispensable role for Avshalomov's staged works over the following decade. Avshalomov was so impressed with Singer's skills during production rehearsals that he composed a *Concerto for Piano in G, on Chinese Themes and Rhythms* for Singer during a holiday in Hangzhou in the summer of 1935. The three-movement concerto premiered on January 19, 1936, with Singer performing on an "enormous Bluthner concert grand which Knud Jordan had bought for the occasion" (Avshalomov 2001, 92). According to the *China Press*, reporting on the record numbers of SMO audiences for 1936, the *Concerto in G* "had an enormous success and had to be repeated, by general request, at the following concert" ("1936 Concert Attendance Sets Record" 1937, 9). A special follow-up performance was thus added for February 2.

The enthusiastic reception was due to a combination of factors relating to compositional approach and virtuosic performance and was likely bolstered by featuring a Russian composer-soloist duo as part of an SMO season frequented by Russian audience members in the manner of the special Russian concerts discussed in chapter 4. Basing a piano concerto on Chinese themes was itself as innovative as Tcherepnin's "Hommage" had been the year before. With assistance from Shen Zhibai, Avshalomov adapted traditional Chinese materials in multiple ways. According to Qin Pengzhang, the first movement was based on incomplete fragments of Chinese folk tunes, while the second movement quoted an old Chinese melody from Kunqu opera that was selected by Shen (Jiang et al. 1994, 476). The third movement paralleled "Hommage" by including materials composed in the style of the *pipa* tune, but here the Chinese instrumental idioms are mimicked in both the orchestra (via strummed chords in the violins) and rapidly repeating notes in the piano, which persist over the orchestra throughout the eight-minute movement.[23] As Tcherepnin had thrilled Chinese audiences with his piano dexterity, Singer's brilliant execution, especially of the allegro finale, earned similar plaudits in each performance.

The *Concerto in G* broke other experimental ground during the January 19 premiere. After the concerto finale concluded, an ensemble of fourteen Chinese instrumentalists, including Wei Zhongle, took the stage with Singer and Avshalomov, and the concerto's middle movement was performed a second time in an alternate version scored by the composer for Chinese instruments and solo piano. This was the first time a concerto was performed in this way. Since then, hundreds of concertos have been written that mix Chinese and Western instruments in various manners.[24] The Chinese instrumental version was not performed at later concerts, but the *Concerto in G* became one of Avshalomov's most successful pieces, gaining five SMO performances with Singer between 1936 and 1946. It was also recorded by Avshalomov, Singer, and the SMO on April 23–25, 1936, and released by Columbia as a four-sided LP that year.[25]

Avshalomov and Singer maintained a close partnership in other ways. Singer was also a fine composer, and Avshalomov conducted Singer's *Prelude, Fugue & Allegro* with the SMO in March 1939. They interacted with newly arrived refugees from Europe, including a Russian-Jewish cellist, Roman Dukstulsky, who had played in the symphony in Stockholm, for his debut chamber performance. Also, according to Shen Zhibai scholar Zhao Jiazi, Avshalomov helped Singer take on piano students, including Shen Zhibai and the son of *The Great Wall* sponsor Jiang Chunfang (Jiang et al. 1994, 324). He thereby joined the many Russian pianist-musicians who, at least in part, made their livelihoods as Western music pedagogues in Shanghai.

The close friendship between Avshalomov and Singer helped them endure the war years under the Japanese occupation. They were both able to compose under extraordinary hardship, and both appear to have been inspired by the defense of Russia against Nazi invasion, as well as from their own experience with the Japanese, who were German allies. Avshalomov took Soviet citizenship at some point during the war and participated in Soviet-sponsored events. He wrote to Jacob in December 1945 that "during the war Grischa has composed a remarkable piece for orchestra and chorus, entitled '28', [for] the heroes who stopped Hitler from taking Stalingrad. . . . I have conducted it here in the Soviet Club" (Avshalomov 2001, 210). With patriotic fervor reaching its heights during the war period, Soviet functionaries in China had beckoned Russian émigrés to return to the motherland during that period. According to Jacob Avshalomov, Grischa Singer accepted, returned to the Soviet Union, and "made a fine career there" (2001, 216). The March 1946 *Concerto in G* performances with the SMO mark their collaborative farewell.

The Great Wall

Ashalomov considered moving to the Soviet Union as well. But he had set his sights on finding success in the United States since his collaboration with IAT, and he was intent on playing out that option first. By harboring multiple, if not incompatible loyalties, Avshalomov set himself on a course that became increasingly difficult to manage. As the crisis with Japan turned into all-out war, many Westerners left China, and numerous Chinese moved to the interior of the country. Those who stayed in Shanghai faced struggles on numerous fronts: daily survival; internment, restriction, and harassment from the Japanese occupation; bombardment and antiaircraft artillery; and increasing tension between Kuomintang (KMT) and CCP partisans. For Shanghai Russians like Avshalomov and Singer, there were growing enticements from various sources to support Soviet efforts.[26] It is clear that both Avshalomov and Singer grew closer to the Soviet Russian community between 1935 and 1945. In Avshalomov's case, this coincided with his increasing contact with the CCP.

Shanghai's Soviet population was small in relation to the tens of thousands of Russians who lived there in the first half of the twentieth century. According to Ristaino, a 1942 census listed 1,666 registered Soviet citizens in the main areas of Shanghai (2000, 209, note 42). The Shanghai Soviets could count on only fluctuating consular protection and services through the 1940s according to shifting relationships between (1) the KMT and CCP, (2) the CCP and Soviet representatives, (3) China, invading Japanese forces, and their Axis power partners (especially Germany), and (4) China, the United States, and other Allied powers fighting against Germany and Japan. The Soviet Union, however, also promoted its interests with the Chinese (including the CCP) and Russian communities in Shanghai via official Soviet media organs (such as the news agency TASS), local pro-Soviet publications (such as *Novosti Dnia* and *Novaia Zhizn*), and Soviet-backed organizations (such as the aforementioned Soviet Club), which formed further subsidiary associations for social, cultural, economic, and political purposes.

Avshalomov had tangible contacts with both Russian and Chinese segments of these Soviet-backed groups. But references to his participation in the Russian community mainly appear in passing, suggesting more limited contact, whereas his proximity to the Soviet-backed CCP and leftist Chinese artists is more demonstrable until the American military appeared in late 1945. Soviet-Chinese contacts assumed a variety of forms in different parts of China, and Chinese leftists themselves operated through different networks, sometimes overlapping and sometimes separate. Avshalomov had been acquainted since the early 1930s with the aforementioned leftist Chinese composers and artists via his work in film and theatrical productions. As he sought new sources of sponsorship in 1939–1940, he met Jiang Chunfang, a translator of Russian films, which linked Avshalomov, at least indirectly, to the Soviet TASS agency. Jiang had joined the CCP in 1932 and started working in the underground Shanghai party's cultural committee from the late 1930s. Jiang headed a number of Chinese-language publications supported by TASS, including the Shanghai newspaper *Shidai Ribao* (Epoch Daily), of which he was the founder-editor and for which Shen Zhibai began working in 1945. After 1949, Jiang was the head of the Shanghai Russian Language School and the general editor of the Greater

Chinese Encyclopedia. He oversaw translations of major Russian communist texts into Chinese.

One of Jiang's tasks with the CCP was to develop ties in the Peking Opera community for the purpose of promoting reformed theatrical works and enhancing mass mobilization against the Japanese. Jiang had been assigned to support Avshalomov, and he found him during a moment of high need when *Incense Shadows* rehearsals were underway but without solid sponsorship. Jiang helped arrange new Peking Opera actors from the I You Association for the casts. According to Jiang Chunfang, the 1941 performances were copresented by the CBA and the I You Association in conjunction with the Chinese Red Cross, which was arranged through Jiang's contacts, as a benefit for a new I You Hospital (Jiang et al. 1994, 332). Jiang further assisted Avshalomov and the CBA for the December 1942 *Incense Shadows* and *Buddha* performances.

In the early 1940s, the composer tried to maintain his focus on getting works composed, rehearsed, performed, and if possible taken abroad. His collaborations with Singer, the SMO, the CBA, and Jiang Chunfang carried him through December 1942. But the height of the war curtailed his public activity from 1943 through the Japanese surrender in 1945. Avshalomov had lost his position at the Municipal Library early in the war and no longer had regular means of survival. At that time, Jiang and the Underground Party helped support him so that he could continue to compose experimental works. Especially instrumental in this respect was Jiang's good friend Yuan Likang, not a party member, who provided vital financial support to Avshalomov throughout the war.

Jiang and the Underground Party were searching for ways to involve Avshalomov in their propaganda efforts, initially against the Japanese, but also in view of ongoing tension with the KMT. In Mao Zedong's 毛泽东 base at Yan'an in Shaanxi Province, attempts were underway to present reformed opera that directly carried the party line, as with the opera *White Haired Girl* (*Bai Mao Nu*), which premiered in 1945. Shanghai remained under Japanese control, which had been wrested from the KMT and Western powers. The Underground Party was interested in bringing Avshalomov to the resistance base of the communist-led New Fourth Army in northern Jiangsu Province to compose and perform there, but instability in the area, and likely hesitation on Avshalomov's part, prevented that. Any new production in Shanghai had to be created with caution, not knowing where the tides of power would shift.

Yuan Likang was an arts aficionado, and after seeing a rerun of *Incense Shadows* in 1941, he gained interest in supporting Avshalomov's works more directly. Through Avshalomov and Jiang, Yuan also acquainted himself with Shen Zhibai and began exploring options for promoting operatic reform with Jiang and another Shanghai Underground Party operative, Jiang Wendao 江闻道. Yuan recalled, "as a result of discussions among the three of us, Jiang

Chunfang, Jiang Wendao and I believed that [Avshalomov and Shen Zhibai] had found the right path for theatrical-musical reform. So with the three of us (Jiang, Jiang, and myself) as the core, we established the 'Chinese Ballet and Music-Drama Association' [CBMDA] to oversee all the operations. We invited Shen Zhibai to be the consultant and used Avshalomov's work *The Great Wall* as the experimental performance" (Jiang et al. 1994, 461–462).

The Great Wall was Avshalomov's finest and most monumental work.[27] It extends more than two hours in length with a cast of more than fifty, accompanied by a large orchestra, advanced lighting techniques, and elaborate scenery, costumes, and makeup. Written in 1943–1944, the hybrid music drama exceeded the *The Soul of the Chin, Incense Shadows*, and the other staged works in melding Chinese and Western musical and theatrical elements. In *Kuan Yin*, Avshalomov had written a veritable opera, where the vocal music was central and the orchestra supported the voices. In the works of the 1930s, Avshalomov transformed the notion of Chinese opera toward a primarily symphonic-dance genre, where references to operatic gestures, costumes, myths, and melodies remained but the works were devocalized into pantomime ballets. *The Great Wall* further transfigured the synthetic mixture by adding back in limited vocal elements, but choral singing is prevalent and solo singing is limited to a single folk song ("Meng Jiang Nu"), while dialogue is generally declaimed in the manner of Chinese opera. Above all, the work is musically driven: the symphonic orchestra is ever-present in the manner of melodramatic film music, relying heavily on Chinese folk tunes as its musical basis and incorporating body movements of the Peking Opera (see figure 7.1).

To serve the purposes of the Underground Party, the plot adapted the Chinese myth of Meng Jiang Nü as an allegorical attack on the corrupt elements of the KMT. Here Meng Jiang sacrifices herself at the Great Wall in an act of

Figure 7.1 Stage tableau in *The Great Wall* ("Meng Jiang Nü" 1946, 33)

vengeance against Emperor Qin Shi Huang for the cruel death of her husband, Wan Xiliang. The 1945 cast included popular figures in the Shanghai artist world, including Cao Xueqin (Chao Hsueh Ching 曹雪芹), Cheng Shaoyu 程少余, and Qiu Yucheng 邱玉成. The magnitude of the production was unprecedented. Under the CBMDA, the Underground Party quietly helped organize the entire production as Avshalomov completed it. To raise funds, Yuan Likang solicited loans from banks, currency dealers, and friends and relatives, with some help from the treasury of the Underground Party. As the war ended, Avshalomov resumed correspondence with his son Jacob, and in a letter dated November 13, 1945, he described the process as the premiere approached:

> Now the "Great Wall" is scheduled for performances on the 26th of this month, but God knows what difficulties confront me on all sides—social, political (and personal) not to mention financial. . . . This entire experiment I am now trying . . . will not, I am afraid, be appreciated by the general public, and that means financial loss which may preclude further support from my group of Chinese. . . . During six months before the end of the war we rehearsed but had to keep quiet on account of Japs; twice had to dissolve and start again, and now I do not know whether I can bring it to a successful performance. (Avshalomov 2001, 202)

The CBMDA and Underground Party supporters, however, showed great solidarity and pride behind the work. Avshalomov had been sought because of his proactive role in musical reform and proven stature in the Shanghai musical world. The communists were eager to reach the masses through familiar forms that could be altered to carry anti-imperialist and antifeudalist messages. For this purpose, they also needed individuals capable of organizing a musical effort that would help rouse the spirit of national resistance. Ideally, they sought the combination of perceived "strength" via Western symphonic instrumentation and "familiarity" via national markers of folk and theatrical music. An ideologically committed, technically capable foreigner who could help promote the CCP cause both domestically and internationally would prove valuable.

To Avshalomov, his experiments were more "ideological" in terms of national aesthetics than party politics: developing an indigenous, modern musical language along the lines of European art music. Avshalomov was motivated by his own unique migratory experience, as well as his contact with various musical networks in China. And like Tcherepnin, he hoped that Chinese music could be developed based on its traditional forms with a strong but limited infusion of Western techniques and instrumentation. He feared both all-out Westernization and obstinate clinging to old forms. But his goal was always sublimation, striving to elevate the human experience through the highest art forms possible. He was, therefore, fundamentally driven by aesthetic concerns and artistic intention rather than by partisan or class politics.

Artistic preference is what aligned him more closely with reform advocates like Jiang Chunfang, Mei Lanfang, and Fu Lei than with leftists like Ren Guang, Nie Er, He Luting, and Tian Han 田汉, who focused on maximum, rapid, mass mobilization by direct appeal. To them, song melodies that were easily recognized, learned, and sung in unison without intricate textures, harmony, dissonance, and rhythm were the formula for national salvation. Avshalomov interacted with the leftists, who had been active both in the Soviet Friends Society and in music that was aimed at promoting national strengthening. Critical reviews published by Nie Er (of *Hutungs* and *Incense Shadows*) in 1935 and Tian Han (of *The Great Wall*) in 1947 expressed ambivalence toward Avshalomov's language, implicitly because its symphonic complexity challenged the ears of listeners with limited exposure to Western music. This, together with its romanticized thematic content (in terms of dramatic plot), would not adequately serve the needs of realism and mass appeal (see Nie 1935 and Tian 1947).

Fu Lei, however, had aligned himself with Avshalomov's reformist approach in the years following the Grand Chinese Evening. Fu eventually began associating with Shen Zhibai and Jiang Chunfang through Avshalomov. During the Japanese occupation in the 1940s, they met with other Shanghai artists at biweekly "tea meetings" to discuss the reform of China's arts. On the eve of *The Great Wall* premiere, Fu Lei, Shen Zhibai, Mei Lanfang, Zhou Xinfang 周信芳, and numerous other prominent figures coauthored a highly politicized endorsement of the work in Shanghai newspapers *Shidai Ribao*—which Jiang Chunfang ran for Soviet TASS—and *Dagongbao* on November 25, 1945.[28]

The CBMDA also promoted *The Great Wall* as "China's First Music Drama" in local magazines and other dailies.[29] The promotion assumed an aura of polemics and didactics. For example, the December 1, 1945, issue of *Shidai* (Epoch)[30] asked readers to consider a number of fundamental questions:

1. Can operatic performance practices that have already become highly formalized and representative of a lost life become elements for blending into a systematic organization to form a unified set of artistic works, giving them new life? . . .
2. Can old Chinese operatic gestures, with their special classical form and style, find an appropriate manner for being incorporated on stage with other theatrical arts, such as scenery, lighting, and colors, so that they form a synthesis? . . .
3. Is it possible to use modern instrumental music that is used throughout the globe on the opera stage and still maintain Chinese folk flavor,

spirit, and old operatic techniques when they are blended [on the modern stage]? . . .

. . . "The Great Wall" answers all these questions with certainty. . . . [It] fulfills this enormous task and in reality solves these problems. ("Zhongguo diyibu yinyueju" 1945, n.p.)

These queries, like the experiments of *The Great Wall* and other Avshalomov works, were clearly aimed at Shanghai's educated, urban, cosmopolitan elite. Despite its political themes of anticorruption and antioppression, the artistic intent of the production would have been viewed as exclusionary by left-wing artists seeking greater mass appeal.

The production achieved unexpected popularity during its opening week-long run, however, and Avshalomov found himself in the Shanghai spotlight. He and his productions had already made him an unlikely conduit for networking among Chinese artists. After the success of the 1945 *Great Wall* run and follow-up performances in March 1946,[31] he was a hero of the CBMDA, with plans to take the production to the United States and preparations already being made for his next production, the combined symphonic poem and opera-ballet *Phoenix* on a poem by Guo Moruo 郭沫若 for orchestra, dancers, tenor and alto soloists, and chorus.

As a demonstration of his success, an unusual capstone event took place on May 27, 1946. Avshalomov, back in his home on Linsen West Road (today's Huaihai Xilu), hosted a garden party at which a trial performance of *Phoenix* and other new compositions were given. According to Xu Buzeng, "this was the last public activity to be held by the [CBMDA]" (Xu 2006, 43). Among the many guests in attendance were Guo Moruo, Tian Han, Xia Yan, Mr. and Mrs. Yu Ling, Shen Zhibai, Wei Zhongle, Zhou Xinfang, Li Huifang, Cao Xueqin, Lü Junqiao, Li Lilian, Ouyang Shandao, Ma Sicong, and various Chinese and foreign members of the literary, music, and theater world. "It can be said that all the most noteworthy personalities were assembled in one place" (2006, 43).

Phoenix did not receive an official premiere, however. The success of Avshalomov's collaboration with the CBMDA came to a halt due to political vicissitudes arising from the end of the war. Already on December 27, 1945, Avshalomov penned a marathon letter to Jacob, which marked a turning point in his life and, unwittingly, heralded the end of his days in China.[32] According to the letter, the CBMDA ran a deficit of two million Chinese dollars (US$3,000) for *The Great Wall*, a failure that Avshalomov attributed to amateurish organization of the business side of the enterprise. Jiang, Yuan, and the Underground Party were no longer in a position to finance a tour to the United States without Chinese governmental support.

Instead, Avshalomov's fortunes shifted with the arrival of the American military temporarily stationed in Shanghai. The Chinese War Area Service Corps (WASC) had been set up early in the war to support Americans fighting against the Japanese in China. According to Avshalomov, the early *Great Wall* performances attracted top American military, including US Lt. Gen. A. C. Wedemeyer and his assistants, as well as WASC staff in Shanghai to support them. In addition, WASC and a conglomerate of Allied military administrators had taken over the SMO and were in need of guest conductors to maintain stability as they searched for a new permanent conductor in place of Mario Paci, who had been accused of collaborating with the Japanese. The director of the Shanghai WASC headquarters, Gen. Ernest K. Moy, was scouting possible transitional conductors, and he remembered Avshalomov from the Grand Chinese Evening in 1933, which he had attended. Moy invited Avshalomov to serve as one of the SMO conductors for several months. When Avshalomov's conducting earned praise at his first SMO concert, immediately on the heels of *The Great Wall* success, he found himself receiving invitations from the American military to take *The Great Wall* to the United States. This placed Avshalomov in a unique imbroglio: he had been supported by the communist-backed CBMDA and had taken Soviet citizenship during the war, and now the increasingly anticommunist Americans, who were allied with the KMT (which had been the allegorical target of *The Great Wall*), were pressing for his support.

The first half of 1946 signaled a steady shift away from the CBMDA. At the urging of General Wedemeyer, Chiang Kai-Shek (Jiang Jieshi) 蒋介石 and his wife Soong Mei-Ling (Song Meiling, Mme. Chiang Kai-Shek) 宋美龄 decided to back *The Great Wall* for a US tour, to be preceded by a series of performances in Nanjing and Shanghai in late 1946. Gen. J. L. Huang (Huang Renlin) 黄仁霖 was a personal attaché to the Chiangs and was in charge of supporting the American military during the Marshall Plan after World War II. Huang arranged for Avshalomov to meet Mme. Chiang in April 1946, after which it was decided that they would set up the Chinese Dance Drama Company (CDDC) to take over the production. The CDDC was formally established on June 9, 1946, just two weeks after the final CBMDA event, under the patronage of Mme. Chiang. Huang assumed personal responsibility for the project.

J. L. Huang became a great source of anxiety for Avshalomov over the coming year. The allegory of *The Great Wall* was not lost on Huang, and he exerted increasing personal pressure on Avshalomov to make changes to the script and to assemble a new, KMT-friendly cast and production team. He also requested Avshalomov to form an all-Chinese orchestra in Nanjing, which Avshalomov felt did not yet have the training to reach the standard of the SMO players he was accustomed to. Furthermore, Huang demanded that he renounce his Soviet citizenship and assume Chinese citizenship for purposes of public façade and so he could place Avshalomov firmly under his control. At the same time, Avshalomov felt the resentment and accusations from his previous backers as the Civil War intensified and CCP made gains. The Nanjing-Shanghai performances of November-December 1946 under the CDDC were hailed as a great success, but by early 1947 the US tour was canceled and Avshalomov indicated that he was "positively in fear of remaining here" (Avshalomov 2001, 244). Polarized between the CBMDA and CDDC, he took the opportunity in October 1947 to go to the United States, ostensibly to solicit *Great Wall* sponsorship there. Within two years, however, KMT forces fled to Taiwan. As the United States and China became estranged for the next two decades, so too did Avshalomov lose touch with his many Chinese counterparts.

Tcherepnin and Avshalomov: Shanghai Shadow Play

The discussion of Tcherepnin and Avshalomov places their activities within the immediate historical context of China, but set against the backdrop of their Russian origins: both engaged China due to the epochal change of the Russian Revolution; both contributed to China's musical modernization as part of their own migratory journeys; both took leave of China under emotional stress but experienced cathartic releases as they moved on. Their musical agency in China was defined by the personal and professional relationships they engaged in. Tcherepnin enjoyed celebrity status throughout his short stays in China, but faced the hardships of war, divorce, and financial self-reliance after leaving in 1937. Once he surmounted those difficulties, he and Ming found great happiness with their new family after they secured a stable lifestyle in the United States after 1948.

Avshalomov faced a different post-China future. In early 1947, he wrote—rhetorically—to Jacob, "at least in the US I could starve in peace" (2001, 244). The reality for his final years in New York was not far from that prophecy. Avshalomov's move from China at first appeared a quiet, ephemeral catharsis, an escape to obscurity without resolving personal or professional conflicts. When Russians fled to China for refuge, Avshalomov moved there for opportunity, out of choice because he felt at ease among its mixed communities. Such ease made him perhaps more genuinely "Eurasian" than was Tcherepnin, who exhibited that identity more in ideal than in practice. The uncertain identity led Avshalomov to straddle sometimes tense borders. Professionally, he became entangled in party factionalism as few other Shanghai Russians could imagine and fled China as numerous White Russians had fled the Bolsheviks. The professional ties he had cultivated over decades were largely dissolved. Jiang Chunfang, Shen Zhibai, and the many CBMDA colleagues appear to have forgiven, or at least understood,

Avshalomov's shifts in allegiances. In the new PRC, Avshalomov was invited back to help establish music institutions. Only when Aaron's son Jacob returned to China for concerts commemorating Aaron's work in the 1980s, however, did a symbolic reconciliation take place, posthumously.

Avshalomov's closest personal Shanghai ties were never mended. In contrast to Tcherepnin's status as "musical master," Avshalomov was a lifelong musical aspirant, seeking to establish a higher place for himself from the ground up. His experimental compositions and collaborations required boundless mental and physical exertion. As a result, his marital and family relations often took second place to professional endeavors, and yet he was in constant need of female companionship. Avshalomov did not maintain cordial relations with his first wife after their separation. For a time, Esther forbade contact between Aaron and Jacob until Jacob was able to join his father in Shanghai as an adult. When Aaron planned to marry Tatiana, he unilaterally initiated divorce proceedings with Esther in the Chinese court in 1938 after she and Jacob had already moved to the United States. The divorce was granted, and Aaron married Tatiana shortly thereafter. A scandal ensued in 1939, however, when it was discovered that Esther had attempted revenge. Aaron and Tatiana had hoped to visit the United States in the 1930s, and Esther tried to have their visa applications denied. As covered in the Russian and English press, through "voluminous correspondence" with the US Consulate, Esther challenged the validity of the Chinese divorce and accused Avshalomov of bigamy ("Divorce Challenged" 1939, 430). A court case ensued, and while the new marriage held, Aaron did not gain a visa to the United States until 1947.

Before the scandal subsided, Aaron was already finding new interest in Indira Devi, with whom he collaborated on the *Indian Dances* and *Buddha and the 5 Planetary Deities*. Devi was in fact the Russian Evgeniya (Eugenia) Peterson, from the area of modern Latvia, who was married to a Czech diplomat named Jan Strakaty (Goldberg 2015). She assumed the name Indira Devi after moving to India from Europe. Devi assisted with Avshalomov's other 1940 productions and was listed as an "Honorary Secretary" for the CBMDA in the 1945 performances. Avshalomov became enchanted with Devi, and the two maintained an extramarital affair throughout the war. The temporary breakups and reconciliations caused tremendous hardship for Aaron's second wife Tatiana, which also displeased Jacob. Devi was not committed to Avshalomov, however, and she tried to leave for India at one point, only to return to Shanghai. She then moved to Los Angeles, and according to Goldberg, part of Avshalomov's impetus for going to the United States was to follow her (2015, 151). Is it possible that Avshalomov's quagmire in 1946–1947 involved both political and romantic trappings? He left Tatiana in Shanghai in 1947, though he professed hopes of bringing her to the United States later.

Once in the United States, however, Avshalomov joined Devi in Los Angeles, and she supported him financially for a time. He expressed deeply conflicted feelings toward Tatiana and Devi, as Tcherepnin had experienced a decade earlier. Around the time of Avshalomov's Shanghai departure, a letter was sent to the US Consulate there accusing Devi of being a Soviet spy. Devi was resolutely defended by American personnel who had known her in Shanghai, and some suspected the letter had been sent by a spiteful Tatiana (2015, 161–162). Though unsubstantiated, the accusation created prolonged difficulties for Devi, given the anticommunist atmosphere in the United States. Avshalomov and Devi parted ways not long after. Tatiana did not join him in the United States, though they never divorced. Avshalomov subsequently settled in New York City and found new companionship with Maria Reeves until his death from cancer in 1965.

From this standpoint, the paths of Avshalomov and Tcherepnin appear oblique. During the mid-1930s they both lived in Shanghai (and for a time, later, in New York). There is, surprisingly, no mention in any of the literature that they ever met or were acquainted with each other. The two eminent Russian composers had many mutual contacts, such as Shen Zhibai, Mei Lanfang, Paci and the SMO, Aksakov and the Russian press, Xian Xinghai, He Luting, and A. Strok. Not being of conservatory stock, Avshalomov had a limited connection to the National Conservatory, though he at least engaged in guest lectures there. There is no indication that Xiao Youmei or the Russian faculty took a significant interest in Avshalomov. The scope of his experimental compositions and performances dwarfs that of Tcherepnin within the Shanghai sphere. But Tcherepnin's Russian master lineage, international prestige, and keyboard virtuosity placed him in a class of the "honorary" elite, which Avshalomov could only aspire to. Avshalomov hoped, in vain, that his Chinese experiments would elevate him to new heights of opportunity in the United States. But his Shanghai accomplishments had come over years of scrambling to build a reputation from nothing, forging local collaborative networks in spite of his lack of international recognition. Tcherepnin, on the other hand, was handed exclusive opportunities virtually off the boat.

Ultimately, the lives of both composers must be considered within the historical epoch of Russia, China, and the West. Both individuals were products of political change in Russia, whose own musical, cultural, and political modernity had been largely shaped by an agonistic dependence upon Europe. Both men straddled identity borders between East and West, at once encouraging the Chinese musical community to find a distinctively national path to modernity, even as they created their own experimental models for this purpose and for personal opportunity. Both émigré composers carried out valuable work in China while experiencing joys and challenges in their private lives. And in China, both composers received posthumous "revivals" beginning in the 1980s, after the first turbulent decades of the PRC had subsided. Tcherepnin had regularly been regarded as the foremost foreign influence on Chinese musicians. Numerous articles, often repeating erroneous information, testify to the respect that his name garners among conservatory-trained musicians even today. Recognition of Avshalomov's contribution to modern Chinese music development has been more recent. Whereas Tcherepnin served as a model for modern Chinese piano compositions as a "Eurasian" Russian, Avshalomov furthered China's symphonic-theatrical reform as a localized non-Chinese.

The chapters on Tcherepnin and Avshalomov attempt to establish the vast web of links in time, space, and culture that were formed by the unique diasporic experience of both composers in China. Upon leaving, Tcherepnin operated atop the Western classical music world, and recent studies indicate that a strong sense of Russianness was revived in him later in life. His time in Asia was brief, but his union with Ming ensured that he kept one eye on China during his final decades in the United States and Paris. Avshalomov seems not to have been as strongly driven by Russian nationalist feeling. Rather, he accepted and worked with his Russianness as a natural part of his identity. Musically, Avshalomov remained dedicated to his own brand of Chinese music to the end. Innately, both composers understood from their own heritage the challenges of finding one's own identity when existing on the margins of the European-based global music order. Likewise, their contributions could never be fully accepted as coming from "within" Chinese culture, but there is recognition in China that they were something more than "outsiders." Avshalomov and Tcherepnin navigated the border of Chinese and international networks more naturally and successfully than most other foreigners of the interwar period. Yet they were always aware that Chinese musicians would ultimately be the ones to effectuate China's new musical direction.

EPILOGUE

WHEN Tcherepnin visited Shanghai in 1934, Shanghailanders responded with a cartoon titled "Shanghai the Melodious" (1934) that highlighted the sonic multi-plicity of the city. Such a unique feature of Shanghai's soundscape was also aptly described by Andrew Jones' monograph *Yellow Music* (2001). Yet Russian émigré musicians that were crucial actors of such a soundscape have been mostly over-looked in studies on Russian emigration (Raeff 1990; Raymond and Jones 2000; and Ristaino 2000, 2001), music in Shanghai (Jones 2001), and contemporary Chinese music, including Liu Ching-Chih's *A Critical History of New Music in China* (2010). Without the many Russian and later Jewish émigré musicians in Shanghai, the city's musical scene would have been very different. These refu-gee musicians worked as restaurant entertainers, playing in jazz bands and pop music orchestras of recording companies and movie theaters. The best trained were employed by the city's cultural icon, the Municipal Orchestra, as tempo-rary and permanent players, whereas the lesser ones were taken on by an array of symphony orchestras and brass bands, adapting to various forms of local music and anticipating the sonic hybridity of China's global soundscape today.

Fast-forwarding to the twenty-first century, not only in Shanghai but in other Chinese cities, Western classical music is flourishing. Taking Shanghai as an example, a recent study registered the following statistics: among the 227 per-forming events from December 25, 2014, to January 4, 2015, there were at least 41 New Year's concerts with more than sixty thousand estimated attendees (Yang 2015). Even symphony orchestras of the West are now turning to China to invig-orate the stagnant institution. For instance, the Philadelphia Orchestra launched its China Residency program in 2013. Its past tour of Asia and China, accom-panied by the many activities connected, was deemed a major success ("The Philadelphia Orchestra's 2014 Tour" 2015).[1] The New York Philharmonic, too, launched a four-year Shanghai Orchestra Academy and Residency Partnership program with the Shanghai Conservatory of Music in 2014 ("Shanghai Orchestra Academy" 2015).

In fact, China's prosperous Western music scene has attracted international attention since the beginning of the twenty-first century. In October 2005, for example, what was described as "one of the most significant East-West cultural exchanges of our time," Beijing's Poly Theatre featured Nuremberg Opera's production of Richard Wagner's *Der Ring des Nibelungen* (Morrison 2005, 23). While the event was deemed unprecedented, Western reporters and Chinese concertgoers were probably not aware that Western music in China had a much longer history,[2] and Western operas were already a part of Shanghai's soundscape in the 1930s, as discussed in chapter 2. The Shanghai Opera management's 1937 lament of lacking a proper operatic venue was answered three-quarters of a century later. China is now proud to present its world-class operatic facilities even though performances of Western operatic works are far from frequent. Shanghai is the city that has led the trend with the opening of its Shanghai Grand Theatre in 1998.[3] Beijing's National Center for Performing Arts, opened in 2007, has an opera hall that can accommodate an audience of over two thousand. The Guangzhou Opera House in southern China, opened in 2010, is stunning in design and acoustics. It was also a dream come true for the Iraqi-born British architect Zaha Hadid, whose earlier competition-winning design for the Cardiff Bay Opera House at last found materialization in China.[4] In fact, the flourishing of performance halls in China is not limited to major cities like Beijing and Shanghai but can also be found in secondary cities such as Dalian and Wuhan. While these emerging venues testify to the prosperous Western musical scene in China's cultural landscape, we would like to emphasize that they have their roots in cosmopolitan Shanghai's musical scene that was greatly enlivened by Russian émigrés.

Human migration is due to many factors, both voluntary and involuntary, and the impact of migration can be profound on both the immigrants and the hosting country. The Russian emigration to Shanghai is a case in point. These émigrés struggled to survive in an alien land such as Shanghai; they tried to make the best of their situations, forming self-help and professional organizations to help each other; they gradually built a community of their own, establishing their own churches and schools to promote Russian cultural heritage among their youth and form a network generally regarded as a "diaspora." The characteristics and features of this community have been examined in chapter 1 and the unfair treatment they received is covered in chapter 3.

Unlike other diasporas in which the practice of music from home functioned to foster solidarity among its members, the role of music in Shanghai's Russian community was a complex one, as was discussed in chapter 2. Émigrés formed an array of literary and art societies to unite like-minded individuals, and music activities were commonly deployed to build cohesion within each of the groups. But because some of these groups were nationalistic in character and others cosmopolitan, different interactions with Shanghai's different communities were evident. Contrary to the general understanding of the features of diaspora suggested by Cohen (1997), Slobin (1992), and Zelensky (2009), music let Shanghai's Russian émigrés reach out rather than shrink back. For example, Russian choirs and the Russian opera, as testified by many primary source accounts, did not just serve the Russian community but were also enjoyed by audiences of the international and Chinese communities. In fact, a few of these performances even afforded Chinese musicians performing opportunities that helped China nurture its first generation of highly successful Western music practitioners, some of whom have since become renowned musical figures.

That the Shanghai Russian community transcended diaspora boundaries was evident in its impact on the Shanghai Municipal Orchestra (SMO), as discussed in chapters 3 and 4. Accounting for more than 50 percent of the SMO's players, Russian musicians were also frequently featured as soloists in the orchestra's regular concerts as well as in its special Russian concerts. These musicians were also crucial in large-scale choral concerts deployed by SMO director Mario Paci to bring Shanghai's different musical communities together.

Most important of all, it is the Russian pedagogues affiliated with the National Conservatory that have left an indelible mark on Chinese musical development. They were responsible for producing the first generation of renowned Chinese performers who went on to become leading musical figures of China in the second half of the twentieth century, which is the focus of chapter 5. In fact, Russians émigrés in the 1930s and 1940s were aware of Russian musicians' success at the National Conservatory. They compared themselves to the Italian musicians working in Saint Petersburg during the late eighteenth and early nineteenth centuries; the Italian musicians shaped the development of Russian music while in Russia, whereas the musicians in China shaped Russian music from abroad (Aksakov 1933, 4). The pride that many Russians took in teaching at the National Conservatory can also be detected in the memoirs of Russians who lived in Shanghai, although on occasions they exaggerated their importance.[5]

China's Western-inclined trajectory in music development would probably have happened irrespective of whether it employed Russian pedagogues or not. The National Conservatory was founded to answer to the musical and cultural changes of the country at the time, and it did not compete with rival private institutions in terms of funding and staffing. While the programs of both the National Conservatory and Russian conservatories were based on German models, Russian pedagogues undoubtedly brought the rigorous professional standards of leading conservatories in the West to their work and their students in Shanghai. This set a solid foundation for Western music development in the

People's Republic of China (PRC) and other Chinese diaspora such as Hong Kong and Taiwan, to where some of these early conservatory graduates moved after the founding of the PRC in 1949. For instance, the singer Hu Ren, who was Shushlin's student and was featured as soloist in a number of SMO's choral concerts, emigrated to Hong Kong and founded the Hong Kong Music Institute in the 1950s. This institute helped to train many Hong Kong musicians before the colony's first government-funded conservatory, the Hong Kong Academy for Performing Arts, was established in 1984.[6]

Tracing the success of Russian pedagogues' students in chapter 5 led us to a discussion about diaspora being a source of cultural transformation, be it on its host community or on its own. While the development of Western music in China exemplifies the former, the experiences and compositions of the two Russian émigré composers, Alexander Tcherepnin and Aaron Avshalomov, the focus of chapters 6 and 7, are an example of the impact of cultural encounter on creativity. These two composers' synthesizing Chinese elements into their musical language following their contacts with Chinese culture were not only compositional innovations, but also emotional catharses to negotiate personal experiences and émigré identities, thus refuting the notion of "chinoiserie." Their endeavors were a harbinger of Chinese new music and intercultural music that became an important feature of music in the late twentieth century and twenty-first century.

In studies of diaspora, particularly in its cultural manifestation, identity is often a central issue, as testified by the articles in *Russian Émigré Culture* (2013) (see for example chapters by Dubinets, Fortunova, Leveillé, Radecke) as well as in other studies mentioned in this volume's introduction (see for example Zelensky 2009; Wong 2004; and Zheng 2010). Even though identity is a theme that recurs in our volume, our research data points out that identity is intricate, whether it refers to the individual or to the manifested cultural objects, let alone the notion of identification, the complexities of which have been explained by Stuart Hall in great length (1996, 2–4). In fact, layers of identities are embedded in different works of different émigré composers. The Chinese-influenced works of a cosmopolitan composer like Tcherepnin and of a Chinese-inclined composer like Avshalomov raise questions about the theoretical usefulness of existing discourse on diaspora and identity. Even the cosmopolitan works of a diaspora-inclined composer such as Aksakov illustrate the elusiveness of Russian diaspora identity. While there might have been a perceived "Russian cultural identity" in reality or in imagination, cultural encounters inevitably lead to individuals' new hybrid identity or identities as reflected in their cultural manifestations.

As Nicholas Cook has pointed out, "[a]ll encounters, musical or otherwise, are conditioned by socioeconomic context, by history, by ideology" (2012, 193).

The different encounters among the Russian network and the international and Chinese ones in interwar Shanghai were no exceptions. How the Russian émigrés ended up in Shanghai; how Shanghai, the semicolonial city in China, became the port of last resort for these émigrés as well as for an array of Shanghailanders from different origins; how the various communities in Shanghai benefited from the presence of a large number of Russian musicians as well as the rich Russian musical tradition; how the Russian pedagogues found livelihood and satisfaction in performing and teaching music for their own community as well as beyond; how cultural encounters enriched the compositional subject matters and musical language of émigré composers such as Tcherepnin and Avshalomov; and, most of all, how all these played a part in Chinese musical development were all consequences of socioeconomic-historic conditioning. All this happened, seemingly, beyond the control of any single individual. But it is after all many different individuals' endeavors that made up the whole picture. The Russian community's "musicking" in interwar Shanghai—to borrow a term coined by Christopher Small (1998) to refer to music as an act of performing, participating, and listening—resulted in what is best described in Slobin's words, "the musical interplay—the cultural counterpoint between individual, community, small group, state, and industry" (1992, 4).

First, the goal of our volume is to reveal different forms of musicking in interwar Shanghai as a contact zone registering transnational sociocultural relations, aesthetics, and ideology. Such an aspiration is in tune with "relational musicology" as advocated by Georgina Born (2010) and Nicholas Cook (2012). "Relational musicology" as a disciplinary practice comes in many forms, including cross-cultural music analysis as proposed by Born and Cook. Our book's objective to unravel otherwise overlooked connections between the Russian community and other communities not only articulates the contributions made by the Russian émigrés, but also challenges some of the well-established conceptions about diaspora. We would like to propose that such an approach toward the study of emigration should appear as imperative in sight of what's going on around us: Britain voting to leave the European Union, the US president issuing an executive order to build a wall along the US-Mexican border to prevent illegal immigration and the overall skepticism toward immigrants. Our research points out the benefit of emigration with many examples. Shanghai's prosperity during the interwar period was in part due to its open-door policy to immigrants, and Russian émigrés' roles in fostering the city's cultural landscape should be better remembered.

Second, just as "relational musicology" advocates "a fully relational and reflexive, social and material conception of all musics" (Cook 2012, 198) and the need for musicology to "addresses different orders of the social in music and their complex interrelations" (Born 2010, 235), our volume is not bound by music as text, but instead we let musical materiality speak for itself as well as for the actors it represents. For instance, it is through different Russian musical and artistic organizations and societies that the role of music in the diaspora is revealed. Then it is through the musicians' interactions with the SMO that the émigré experience is further explored. In addition, the émigré musicians' triumphs are demonstrated through the SMO's Russian concerts showcasing them as soloists and through their long-lasting contribution made by their teaching of Chinese students at the National Conservatory. Only the last two chapters turn to musical text. Through the intercultural works of the Russian émigré composers Tcherepnin and Avshalomov, issues of musical and cultural identity are addressed in the context of the composers' social and cultural networks.

Third, this volume contributes to "relational musicology" in the sense that it challenges idealistic dichotomies that often mark such a notion, namely East versus West, local versus global, diasporic or nationalistic versus cosmopolitan, victim versus victor, we versus the others, and last but not least serious music versus popular music, etc. As the musical scene in Shanghai showed, East and West, be that sonically and culturally, were more connected than we nowadays assume. This is indicated by many features like the Russian New Year ball, a fashionable event celebrated beyond the Russian community, or how Peking Opera star Mei Lanfang was open-minded enough to try out new artistic forms with Avshalomov, and many others.

Last, we would like to point out that this volume is the embodiment of "relational musicology" in itself, adopting a collaborative mode of investigation into a subject that demands interdisciplinarity at many different levels of the research. If the study had been taken up by a Russian historian alone, the study would most likely have focused on the diaspora only. Likewise, a musicologist would have likely focused only on the intercultural works of Tcherepnin and Avshalomov. In the same vein, a Chinese music specialist would have missed out on the rich Russian sources altogether. The triauthorship thus brings together different fields of expertise, language skills, methodologies, and perspectives that would not have been possible had the volume been taken up by a single author. The exchange of ideas, the cross-reading of chapters, the different attempts to unify stylistic matters, though quite challenging at times, were a unique but rewarding experience that has also had an impact on each of us. As our research journey on this fascinating topic is coming to an end with this epilogue, we propose that "relational musicology" is not only "relational" but should also be "collaborative" and "networked," which we hope will also have an impact on Russian and Chinese music historiography in the twenty-first century.

Richard Taruskin has pointed out that the history as well as the historiography of Russian music is entwined with nationalism and politics.[7] The Chinese-Russian conductor-scholar Tszo Chzhenguan has also remarked that Russian émigré musicians in China have long been an unwelcome subject in the former Soviet Union due to government's ideology of treating émigrés as traitors (2011, 55). Even though interest in émigré culture has been on the rise after the fall of the Soviet Union, our volume is groundbreaking in the sense that it is the first to explore such a subject matter in English-language literature.

On the Chinese side, politics has been and still is entwined with the country's musical development and music discourse.[8] The founding of the PRC and the coming to power of the Chinese communist regime brought an end to the Shanghai Russian diaspora as émigrés were driven out of the country. Sino-Russian relations continued, but in a different form. Seeing the Soviet Union as the future of the PRC, the new nation's development in the first decade closely followed Soviet models. Music was no exception. In the 1950s, a team of Soviet experts was brought in to teach at the newly founded Central Conservatory and also at the National Conservatory, which had its name changed to the Shanghai Conservatory. Likewise, the best of the country's music students were sent to study at Soviet conservatories. The Soviet music education system, its teaching materials, pedagogical methods, and music aesthetics were all transplanted to the PRC, wholeheartedly incorporated into the Chinese music education system by Chinese musicians. The connection of the two country's musical practices was further strengthened by numerous cultural exchanges at the time, with Soviet musicians and music groups visiting and performing in the PRC and vice versa. Such a trend continued until the two nations' diplomatic relations soured in the early 1960s.[9]

Even though Russian/Soviet musicians of these two phases of Sino-Russian relations have since died, their legacy continues through their students and the students of these students. In 2009, the first ever conference on Sino-Russian musical exchange was held at Harbin Normal University to mark the sixtieth anniversary of Sino-Russian diplomatic relations. It attracted more than a hundred participants, including delegates from Russia, students of Soviet pedagogues, and scholars of Russian music and Sino-Russian musical studies. The conference papers were published two years later (Tao 2011). Both the conference and the proceeding were not only unprecedented, but they were also a watershed in PRC history. The state's permission for musicians to publicly reflect on the country's indebtedness to the Soviet Union and Russia was a goodwill gesture despite the two nations' political and ideological differences in the twenty-first century.

For the older generation of Chinese musicians, recognizing the contributions of the Russian/Soviet pedagogues, like the rehabilitation of musicians whose reputations were denigrated during the Cultural Revolution, was of a healing nature. As a matter of fact, this group of musicians, rigorously trained by foreign musicians that were dubbed "foreign devils" at the time, were targeted victims of political persecution. The Shanghai Conservatory was the most severely affected among all music institutions due to its concentration of "cosmopolitan" professors, who had received systematic training from Westerners or in the West, as opposed to the "populist" camp of musicians,[10] who were largely self-taught. Many were imprisoned or sent to labor camps, and more than a handful committed suicide.[11]

Precisely because of such close ties between the PRC and the Soviet Union in the 1950s, it is not a surprise that the subject of Russian émigré musicians in Shanghai was taboo in the PRC for a long time. Due to strict state control and widespread communist ideology, foreign musical influence was considered a sensitive topic prior to 1980. At the time, even important Chinese musical figures were left out in Chinese music historiography (Huang 2005, 138), so it is not a surprise that Russian émigré musicians in Shanghai suffered the same fate.[12] Only after the 1980s did commemorative articles about these Russian teachers begin to appear. The burgeoning of research and the affirmation of their contributions are, however, evident in recent publications. For example, both Boris Zakharov and Vladimir Shushlin were each mentioned in more than a hundred articles published between 2013 and 2016 on Chinese pianism, Chinese vocal performance, the Shanghai Conservatory, contemporary Chinese music, and the lives of various Chinese musicians and composers.[13]

In 2014, a photo exhibit titled "Russians in Shanghai: 1930's" was held in Shanghai to mark Russian president Vladimir Putin's visit (Mihailova 2014). The exhibit was held at the Cathedral of the Mother of God, an extant Russian orthodox church located in the former French Concession built in the 1930s with donation from émigrés,[14] one of the few physical traces of the Russian presence in Shanghai. In 2017, the centenary year of the Russian Revolution, the global scholarly community has taken interests in its impact, as evident in conferences that address its specters as well as the impact of migration on development of new communities and identities and the circulation of ideas, skills, and goods.[15] It so happens that our volume makes a timely contribution to this paradigm shift in Russian studies, as we provide new insights into an otherwise overlooked aspect of Russian migration and its impact on the global musical scene outside the West. After all, migration is about breaking old networks and creating new ones. As demonstrated by the Russian emigration in Shanghai during the interwar period, music was and is a powerful tool for connectivity. Indeed, one of the networks the Russian émigré musicians established was intricately connected to what the National Conservatory in Shanghai aspired to back then and what most Chinese still hope for today: *gen shijie jiegui*, meaning to be connected to the rest of the world, be it through music or other means.

NOTES

Introduction

1. There is a large body of literature on Shanghai's cultural scene in the 1930s. See for instance Lee (1999), Shi (2001), Jones (2001), Stock (2002), Enomoto (2003), and Zarrow (2006).

2. For further discussion on the development of Chinese "xin yinyue," see for instance Melvin and Cai (2004), Li (2010), and Liu Ching-Chih (2010). The term "xin yinyue" (new music) can be confusing, as it is used by some Chinese scholars to refer to contemporary music in China. For example, Qian's monograph *Zhongguo xin yinyue* (2005) is entirely devoted to contemporary music composed by Chinese composers after the 1980s.

3. Yang would like to thank Simo Mikkonen for drawing her attention to this newspaper report as well as providing a summary of its contents.

4. See for example Berkowitz (1982), Scott (2000), and Jackson and Oliver (2003).

5. The three elements of a network—nodes, links, and mesh—can easily be mapped to the different facets of an investigation, the mesh referring to the overall structure, the nodes the different points or facets, and links the crossings that connect the nodes (Loon 2006, 307).

6. For instance, a musical trade imbalance between the core and periphery nations is revealed through using a network analysis (Moon, Barnett, and Yon 2010). Cheung's study of Chinese musical modernity in Shanghai (2012) uses the concept of network to explore the divide and connections between two antagonistic music institutions in Shanghai's Chinese community, the National Conservatory and the Great Unity (Chinese Music Reform Club).

7. Actor Network Theory (ANT) is better known as a method than a theory apt for exploring the heterogeneous chain of associations connected to human, nonhuman, or collective actors that are multidimensional as well as entangled. Originating in the study of science and technology, ANT is found in the works of Bruno Latour, Michel Callon, John Law, and others. According to Latour, the "actor" or "actant" in ANT is a "semiotic definition" in that it "can literally be anything provided it is granted to be the source of an action" (Latour 1996, 373). That is, human actions can be seen through objects, which are "agents," so to speak, and the notion of "agency," of "materiality," is one of the major contributions of ANT. Latour also emphasizes the importance of treating the actor/actant as "infinitely pliable, heterogeneous, that they are free associationists, know no differences of scale, that there is no inertia, no order, that they build their own temporality" (Latour 1996, 374). For studies on ANT, see

for instance Mol and Law (1994), Latour (2005), Shiga (2007), Mützel (2009), Mol (2010), and Piekut (2014).

8. For instance, both Western popular music and jazz were introduced to Shanghai during the interwar period. See Jones (2001).

9. The other ports opened were Guangzhou (Canton), Xiamen (Amoy), Fuzhou (Foochow), and Ningbo (Ningpo) (Bard 2009, 45).

10. *All About Shanghai and Environs* provided a chronology and history of early Shanghai up until 1934 in the last part of the volume (203–211).

11. For further discussion on the opportunities generated by Shanghai's treaty port status, see Bickers and Henriot (2000), which is devoted to exploring the development of new communities in East Asia, including Shanghai, as a result of imperialism and colonialism.

12. See Yang (2017).

13. At the time, Finland was an autonomous part of the Russian Empire, with its own currency, administration, and border control. Finland declared independence in December 1917.

14. For more information on the musical life in Harbin, see Liu Yinyin and Liu Xueqing (2002).

15. The volume has a broad scope, interpreting Sino-Russian musical relations to encompass anything that has to do with the two nations musically. The contents of the volume largely focus on the post-1949 period of Sino-Russian relations.

16. Bian's article (2011) repeats his earlier article on Avshalomov. Wang Yanli's (2011) is also an exact repetition of her study on the SMO and its Russian elements to be mentioned in a later part of this volume. Luo Qin's (2011) article about the application of his concept of diaspora to the Russian émigrés in Shanghai repeats the ideas in his 2010 article. Zuo Zhenguan is known as Tszo Chzhenguan in Russian transliteration. Zuo is a Chinese-Russian musician whose mother is Russian and who emigrated to the former USSR with her mother during China's Cultural Revolution. He is the concertmaster of the Russian Philharmonic and has published a volume on Russian musicians in Shanghai (2014).

17. That was particularly the case when the number of Soviet émigrés increased in the 1930s.

18. Just browsing through the list of some of the Russian organizations already established in 1926 would provide glimpses of the complexity of the Russian community, namely the Union of Russian Army and Navy Men, the Russian Orthodox Confraternity, Far Eastern Cossacks Group, the Union of Russian Cossacks, Uralo-Siberian Labor Association. These were some of the organizations listed in the formation of the Union Russian Association in 1926, which was probably an early form of the Russian Emigrants Committee. See Shanghai Municipal Archive (SMA), U1-3-2859, 2, and Wang (1993, 433–490) for further discussions on these organizations.

19. The Chinese scholar Luo Qin 洛秦 (2010, 2011) has used the notion of diaspora to interpret the musical phenomenon of the Russian musicians in Shanghai, though neither the theory nor the evidence have been adequately explained.

Chapter 1: Between Limbo and a Haven

1. In the summer of 1929, Chinese warlord Zhang Xueliang 张学良 seized control of the Manchurian Chinese Eastern Railway from the Soviet Union. Soviet military intervention quickly restored control back to the Soviets. This, however, underlined the precarious position of Harbin, which stood in a key junction of the railway.

2. The event was publicized with a sizable picture featuring Czechoslovak folk costumes and folklore.

3. Viktor Serbsky was one of the pen names of the chief editor Lev Arnoldov.

4. This was a separate afternoon issue of *Shanghai Zaria*.

5. For example, the artists Baturina and Velikanov, a couple, went to Soviet Russia in 1935. A. Siziakova and E. Suvorin were also reported to be moving to Soviet Russia to serve in the Kiev Opera and Operetta ("Teatralnaia Khronika" 1935; "Khudozhestvennaia Khronika" 1935).

6. Severny was one of the backbones of Shanghai's artistic community, an author who—despite his writings—yearned to return to the Soviet Union in the 1940s. His wife was against it, apparently, and they returned only in 1954, after Stalin's death. He was not persecuted, and after some years he managed to move close to Moscow, if not into the metropolis itself.

Chapter 2: Networking the Diaspora

1. Melodeclamation was the combination of poetry and music. Performers were not typically singers, but specialized in reciting poetry and, at least in Shanghai, were often poets themselves.

2. This was the yearbook of Russian artistic organization "Vostok," later known as "Shatior."

3. The other major Russian artistic organizations in the 1930s were called Monday, Tuesday, and Friday, for the same reason. The Jewish artistic association convened on Thursdays and was considered by many to be a Russian association as well. Several ethnic Russians performed at the Jewish Club and were members of the association.

4. Members included Vladimir Shushlin (opera artist working at the conservatory) and Zinaida Pribytkova (theater director, also teaching piano at the conservatory), Eduard Elirov (ballet director), Valentil Val (actor), V. V. Panova-Rikhter (actor and dancer), P. A. Diakov, and many others.

5. Khisamutdinov refers to the relocation to Cafe Renaissance in 1937, but advertisements suggest that KhLAM was convening at Cafe Renaissance already in autumn 1935 (Khisamutdinov 2010, 220). Cafe Renaissance was in the French quarter. On Wednesdays, artists were said to spend a whole day there, starting with lunch at noon, happy tea at 5 p.m., and a modern dinner at 8 p.m. (Advertisement 1935a).

6. Most likely, grotesque was used as shorthand to refer to absurd performances bordering on fantastic, as well as the use of imaginative, sometimes ugly human and animal forms.

7. Several Russian newspapers reported comings and goings of artists during the 1920s and 1930s. Sometimes Shanghai Russians would take fixed contracts of some months in places like Manila or Singapore, and sometimes they would go for tours of several months throughout Asia. Particularly active as organizer of Russian tours was impresario A. Carpi.

8. The Russian Social Union was an important Russian society involved in charity, cultural and social work involving many Shanghai Russians.

9. The exact date of establishment could not be ascertained. Most likely it was established in 1931, since the first events organized by the society took place early in 1932.

10. The choir circle went unnamed, at least in the Russian media. It was simply referred to as an amateur choir circle led by Mashin.

11. An advertisement of the concert had Mashin's name printed in all capital letters (Advertisement 1929).

12. Shushlin eventually returned to the Soviet Union from Shanghai in 1956 and taught at the Moscow Conservatory until 1974. He passed away in 1978. Victor Chernomortsev and Nikolay Gutorovich both mention having Shushlin as their vocal teacher at the Moscow Conservatory in the mid-1960s (Baosia Liu 2010, 381–382).

13. The exact founding year of the Russian Operetta is difficult to ascertain. It moved back and forth between Harbin and Shanghai until the 1934–1935 season, when the group made Shanghai its permanent home. Key figures of the Russian Operetta were Zinaida Bittner and Lev Rozen.

14. Sze Yi-Kwei (1915–1994) made his successful US debut in 1947, sang in the best opera houses around the world, and taught at Eastman School of Music as a professor. Marie Wong (occasionally spelled Waung), however, seems to have disappeared in the 1940s, leaving few traces, although her debut received more attention than Sze's and she was predicted to have a bright future in the field of opera.

Chapter 3: An Imperfect Musical Haven

1. Even though the Chinese scholar Wang Yanli (2010) has published a study on Russian musicians' relationship with the SMO, Wang seems to have overlooked the musicians' contracts at the SMA.

2. This quote originated from Japanese musicologist Hisao Tanabe's memoir (1970, 247), which was quoted in Enomoto (2009, 102–103).

3. For studies on the SMO, See Han (1995), Bickers (2001), Enomoto (2009), Wang Yanli (2010, 2012), Tang (2014), and Pang (2015).

4. The member also stated, "We should like to be able to tell people everywhere that it does not matter what music is brought out in Paris, or Vienna, or London, or wherever it may be, if we cannot afford to go home and hear that music we can get it here in our midst. That is a very great thing to be able to say considering the disabilities of life in the Far East, and for the comparatively small sum of Tls.54,000 a year" (*Municipal Gazette* 1921).

5. Buck's repertoire consisted of works of Mozart, Haydn, Beethoven, Schubert, Schumann, Berlioz, Massenet, Sibelius, Bizet, Elgar, Tchaikovsky, Smetana, Liszt, Saint-Saëns, Weber, Mendelssohn, Leoncavallo, etc. (Shanghai Municipal Orchestra Concert Programs 1912).

6. The orchestra's player list was printed in the *North China Desk Hong List* annually. In the list, Western and Filipino players were listed separately.

7. For a biography on Paci, see his autobiographical note in the *Souvenir Program of Farewell Concert* held on May 31, 1942, 13–16. Also see his daughter's biography (Zakharoff 2005).

8. As stated in the council minutes, it was agreed that it was better to allow the group "to revert in the meantime to what it was before any German Musicians were engaged, a Band which is not in any sense an orchestra, but which is merely able to fulfill the requirements of a Manila Band, to give performances in the Public Garden and to play in dances, etc." (*The Minutes* 1917–1919, 151). The *North China Desk Hong List* 1919 registered only seven Western and twenty-one Filipino musicians (144).

9. It was an operatic concert with selections from Donizetti, Gluck, Massenet, Rossini, Richard Strauss, and Wagner. The soloist was H. V. Heidenstam.

10. Paci's letter was dated July 12, 1920, addressed to the secretary of the council (SMA U1-3-867, 1).

11. Letter to the assistant secretary of the council J. M. McKee, December 12, 1921. In the

letter, he requested that the financial controller pay for four extra musicians who had played for their service in November (SMA U1-3-286, [n.p.]).

12. Ibid.

13. Tls. is the short form for "taels," which was the English translation of the old Chinese silver currency unit "liang." While this old Chinese currency went into disuse in the early twentieth century, the Municipal Council in Shanghai continued its use until March 1, 1933, when the Chinese National Government abolished it. The exchange rate of Tls. and Chinese dollars was around 1:1.39. Banks in Shanghai were said to be able to take advantage of the currency exchange. Thus the SMO musicians' salary was paid in Tls. prior to 1933 and in Chinese dollars after that (1936, 23–24). The following list of food prices in *Shanghai Zaria* dated January 16, 1929, provides a sense of the living cost at the time: apples and bananas, 20 cents per pound; corn, 10 cents per pound; rice, $13 per 200 pounds; white bread, 60 cents per pound; black bread, 12 cents per pound; pork, 40 cents per pound; lamb, 25 cents per pound.

14. This is based on a pay-scale list of Filipino musicians from 1925. In the list, for instance, the European musician Percu's pay was listed as Tls.205, whereas all the Filipino musicians' pay was from Tls.145 to Tls.160 (SMA U1-3-863, 180).

15. Original transliteration of the Russian musicians' names as they appeared in SMO contracts are presented in brackets the first time they appear in the text. But when a musician's name appears in a direct quote from an original source, its original transliteration is kept for the sake of flavor and historical accuracy.

16. Letter addressed to the council by Ponomariov upon the grief for the discontinuation of his service for the band after September 30, 1921 (SMA U1-3-297, 11–12).

17. Paci to N. O. Liddell, January 10, 1920, regarding the employment of Ponomariov (SMA U1-3-297, 2–3).

18. According to Paci's letter to the council secretary, Liddell, September 20, 1920 (SMA U1-3-097, 8 or 9).

19. Paci to McKee, December 15, 1922.

20. Paci to J. M. McKee of the council, November 19, 1923 (SMA U1-3-097, 32).

21. The Chinese composer Nie Er also wrote jealously in his diary about the high salary of his teacher Podushka and Paci (1985, 346).

22. Paci to the secretary of the council regarding Schvaikowsky's condition of service, September 21, 1932.

23. Information based on figures provided in the Shanghai Municipal Council Reports, quoted in Wang Yanli (2015, 218–220).

24. The expenditure of 1926 was Tls.130,320; of 1927 Tls.149,681.03; and of 1928 Tls.143,873.73. Wang Yanli (2015, 220–221).

25. Letter to Paci, undated but attached to Paci's letter to the secretary, E. S. B. Rowe, December 27, 1925.

26. Minutes of the Band Committee, May 1, 1923.

27. Letter, March 13, 1922. In the letter, Paci mentioned that when Hayek was hired as a temporary musician, he used the name J. Gay because when Hayek came to Shanghai two years before that, he found that people had a hard time pronouncing his name and that the sound "H" in Russian sounded like "G" in English.

28. In the letter, Paci mentioned to Hayek that employers included the Astor House, Palace Hotel, and Apollo Theatre.

29. Details mentioned in the letter of March 13, 1922, as well as another letter to McKee of April 3, 1922.

30. The letter of March 30, 1922, was very long.

31. The lawyer representing Hayek was Alexander N. Fishman, and his letter to McKee was dated April 4, 1922.

32. Letter, April 5, 1922, to the secretary of the Municipal Council.

33. Paci emphasized in the letter of April 13, 1932, that "it was necessary for the orchestra to have the trumpet," thus it was recommended that the said Russian musician be hired on a temporary contract.

34. Letter of appointment, April 15, 1932, sent by the deputy secretary to the secretary of the council recommending the hiring of Phedorov-Kozmenke at Tls.165 per month.

35. Paci to the secretary of the council, February 23, 1928.

36. Paci to the secretary of the council, March 12, 1928.

37. Mentioned in a list of Filipino musicians' pay rates.

38. Respective years of the Municipal Band and Orchestra listing in *China Hong Desk List*.

39. It should be noted that the pay-scale system approved in 1926 was quite different from what Paci proposed in 1923. In Paci's original proposal from 1923, he simply wanted to divide the musicians between "principal instruments" and "second instruments." Letter to J. M. McKee, February 2, 1923. A more sophisticated system was proposed again in 1924, with category A consisting of the assistant conductor, the concertmaster or soloist(s), the harpist and pianist, and leader of the second violins; category B consisting of the rest of the "principal instruments" including the timpani; and category C the rest of the instruments. Letter to J. M. McKee, October 9, 1924. Such a format was authorized in 1925. Note from the acting secretary to the treasurer and comptroller, stating that this classification and pay of European musicians is to be in effect from January 1, 1925 (SMA U1-3-2339, 1–18). It is not clear what caused the pay structure to change again in 1926.

40. A memo addressed to the conductor stated that "the Council has decided that, with effect from May 26, 1926, the holders of the following posts are to be considered the permanent nucleus of the Orchestra and Band, and will serve under 'A' form agreements carrying the usual Municipal privileges." (SMA U1-3-2884, 58). The memo is not dated and seems to be a draft.

41. Such was the explanation Paci provided for the Municipal Council to justify Podushka's pay-raise request. He wrote, "although Mr. Podushka's services have been quite satisfactory, he is in my opinion not a good enough Viola-player to be definitely engaged as the First in our Orchestra." Paci to the secretary, January 10, 1927 (SMA U1-3-2031, 6).

42. Paci to the treasurer and controller, April 17, 1931.

43. Paci to J. M. McKee, the assistant secretary of the council, February 14, 1923, regarding Poduska's contract.

44. Podushka's letter of January 7, 1927, was attached to Paci's letter of January 10, 1927.

45. Paci to the secretary of the council, September 21, 1932, regarding Schvaikowsky's condition of service, in which he explained the intricacy of the temporary contract as well as why Podushka was treated differently (SMA U1-3-2574, 64 or 65).

46. Letter to the secretary of the council, February 3, 1928, 11 or 42. Paci's explanation falls apart under scrutiny. First, it would be hard to see why Shevtsov did not want to be bound by the Form "A" agreement. Apparently, if he were on a Form "A" agreement, it would not be possible for Paci to hire another cellist from Italy. In other words, even though Shevtsov was good and Paci was willing to reward him financially like other principal players, Paci did not want to give up the possibility of hiring someone "better" from abroad.

47. "Renewal of Agreement," January 16, 1931.

48. Letter to the secretary by Paci on behalf of the two musicians, February 11, 1930.

49. "Renewal of Agreement," May 19, 1931.

50. See for instance discussion in Ablova 2007 and Van 2008. This is also identified in Mikkonen's research, as evident in many reports of crimes committed by Russian refuges and the refugees' alcohol problems ("Za pianstvo i poproshainichestvo" 1929, 7; "Za pianstvo" 1929, 3). There were also frequent reports of suicides and sometimes several attempts in a day ("Pokushenie na samoubiistvo" 1929, 3; "Shankhaiskii den" 1929, 5). The late-night work also subjected musicians to robberies, such as when a group walking at four o'clock in the morning on Avenue Joffre were beaten by a group of young hooligans ("Izbienie muzykanta" 1930, 4). These were just a few of the many that Mikkonen referred to in an earlier version of chapter 1. I am grateful to him for letting me use a few of the sources here.

51. Paci to the council secretary, Liddell, January 22, 1921. He complained about the early arrival of two musicians from London—first oboist Griffiths and first baritone and cellist Coles—without John Pook & Co cabling him in advance so he could release the current musicians accordingly (SMA U1-3-1006, [n.p.]).

52. Paci to McKee, assistant secretary, March 4, 1924, in which the terms of the agreement with Schvaikowsky were stated. He was to be refunded for a sum up to Tls. 85 for his traveling expenses (SMA U1-3-2574, 1 or 2).

53. Handwritten letter, March 12, 1924 (SMA U1-3-2574, n.p.).

54. Paci to McKee, January 5, 1925, regarding Schvaikowsky's definite engagement (SMA-U1-3-2574, 5 or 6).

55. His leave was a discussed item at the meetings of the Staff Committee. First Paci suggested seven instead of the eight months of leave he was entitled to. Then the committee was doubtful as to what would happen during his leave if the SMO were to be disbanded if it did not gain enough support from the taxpayers. Letters forwarded by the deputy secretary to the Orchestra and Band and Staff Committee, no dates (SMA U1-3-2574, 25–26 or 26–27). As mentioned in his next contract dated January 16, 1931, he took a long leave in 1929 (SMA U1-3-2574, 31).

56. "Renewal of Agreement," January 31, 1928 (SMA U1-3-2574, 19–20).

57. "Renewal of Agreement," January 16, 1931 (SMA U1-3-2574, 31).

58. Letter, April 1, 1932 (SMA U1-3-2574, 49).

59. Letter, June 24, 1932 (SMA U1-3-2574, 51 or 52).

60. The council compiled a detailed list of Schvaikowsky's debts. He owed a total of $1,767.70 to the China Finance Corporation and to many individuals, restaurants, and shops (SMA U1-3-2574, 67 or 68).

61. "Orchestra & Band—Musician S. Schvaikowsky—Termination of Services and Re-engagement," apparently extracted from the minutes of a committee meeting (SMA U1-3-2574, 121–122 or 122–123).

62. Paci's five-page letter was filled with details of the event, as well as his own interpretation of the incident (SMA U1-3-2574, 128–132 or 129–133).

63. There was an undated note by R. Winter addressed to the secretary with the following: "The Police have enquired of pawn shops in both the Concession and Settlement, which accept musical instruments but can find no trace of the particular instruments having been pawned. It is suggested by them that the instruments may have been sold to a second-hand dealer and afterwards repurchased, which could not be traced" (SMA U1-3-2574, 144).

64. Paci's grounds for dismissal were as follows: (1) disobeyed instructions in not attending the rehearsal on February 11; (2) disobeyed instructions to bring the oboe, which was the council's property; and (3) took away a trumpet from the office of the Orchestra and Band without the permission of the owner. Paci's letter, February 13, 1933 (SMA U1-3-2574, 146–148).

65. R. Winter to the secretary, report, March 11, 1933. The report was said to be read by Schvaikowsky, who agreed to its contents (SMA U1-3-2574, 143).

66. According to Schvaikowsky's wife, her husband's "behavior in the latest days should be explained by his chronical [sic] sickness during which he is losing all his will and power to conscious actions." Letter, February 21, 1933 (SMA U1-3-2574, 137).

67. In the letter from Schvaikowsky's daughter, she wrote that her education "is a[t] stake" and that her father, "if given another opportunity, promises to spare no efforts to give every satisfaction to the Council and his superiors." Letter, no date (SMA U1-3-2574, 139).

68. Council minutes, March 15, 1933, extracted and included in Schvaikowsky's file.

69. Paci, letter, March 16, 1933, accompanied by Schvaikowsky's undated letter (SMA U1-3-2574, 154).

70. Letter, February 20, 1935 (SMA U1-3-2574, 175).

71. Letter by G. Godfrey Philips, February 21, 1935 (SMA U1-3-2574, 180).

72. The works played included Lalo's Cello Concerto in D minor, Dvořák's Cello Concerto in B minor, Saint-Saëns's Cello Concerto No. 1 in A minor, Haydn's Cello Concerto No. 2 in D minor, and Beethoven's Triple Concerto in C major (SMO Concert Program).

73. These works included Volkmann, Serenade No. 3 in D major for Cello and Strings; Zandonai, *Serenata medioevale*; Popper's *Requiem* for three cellos and orchestra; and Herbert, Cello Concerto No. 2 in E minor (SMO Concert Program).

74. Namely, Mozart's Concerto for Harp and Flute in C major with Spiridonov, Zabei's Harp Concerto in C minor, and Sgambati's Piano Concerto in G minor, op. 15 (SMO Concert Program).

75. Some of these chamber works performed included Tchaikovsky's String Quartet No. 1 in D major, Schubert's Octet in F major, Mendelssohn's String Quartet No. 1 in E-flat major, Gretchaninov's Piano Trio No. 1 in C minor, and Rimsky-Korsakov's Piano Quintet in B flat major, to name but a few (SMO Concert Program).

76. Even though the article is long, no specific author is identified.

77. According to Zakharov, who performed regularly at these chamber music concerts, "[t] hough there is only a small group of music lovers in Shanghai[,] the musicians find it a pleasure to work before them. They are appreciative and warmly responsive to something which stirs them" (Lewis 1931, 13).

Chapter 4: Sounding Russian in a Metropolis

1. Most of the concert reviews in Shanghai's English-language newspapers were published anonymously or with the authors identified only with initials. It is therefore almost impossible to know the background of these critics. So it is only fair to assume those who wrote for the English-language newspapers were written with Shanghai's English-speaking readers in mind, as there were also French, German, Russian, and Hebrew and Yiddish newspapers for their own specific readerships.

2. Such a view is evident in Guo-huang Han's study of the SMO (1995) and is reiterated in Enomoto's monograph on the institution (2009). Pui Ling Pang's dissertation (2015) also does not point out this unique programming feature of the SMO. Such a feature is only recognized in Wang Yanli's study (2015).

3. For example, relevant concerts took place on the following dates: May 1, 1921; October 16, 1927; January 14, 1934; March 10, 1935; April 11, 1937; May 26, 1940; and November 28, 1943 (SMO Concert Program).

4. Tchaikovsky's Symphony no. 6 and Dvořák's Symphony no. 9, the so-called New World Symphony, were said to be promised to the audience in the first review, and it was mentioned in the 1910 review that Tchaikovsky's Symphony no. 6 had been played.

5. This information is based on concert announcements in *The Municipal Gazette* (1908–1921). The repertoire list that the present author compiled also showed no premiere of Tchaikovsky's works during Paci's tenure, suggesting that what he played had been established already by his predecessor.

6. This is a view held by the British musicologist and music critic Stephen Walsh, who heard a simplified version of this chapter at the conference titled "Russian Émigré Culture: Transcending the Borders of Countries, Languages and Disciplines," held at Saarland University, Saarbruecken, Germany, November 12–15, 2015. I am most grateful for his input.

7. The premiere of *The Firebird Suite* was on March 29, 1923, in a concert titled "Modernism.Impressionism" (SMO Concert Program).

8. It was repeated again on March 3, 1929; December 8, 1929; April 20, 1930; November 29, 1932; March 19, 1933; April 7, 1935; January 17, 1937; March 27, 1938; December 22, 1940. The premiere of the "Sacrificial Dance" from *The Rite of Spring* was on November 12, 1933; the premiere of *Petrushka* was on June 4, 1944. Both were accompanied by ballet performances.

9. The SMO's performance of Shostakovich's work in 1936 was unusual, as very few Soviet works were played outside of the then USSR at that time. The work had only been completed in 1933 and was premiered in Shanghai on January 5, 1936. It was given a repeat performance on April 5 of the same year, after which it was played again only in 1945.

10. The Shanghai Symphony Orchestra archive reported they had no extant score of Sergei Aksakov.

11. He was one of the founders of the First Russian Music School in Shanghai in 1937, as was discussed in chapter 2. In its January concert, he was reported to have also given a lecture on the Russian composer A. S. Arensky ("Kontsert Pervoy Russkoy" 1937, 7), an act to propagate the lineage of Russian music.

12. There were five concertgoers who wrote to the *North-China Daily News*. Their responses were reprinted in the *North-China Herald* (November 2, 1938, 203).

13. Take for instance a reader's letter to the editor of the *North-China Herald* dated March 8, 1940, in which he complained about the Municipal Orchestra giving "us an absolute surfeit of Italian music at the weekly concerts" and declared that it was "the ratepayers of the International Settlement who pay the piper and are therefore entitled to call the tune." The letter also pointed out that even though the Sunday concerts were often well attended, "one has only to see the crowd disperse after a concert, nine-tenths of them going off in the direction of Avenue Joffre." ("Municipal Orchestra" 1940, 421).

14. For more discussion on music and utopia, see Saffle and Yang (2010).

15. Shushlin's life and musical career were examined in chapter 2 and his contributions to Chinese vocalism are examined in chapter 5.

16. In the same issue of the newspaper report on the concert, there was a long article on the composer ("Richard Wagner" 1908, 593).

17. Selivanov's contribution to the Russian community was covered in chapter 2.

18. The SMO's presenting these Wagner concerts in 1922 prompted a local music lover to write about his personal aspiration for Shanghai to stage a Wagner opera. For the writer concerned, and presumably many others in Shanghai, staging a Wagner opera was comparable to living the dream of having what was in a metropolis: the museum, library, and the art gallery. Quite proud of the standard of the SMO, he wrote that "such an orchestra as

Shanghai possesses today has never been heard east of Suez. . . . So far as the orchestral work is concerned, there appears no insuperable obstacle to mounting a Wagner music-drama" ("A Wagner Opera in Shanghai" 1922, 281).

19. Based on the budget proposal submitted by Paci to the Municipal Council: "Special Concert by Municipal Orchestra" (SMA U1-4-041-901-920, 370–372).

20. Mentioned in literature but also confirmed by personal correspondence with Zakharov's grandson Andrew Behr.

21. One concert was held on April 30, 1933, and the other on April 27, 1936.

22. He started piano at age six and studied with a Madame Dillon at the Glazunov Academy. He was said to have given his first recital at the age of ten ("Shanghai To Hear" 1935, 3).

23. Recommended by de Kryger, the assistant conductor of the SMO (SMA U1-4-041-0828, 37).

24. There is a short biography of him on this website of Russian celebrities: http://persona.rin .ru/eng/view/f//35739/vedernikov, accessed December 18, 2015.

25. In the concert, he played the first movement of Beethoven's Piano Concerto no. 3, Arensky's *Bigarrares*, and Chopin's *Etude* op. 10, no. 4 ("Program for Afternoon" 1936, 11).

26. Paci to the council secretary, April 18, 1940, regarding "Suggestions and Recommendations for a 'Tchaikovsky Festival' to Be Held in Celebration of the Centenary of the Master's Birth" (SMA U1-4-913, 127–130).

27. Mentioned in the liner note of a contemporary music recording titled "London/Nowak" released in 1981, in which he played Lionel Nowak's "Soundscape for Piano" (CRI: CRL 470. Information based on DRAM at https://www.dramonline.org/albums/london-nowak, accessed December 29, 2015).

28. He performed regularly at Bennington College's faculty concerts, of which the program notes are accessible at https://crossettlibrary.dspacedirect.org/handle/11209/4/discover? filtertype_0=author&filtertype_1=author&filter_0=Schonbeck%2C+Gunnar+-+Clarinet& filter_relational_operator_1=equals&filter_1=Neuman%2C+Maxine+-+Cello&filter _relational_operator_0=equals&filtertype=author&filter_relational_operator=equals&filter =Havsky%2C+Vladimir+-+Piano, accessed December 20, 2015.

29. He was a resident of Croton on Hudson, New York. Information based on "Celebrity Obituaries" (http://www.tributes.com/obituary/show/Vladimir-Havsky-86970967, accessed December 20, 2015).

30. The Kolchin choir consisted of twenty-two professional singers hired for a fee of $300 plus a share of the revenue gained from the performance, mentioned in a memo by Paci regarding the 1940 performance (SMA U1-4-913, n.p.).

31. Letter to the secretary of the Municipal Council dated August 3, 1935 (SMA U1-4-934, n.p.). The file also contains Metzler's letter to the secretary as well as a detailed proposal plus a tentative budget for the permanent employment of a choir of various sizes.

32. For more discussion of the 1936 concert, see Yang (2013).

33. Paci to the council secretary, April 18, 1940, pertinent to "Suggestions and Recommendations for a 'Tchaikovsky Festival' to Be Held in Celebration of the Centenary of the Master's Birth" (SMA U1-4-913, 127–130).

Chapter 5: Foundations of New Chinese Music

1. The translation of this passage was by Andrew Behr, the grandson of Boris Zakharov. Behr kindly translated this passage for me, whereas I translated a Chinese article on Zakharov

in return. This newspaper clipping was among the research materials Neil Edmunds collected before passing away in January 2008. Edmunds' materials were given to me, thanks to his parents' generosity, which I passed onto Mikkonen, but due to problems in matching clippings with citations, we were not able to use his materials directly, including this one. But knowing the students in the photograph and the dates the graduation took place, Mikkonen was able to locate the citation in the newspaper.

2. Information given in the National Conservatory's record of the first cohort of graduates issued in 1933 ("Jinian Yu Yixuan danchen . . ." 2009).

3. As Slavianova left the conservatory in 1931, Yu was transferred to study with the head of the vocal department Zhou Shu'an ("Jinian Yu Yixuan danchen . . ." 2009).

4. Li received a scholarship to study in Belgium in 1934, Qiu went to the United Kingdom, and Yu pursued a master's degree at Cornell University in 1935 (Luo and Qian 2013, 123).

5. For details of its various names from 1927 to 1956 as well as its many relocations during the period, see Ding (1987, 60).

6. Nonetheless, the name National Conservatory was officially used by the institute only from 1927 to 1929. When it was downgraded to a technical college in 1929, its name was changed to the National Institute of Music (Guoli yinyue zhuanke xuexiao), which lasted until 1937. Due to the Sino-Japanese War, the Nationalist government stopped its funding and the conservatory became a private institution, and its name changed to the Private National Institute of Music as well as various other names during the war years. In this chapter and also throughout the entire volume, the institution is referred to as the National Conservatory of Music, or simply the National Conservatory or the conservatory.

7. The May Fourth Movement was a student-led movement in reaction to the Chinese government's lack of resolve to face the international peace settlement at the end of World War I that disadvantaged China's territorial rights by allowing the possibility of Japanese inheriting German privileges in the Shandong Province. Intellectuals, workers, and merchants rallied to prevent the Chinese government's signing the Treaty of Versailles, and the movement was considered a victory for democracy that engendered a new political confidence among Chinese youth and intellectuals. It heralded changes that included the rejection of Confucianism and the replacement of classical written Chinese (*wenyan*) with the colloquial and more widely understood spoken Chinese (*baihua*). The success of the May Fourth Movement also prompted an increase in the number of trade unions and newspapers and a desire for education, as well as boosting the membership of the Nationalist government and popularizing novel ideas such as socialism and communism. For further information about the May Fourth Movement and its effects, see Chesneaux et al. (1977, 65–103) and Schwarcz (1986).

8. For more details of Cai Yuanpei's ideas, see Cai Jianguo (1997).

9. Such a view was expressed in the preface to the inaugural issue of the National Conservatory's magazine *Yinyueyuan yuankan* (Conservatory music magazine) (May 1928), quoted in Enomoto (2003, 114).

10. For more information on Xiao Youmei's life, see Zhang Jigao (1982) and Yu Shaohua (1982).

11. Xiao successfully completed a doctoral thesis titled "Eine Geschichtliche Untersuchung über das Chinesische Orchester bis zum 17 Jahrhundert" (A Study of the History of Chinese Orchestra until the Seventeenth Century) at the University of Leipzig.

12. Some, such as Schimmelpenninck and Kouwenhoven (1993), have regarded the founding of the conservatory as Xiao's act to "upgrade" Chinese traditional music to make it fit in with Western musical and educational conventions (63).

13. Despite Cai Yuanpei's political connections that were hoped to ensure the institution's future, the conservatory's first years were plagued by instability and financial crisis. The monthly grant of $3,000 turned out to be only $2,600 a month for the first year of the conservatory's existence, and the amount was capped at $5,000 per month until 1933 regardless of the increase in student numbers and inflation. Only three months after the conservatory opened in November 1927, it was forced to move from its initial home at No. 56, Rue Dolfuss (now Nanchang Road) to Avenue Joffre (now Huaihai Road), and a combination of the financial crisis and Japanese bombing saw it move eight times in the first ten years of its existence. A government grant of $80,000 was finally awarded to the conservatory in 1934 for construction of its own building. There were ongoing fund-raising activities organized by the conservatory's Fund Raising Committee to support various initiatives including the construction of new buildings (Ding 1987, 60, 81–86).

14. For more about Shanghai, see this volume's introduction as well as A. Feuerwerker (1983).

15. *Yinyue xueyuan yuankan* (The conservatory magazine), inaugural issue reprinted in Luo and Qian (2013, 21).

16. *Guoli yinyueyuan yilan* (A guide to the National Conservatory of Music), 1928, reprinted in Luo and Qian (2013, 24).

17. There is no clear explanation in current literature about why the Nationalist government decided to reorganize the structure of the conservatory. Funding could have been an issue.

18. Two Western-trained Chinese pedagogues joined in 1929. One was Zhou Shu'an, a graduate of Radcliffe College and the New England Conservatory of Music, who was in charge of the vocal department as well as teaching aural training. The other was Huang Zi (also known as Huang Tzu), a graduate of Oberlin College and Yale University, who was to teach composition, harmony, and Western music history (Luo and Qian 2013, 32).

19. *Jiao zhiyuan xingming lu* (Directory of faculty and staff), 1929, reprinted in Luo and Qian (2013, 44).

20. The list of Russian faculty members after 1929 was based on Wang (2007, 57–58).

21. Such an impression is based on a search with the keyword "National Conservatory" through Shanghai's English-language newspaper databases, which generate voluminous articles on the activities of the conservatory. Two such reports are mentioned at the beginning of this chapter and in the introduction of this volume.

22. The present Shanghai Conservatory of Music includes thirteen departments: namely, musicology and theory, composition, conducting, piano, vocal and opera, orchestral instruments, Chinese orchestral instruments, education, musical theater, music engineering, contemporary instruments and percussion, arts administration, and the upcoming digital media. The last five departments in this list were established only after the new millennium.

23. That was the same rate as the salary of the Chinese professors at the conservatory or that of the average players at the SMO. Actually, many conservatory students were hired before they even graduated due to the solid training they received as well as the high level of their performance skills (*Xiaoshe lecheng jiniankan* 1935, 85).

24. Statistics of student enrollment numbers and their place of origin can be found in *Xiaoshe lecheng jiniankan* (1935, 103).

25. His name is mentioned in more than one hundred Chinese articles on Chinese pianism, many only in passing.

26. Information from Andrew Behr, Zakaharov's grandson, in correspondence with the

present author, October 2, 2015. For a description of Zakharov's early career, see Kruzenshtern (1933). For Zakharov's playing and character, see Philips (2006, 237–240, 713).

27. According to Behr, his mother, Zakharov's daughter Tatiana, was born in 1917. Tatiana was the only child of Zakharov and Cecilia Hansen. Hansen and Zakharov parted, as explained by Behr, because of Zakharov's gambling. Correspondence, October 2, 2015. It seems Zakharov was not able to free himself of his gambling habit even after he settled in Shanghai. He was said to be penniless when he died, so his funeral was paid for by his friends despite the handsome monthly salary he made (see Zhao 1996).

28. Hansen's Asia tour and her stop in Shanghai in the summer of 1928 were highly publicized. Between June and October, there were at least a dozen articles in various Shanghai newspapers on the event.

29. The average salary for a full-time professor was $200 (local currency) per month, whereas Zakharov's was $400 per month (Ding 1982, 4). Zakharov's contract for academic year 1937 to 1938 was reproduced in Wang (2007, 61).

30. Zakharov's appointment was after the sacking of Wang Ruixian (王瑞娴) and Li Enke (李恩科). Wang taught the piano whereas Li was head of academic matters. The instructors were sacked because of their involvement in the students' protest in the summer of 1929 (Bian 1996, 16).

31. In the press reports on Hansen's tour and concert, Zakharov was not mentioned. See, for instance, "A famous woman violinist" (1928, 567); "World-famous musicians . . ." (1928, 236); "Great violinists" (1928, 530). According to Behr, by then there was not much left in their relationship but just concert engagements. Correspondence, October 5, 2015.

32. Ding Shande nonetheless did not pursue the route of a world-class pianist but instead furthered his study in composition at the Paris Conservatory of Music from 1947 to 1949. Eventually he became senior professor of composition and the vice president at the Shanghai Conservatory (1956–1984).

33. Wei Hanzhang emigrated to Hong Kong in 1950 and founded the Hong Kong Music Institute (then known as the Hong Kong Sacred Music Institute), which was modeled on the curriculum of the National Conservatory and was responsible for training the first generation of local musicians before professional musical training was systematized in the former colony.

34. For details about Jiang's study at the conservatory, see Xiao and Qian (2013).

35. Zakharov also taught a number of non-Chinese students, including Andrei Iartsev, Elena Gora, Tamara Markitant, Vladimir Havsky, and Fausta Sakharova. Sakharova was later appointed as a pedagogue at the conservatory. For more on Havsky, see chapter 4.

36. Liao Fushu was a student of the conservatory and was then hired as an administrative staff member in 1934 (*Xiaoshe luocheng jinian kan* 1935, 84). In the 1980s and 1990s, he wrote a number of eyewitness accounts about the Western pedagogues in the early history of the institution.

37. His name was listed in the conservatory's faculty list from 1930 as a part-time teacher (Zhang 2010a, 16). He was listed as joining the conservatory in August 1930 (*Xiaoshe luocheng jinian kan* 1935, 87).

38. Her death was mentioned in Wang (2007) as occurring in September 1938, but it was mentioned in Yang (1991) as occurring in November 1937.

39. She was not on the faculty list or prior faculty list in *Xiaoshe luocheng jinian kan* (1935), the commemorative publication for the completion of the school building.

40. The repertoire included *Xiaopin* (Miniature), *Datiqin mofan qu xuan* (Cello model works), *Boba datiqin qu xuan* (Boba cello pieces), *Geju Yesijia de chaqu* (Arias from the opera

Yeska), *Yinyuehui de bolanwu* (Concert polonaise), *Pipa zhisheng* (The sound of *pipa*). All these were published by the conservatory through the Commercial Press. In *Xiaoshe luocheng jinian kan* (1935, 101).

41. The works published by the conservatory also included Tcherepnin's *Wusheng yinjie de gangqin jiaokeshu* 五聲音階的鋼琴教科書 (A piano textbook based on the pentatonic scales) and Aksakov's *Gangqin quji* (Piano album) among a few other titles by Chinese faculty members.

42. Mentioned in biographies of these musicians in Xiang (1994, vol. 2, 238, 354, 542).

43. The Chinese Musicians Association is the leading professional organization to impart party ideology to Chinese musicians. Lü Ji also studied with another Russian, the singer Vladimir Shushlin, and had been a member of the Communist Party since 1935.

44. Nie Er mentioned his lessons with Aksakov in a letter to his brother dated August 28, 1934.

45. The impression is based on interviews in Shanghai on July 2, 2005, and June 31, 2006, respectively, with Wang Zhicheng, the Chinese expert on Russians immigrants in Shanghai, and Anna Michaels, a former resident of the French Concession who is half Russian and half Italian. Both spoke about the amicable relationships between the Russians and the Chinese. Anna, who goes to Shanghai regularly to be in touch with her past, spoke strongly about the "Chineseness" in her upbringing.

46. One concert was held at the YMCA in which Podushka played a solo, and Nie Er was slightly disappointed by the occasion.

47. The concert featured a Wagner and Beethoven program.

48. The concert Li Delun referred to was held on August 24, 1940. It was an open-air concert held in Jessfield Park with the following program: Grieg's Piano Concerto in A minor played by Wu Leyi (Lois Woo), followed by Rimsky-Korsakov's *Flight of the Bumblebee* and Tchaikovsky's *The Nutcracker: Arabian Dance*, with Doris Yanover as the dancer.

49. The quartet consisted of Kluge and three other Chinese students taking cello as minor instruments, including pianist H. M. Li (Lee Hsien Ming), the flutist C. H. Lao (Lao Jingxian 劳景贤), and a Mr. A. Chen (Shen Songbai 沈松柏), probably an elective student.

50. Zakharov performed as soloist at many of SMO's chamber music concerts as well as serving on the SMO's Music Committee from 1940 to 1942. In fact, he was the only Russian musician ever given such a position (Wang Yanli 2015, 64). A list of SMO Music Committee members can be found in Wang Yanli (2015, 62–64). Aside from the conductor, the committee consisted of representatives of the Municipal Council as well as respected musicians from the Shanghai community.

51. Her repertoire included Chopin's two concertos on April 7 and August 24, respectively, and Liszt's Piano Concerto no. 1 on December 15, 1940. In the following year, she played a solo concert on May 4 and Schumann's Piano Concerto in A minor on November 30. In 1942, she played Tchaikovsky's Piano Concerto no. 1 on May 24 and played it again in January 1943; on March 14 of that year, she played Liszt's Piano Concerto no. 1.

52. Actor/actant are terms used in Actor Network Theory (ANT). According to Latour, the "actor" or "actant" in ANT is a "semiotic definition" in that it "can literally be anything provided it is granted to be the source of an action." The entity chosen to be seen as the "actor" or "actant" "including the self, society, nature, every relation, every action, can be understood as a 'choice' or a 'selection' of finer and finer embranchments going from abstract structure—actants—to concrete ones—actors" (Latour 1996, 373). That is, human actions can be seen through objects, which are "agents" so to speak, and the notion of "agency," of "materiality,"

is one of the major contributions of ANT, which above all looks at both human and nonhuman actors equally, regarding them as "paying the *same semiotic price*" or in "symmetry." The actant is considered "mediator" rather than "intermediary" (Latour 1996, 374). Furthermore, Latour emphasizes the importance of treating the actor/actant as "infinitely pliable, heterogeneous, that they are free associationists, know no differences of scale, that there is no inertia, no order, that they build their own temporality" (Latour 1996, 374). That is, the actant can itself grow to become a network of its own by generating *transformations* "manifested by the many unexpected *events* triggered in the other mediators that follow them along the line" (Latour 2005, 107).

53. Such was a phrase used in the review of the concert of Xia Guoqiong and Wang Wenyu held on January 24, 1937 ("Xia Guoqiong . . ." 1937, 15).

Chapter 6: From "Folk Cure" to Catharsis

Epigraph. Chang Chi-Jen (1986, 126).

1. Beiping was the name of China's current capital Beijing under the Republic of China.

2. For a full catalogue of works, see Folkman (2008, 510); Korabelnikova (2008, 211); Arias (1989).

3. The nine-step scale is formed by a series of nine semitones and whole tones occurring within an octave in repeating order of half-half-whole-half-half-whole-half-half-whole. Interpoint is a contrapuntal method of combining several linear elements in various independent manners. See Wuellner (1974, 65).

4. Tcherepnin passed away in Paris in 1977.

5. Many of these details were not verifiable until Tcherepnin's autobiographical materials (PSF) and the diaries of Tcherepnin's first wife Louisine Peters Weekes recently became available. Tcherepnin himself had inaccurately recalled the exact dates of his Asian activities to Guy Wuellner in 1971. See Wuellner (1974, 88).

6. As explained below, Tcherepnin traveled with his wife and stepdaughter, and he had daily obligations for sightseeing and socializing with them. He regularly worked four hours each morning and scheduled other musical work around family obligations. See Xiao Youmei (1934, 2).

7. For further details, see also Tcherepnin (1935, 397); Jiang (1982, 4); Qian and Zhang (2011, 8).

8. Qian and Zhang (2011, 14) also state that Tcherepnin performed at Saint John's University during his first Shanghai visit. Frank Ma (1937, 9) states that two concerts were given at the Grand Hotel de Pekin in March 1937, but so far documentation has been found for only the March 1 concert.

9. Strok had Latvian origins but was considered Russian by other Russians because he was born in Russia and communicated in Russian. He was also a key figure for many Russian musicians because he hired for tours in Asia. Thanks to Simo Mikkonen for providing this information.

10. Strok was based in Japan but had relatives assisting him in China operations. See PSF, second unpublished Alexander Tcherepnin autobiography covering 1899–1937 (no date, 155–157). The autobiography was drawn from detailed diaries that Tcherepnin kept in Russian over decades, as well as clippings and personal materials he kept.

11. Tcherepnin traveled to Asia with his first wife, Louisine Peters Weekes, but eventually divorced her and married Lee Hsien Ming. These relationships are discussed in detail below.

12. Zakharov was also the teacher of Lee Hsien Ming. He "introduced" her to Tcherepnin at his home in the spring of 1934, unaware that the two had already met briefly. See PSF, Tcherepnin autobiography (158).

13. PSF (157). "Vostok" was a Russian society dedicated to national poetry and literature. Tcherepnin remarked of the group that "all of them were Sinophiles, believed in Sino-Russian collaboration" (157).

14. Tcherepnin played the orchestra part on the piano and sang all the roles himself (Folkman 2008, 174).

15. See chapter 4 in this volume.

16. According to Tcherepnin, "the hall was overcrowded" for the May SMO concert at the Grand Theatre (PSF, 157). SMO records, however, indicate that the Grand, with a capacity of 1,953 seats, attracted an audience of 573. The Lyceum Theatre used for the November concert had a capacity of around 700. See SMA U1-4-259 and U1-4-893 [Statement of Attendance and Receipts]. Thanks to Yang Hon-Lun for providing this information.

17. Internal SMO documents reveal that Strok did not approach the SMO for approval of the May 13 concert until April 27, 1934. See SMA U1-4-284. Similarly, internal requests to approve the November 25 concert budget were not made until November 16. See SMA U1-4-259. Thanks to Yang Hon-Lun for bringing this file to my attention. According to Tcherepnin, the tour concert dates lacked coordination, in general, "due to the fact that they were set by different managers" (PSF, 155).

18. See "Vecher A. N. Cherepnina v 'Vostoke'" (1934, 9); "Recital at A. W. C." (1934, 19); and "Municipal Orchestra Concert" (1934, 15).

19. Chang states that Tcherepnin met Xiao through Zakharov in 1934 (1986, 1). For more information on Xiao Youmei, see chapter 5 in this volume.

20. PSF (157).

21. For a related discussion of Western timbral development and the twentieth-century inclusion of Chinese instruments, see Winzenburg (2017).

22. Mexican currency was offered due to the then relative instability of the Chinese yuan.

23. Tcherepnin's other compositions with Chinese elements included vocal, instrumental, and theatrical works. See Chang (1986, 192).

24. Aaron Avshalomov had already experimented in mimicry of Chinese instruments in orchestral settings. See the following chapter.

25. Italics added for emphasis.

26. The first two royalty reports sent to Tcherepnin from the Commercial Press indicate that 426 copies were sold in the first six months of publication, while 130 copies were sold in the second six-month period. It is unclear whether significant bulk sales were made in following years for the purpose of promoting the book in piano curricula. See PSF (no file number). Tcherepnin's Japanese agent offered to reprint the Concert Etudes in 1938, "as there is no more Commercial Press in Shanghai." See PSF, letter from Yeinen Yuasa, August 29, 1938.

27. PSF (160).

28. Ming Tcherepnin also performed modern Chinese piano music after 1937. See Chang (1986, 90–93). Programs and news clippings kept by Tcherepnin show the extent to which the works were performed on tours across North America, Scandinavia, Eastern and Western Europe, and North Africa (see PSF), especially until 1948.

29. According to news reports, audiences for each Beiping performance generally numbered several hundred.

30. Ryuginsha is the Japanese name for *Longyinshe* (Dragon Song Agency).

31. It is unclear exactly when Ryuginsha ceased publication. Kumazawa (2005, 68) states

that it continued at least until 1940, while Chang says it closed in 1939. Tcherepnin wrote in 1965 that he maintained it until 1937. See Chang (1986, 85) and Korabelnikova (2008, 109).

32. Tcherepnin also worked closely with young Japanese composers and sponsored a separate competition in Japan for orchestral works that incorporated Japanese themes.

33. Jiang became especially vulnerable because of his associations with Japan and Tcherepnin in the tumultuous decades from the 1940s, and he was subject to persecution at various times.

34. Tcherepnin's concerts outside of Asia increasingly focused on works by the Chinese composers over the Japanese composers from the late 1930s to the late 1940s, especially when he partnered with Lee Hsien Ming in performance and on tour. The publishing collection, however, included more Japanese works of greater variety than the Chinese pieces, which were all piano and vocal.

35. Letters Tcherepnin received from his Japanese Ryuginsha agent Yuasa Yeinen from 1937 to 1940 reveal the intricate cultural-political position facing Chinese-Japanese ventures such as Ryuginsha as Japan extended its control over parts of China (PSF, Tcherepnin correspondence with Yuasa Yeinen).

36. August 4, 1926. Louisine was the granddaughter of sugar magnate Charles Elder and the daughter of Samuel Peters, who made his fortune in coal. She passed away in 1952. In order to avoid confusion when referring to Tcherepnin's first and second wives, as well as other family members (also applicable to Avshalomov), I use given names in chapters 6 and 7 where I deem that they will provide a clearer narrative.

37. Tcherepnin's autobiography offers an extended account of his relationship with Louisine (PSF, 85–190).

38. In the first Tcherepnin biography, Reich does not even mention Louisine by name. Korabelnikova mentions Louisine just twice in her biography (2008, 78 and 113).

39. Tcherepnin did not openly discuss his relationship with Louisine for decades. The subject is carefully broached in Folkman's *Compendium*. See Folkman (2008, viii, xi–xii).

40. Folkman cites Louisine's personal reasons for giving her consent (2008, 167).

41. By 1932, Louisine had estimated that she had given Tcherepnin's parents half a million francs just in the first seven years of the relationship. Though resentful of the tension caused, Tcherepnin does not dispute this figure. See PSF (148).

42. Louisine's entry from November 14, 1934, suggests that she was privy to the competition jury's decision to award four more prizes. See LPW (1923–1946).

43. See Liang Maochun (2014, 26); Ma (1935a, 6); and PSF, Alexander Tcherepnin correspondence with Koh Bunya (Jiang Wenye).

44. Diary entry of July 4, 1935.

45. March 12, 1938.

46. September 24, 1938.

47. November 9, 1938.

48. The *Compendium* does not clarify the exact date of their marriage, with events and dates especially unclear between March 1937 and late 1938. See Folkman (2008, 41 and 181). The Tcherepnin autobiography breaks off in 1937, just prior to the period in question (PSF, 190; Folkman 2008, xi).

49. Willi Reich is vague in his account of Tcherepnin's marital relations, stating only that "shortly before the outbreak of World War II, Tcherepnin received a divorce from his first wife and married Lee Hsien Ming" (Folkman 2008, 41). In correspondence with Reich, Tcherepnin expressed his desire to limit discussion of the first marriage (PSF, letter to Willi Reich, September 27, 1965; Folkman 2008, viii).

50. See Lam (1957, 11) and "Tcherepnin: One of the Great Masters" (1950, 8).

51. A handwritten anniversary greeting in French from August 24, 1944, does not clearly identify the wedding year (PSF, no file number).

52. See July 11, 1935; August 3, 1935; September 24, 1937; September 24, 1938; February 7, 1939.

53. August 2, 1946. Peter was Ming and Alexander Tcherepnin's first child and is chairman of the board of the Tcherepnin Society.

Chapter 7: Partnering with the Shanghai Arts Community

Epigraph. Arnoldov (1933). This passage was translated by Riikkamari Muhonen.

1. Performed at that time under the title *The Soul of Kin Sei.*

2. For biographical details, see Winzenburg (2012, 2013, 2015) and Avshalomov (2001).

3. See Winzenburg (2015).

4. I emphasize the relative depth here in order to refute claims that Avshalomov engaged in "Chinoiserie" in the manner of eighteenth- and nineteenth-century European composers on account of his being non-Chinese. See Liang Maochun (2014).

5. See, for example, Jiang et al. (1994); Wang Yuhe (2009, 289–290); Liu Ching-Chih (2010); Man (2011).

6. Avshalomov's experimentation was a creative response to the theoretical reform discussion, which gained momentum through the first half of the twentieth century, involving whether and how theatrical, musical, and literary aspects of the predominant traditional Chinese opera might be changed or developed for purposes of wider political and social reform in China. In practice, *yangbanxi* "model dramas" and other works of the later twentieth century adopted similar practices to the earlier experiments by Avshalomov. See Winzenburg (2015).

7. For further background of Jewish musical and cultural life in Shanghai, see Goldstein (2015), Rosenson (1998), and Xu (1991, 1998).

8. This work appeared under various titles, including *In Hutungs of Peking*, "A Sketch in Sounds 'In Hutungs of Peiping' for Grand Orchestra," and *Peiping Hutungs.*

9. *Hutungs* was performed by major North American orchestras, including those in Philadelphia, Los Angeles, Cincinnati, and elsewhere. New York Public Library of Performing Arts JPB 89–35.

10. Avshalomov also conducted for other organizations, such as the Shanghai Choral Society.

11. *Hutungs* was recorded on Columbia Records by the SMO in 1937 and later on multiple occasions in North America and Russia. It was also published commercially by Ricordi.

12. Shen continued to serve as an invaluable behind-the-scenes musical and theatrical advisor to Avshalomov on his dramatic and symphonic works. See Jiang et al. (1994, 333, 461); Winzenburg (2012).

13. Traditional Chinese theater such as Peking Opera generally utilizes minimal stage props and scenery. Instead, symbolic references are made to objects, passage of time and distance, and scenic backdrop via physical, musical, and poetic gestures.

14. The net ticket intake of $5,086 was far higher than for the other three special May concerts, which took in between $2,200 and $3,700. SMA U1-4-365.

15. The ballet assumed different English and Chinese titles for different performances. In English, it was performed as *Incense Shadows* in 1935 and 1941 and *The Dream of Wei Lien*

in 1936 and 1942. The Chinese title was *Xiangzhuan huanjing* 香篆幻境 in 1935, *Niao luo meng* 茑萝梦 in 1936, and *Gusha jingmeng* 古刹惊梦 in 1941 and 1942. See Jiang et al. (1994, 332).

16. The review was written shortly before Nie's death in Japan. Nie, via He Luting, had Avshalomov orchestrate "The March of the Volunteers" for the film *Children of Troubled Times*. The song has since become the national anthem of the PRC. See Winzenburg (2012, 69).

17. The *Incense Shadows* score is dedicated to Jordan. Alla Grigorievna frequently wrote reviews for the Russian-languague newspaper *Slovo*, using her given name only without surname.

18. Jacob Avshalomov attributes the small audiences to tension caused by the Xian Incident, in which Chiang Kai-Shek was kidnapped, just as the production opened. See Avshalomov (2001, 74).

19. Part of the failure was due to increasing war tension and inadequate financial assurances for traveling production members. Avshalomov also discovered later that impresario A. Strok had intentionally spoiled his chance with Columbia because Avshalomov had refused to take on Strok as his manager. See Avshalomov (2001, 202). See also "Chinese Ballet Talent Sought" (1937, 14).

20. Avshalomov complained that most of his foreign friends had left China by mid-1939. See Avshalomov (2001, 147).

21. Singer was often referred to by the nickname "Grischa." He was mentioned in chapter 4 among the talented generation of Russian émigré pianists, such as Tolya Vedernikov and Vladimir Havsky, to perform with the SMO.

22. Thanks to Simo Mikkonen for providing this biographical information.

23. There is no evidence in the literature to suggest that Avshalomov was inspired by "Hommage" in his conception of the concerto. Avshalomov wrote the work six months after Tcherepnin premiered his piece in Beiping. It is plausible, if not likely, that Avshalomov at least heard about Tcherepnin's piece. There is little chance he would have heard it or seen the score before writing his own concerto, however.

24. See Winzenburg (2012, 2013, 2017). Avshalomov also wrote *3 Short Pieces for Erhu [fiddle] and Orchestra* for Wei Zhongle, which were performed with the SMO in 1941.

25. See "Avshalomoff Music Will Be Recorded" (1936, 9). It was recorded at the Columbia-Pathé studio on 1099 Xujiahui Road.

26. Avshalomov complains of being "threatened by both Japanese and Russians" during the war, but he is careful not to explicate where Russian pressure is coming from. See Avshalomov (2001, 183).

27. For details of *The Great Wall*, see Winzenburg (2012, 2015).

28. For a full translation of the letter, see Winzenburg (2015).

29. For example, see "Zhongguo diyibu yinyueju Meng Jiang Nü" (1945).

30. The *Shidai* magazine cover also included its English title *Music Epoch*. This was another Soviet TASS-supported publication that Jiang established in 1942. See Man (2011, 166).

31. The March performances were held as a fundraiser for the China Welfare Fund, sponsored by Soong Ching-Ling (Song Qingling 宋庆龄, Mme. Sun Yat Sen). In all, they netted an extraordinary sum of eighteen million dollars (US$27,000) for the fund. See Avshalomov (2001, 231).

32. See Avshalomov (2001, 207). The following summary paraphrases details from his letter.

Epilogue

1. As mentioned on the Philadelphia Orchestra website, the orchestra and its current music director Yannick signed a five-year agreement with both Beijing's National Center for Performing Arts and Shanghai Media Group, continuing the strong ties between the orchestra and the Shanghai audience. https://www.philorch.org/history#/, accessed February 27, 2017.

2. See for instance Yang and Saffle (2017), a study that includes a theoretical introduction to various critical theories pertinent to cross-cultural studies and twelve chapters on different forms of musical encounters between China and the West from different historical periods.

3. Information posted on Shanghai Grand Theatre's official webpage at http://www.shgtheatre.com/jsp/portal/center.jsp?branchID=1000002152, accessed on January 2, 2017.

4. Zaha Hadid's design won the international competition for the Cardiff Bay Opera House in Wales, which was planned in the 1990s but never built. This is discussed in Crickhowell 1997.

5. For example, Petr Balakshin, referring to the fact that the Russian pedagogues' teaching methods were based on their experience as students of the Moscow or Saint Petersburg Conservatory, noted that "the first Chinese conservatory adopted the program of Russian conservatories, and from that moment established itself as the center of music education for all China" (1958, 351).

6. It is interesting to note that Russian émigrés had also left an impact on Hong Kong's musical scene and food culture. One of the early conductors of the Hong Kong Philharmonic was the Russian violinist Solomon Bard from Harbin and then Shanghai. Many Russian refugees who came to Hong Kong opened cafes selling dishes such as borscht and shaslik, which have been assimilated into local restaurants' menus to the extent that nobody knows the dishes' origin anymore (Wordie 2007, n.p.).

7. The history as well as the historiography of Russian music is entwined with nationalism and politics, as has been pointed out by Richard Taruskin in "Some Thoughts on the History and Historiography of Russian Music" (2009), a reworking of an earlier article he wrote in 1985. In a way, the same happened in Chinese music historiography regarding the contribution of Western musicians. As evident in Taruskin's various monographs on Russian music (for instance 2009 and 2016) as well as Francis Maes' *A History of Russian Music* (2002), there is a hiatus on Russian émigré musicians abroad, which hopefully will get a mention in future historiography of Russian music.

8. Assessing Russian musicians' roles in the development of Chinese music in China is not an easy task, particularly for Chinese historians. First of all, many of the historical records in the PRC were destroyed during the Cultural Revolution, and those that remain are not always accessible to researchers. Archive policies in the PRC change from time to time and from place to place. For instance, the Shanghai Symphony Archive is most receptive to foreign investigators, giving free access to its concert programs and other archival materials the institution holds. But the Shanghai Conservatory of Music only allows access to its special collection of printed materials, which include early publications of the National Conservatory. Archival records such as students' enrollment or faculty contracts are barred from use by foreigner researchers. The Shanghai Municipal Archive's policies have also changed over time. Hard copies of archival records of the Municipal Council had been available in Yang and Edmunds' visit in 2005 and 2006, but are now only available through microfilms that cannot be photocopied and as of 2015 are seemingly now only open to Chinese nationals.

9. The conference proceedings for Sino-Russian Musical Exchange edited by Tao Yabing

(2011) collects many reminiscences of musicians who studied with Russian experts at the Central Conservatory as well as at Soviet conservatories. The volume includes studies on the influence of the Russian education system on the Chinese ones. The transmission of Russian songs is also a topic that has attracted a lot of scholarly attention.

10. The terms "populism" and "populist" were used by Richard Kraus in his seminal volume *Pianos and Politics in China* to refer to believers in resisting the cosmopolitan's embrace of Western art as well as in minimizing the impact of the West (1989, 29).

11. As the Cultural Revolution is still a sensitive subject in the PRC, little is known about the intelligentsia who committed suicide at the time. There are a couple of lists compiled by individuals regarding famous professors who committed suicide. In various writings, it is mentioned in passing that seventeen people related to the Shanghai Conservatory took their lives, whereas a Chinese scholar from Shanghai told me that twelve professors committed suicide, while quite a few took their lives with their family members.

12. The Chinese musicologist Wang Yuhe 汪毓和's authoritative official history of contemporary Chinese music (1984, 1994, 2002, and 2006) is a case in point. The contributions of Xiao Youmei and naturally the Russian pedagogues of the National Conservatory were entirely left out in his earlier discourse but were included in the 2009 version.

13. This is based on a search with their names in Chinese in *China Academic Journals Fulltext Database*. Naturally, some mention them in greater details whereas others just in passing.

14. The Russian Orthodox Church, Department of External Church Relations website, https://mospat.ru/ru/2014/05/21/news102668/, accessed on June 25, 2018, provides an English translation by Katherine Ilachinski. It says that the Cathedral of the Mother of God "Surety of Sinners," designed by the Russian architect J. L. Lihonosa, was founded in 1933 with donations from émigrés, and the construction was completed in 1937. The article provides a short description of the history of the structure after it was closed for worship during the Cultural Revolution. When Yang and Mikkonen visited it in January 2016, the building was empty, and part of it was used a restaurant. The building is located at 55 Xinle Road.

15. For instance, the event "Specters of Communism. A Festival on the Revolutionary Century" held in Munich, Germany, from November 16 to 21, 2017, and the conference "A Century of Movement: Russian Culture and Global Community Since 1917" held at the University of North Carolina at Chapel Hill in the United States from October 12–13, 2017.

BIBLIOGRAPHY

"1936 Concert Attendance Sets Record." 1937. *China Press*, February 26, 9.

"A Famous Woman Violinist: Cecilia Hansen, Peer of Musicians of Her Sex, Coming." 1928. *North-China Herald and Supreme Court & Consular Gazette*, June 30, 567.

"A Wagner Opera in Shanghai." 1922. *North-China Herald and Supreme Court & Consular Gazette*, February 4, 281.

Ablazhei, N. N. 2007. *S vostoka na vostok: Rossiiskaia emigratsia v Kitae* (From east to east: Russian emigration in China). Novosibirsk: Institut Istorii SO RAN.

Ablova, N. E. 2007. *Dalnevostochnaia vetv' Russkogo zarubezhia* (Far Eastern branch of Russia Abroad). Minsk: Respublikanskii institute vyshei shkoly.

"Advances Made By Municipal Orchestra Shown By Contrast with Cruder and Earlier Days." 1928. *China Press*, April 8, 5.

Advertisement. 1928. *Shankhaiskaia Zaria*, February 24, 2.

Advertisement. 1929. *Shankhaiskaia Zaria*, February 24, 2.

Advertisement. 1930. *Shankhaiskaia Zaria*, March 30, 2.

Advertisement. 1932a. *Slovo*, January 31, 2.

Advertisement. 1932b. *Slovo*, May 4, 2.

Advertisement. 1935a. *Feniks*, no. 12:17.

Advertisement. 1935b. *Feniks*, no. 17:15.

Advertisement. 1936a. *Slovo*, April 20, 4.

Advertisement. 1936b. *Slovo*, January 21, 2.

Advertisement. 1936c. *Slovo*, January 23, 3.

Advertisement. 1937. *Slovo*, December 15, 2.

Advertisement. 1938. *Slovo*, March 6, 2.

Advertisement. 1946. *Novosti Dnia*, April 25, 4.

Aksakov, Sergie. 1933. "Molodye kitaiskie artisty" (Young Chinese artists). *Vecharnaia Zaria*, June 10, 4.

———. 1935. "Muzyka (Music)." *Vrata 2*, 242–243.

———. 1936. "Muzykalnye zametki (Musical notes)." *Shankhaiskaia Zaria*, January 19, 10.

All About Shanghai and Environs: A Standard Guide Book. Edition 1934–1935. Shanghai: The University Press.

"Anshlag na 'Karmen'" ('Carmen' sold-out). 1937. *Slovo*, November 14, 6.

Arias, Enrique Alberto. 1989. *Alexander Tcherepnin: A Bio-Bibliography*. New York: Greenwood Press.

Arnoldov, L. 1933. "O kitaiskoi muzyke" (On Chinese music). *Shankhaiskaia Zaria*, May 23, 6.

"Avshalomoff Music Will Be Recorded." 1936. *China Press*, April 22, 9.

Avshalomov, Jacob, and Aaron Avshalomov. 2001. *Avshalomovs' Winding Way: Composers Out of China—A Chronicle*. N.p. Xlibris.

"B. S. segodnia v Taun-Kholle" (B. S. today at Town Hall). 1929. *Shankhaiskaia Zaria*, February 23, 6.

"B. S. Zakharov i laureaty: Istoricheskii vypusk Natsionalnoi Konservatorii" (Professor B. S. Zakharov and his Prize-Winners: Historic graduates of the National Conservatory). 1933. *Shankhaiskaia Zaria*, July 7, 6.

Bakich, Olga. 1986. "A Russian City in China: Harbin before 1917." *Canadian Slavonic Papers* 28, no. 2: 129–148.

Balakshin, Petr. 1958. *Final v kitae* (Finals in China). Vol. 1. San Francisco: Sirius.

Bard, Solomon M. 2009. *Light and Shade: Sketches from an Uncommon Life*. Hong Kong: Hong Kong University Press.

Baumann, Martin. 1995. "Conceptualizing Diaspora: The Preservation of Religious Identity in Foreign Parts, Exemplified by Hindu Communities Outside India." *Temenos* 31: 19–35.

Berkowitz, William R. 1982. *Community Impact: Creating Grassroots Change in Hard Times*. Cambridge, MA: Schenkman Publishing Company.

"Bez raboty. . . ." (without work). 1930. *Shankhaiskaia Zaria*, May 3, 3.

Bian Meng 卞萌. 1996. *Zhongguo gangqin wenhua zhi xingcheng yu fazhan* 中国钢琴文化之形成与发展 (The formation and development of Chinese piano culture). Beijing: Huayue Chubanshe 华乐出版社.

Bian Zushan 卞祖善. 2011. "Ta ba yisheng xiangei le zhongguo minzu yinyue shiye: jinian ahlong. Ahpuxialuomufu danshen 115 zhounian" 他把一生献给了中国民族音乐事业—纪念阿镗.阿莆夏洛穆夫诞辰115周年 (He devoted his life to the cause of Chinese national music—to commemorate Aaron Avshalomov's 115th anniversary). In *Zhonger yinyue jiaoliu: shishi huigu yu dangdai fansi* 中俄音乐交流: 史事回顾与当代反思 (Sino-Russian musical exchange: Historical review and contemporary reflections), edited by Tao Yabing 陶亚兵, 105–116. Beijing: Renmin yinyue chubanshe 人民音乐出版社.

Bickers, Robert. 1998. "Shanghailanders: The Formation and Identity of the British Settler Community in Shanghai 1843–1937." *Past and Present* 159: 161–211.

———. 1999. *Britain in China: Community Culture and Colonialism, 1900–1949*. Manchester: Manchester University Press.

———. 2001. "'The Greatest Cultural Asset East of Suez': The History and Politics of the Shanghai Municipal Orchestra and Public Band, 1881–1946." In *Ershi shiji de Zhongguo yu shijie lunwenji* 二十世纪的中国与世界论文集 (Twentieth-century China and the world proceedings), vol. 2, edited by Chang Chi-hsiung, 835–875. Taibei: Institute of History, Academia Sinica.

Bickers, Robert, and Christian Henriot, eds. 2000. *New Frontiers: Imperialism's New Communities in East Asia, 1842–1953.* Manchester: Manchester University Press.

"Blestiashchii triumf Toli Vedernikova" (The great triumph of Tolya Vedernikov). 1935. *Shankhaiskaia Zaria,* April 1, 5.

Boguslavsky, Boris. 1928. "Nasha anketa o shkole, otvet Bor. Boguslavskago" (Our questionnaire about the school, Bor. Boguslavsky's reply). *Shankhaiskaia Zaria,* February 18, 5.

"Boris Godunov." 1937. *Slovo,* October 19, 4.

Born, Georgina. 2010. "For a Relational Musicology: Music and Interdisciplinarity, Beyond the Practice Turn." *Journal of the Royal Musical Association* 135, no. 2: 205–243.

"Boy Pianist Plans Farewell Concert Here." 1935. *China Press,* September 24, 3.

Brickner, Rachel K., ed. 2013. *Migration, Globalization, and the State.* New York: Palgrave Macmillan.

Cai Jianguo 蔡建国. 1997. *Cai Yuanpei yu jindai Zhongguo* 蔡元培与近代中国 (Cai Yuanpei and contemporary China). Shanghai: Shanghai shehui kexueyuan chubanshe 上海社会科学院出版社.

"Capacity House Pays Tribute to Mms. Tomskaya." 1928. *China Press,* April 3, 4.

Caughey, John Hart. 2011. *The Marshall Mission to China, 1945–1947: The Letters and Diary of Colonel John Hart Caughey.* Edited by Roger B. Jeans. Lanham, MD: Rowman & Littlefield.

Chang Chi-Jen. 1986. "Alexander Tcherepnin: His Influence on Modern Chinese Music." PhD dissertation, Columbia University Teachers College.

Chao Mei-Pa. 1937. "The Trend of Modern Chinese Music." *Tien Hsia Monthly* 4: 269–286.

"Chekho-slovatskii muzykal'no-literaturnyi chai" (Czecho-Slovak musical and literary event). 1930. *Shankhaiskaia Zaria,* February 2, 3.

Cheng Naishan 程乃珊. 2007. "Bai e shengyue jiaoshou Su Shilin he ta de Zhongguo xuesheng Wen Kezheng" 白俄声乐教授苏石林和他的中国学生温可铮 (Russian vocal pedagogue and his Chinese student Wen Kezheng). *Dangan chunqiu* 档案春秋 10: 59–60.

Chesneaux, J., et al. 1977. *China from 1911. Revolution to Liberation.* Hassocks: Harvester Press.

Cheung, Joys Hoi Yan. 2008. "Chinese Music and Translated Modernity in Shanghai, 1918–1937." PhD dissertation, University of Michigan.

———. 2012. "Divide and Connections in Chinese Musical Modernity: Cases of Musical Networks Emerging in Colonial Shanghai, 1919–1937." *Twentieth-Century China* 37, no. 1: 30–49.

"Chinese Ballet Talent Sought." 1937. *China Press,* June 23, 14.

"Chinese Ballet To Use Modern Stage Make-Up." 1933. *China Press,* May 3, 4.

"Chinese Pantomime-Ballet Sunday Will Be Unique In Local Art Annals." 1933. *China Press,* May 20, 12.

Clifford, James. 1994. "Diasporas." *Cultural Anthropology* 9: 302–38.

———. 1997. *Routes: Travel and Translation in the Late Twentieth Century.* Cambridge, MA: Harvard University Press.

Cohen, Phil. 1999. "Rethinking the Diasporama." *Patterns of Prejudice* 33, no. 1: 3–22.

Cohen, Robin. 1997. *Global Diaspora: An Introduction*. London: UCL Press.

Cohen, Robin, and Gunvor Jónsson, eds. 2011. *Migration and Culture*. Northampton, MA: Edward Elgar Publishing.

Collins, Tim. 2010. "'Tis Like They Never Left: Locating 'Home' in the Music of Sliabh Aughty's Diaspora." *Journal of the Society for American Music* 4, no. 4: 491–507.

"Composer Congratulated." 1938. Letter to the Editor, *North-China Daily News*, October 28, reprinted in *North-China Herald*, November 2, 203.

"Composer's Recital Given Here." 1934. *Peking & Tientsin Sunday Times*, June 3.

Cook, Nicholas. 2012. "Anatomy of the Encounter: Intercultural Analysis as Relational Musciology." In *Critical Musicological Reflections: Essays in Honour of Derek B. Scott*, edited by Stan Hawkins, 193–208. Farnham: Ashgate.

Cover page. 1928. *Shankhaiskaia Zaria*, April 15, 1.

Crickhowell, Nicholas. 1997. *Opera House Lottery: Zaha Hadid and the Cardiff Bay Project*. Wales: University of Wales Press.

Dai Penghai 戴鹏海. 1990. "Heyi wei sizhe" 何以慰死者 (How to comfort the dead). In *Wenhua lingmiao bozhongren: Jiang Chunfang* 文化灵苗播种人姜椿芳 (A sower of cultural seedlings: Jiang Chunfang), 33–38. Shanghai: Zhongguo wenshi chubanshe 中国文史出版社.

———. 1991. "Zhongguo di yige kai gangqin yanzouhui de yinyue jia—wei 'Ding Shande yinyue shengya liushi zhounian' er zuo" 中国第一个开钢琴演奏会的音乐家——为 "丁善德音乐生涯六十周年" 而作 (First musician to give a piano recital in China—written for 'Ding Shande's 60th musical career'). *Yinyue aihao zhe* 音乐爱好者 (Music Lover) 5: 6–7.

———. 1993. *Ding Shande ji qi yinyue zuopin: Shanghai yinyue xueyuan xiandai yinyuexue hui di sijie nianhui lunwenji* 丁善德及其音乐作品:上海音乐学院现代音乐学会第四届年会论文集 (Ding Shande and his music: Proceedings of the Contemporary Music Society of the Shanghai Conservatory of Music's fourth annual meeting). Shanghai: Shanghai yinyue chubanshe 上海音乐出版社.

"Dairen Maru." 1932. *Slovo*, May 18, 6.

"Damskii klass shkoly fizicheskogo razvitiia L. Knizhe" (Women's class of L. Knizhe's school of physical development). 1927. *Solntse*, no. 1: 4.

"Deiateli iskusstva" (Art professionals). 1928. *Shankhaiskaia Zaria*, April 6, 5.

Ding Shande 丁善德. 1982. "Nanyi wangque de huiyi: huainian Xiao Youmei xiansheng" 难以忘却的回忆——怀念萧友梅先生 (Unforgettable memories: Missing Mr. Xiao Youmei). *Yinyue yishu* 音乐艺术 (Journal of the Shanghai Conservatory of Music) 3: 2–4.

———, ed. 1987. *Shanghai Yinyuexueyuan jianshi* 上海音乐学院简史 (A brief history of the Shanghai Conservatory of Music). Shanghai: Shanghai yinyue xueyuan chubanshe 上海音乐出版社.

"Divorce Challenged." 1939. *North-China Herald and Supreme Court & Consular Gazette*, June 7, 430.

"Doktor Voronov v Shankhae" (Doctor Voronov in Shanghai). 1935. *Prozhektor*, no. 8: 13.

Dorfman, Ben. 1935. "White Russians in the Far East." *Asia* (March): 166–172.

"Dukhovnyi kontsert" (Spiritual concert). 1928. *Shankhaiskaia Zaria*, April 6, 4.

Dyer, Richard. 2002. *Only Entertainment*, 2nd edition. New York: Routledge.

Dubinets, Elena. 2013 "Contemporary Émigré Composers: How Russian Are They?" In *Russian Émigré Culture: Conservatism or Evolution?*, edited by Christoph Flamm, Henry Keazor, and Roland Marti, 269–286. Newcastle upon Tyne: Cambridge Scholars Publishing.

"The Easter Sunday Concert at Lyceum: Brilliant Performance by Municipal Orchestra and Choral Societies." 1940. *North-China Daily News*, March 26, 2.

Enomoto, Yashiko (Jiaben Taizi) 榎本泰子. 2003. *Yueren zhi du—Shanghai: Xiyang yinyue zai jindai Zhongguo de fachu* 乐人之都:上海:西洋音乐在近代中国的发轫 (A musician's capital: Shanghai: The origins of Western music in modern China). Shanghai: Shanghai yinyue chubanshe 上海音乐出版社.

———. 2009. *Xifang yinyuejia de Shanghai meng: gongbuju yuedui chuanji* 西方音乐家的上海梦:工部局乐队传奇 (Western musicians' Shanghai dream: The legend of the Municipal Orchestra). Translated by Zhao Yi 趙怡. Shanghai: Shanghai cishu chubanshe 上海辞书出版社.

"Eshcho o Fauste" (Again about Faust). 1937. *Slovo*, October 7, 4.

"Evgenii Onegin" (Eugene Onegin). 1937. *Slovo*, October 12, 4.

"Evropa interesuetsia kitaiskoi i iaponskoi muzykoi" (Europe takes an interest in Chinese and Japanese music). 1936. *Shankhaiskaia Zaria*, May 21, 5.

"F. I. Shaliapin v Shankhae (F. I. Chaliapin in Shanghai)." 1936. *Shankhaiskaia Zaria*, January 21, 6.

"F. I. Shaliapin v Shankhae" (F. I. Chaliapin in Shanghai). 1936. *Slovo*, January 21, 3–4.

"F. I. Shaliapin v Shankhae" (F. I. Chaliapin in Shanghai). 1936. *Feniks*, no. 22: 14–15.

Fairclough, Pauline. 2016. *Classics for the Masses. Shaping Soviet Musical Identity under Lenin and Stalin*. New Haven, CT: Yale University Press.

Feuerwerker, A. 1983. "The Foreign Presence in China." In *The Cambridge History of China*, edited by J. K. Fairbank, 128–132. Cambridge: Cambridge University Press.

"Final Concert in Carlton: Special Programme Given by M. Zakharoff." 1933. *North-China Daily News*, May 1, 12.

Flamm, Christoph. 2013. "'My love, forgive me this apostasy': Some Thoughts on Russian Émigré Culture." In *Russian Émigré Culture: Conservatism or Evolution?*, edited by Christoph Flamm, Henry Keazor, and Roland Marti, 1–18. Newcastle upon Tyne: Cambridge Scholars Publishing.

Flamm, Christoph, Henry Keazor, and Roland Marti. 2013. *Russian Émigré Culture: Conservatism or Evolution?* Newcastle upon Tyne: Cambridge Scholars Publishing.

Flamm, Christoph, Roland Marti, and Ada Raev, eds. 2018. *Transcending the Borders of Countries, Languages, and Disciplines in Russian Émigré Culutre*. Newcastle upon Tyne: Cambridge Scholars Publishing.

"Floriia Toska" (Floria Tosca). 1938. *Slovo*, January 29, 2.

Folkman, Benjamin. 2008. *Alexander Tcherepnin: A Compendium*. New York: The Tcherepnin Society, Inc.

———. 2013. "Yalishanda Qierpin: Huodong zai Zhongguode Ou Ya zuoqujia" 亚历山大.齐尔品: 活动在中国的欧亚作曲家 (Alexander Tcherepnin: A Eurasian composer in China). Translated by Wu Weiyi 伍维曦. *Yinyue yishu (Shanghai yinyue xueyuan xuebao)* 音乐艺术 (上海音乐学院学报) (Journal of the Shanghai Conservatory of Music) 2: 17–21.

Fonteyn, Margot. 1998. "Margot Fonteyn, Aged Twelve, Dances in Shanghai." In *Shanghai: Electric and Lurid City: An Anthology*, edited by Barbara Baker, 99–104. Hong Kong: Oxford University Press.

Fortunova, Anna. 2013. "Russian Collective Identity in Exile and Music in Berlin 1917–1933." In *Russian Émigré Culture: Conservatism or Evolution?*, edited by Christoph Flamm, Henry Keazor, and Roland Marti, 139–150. Newcastle upon Tyne: Cambridge Scholars Publishing.

Fu Lei 傅雷. 1933. "Cong 'Gongbuju Zhongguo yinyuehui' shuo dao Zhongguo xiju he yinyue di qiantu" 从'工部局中国音乐会'说到中国音乐与戏剧底前途 (A discussion of China's musical and theatrical future from the 'SMO Chinese Concert'). *Shishi Xinbao* 时事新报, May 28, 4.

Fu Shu 辅叔. 1935. "Xiao shi" 校史 (School history). In *Xiaoshe luocheng jinian kan* 校舍落成纪念刊 (Commemorative publication for the completion of the school building). In *Guoli yinyue juanke xuexiao xiaoshe lecheng jinian tekan* 国立音乐专科学校校舍落成纪念特刊 (Special issue to celebrate the completion of the school building of the National Music Institute), edited by Conservatory Book Committee, 9–26. SMAY8-1-468.

"G. Kudinov—Rigoletto." 1937. *Slovo*, November 21, 2.

Gamsa, Mark. 2010. *The Reading of Russian Literature in China: A Moral Example and Manual of Practice*. New York: Palgrave Macmillan.

"Ganina." 1936. *Feniks*, no. 23: 15.

"Gao Zhilan: Wo cong wei likanguo yinyue" 高芝兰：我从未离开过音乐 (Gao Zhilan: I have never left music). An interview with Gao Zhilan by Mu Ran posted on the website "Xingwang" on September 24, 2003. http://www.newstarweekly.com/phpcode/web/view_detail.php?news_art_id=25014. Accessed on March 5, 2016.

"Godovoe sobranie KhLAMa" (Annual meeting of KhLAM). 1937. *Slovo*, May 19, 4.

"Godovshchina 1 Russkoi Muzykalnoi shkoly." 1937. *Slovo*, January 22, 2.

Goldberg, Michelle. 2015. *The Goddess Pose, The Audacious Life of Indra Devi, the Woman Who Helped Bring Yoga to the West*. New York: Alfred A. Knopf.

Goldstein, Jonathan. 2015. Jewish Identities in East and Southeast Asia: Singapore, Manila, Taipei, Harbin, Shanghai, Rangoon, and Surabaya. Berlin: De Gruyter Oldenbourg.

"Gounod's Faust Well Received." 1937. *Shanghai Evening Post & Mercury*, October 6.

"Grand Benefit Concert." 1937. *North China Herald*, December 15, 421.

"Great Violinists." 1928. *North-China Herald and Supreme Court & Consular Gazette*, September 29, 530.

Guan Liren 关立人. 1994. "Wei renmin de liyi yu weilai er sikao" 为人民的利益与未来而思考 (Think for the benefit and future of the people). In *Zhongguo jinxiandai yinyuejia zhuan* 中国近现代音乐家傳 (Biographies of contemporary Chinese musicians), edited by Xiang Yanshen, vol. 2, 12–30. Liaoning: Chunfeng wenyi chubanshe 春风文艺出版社.

Guo Youshou 郭有守. 1947. "Zhongguo zhi ying nügaoyin geren zai Bali" 中国之莺女高音歌人在巴黎 (Bird of China soprano songster in Paris). *Shen Bao* 申报, May 4, 7.

"Guoli yinyue yuan zhaosheng" 国立音乐院招生 (National Conservatory of Music recruitment). 1927. *Shen Bao* 申报, September 1, 2.

Hall, Stuart. 1996. "Introduction: Who Needs Identity." In *Questions of Cultural Identity*, edited by Stuart Hall and Paul Du Gay, 1–17. London: Sage Publications.

Han Guo-huang 韩国璜. 1995. "Shanghai gongbuju yuedui yanjiu" 上海工部局乐队研究 (A preliminary study of Shanghai Municipal Orchestra). *Yishuxue* 艺术学 (Study of the arts) 14: 143–203.

He Luting 贺绿汀. 1991. *He Luting quanji* 贺绿汀全集 (He Luting collected works). Shanghai: Shanghai yinyue xueyuan chubanshe 上海音乐学院出版社.

———. 1982. "Huainian Qierpin xiansheng 怀念齐尔品先生 (In remembrance of Mr. Tcherepnin)." *Yinyue yishu* 音乐艺术 (Journal of the Shanghai Conservatory of Music) 3: 1–2.

HIA (Hoover Institution Archives). Georgy Vasilievich Kudinov (George Koudinoff) Papers.

Howard, Joshua. 2012. "Introduction: Contesting China's New 'National' Music." *Twentieth-Century China* 37, no. 1: 2–4.

Hsia, Ching-Lin. 1929. *A Historical Review of the International Settlement. Its Future Development and Possibilities Through Sino-foreign Co-operation*. Shanghai: Kelly and Welsh Limited.

Huang Xudong 黄旭东. 2005. "Ershi shiji sishi niandai zhongguo zuigao yinyue xuefu—Guoli Yinyueyuan shujie" 二十世纪四十年代中国最高音乐学府—国立音乐院述介 (Highest institute of music in the 1940s of the twentieth century: Introduction to the National Conservatory of Music). In *Nongfu ji—yinyue shishi menwai tan* 弄斧集 (Giving it a try collection), 158–177. Beijing: Zhongyang yinyue xueyuan chubanshe 中央音乐学院出版社.

Huang Zi 黄自. 1934. "Zeyang caike chansheng wuguo minzu yinyue" 怎样才可产生吾国民族音乐 (How can we produce our national music). *Shanghai Chenbao* 上海晨报, October 21, 9.

"Huanying Qierpin yinyue yanzouhui mingwan juxiing" 欢送齐尔品音乐演奏会明晚举行 (Tcherepnin welcoming concert to be held tomorrow evening). 1935. *Shijie Ribao* 世界日报, January 18, 7.

Huo Yeji 火页寄. 1935. "Hanyou zhongda yiyi de yinyue yanzouhui" 含有重大意义的音乐演奏会 (A music performance of great significance). *Dagongbao* 大公报, January 24, 15.

"I. A. T. Outgrowing Its Quarters." 1935. *North-China Herald and Supreme Court & Consular Gazette*, October 9, 60.

"Imeniny i vystavka khudozhnika A. D. Safronova" (Jubileum and exhibition of artist A. D. Safronov)." 1936. *Slovo*, April 19, 5.

"In the Russian Colony." 1938. *North-China Herald and Supreme Court & Consular Gazette*, December 14, 454.

"In the Russian Colony." 1939. *North-China Herald and Supreme Court & Consular Gazette*, April 5, 21.

"'Incense Shadows' An Experiment." 1935. *North-China Daily News*, February 28, 14.

"Interviu o predsedatelem sodruzhestva KhLAM B. M. Zhozefo-Shchik" (Interview with the chairman of association KhLAM B. M. Zhozefo-Shchik)." 1940. *Slovo*, December 6, 4.

Isurin, Ludmila. 2011. *Russian Diaspora: Culture, Identity, and Language Change*. New York: De Gruyter.

"Izbienie muzykanta" (Beating of a musician). 1930. *Shankhaiskaia Zaria*, April 13, 4.

Jackson, John, and Tony Oliver. 2003. "Personal Networks Theory and the Arts: A Literature Review with Special Reference to Entrepreneurial Popular Musicians." *Journal of Arts Management, Law, and Society* 33, no. 3: 240–256.

Jiang Chunfang 姜椿芳. 1983. "Yige zhili yu Zhongguo minzu yinyue yanjiude waiguoren: Along Afuxialuomufude zhuzhang yu shijian" 一个致力于中国民族音乐研究的外国人——阿龙•阿甫夏洛穆夫的主张与实践 (A foreigner who dedicated himself to Chinese music research: Aaron Avshalomov's advocacy and practice). *Yinyue aihaozhe* 音乐爱好者 (Music lover) 1: 40–41.

Jiang Chunfang 姜椿芳, Qin Pengzhang 秦鹏章, Yuan Likang 袁励康, and Zhao Jiazi 赵佳梓. 1994. "Huiyi Shen Zhibai xian sheng 回忆沈知白先生 (Commemorating Mr. Shen Zhibai)." In *Shen Zhibai Yinyuelun Wenji* 沈知白音乐论文集 (Collected music theoretical works of Shen Zhibai), edited by Jiang Chunfang 姜椿芳 and Zhao Jiazi 赵佳梓, 323–500. Shanghai: Shanghai yinyue chubanshe 上海音乐出版社.

Jiang Dingxian 江定仙. 1982. "Jinian Qierpin 纪念齐尔品 (Remembering Tcherepnin)." *Zhongyang yinyue xueyuan xuebao* 中央音乐学院学报 (Journal of the Central Conservatory of Music) 4: 3–12.

———. 1994. "Yuyu wangshi kan ziwei—zuoqu jia Jiang Dingxian zizhuan" 悠悠往事堪自慰:作曲家江定仙自传 (Comfort from old memories: Composer Jiang Dingxian's autobiography). In *Zhongguo jinxiandai yinyuejia zhuan* 中国近现代音乐家傳 (Biographies of contemporary Chinese musicians), edited by Xiang Yanshen, vol. 2, 296–306. Liaoning: Chunfeng wenyi chubanshe 春风文艺出版社.

Jin Shenghua 金圣华. 1994. *Fu Lei yu ta de shijie* 傅雷与他的世界 (Fu Lei and his world). Hong Kong: San lian 三联.

"Jinian Yu Yixuan danchen 100 zhounian" 纪念喻宜萱诞辰100周年 (Commemorate the 100th Birthday of Yu Yixuan)." 2009. Posted September 11, 2009, on the website of the Shanghai Conservatory of Music. http://www.shcmusic.edu.cn/view_0.aspx?cid=370&id=2&navindex=0. Accessed on December 26, 2015.

Jones, Andrew. 2001. *Yellow Music: Media Culture and Colonial Modernity in the Chinese Jazz Age*. Durham, NC: Duke University Press.

K dniu russkoi kultury (Days of Russian culture). 1933. *Odnodnevnii zhurnal* (One-day journal). Shanghai, no publisher mentioned.

"K stoletiiu natsionalnoi opery" (On the hundredth anniversary of national opera). 1938. *Slovo*, March 6, 1.

"Kak eksportiruet devushek v Shankhai (How women are exported in Shanghai)." 1930. *Shankhaiskaia Zaria*, August 29, 6.

"Kak gotovit' bliny" (How to make blinys). 1928. *Shankhaiskaia Zaria*, February 19, 6.

"Kamernye kontserty" (Chamber concerts). 1929. *Shankhaiskaia Zaria*, September 27, 6.

Khisamutdinov, A. A., et al. 2010. *Russkie v Kitae. Istoricheskii obzor* (Russians in China. Historical survey). Shanghai: Russkii klub v Shankhae.

"Khoreograficheskaia mifologiia na shankhaiskoi stsene: k postanovke baleta 'V oblakakh fimiama'" (Choreographic mythology on the Shanghai scene: The production *Incense Shadows*). 1935. *Shankhaiskaia Zaria*, March 11, 5.

"Khorovoi Kruzhok" (Amateur choir). 1928. *Shankhaiskaia Zaria*, February 11, 3.

"Khudozhestvennaia Khronika" (Artistic chronicle). 1935. *Prozhektor*, no. 18: 18.

Koliesnikova, Evgeniia. 1926. *Russkii emigrantskii almanakh Rossiia* (Russian émigré almanac "Russia"). Shanghai: Rossiia.

"Kompozitor A. N. Cherepnin v 'Shatre'" (Composer A. N. Tcherepnin at 'Shater'). 1937. *Emigrantskaia Mysl*, January 24, 4.

"Konchina A. N. Rusanova" (Death of A. N. Rusanov). 1936. *Slovo*, July 14, 9.

"Kontsert Kardashevskikh" (Kardashevskys' concert). 1930. *Shankhaiskaia Zaria*, April 11, 4.

"Kontsert 1-oi Russkoi Muzykalnoi Shkoly." 1937. *Slovo*, January 24, 7.

"Kontsert LAO" (LAO's concert). 1928. *Shankhaiskaia Zaria*, February 7, 5.

"Kontsert molodogo kitaiskogo pianist" (Concert of the young pianist). 1935. *Shankhaiskaia Zaria*, May 12, 13.

"Kontsert orkestra o-va bogemy" (Concert of Bohemian association's orchestra). 1937. *Slovo*, April 18, 2.

"Kontsert Pervoy Russkoy Muzikalnoy Shkoly" (Concert of the First Russian Music School). 1937. *Slovo*, January 24, 7.

"Kontsert RMO" (RMO's concert). *Novyi Put*, November 22, 5.

"Kontsert russkoi kapelly" (Concert of the Russian cappella). 1929. *Shankhaiskaia Zaria*, February 26, 3.

"Kontsert shankhaisikikh pevtsov" (Concert of singers of Shanghai). 1930. *Shankhaiskaia Zaria*, May 4, 4.

"Kontsert studii P. N. Mashina" (P. N. Mashin's studio's concert). 1929. *Shankhaiskaia Zaria*, June 8, 6.

Korabelnikova, Ludmila. 2008. *Alexander Tcherepnin: The Saga of a Russian Émigré Composer*. Translated by Anna Winestein. Edited by Sue-Ellen Hershman-Tcherepnin. Bloomington: Indiana University Press.

Kraus, Richard. 1989. *Piano and Politics in China: Middle-Class Ambitions and the Struggle over Western Music*. Oxford: Oxford University Press.

Kreader, Barbara. 1984. "Zhongguo guoqu he xianzai de gangqin jiaoxue : fang gangqin jia Li Xianmin 中国过去和现在的钢琴教学—访钢琴家李献敏 (China's past and present piano teaching: Interview with pianist Li Xianmin). Translated by Quyang Meilun. *Yinyue yishu* 音乐艺术 (Journal of the Shanghai Conservatory of Music) 4: 16–21.

Kriukov, A. P. 1923. *Russkie Pesni* (Russian songs). Shanghai: A. P. Kriukova's press.

Kruzenshtern, Iu. 1933. "20 let muzykalnoi deiatelnosti. Nasha beseda s B. S. Zakharovym (20 years of musical activities. Our interview with B. S. Zakharov)." *Vechernaia Zaria*, April 22, 8.

"Kruzhok liubitelei" (Amateur circle). 1930. *Shankhaiskaia Zaria*, April 11, 3.

"Kul'turnyia zadachi Shankhaia" (Culture as Shanghai's task). 1929. *Shankhaiskaia Zaria*, February 19, 2.

Kumazawa, Ayako 熊沢彩子. 2005. "Yalishanda Qierpin yu Zhong Ri zuoqujia" 亚历山大·齐尔品与中日作曲家 (Alexandar Tcherepnin and Chinese and Japanese composers). *Zhongyang yinyue xueyuan xuebao* 中央音乐学院学报 (Journal of the Central Conservatory of Music) 1: 64–71.

Lai Yuege 赖越歌. 2014. "Zhong bai youyi de shizhe: Su Shilin de 'gesheng' piaodang zai zhongguo" 中白友谊的使者—苏石林的 '歌声' 飘荡在中国 (The messenger of

Sino-Russian friendship: Shushlin's singing wafts in China). *Yinyue daguan* 音乐大观 (Music magazine) 12: 59–60.

"Lakme i Traviata" (Lakmé and La Traviata). 1938. *Slovo*, January 29, 2.

Lam, Jeanette. 1957. "Composer's Kin to Hear 'Lost Flute' in Hawaii." *The Saturday Star-Bulletin, Honolulu*, January 12, 11.

Latour, Bruno. 1988. *The Pasteurization of France*. Translated by A. Sheridan and I. Law. Cambridge, MA: Harvard University Press.

———. 1996. "On Actor-Network Theory: A Few Clarifications." *Soziale Welt* 47, no. 4: 369–381. http://www.jstor.org/stable/40878163. Accessed on December 25, 2015.

———. 2005. *Reassembling the Social: An Introduction to Actor-Network-Theory*. New York: Oxford University Press.

Lau, Frederick. 2008. *Music in China: Expressing Music, Expressing Culture*. New York: Oxford University Press.

Lee Hsien Ming (Tcherepnin). 1984. "For the Love of Music." An interview with Lee Hsien Ming by David Dubal on WNCN-FM, New York, posted on YouTube on March 4, 2013. https://www.youtube.com/watch?v=_CQLeLCkmAs. Accessed on August 28, 2017.

Lee, Leo Ou-fan. 1999. *Shanghai Modern: The Flowering of a New Urban Culture in China, 1930–1945*. Cambridge, MA: Harvard University Press.

Leveillé, Anya. 2013. "Slavic Charm and the Soul of Tolstoy: Russian Music in Paris in the 1920s." In *Russian Émigré Culture: Conservatism or Evolution?*, edited by Christoph Flamm, Henry Keazor, and Roland Marti, 165–178. Newcastle upon Tyne: Cambridge Scholars Publishing.

Lewis, Herb. 1931. "Shanghai, a Bleak Cathedral of Commerce, Finds Its Soul in the Stirring, Wild Melodies from the Hearts of Russian Artists." *China Press*, December 12, 13.

Li Hexie. 1984. "Jacob Avshalomov and Chinese Music." *China Reconstructs* 33, no. 1: 38–40.

Li Lanqing 李岚清. 2010. *Shanghai: Zhongguo jin xiandai yinyue de yaolan* 上海:中国近现代音乐的摇篮 (Shanghai: Cradle of China's contemporary and modern music). Shanghai: Wenhui chubanshe 文汇出版社.

Liang, Luo. 2014. *The Avant-Garde and the Popular in Modern China: Tian Han and the Intersection of Performance and Politics*. Ann Arbor: University of Michigan Press.

Liang Maochun 梁茂春. 2014. "Qierpin gen wo xue pipa—Cao Anhe huiyi Qierpin" 齐尔品跟我学琵琶——曹安和回忆齐尔品 (Tcherepnin's *pipa* studies with me: Cao Anhe remembers Tcherepnin). *Gangqin yishu* 钢琴艺术 11: 25–30.

Liao Fushu 廖辅叔. 1991. "Guanyu Qierpin" 关于齐尔品 (Regarding Tcherepnin). *Zhongyang yinyue xueyuan xuebao* 中央音乐学院学报 (Journal of the Central Conservatory of Music) 1: 89–90.

———. 1998. "Su Shilin ershi zhounian ji" 苏石林二十周年祭 (Twentieth anniversary of Shushlin's death). *Zhongyang yinyue xueyuan xuebao* 中央音乐学院学报 (Journal of the Central Conservatory of Music) 2: 94–96.

———. 2001. "Mianhuai laoyou Jiang Dingxian" 缅怀老友江定仙 (Recalling my good friend Jiang Dingxian). *Zhongyang yinyue xueyuan xuebao* 中央音乐学院学报 (Journal of the Central Conservatory of Music) 2: 90–91.

Liu, Baosia. 2010. "V. G. Shushlin i vokalnoe obrazovanie v Kitae" (V. G. Shushlin and vocal education in China). In *Upravlenie v sotsialnykh i ekonomicheskikh sistemakh* (Management in social and economic systems). Materialy XIX mezhdunarodnykh nauchno-prakticheskoi konferentsii (Materials of the XIX international scientific-practical conference). Minsk, May 18, 381–382.

Liu, Ching-Chih. 2010. *A Critical History of New Music in China*. Translated by Caroline Mason. Hong Kong: Chinese University Press.

Liu Xinxin 刘欣欣 and Liu Yueqing 刘学清. 2002. *Harerbin xiyang yinyueshi* 哈尔滨西洋音乐史 (The history of Western music in Harbin). Beijing: Renmin yinyue chubanshe 人民音乐出版社.

Liu Xuean 刘雪庵. 1983. "Huainian Eguo zuoqujia Cheliepuning" 怀念俄国作曲家车列普宁 (Commemorating the Russian composer Tcherepnin). *Yinyue yu yinxiang* 音乐与音响 (Music and acoustics) 120: 44–46.

Liu Yang 刘洋. 2006. "Qiantan Wen Kezheng yu Su Shilin dui Zhongguo shengyue jiaoyu de gongxian" 浅谈温可铮与苏石林对中国声乐教育的贡献 (Discussion of Wen Kezheng and Shushlin's contribution to Chinese vocal education). *Minzu jiaoyu yanjiu* 民族教育研究 (Journal of research on education for ethnic minorities) 6: 109–112.

"Local Concerto: A Critic Criticized." 1938. Letter to the Editor of the *North-China Daily News*, October 24. Reprinted in *North-China Herald*, November 2, 203.

Loon, Joost van. 2006. "Network." *Theory, Culture & Society* 23, no. 2–3: 307–322.

LPW (Louisine Peters Weekes). 1923–1946. *Diaries of Louisine Peters Weekes, 1923–1946.* Vols. 1–14. Cambridge, MA: Eda Kuhn Loeb Music Library, Harvard University.

Luo Qin 洛秦. 2010. "Yinyue wenhua shixue shijiao zhong de lishi ynjiu yu minzu zhi fangfa—20 shiji sanshishi niandai shanghai e'qiao 'yinyue feidi' de lishi xushi ji qi wenhua yiyi chanshi" 音乐文化诗学视角中的历史研究与民族志方法—20 世纪三四十年代上海俄侨 '音乐飞地' 的历史叙事及其文化意义阐释 (Music cultural poetics in the perspective of historical and ethnographic research: Shanghai Russian émigrés' "music diaspora" from the twentieth century's 30s and 40s, a historical narrative and the interpretation of its cultural significance). *Yinyue yishi (Shanghai yinyue xueyuan xuebao)* 音乐艺术 (上海音乐学院学报) (Journal of the Shanghai Conservatory of Music) 1: 52–71.

———. 2011. "Wenhua binan, wenhua chuanbo yu wenhua renting: Shanghai e'qiao yinyue feidi lishi xiangxiang de wenhua jiedu" 文化避难、文化传播与文化认同—上海俄侨 "音乐飞地" 历史现象的文化解读 (Cultural refuge, cultural dissemination and cultural identity—A cultural interpretation of the historical phenomenon of Shanghai Russian's 'music diaspora'). In *Zhonger yinyue jiaoliu: shishi huigu yu dangdai fansi* 中俄音乐交流：史事回顾与当代反思 (Sino-Russian musical exchange: Historical review and contemporary reflections), edited by Tao Yabing 陶亚兵, 145–150. Beijing: Renmin yinyue chubanshe 人民音乐出版社.

Luo Qin 洛秦 and Qian Renpin 钱仁平, eds. 2013. *Guoli yinyue xueyuan / guoli yinyue zhuanke xuexiao tujian* 国立音乐学院 / 国立音乐专科学校图鉴 (1927–1941) (National Conservatory/National Music Institute in pictures: 1927–1941). Shanghai: Shanghai yinyue xueyuan chubanshe 上海音乐学院出版社.

Luo Yunyun 罗筠筠. 2001. *Li Delun Zhuan* 李德伦传 (The Life of Li Delun). Beijing: Zhuojia chubanshe 作家出版社.

Ma, Frank. 1937. "Tscherepnine Leaves China." *China Press*, March 14, 9.

Ma Huaxi 冯华熙. 1935a. "Qierpin chu si" 齐尔品去思 (Tcherepnin expresses his thoughts). *Beijing Zaobao* 北京早报, February 8, 6.

———. 1935b. "Zuowan xiehe litang" 昨晚协和礼堂 (Last evening at the Xiehe Auditorium). *Beiping Chenbao* 北平晨报, January 20, 6.

Maes, Francis. 2002. *A History of Russian Music: From Kamarinskaya to Babi Yar*. Translated by Arnold J. Pomerans and Erica Pomerans. Originally published in 1996 as *Geschiedenis van de Russische muziek: Van Kamarinskaja tot Babi Jar*. Berkeley: University of California Press.

"Maestro Pachi o svoei zhizni i o russkikh" (Maestro Paci on his life and the Russians). 1942. *Shankhaiskaia Zaria*, May 31, 5.

Man Xinying 满新颖. 2011. "Afuxialuomufu de Zhongguo ticai yinyue xiju chuangzuo zai 20 shiji Zhonger yinyue jiaoliuzhong de yingxiang" 阿甫夏洛穆夫的中国题材音乐戏剧创作在20世纪中俄音乐交流中的影响 (The influence of Avshalomov's musical-theatrical works with Chinese subject matter within twentieth-century Chinese-Russian musical exchange). In *Zhonger yinyue jiaoliu: shishi huigu yu dangdai fansi* 中俄音乐交流：史事回顾与当代反思 (Sino-Russian musical exchange: Historical review and contemporary reflections), edited by Tao Yabing 陶亚兵, 157–183. Beijing: Renmin yinyue chubanshe 人民音乐出版社.

Mang Kerong 莽克荣. 2004. *Lao Zhicheng chuan* 老志诚传 (Lao Zhicheng biography). Beijing: Zhongguo wenlian chubanshe 中国文联出版社.

Mao Yurun 茅于润 and Zhao Jiagui 赵家圭. 1983. *Dongfang de xuanlü: Zhongguo zhuming zuoqujia Ding Shande de yinyue shenya* 东方的旋律：中国著名作曲家丁善德的音乐生涯 (Eastern melody: The musical life of Chinese composer Ding Shande). Hong Kong: Shanghai shuju youxian gongsi 上海书局有限公司.

Melikhov, Georgii. 2003. *V Belyi Kharbin: Seredina 20-kh* (In White Harbin: mid-1920s). Moscow: Russkii Put.

Melvin, Sheila, and Jindong Cai. 2004. *Rhapsody in Red. How Western Classical Music Became Chinese*. New York: Algora Publishing.

"Members Elected to I. A. T. Committees." 1936. *China Press*, March 25, 4.

"Meng Jiang Nü" 孟姜女 (The Great Wall). 1946. *Wenyi huabao* 文艺画报 1, no. 1: 32–35.

"Meri Wong—Dzhilda" (Marie Waung—Gilda). 1937. *Slovo*, December 2, 2.

Mihailova, Natalya. 2014. "A Photo Exhibit titled "Russians in Shanghai: 1930's" Opens at the Cathedral of the Mother of God "Surety of Sinners" in Shanghai." *Orthodox Christianity and the World*, posted on May 23, 2014. http://www.pravmir.com/photo-exhibit-titled-russians-shanghai-1930-s-opens-cathedral-mother-god-surety-sinners-shanghai/. Accessed on June 25, 2018.

Mikkonen, Simo. 2007. *State Composers and the Red Courtiers. Music, Ideology, and the Politics in the Soviet 1930s*. Jyväskylä: University of Jyväskylä Press.

———. 2009. *Music and Power in the Soviet 1930s: A History of Composers' Bureaucracy*. New York: Edwin Mellen Press.

———. 2011a. "Mass Communications as a Vehicle to Lure Russian Émigrés Homeward." *Journal of International and Global Studies* 2, no. 2: 45–61.

———. 2011b. With Joni Krekola. "Backlash of the Free World: US Presence at the World Youth Festival in Helsinki, 1962." *Scandinavian Journal of History* 36, no. 2: 230–255.

——. 2012. "Exploiting the Exiles: The Soviet Emigration in US Cold War Strategy." *Journal for Cold War Studies* 14, no. 2: 98–127.

——. 2013a. "Winning Hearts and Minds? Soviet Musical Intelligentsia in the Struggle against the United States during the Early Cold War." In *Twentieth-Century Music and Politics*, edited by Pauline Fairclough, 135–154. Farnham: Ashgate.

——. 2013b. "Beyond the Superpower Conflict: Introduction to VJHS Special Issue on Cultural Exchanges during the Cold War." *Valahian Journal of Historical Studies* 8, no. 20: 5–15.

——. 2013c. "Not by Force Alone: Soviet Return Migration in the 1950s." In *Coming Home? Conflict and Return Migration in the Aftermath of Europe's Twentieth-Century Civil Wars*, vol. 1, edited by Sharif Gemie and Scott Soo, 183–200. Newcastle upon Tyne: Cambridge Scholars Publishing.

——. 2018. "Shanghai Russians: Negotiating Cultural Heritage in a Far East Metropolis." In *Transcending the Borders of Countries, Languages, and Disciplines in Russian Émigré Culture*, edited by C. Flamm, R. Marti, and A. Raev, 59–78. Newcastle upon Tyne: Cambridge Scholars Publishing.

Minutes of Shanghai Municipal Council. 1917–1919. Vol. 20. Shanghai Classics Publishing House, 151. Archives Unbound. http://go.galegroup.com.libezproxy.hkbu.edu.hk/gdsc/i.do?&id=GALE%7CSC5106612404&v=2.1&u=hkbu&it=r&p=GDSC&sw=w&viewtype=Transcript. Accessed on October 9, 2015.

Mishin, M. 1937. "Rigoletto—Kudinov." *Slovo*, November 27, 2.

Mittler, B. 1997. *Dangerous Tunes. The Politics of Chinese Music in Hong Kong, Taiwan, and the People's Republic of China since 1949.* Wiesbaden: Harrasowitz.

Mol, Annemarie. 2010. "Actor-Network Theory: Sensitive Terms and Enduring Tensions." In *Soziologische Theorie kontrovers* (Kölner Zeitschrift für Soziologie und Sozialpsychologie, special issue) 50, edited by Gert Albert and Steffen Sigmund, 253–269. Wiesbaden: VS Verlag.

Mol, Annemarie, and John Law. 1994. "Regions, Networks and Fluids: Anaemia and Social Topology." *Social Studies of Science* 24: 641–671.

"Molodaia Churaevka" (Young Churaevka). 1932. *Parus*, no. 8–9: 89.

Moon, Shin-il, George Barnett, and S. L. Yon. 2010. "The Structure of International Music Flows Using Network Analysis." *New Media & Society* 12, no. 3: 379–399.

Morrison, R. 2005. "China Is Embracing Western Classical Music with Unsettling Enthusiasm." *The Times*, October 21, 23.

Municipal Gazette. 1908–1921. *North-China Daily News Chinese and English Newspaper Database* (1850–1951). http://www.cnbksy.com.lib-ezproxy.hkbu.edu.hk/search;JSESSIONID=5fa2b26e-0f9e-47ac-8b83-334bb47e0ff5?isAdminUser=false. Accessed on February 11, 2016.

Municipal Gazette. 1921. Vol. 5, no. 223–270: 98, *North-China Daily News Chinese and English Newspaper Database* (1850–1951). http://www.cnbksy.com.lib-ezproxy.hkbu.edu.hk/search;JSESSIONID=5fa2b26e-0f9e-47ac-8b83-334bb47e0ff5?isAdminUser=false. Accessed on February 11, 2016.

"Municipal Orchestra: A Russian Concert." 1932. *North-China Herald and Supreme Court & Consular Gazette*, May 3, 177.

"Municipal Orchestra Concert." 1934. *North-China Daily News*, May 14, 15.

"The Municipal Orchestra: Concert of Russian Music: Some Numbers as Subject of Controversy." 1930. *North China Daily News*, April 29, 12.

"Municipal Orchestra: Question of Programmes." 1940. *North-China Herald*, March 13, 421.

"The Municipal Orchestra: Special Programme of Russian Music." 1932. *North-China Daily News*, April 30, 12.

Music, Petra. 2008. "The Rest Is History—Mathias Spahlinger and Hans Heinrich Eggebrecht on Utopia in New Music." *Contemporary Music Review* 27, no. 6: 665–672.

"Muzykalnoe obiedinenie i ego tseli, beseda s prof. B. S. Zakharovym" (Musical association and its objectives, interview with prof. B. S. Zakharov). 1929. *Shankhaiskaia Zaria*, October 6, 4.

"Muzykalnye zametki" (Musical remarks). 1932. *Slovo*, May 8, 4.

Mützel, Sophie. 2009. "Networks as Culturally Constituted Processes: A Comparison of Relational Sociology and Actor-Network Theory." *Current Sociology* 57, no. 6: 871–887.

Myers, Helen. 1998. *Music of Hindu Trinidad: Songs from the India Diaspora*. Chicago: University of Chicago Press.

"Na dukhovnom kontserte" (At a spiritual concert). 1930. *Shankhaiskaia Zaria*, April 5, 5.

"Na opere 'Faust'" (At the opera 'Faust'). 1937. *Slovo*, October 6, 4.

"Natsionalnaia konservatoriia. Shirokoe nachinanie v Shankhae" (National conservatory. Great significance for Shanghai). 1929. *Shankhaiskaia Zaria*, September 24, 4.

"Neveselya dela byvshikh Kharbintsev v SSSR" (Unhappy situation of former Harbin residents in the USSR). 1936. *Vechernaia Zaria*, January 18, 4.

"New Music Building for Shanghai U." 1934. *North-China Daily News*, May 22, 10.

New York Public Library of Performing Arts. Aaron Avshalomov Collection. JPB, 89–35.

Nie Er 聂耳. 1935. "Guan Zhongguo yaju 'Xiangzhuan huanjing' hou" 观中国哑剧 '香篆幻境' 后 (After watching the Chinese pantomime *Incense Shadows*). *Dian Tong* 电通 7: n.p.

———. 1985. *Nie Er quanji* 聂耳全集 (The complete writings of Nie Er). Vol. 2. Beijing: Renmin yinyue chubanshe 人民音乐出版社.

Nong 农. 1942. "Zhongguo wujushe yan wu shengxing yu Yindu wu" 中国舞剧社演五生星与印度舞 (The Chinese Ballet Association to perform *Buddha and the 5 Planetary Deities and Indian Dances*). *Shen Bao* 申報, June 13, 7.

North China Desk Hong List. *North-China Daily News Chinese and English Newspaper Database* (1850–1951). http://www.cnbksy.com.lib-ezproxy.hkbu.edu.hk/search;JSESSIONID=5fa2b26e-0f9e-47ac-8b83-334bb47e0ff5?isAdminUser=false. Accessed on February 11, 2016.

"Novaia Russkaia Simfoniia" (A new Russian symphony). 1936. *Shankhaiskaia Zaria*, April 3, 6.

"Novoe obiedinenie 'Shatior'" (New association 'Shatior'). 1935. *Feniks*, no. 12: 18.

Nugent, Walter. 1992. *Crossings: The Great Transatlantic Migration, 1870–1914*. Bloomington: Indiana University Press.

"O tantsakh" (About dances). 1928. *Shankhaiskaia Zaria*, February 23, 5.

Ohashi, Takchiko, et al., eds. 2015. *Shanghai zujie yu lanxin da juyuan: dongxi yishu ronghe jiaohui de juchang kongjian* 上海租界与兰心大剧院: 东西艺术融合交汇的剧

场空间 (Shanghai's International Settlement and Lyceum Theater: A theatrical space for the synergy of East-West arts). Shanghai: Renmin chubanshe 人民出版社.

Ol'chenko, M. 1939. "Russkaia Zhenshchina v izgnanii (Russian woman in exile)." *Russkii Golos*, January 15, 4.

"Operatic Concert at Town Hall." 1920. *North-China Herald and Supreme Court & Consular Gazette*, February 28, 552.

"Opernii kollektiv pod rukovodstvom V. G. Shushlina" (Opera collective under V. G. Shushlin's leadership). 1934. *Vechernaia Zaria*, April 21, 4.

"The Orchestra: A Musician's View. To the Editor of the *North-China Daily News*." 1934. *North-China Daily News*, April 16, 2.

"Organizatsia muzykalnogo obshchestva" (Organizing of musical society). 1929. *Shankhaiskaia Zaria*, November 6, 5.

"Otiezd V. G. Shushlina" (Shushlin's departure). 1930. *Shankhaiskaia Zaria*, May 31, 4.

"Otkliki na prizyv' g. Zhiganova" (Replies to call of Mr. Zhiganov). 1928. *Shankhaiskaia Zaria*, May 29, 5.

"Otkrytye vystavki khud. A. D. Sofronova" (Opening of exhibition of artist A. D. Sofronov). 1936. *Slovo*, April 23, 6.

"Otkrytyi 'Ponedelnik'" (Ponedelnik's opening). 1930. *Shankhaiskaia Zaria*, April 11, 4.

Pang, Pui Ling. 2015. "Reflecting Musically: The Shanghai Municipal Orchestra as a Semi-colonial Construct." PhD dissertation, University of Hong Kong.

"The Past Musical Season." 1910. *The North-China Herald and Supreme Court & Consular Gazette*, May 20, p. 422.

"Patrioticheskii kontsert" (Patriotic concert). 1936. *Vechernaia Zaria*, March 10, 3.

"Pervyi raz v Shankhae 'Korol veselitsia'" (First time in Shanghai: 'The King has fun'). 1932. *Shankhaiskaia Zaria*, April 1, 4.

"The Philadelphia Orchestra's 2014 Tour of Asia & China Residency a Resounding Success!" 2015. http://www.ruderfinnasia.com/en/news/news-archive/2014/%5Cen%5Cnews %5Cnews-archive%5C2014%5Cthe-philadelphia-orchestra%E2%80%99s-2014 -tour-of-asia,-and-china-residency-a-resounding-success!?pid=137. Accessed on December 27, 2015.

Philips, Anthony, trans. 2006. *Sergey Prokofiev Diaries 1907–1914. Prodigious Youth*. London: Faber and Faber.

Picture (with text). 1930. *Illustrirovannaia Zaria*, December 7, 1.

Picture (with text). 1935a. *Feniks*, no. 12: 18.

Picture (with text). 1935b. *Feniks*, no. 17: 15.

Piekut, Benjamin. 2014. "Actor-Networks in Music History: Clarifications and Critiques." *Twentieth-Century Music* 11, no. 2: 191–215.

"Pod novyi god. Bal v Madzhestik" (The New Year. Ball at the Majestic). 1928. *Shankhaiskaia Zaria*, January 14, 4.

"Podobrannyi na ulitse" (Picked up from street). 1929. *Shankhaiskaia Zaria*, March 13, 5.

"Pokushenie na samoubiistvo" (Attempted suicide). 1929. *Shankhaiskaia Zaria*, March 3, 3.

"Poslednyi kamernii kontsert" (Last chamber concert). 1932. *Slovo*, May 18, 4.

"Prof. B. S. Zakharov v Shankhae" (Prof. B. S. Zakharov in Shanghai). 1929a. *Shankhaiskaia Zaria*, January 23, 3.

"Prof. B. S. Zakharov v Shankhae" (Prof. B. S. Zakharov in Shanghai). 1929b. *Shankhaiskaia Zaria*, March 26, 4.

"Prof. Zakharoff at Carlton: Eminent Pianist to Celebrate 20 Years of Music." 1933. *North-China Daily News*, April 22, 18.

"Program for Afternoon Recital Is Given Here." 1936. *China Press*, May 28, 11.

"Proshchalnyi kontsert A. M. Tomskoi" (Farewell concert of A. M. Tomskaya). 1929. *Shankhaiskaia Zaria*, May 10, 4.

PSF (Paul Sacher Foundation). Alexander Tcherepnin Collection. Basel, Switzerland.

Qian Renping 钱仁平. 2005. *Zhongguo xin yinyue* 中国新音乐. Shanghai: Shanghai Conservatory of Music Press 上海音乐学院出版社.

———. 2013a. "Chun zai zhitou yi shifen—gangqin jiaoyu jia Wu Yizhou de xuesheng shidai" 春在枝头已十分—钢琴教育家巫一舟先生的学生时代 (Spring has been on the branches—piano educator Wu Yizhou's student days). *Huangzhong* 黄钟 (Journal of Wuhan Conservatory of Music) 4: 222–226, 252.

———. 2013b. "Qierpin yu guoli yinzhuan" 齐尔品与国立音专 (Tcherepnin and the National Conservatory). *Yinyue yishu (Shanghai yinyue xueyuan xuebao)* 音乐艺术 (上海音乐学院学报) (Journal of the Shanghai Conservatory of Music) 2: 6–16.

Qian Renping 钱仁平 and Zhang Xiong 张雄. 2011. "Lang Yuxiu yu guoli yinzhuan" 郎毓秀与国立音专 (Lang Yuxiu and the National Conservatory of Music). *Yinyue aihao zhe* 音乐爱好者 (Music lover) 10: 46–50.

"Qierpin xiehui zhengqiu Zhongguo zuopin, Xu Shuya de 'Xiaotiqin Xiezouqu' huojiang" 齐尔品协会征求中国作品、许舒亚的《小提琴协奏曲》获奖" (Xu Shuya's Violin Concerto receives Tcherepnin prize for Chinese compositions). 1982. *Yinyue yishu (Shanghai yinyue xueyuan xuebao)* 音乐艺术 (上海音乐学院学报) (Journal of the Shanghai Conservatory of Music) 3: 96.

Radecke, Thomas. 2013 "'I have no country, I have no place': The borderless artistic home of Alfred Schnittke." In *Russian Émigré Culture: Conservatism or Evolution?*, edited by Christoph Flamm, Henry Keazor, and Roland Marti, 257–268. Newcastle upon Tyne: Cambridge Scholars Publishing.

Raeff, Marc. 1990. *Russia Abroad: A Cultural History of the Russian Emigration, 1919–1939*. New York: Oxford University Press.

Raymond, Boris, and David Jones. 2000. *The Russian Diaspora: 1917–1941*. London: Scarecrow Press.

"Recital at A. W. C." 1934. *North-China Daily News*, April 28, 19.

Reich, Willy. 1970. *Alexander Tcherepnin*. Bonn: M. P. Belaieff. In Benjamin Folkman. 2008. *Alexander Tcherepnin, A Compendium*. Translated by Mosco Carner, Marjorie Glock, and Benjamin Folkman. New York: The Tcherepnin Society, Inc.

"Richard Wagner." 1908. *North-China Herald and Supreme Court & Consular Gazette*, June 6, 593.

Ristaino, Marcia. 2000. "The Russian Diaspora Community in Shanghai." In *New Frontiers: Imperialism's New Communities in East Asia, 1842–1953*, edited by Robert Bickers and C. Henriot, 192–210. Manchester: Manchester University Press.

———. 2001. *Port of Last Resort: The Diaspora Communities of Shanghai*. Stanford, CA: Stanford University Press.

Robinson, Harlow. 1998. *Selected Letters of Sergei Prokofiev*. Lebanon, NH: Northeastern University Press.

Rosenson, Harriet P. 1998. "Jewish Musicians in Shanghai: Bridging Two Cultures." In *The Jews of China: Vol. 1: Historical and Comparative Perspectives*, edited by Jonathan Goldstein, 239–250. Armonk, NY: M. E. Sharpe.

"Rossiiskoe muzykalnoe obshchestvo zagranitsei" (Russian musical association abroad). 1933. *Vechernaia Zaria*, April 8, 4.

"Rost dorogovizny v Shankhae" (Rising costliness of Shanghai). 1930. *Shankhaiskaia Zaria*, June 4, 4.

"Russian Charity Concert: A Tchaikovsky Symphony Programme at Town Hall Next Saturday." 1929. *North-China Daily News*, February 19, 12.

"Russian Concert Is New Departure at Town Hall." 1928. *China Press*, October 22, 3.

"Russian Pianist to Present Concert." 1942. *The Proscript: Richmond Professional Institute, College of William and Mary* 4, no. 11 (November 30): 1.

"Russkaia opera v Opera Komik" (Russian opera at the Comic Opera). 1935. *Slovo*, April 28, 4.

"Russkii kontsert" (Russian concert). 1928. *Shankhaiskaia Zaria*, February 10, 4.

"Russkii tsentr Shankhaia, Zaiavlenie d-ra D. I. Kazakova" (Russian center of Shanghai, statement of dir. D. I. Kazakov). 1928. *Shankhaiskaia Zaria*, March 2, 2.

Saffle, Michael, and Hon-Lun Yang. 2010. "Aesthetic and Social Aspects of Emerging Utopian Musical Communities." *International Review of the Aesthetics and Sociology of Music* 41, no. 2: 319–341.

Schimmelpenninck, A., and F. Kouwenhoven. 1993. "The Shanghai Conservatory of Music: History and Foreign Students' Experiences." *CHIME* 6: 56–91.

Schulte, Jörg, Olga Tabachnikova, and Peter Wagstaff. 2012. *The Russian Jewish Diaspora and European Culture, 1917–1937*. Leiden: Brill.

Schwarcz, Vera. 1986. *The Chinese Enlightenment: Intellectuals and the May Fourth Movement of 1919*. Berkeley: University of California Press.

Scott, John. 2000. *Social Network Analysis*. Newbury Park, CA: Sage.

"Segodnia—Bogema" (Today—Bohemians). 1938. *Slovo*, October 19, 2.

"Segodnia 'Faust'" (Today 'Faust'). 1937. *Slovo*, October 5, 4.

"Segodnia pribyvaet F. I. Shaliapin" (F. I. Chaliapin arrives today). 1936. *Slovo*, January 20, 6.

"Segodnia—'Skazki Gofmana'" (Today—'Hoffman's tales'). 1938. *Slovo*, January 16, 2.

Serbsky, Viktor. 1928. "Vse v 'Madzhestik!'" (All to 'Majestic!'). 1928. *Shankhaiskaia Zaria*, January 13, 3.

Sergeant, Harriet. 2002. *Shanghai*. London: John Murray.

Severny, Pavel. 1935a. "Stranitsa Ponedelnika" (Ponedelnik's pages). *Prozhektor*, no. 15: 24.

———. 1935b. "Stranitsa Ponedelnika" (Ponedelnik's pages). *Prozhektor*, no. 18: 24.

———. 1935c. "Stranitsa Ponedelnika" (Ponedelnik's pages). *Prozhektor*, no. 20: 15.

"Shanghai Art Club Musical Section. A Good Start Made: Assistance from Defunct Bodies." 1929. *North-China Herald and Supreme Court & Consular Gazette*. November 16, 256.

Shanghai jiaoxiang yuetuan 125 zhounian 上海交响乐团123周年 (Shanghai Symphony Orchestra 125th anniversary). Shanghai: Shanghai BOAO Media Co. Ltd.

Shanghai Municipal Archive (SMA). 1926. A letter of V. Grosse to Chairman of the Municipal Council. January 6: SMA U-1-3-2859.

———. 1933a. Grand Chinese Evening Tickets Account by S. Moutried and Co. May 22: SMA U1-4-365.

———. 1933b. Letter from Conductor's Office to the Treasurer & Controller, S. M. Finance Department. April 23: SMA U1-4-376.

———. 1933c. Memorandum from the Shanghai Municipal Council Press Information Office. April 26: SMA U1-4-370, 370.

———. 1934a. Letter from Conductor's Office to the Treasurer & Controller, S. M. Finance Department. November 16: SMA U1-4-259.

———. 1934b. Letter from L. Strok per A. Strok to the Secretary, Municipal Band & Orchestra. April 27: SMA U1-4-284.

Shanghai Municipal Orchestra Concert Programs. 1912.

"Shanghai Orchestra Academy and Residency Partnership." 2015. Website of the New York Philharmonic. http://nyphil.org/education/global-academy/shanghai-academy. Accessed on December 27, 2015.

"Shanghai the Melodious." *North-China Daily News*, April 14, 1934, 5.

"Shanghai to Hear Youthful Russian Pianist on Sunday: Tolia Vedernikoff Tells Interviewer He First Touched Keys at Six Years." 1935. *China Press*, July 19, 3.

"Shanghai 'U' Concert." 1937. *China Press*, May 20, 7.

"Shankhaiskaia konservatoriia i russkaia molodezh" (Shanghai Conservatory and Russian youth). 1933. *Vechernaia Zaria*, October 28, 4.

"Shankhaiskaia opera" (Shanghai opera). 1937. *Slovo*, December 18, 4.

"Shankhaiskaia opera pereshla v teatr 'Karlton'" (Shanghai opera moved to Carlton theater). 1937. *Slovo*, December 29, 2.

"Shankhaiskii den. Pokhorony V. Bespalkogo" (Shanghai days. Funeral of V. Bespalkov). 1929. *Slovo*, February 3, 5.

"Shankhaiu nuzhna muzykal'naia shkola. Beseda s prof. B. S. Zakharovym" (Shanghai needs a music school: Interview with Prof. B. S. Zakharov). 1929. *Shankhaiskaia Zaria*, August 3, 5.

Shcherbakov, M. 1931. "Sodruzhestvo 'Ponedelnik'" (Fraternity of 'Ponedelnik'). *Parus*, no. 1: 50.

Sherman, Robert. 1987. "Music; Ossining Director in His Finale." *New York Times*, May 17. http://www.nytimes.com/1987/05/17/nyregion/music-ossining-director-in-his-finale.html. Accessed on December 20, 2015.

Shi, Shumei. 2001. *The Lure of the Modern: Writing Modernism in Semicolonial China, 1917–1939*. Berkeley: University of California Press.

Shiga, John. 2007. "Translations: Artifacts from an Actor-Network Perspective." *Artifact* 1, no. 1: 40–55.

"Shushlin." 1930. *Illustrirovannaia Zaria*, November 9, 5.

"Simfonicheskaia ballada" (The Symphonic Ballade). 1933a. *Shankhaiskaia Zaria*, March 11, 3.

"Simfonicheskaia ballada" (The Symphonic Ballade). 1933b. *Shankhaiskaia Zaria*, March 12, 13.

"Simfonicheskii kontsert o-va bogema" (Symphonic concert of Bohemian's association). 1937. *Slovo*, April 15, 2.

Simpson, John Hope. 1938. *Refugees: Preliminary Report of a Problem*. London: Royal Institute of International Affairs.

"Singer and Composer." 1937. *China Press*, May 23, 4.

Slobin, Greta. 2013. *Russians Abroad. Literary and Cultural Politics of Diaspora (1919–1939)*. Boston: Academic Studies Press.

Slobin, Mark. 1992. "Micromusics of the West: A Comparative Approach." *Ethnomusicology* 36: 1–87.

Small, Christopher. 1998. *Musicking: The Meanings of Performing and Listening*. Middletown, CT: Wesleyan University Press.

"Speshite zapastis biletami na 'Karmen'" (Hurry to reserve tickets for 'Carmen'). 1937. *Slovo*, November 15, 4.

Stock, Jonathan. 2002. *Huju: Traditional Opera in Modern Shanghai*. Oxford: Oxford University Press.

Stokes, Martin, ed. 1994. *Ethnicity, Identity, and Music: The Musical Construction of Place*. Oxford, UK: Berg.

Stuart, Robert. 1937. "The Dream of Wei Lien." *The Musical Times* 78, no. 1128: 173–174.

"Successful Year for Orchestra." 1941. *North-China Herald and Supreme Court & Consular Gazette*, February 26, 334.

"The Sunday Concert." 1919. *North-China Herald*, December 13, 709.

"The Sunday Concerts." 1909a. *North-China Herald and Supreme Court & Consular Gazette*, January 30, 287.

"The Sunday Concerts." 1909b. *North-China Herald and Supreme Court & Consular Gazette*, November 6, 277.

Svetlov, Nikolai. 1934. "Shankaiskaia Churaevka" (Shanghai Churaevka). *Ponedelnik*, no. 3–4: 80.

Tanabe, Hisao. 1970. *Zhongguo zhaoxian yinyue diao cha jixing* (China and Korea, a trip to study music). Tokyo: Ongaku no Tomosha, Shōwa.

Tang, Leang-Li. 1936. *China's New Currency System*. Shanghai: China United Press.

Tang Yading 汤亚丁. 2014. *Diguo feisan bianzouqu: Shanghai gongbuqu yuedui shi (1879–1949)* 帝国飞散变奏曲: 上海工部局乐队史 (1879–1949) (Variations of imperial diasporas: A history of Shanghai Municipal Orchestra). Shanghai: Shanghai yinyuexueyuan chubanshe 上海音乐学院出版社.

Tao Yabing 陶亚兵, ed. 2011. Zhonge yinyue jiaoliu: shishi huigu yu dangdai fansi 中俄音乐交流：史事回顾与当代反思 (Sino-Russian musical exchange: Historical review and contemporary reflections). Beijing: Renmin yinyue chubanshe 人民音乐出版社.

Taruskin, Richard. 2009. "Some Thoughts on the History and Historiography of Russian Music." In *On Russian Music*, 27–52. Berkeley: University of California Press.

———. 2016. *Russian Music at Home and Abroad: New Essays*. Berkeley: University of California Press.

Tassie, Gregor. 2014. *Nikolay Myaskovsky: The Conscience of Russian Music*. Lanham, MD: Rowman & Littlefield.

"Tatsan pereshel k kitaitsam" (Chinese took Tazan). 1932. *Slovo*, May 18, 6.

"Tchaikovsky Memorial Concert: Large Attendance at the Town Hall Saturday." 1929. *North-China Daily News*, February 25, 17.

Tcherepnin, Alexander. 1934a. "Letter to Xiao Youmei." *Yinyue zazhi* 音乐杂志 3: II.

———. 1934b. "Letter to Walter Koons." *Musical Courier* (November 17): 17.

———. 1935. "Music in Modern China." *The Musical Quarterly* 21, no. 4: 391–400.

"Tcherepnin: One of the Great Masters." 1950. *De Paul* (January): 7–8.

"Teatr Muzyka Kino" (Theatre, music, films). 1936a. *Feniks*, no. 19 (January): 14–15.

"Teatr Muzyka Kino" (Theatre, music, films). 1936b, *Feniks*, no. 21 (January): 14–15.

"Teatralnaia Khronika" (Theatre chronicle). 1921. *Novosti teatra*, no. 9: 29.

"Teatralnaia Khronika" (Theatre chronicle). 1935. *Prozhektor*, no. 2: 15.

Tian Han 田汉. 1947. "Yige gudai funü de beiju—ping Meng Jiang Nü" 一个古代妇女的悲剧—评孟姜女 (An ancient woman's tragedy: Review of *The Great Wall*). *Zuojia zazhi* 作家杂志 1: 34–35.

Tölölyan, Kachig. 1996. "Rethinking Diaspora(s): Stateless Power in the Transnational Moment." *Diaspora* 5, no. 1: 3–36.

"Tolya Vedernikov budet igrat kontsert Griga" (Tolya Vedernikov will perform Grieg's concerto). 1935. *Shankhaiskaia Zaria*, March 21, 5.

"Tretii kamernii kontsert" (Third chamber concert). 1930. *Shankhaiskaia Zaria*, April 2, 5.

"Tserkovnyi khor" (Church choir). 1928. *Shankhaiskaia Zaria*, March 13, 4.

Tszo, Chzhenguan [Zuo Zhenguan] 左贞观. 2000. "Muzykal'naia zhizn' russkoi emigratsii v shankhae" (Musical life of Russian émigrés in Shanghai). *Muzykal'naia akademiia* 2: 158–160.

———. 2011. "*Eluosi yinyue jia zai zhongguo* yi shu de xiezuo gongzuo" 俄罗斯音乐家在中国一书的写作工作 (The writing of the book *Russian Musicians in China*). In *Zhonge yinyue jiaoliu: shishi huigu yu dangdai fansi* 中俄音乐交流：史事回顾与当代反思 (Sino-Russian musical exchange: Historical review and contemporary reflections), edited by Tao Yabing 陶亚兵, 53–57. Beijing: Renmin yinyue chubanshe 人民音乐出版社.

———. 2014. *Russkie muzykanty v Kitae* (Russian musicians in China). Saint Petersburg: Kompozitor.

Ufimtsev, Nikolai. 1934. "Shankaiskaia Churaevka" (Shanghai Churaevka). *Ponedelnik*, no. 3–4: 180.

"Ukrainskii vecher" (Ukrainian soiree). 1929. *Shankhaiskaia Zaria*, March 13, 5.

"Uspekh dukhovnogo kontserta" (Success of spiritual concert). 1929. *Shankhaiskaia Zaria*, April 30, 5.

"Uspekh 'Rigoletto'" (Success of 'Rigoletto'). 1937. *Slovo*, November 24, 4.

"Uspekh S. S. Aksakova" (Success of S. S. Aksakov). 1930. *Shankhaiskaia Zaria*, February 25, 5.

"V Drugykh mestakh" (At other places). 1928. *Shankhaiskaia Zaria*, January 14, 4.

"V 'Kavkaz'" (At 'Kavkaz'). 1928. *Shankhaiskaia Zaria*, January 14, 4.

"V Muzykalno-prosvetitelnom obshchetve" (At the musical-educational society). 1932. *Novyi Put*, July 24, 4.

"V sodruzhestve 'Ponedelnik'" (Fraternity of 'Ponedelnik'). 1930. *Shankhaiskaia Zaria*, March 8, 5.

"V turne" (On a tour). 1930. *Shankhaiskaia Zaria*, April 11, 5.

Van, Chzhichen. 2008. *Istoriia russkoi emigratsii v Shankhae* (History of Russian emigration in Shanghai). Moscow: Russkii put.

"Vecher A. N. Cherepnina v 'Vostoke'" (An evening of A. N. Tcherepnin in 'Vostok'). 1934. *Shankhaiskaia Zaria*, May 12, 9.

"Vecher 'Shatra'" (Soiree of 'Shater'). 1936. *Slovo*, April 17, 4.

"Vecher T. Ptitsynoi v KhLAM'e" (Soiree of T. Ptitsyna). 1936. *Vechernaia Zaria*, January 23, 5.

Vertovec, Steven. 2000. "Religion and Diaspora." Paper presented at the conference on "New Landscapes of Religion in the West," School of Geography and the Environment, University of Oxford, September 27–29. http://www.transcomm.ox.ac.uk/working%20papers/Vertovec01.PDF. Accessed on April 1, 2016.

Vivas (unidentified pen name). 1938. "Na premiere 'Zhidovka'" (At the premiere of 'La Juive'). *Slovo*, January 9, 5.

"Vladimir Havsky's Farewell Concert." 1940. *North-China Herald and Supreme Court & Consular Gazette*, November 6, 219.

"Vrata." 1934. *Vrata*. Dalnevostochnye sborniki, no. 1. Vostok: Shanghai, 191–195.

"Vysokie gosti pokinuli Shankhai" (High guests have left Shanghai). 1938. *Slovo*, September 16, 5.

"Wagner Concert." 1908. *North-China Herald and Supreme Court & Consular Gazette*, June 6, 612.

"Wagner Played by Orchestra Here Sunday: Program Sung in 3 Languages at Lyceum." 1938. *China Press*, February 8, 5.

Wang Jia 王佳. 2011. "E'luosi gangqin yishu dui woguo gangqin yishu de yingxiang chutan" 俄罗斯钢琴艺术对我国钢琴艺术的影响初探 (A new study on the influence of Russian pianism on Chinese pianism). *Huanghe zhi sheng* 黄河之声 (Yellow River of the Song) 11: 112–113.

Wang Ren 往仁. 1947. "'Kexue wenjiao yue' liangxiao lexu zai Bali" 「科学文教月」良宵乐叙在巴黎 (A beautiful night of music and narrative in Paris for "science, culture, and education month"). *Shen Bao* 申报, January 10, 9.

Wang, Tianshu. 1999. "Alexander Tcherepnin's Five Concert Studies: An Homage to Chinese Musical Styles, Instruments, and Traditions." DMA dissertation, University of Arizona.

Wang Weide 王维德. 1994. "Gesheng zhong de huainian: nan gaoyin gechang jia Cai Shaoxu" 歌声中的怀念—男高音歌唱家蔡绍序 (Song of nostalgia: Tenor Cai Shaoxu)." In *Zhongguo jinxiandai yinyuejia zhuan* 中国近现代音乐家傳 (Biographies of contemporary Chinese musicians), vol. 3, edited by Xiang Yanshen, 219–229. Liaoning: Chunfeng wenyi chubanshe 春风文艺出版社.

Wang Wen 王文. 2012. "Qierpin wushou yinyuehui lianxiqu zhi Zhongguo fenge ji yanzou jiqiao" 齐尔品五首音乐会练习曲之中国风格及演奏技巧 (Chinese style and technique in Tcherepnin's *Five Concert Studies*). *Yinyue shikong* 音乐时空 5: 42–43.

Wang Xiaoping 王晓平. 2013. "Huainian yinyue jia Yang Shusheng" 怀念音乐家杨树声 (Yearning for musician Yang Shusheng). *Renmin yinyue* 人民音乐 (People's music) 7: 53–55.

Wang Yamin 王亞民. 2013. "Yi zhongguo jin xiandai ganqin jiaoyu zhi fu: Baolishi. Chaha luofa" 忆中国近现代钢琴教育之父——鲍里斯•查哈罗夫 (Recalling the father of modern Chinese piano education: Boris Zakharov). *Gangqin yishu* 钢琴艺术 (Piano artistry) 10: 16–23.

Wang Yanli 王艳莉. 2010. "E'qiao yinyue jia yu gongbuju yuedui jiaowang lishi xintan" 俄侨音乐家与工部局乐队交往历史新探 (Probing into the history of Russian musicians and the Municipal Orchestra). *Renmin yinyue* 人民音乐 (People's music) 5: 37–39.

———. 2011. "E'qiao yinyue jia yu gongbuju yuedui jiaowang lishi xintan" 俄侨音乐家与工部局乐队交往历史新探 (Probing into the history of Russian musicians and the Municipal Orchestra). In *Zhonge yinyue jiaoliu: shishi huigu yu dangdai fansi* 中俄音乐交流：史事回顾与当代反思 (Sino-Russian musical exchange: Historical review and contemporary reflections), edited by Tao Yabing 陶亚兵, 271–282. Beijing: Renmin yinyue chubanshe 人民音乐出版社.

———. 2015. *Shanghai gongbuju yuedui yanjiu* 上海工部局乐队研究 (A study on the Shanghai Municipal Orchestra). Shanghai: Shanghai yinyue chubanshe 上海音乐出版社.

Wang Yanli 王艳莉, Yuan Lin 林媛, and Xin Sui 隋欣. 2012. "Ershi shiji shangbanye xishi guanxian yuedui yu zhongguo yinyuejia guanxi zhi tanjiu: yi Shanghai gongbuju guanxian yuedui weili 20" 世纪上半叶西式管弦乐团与中国音乐家关系之探究——以上海工部局管弦乐队为例 (A study of the relationship between the Western orchestra and Chinese musicians in the first half of the twentieth century: A case of the Shanghai Municipal Orchestra). *Yinyue yanjiu* 音乐研究 3: 22–23.

Wang Yuhe 汪毓和. 1984/1994/2002/2006/2009. *Zhongguo jin xiandai yinyue shi* 中国近现代音乐史 (Recent history of modern Chinese music). Beijing: Renmin yinyue chubanshe 人民音乐出版社.

Wang Zhicheng 汪之成. 1993. *Shanghai eqiao shi* 上海俄侨史 (A history of Russian émigrés in Shanghai). Shanghai: Shanghai sanlian shudian 上海三联书店.

———. 1994. "Jiu shanghai de e'guo qiaomin" 旧上海的俄国侨民 (Old Shanghai's Russian émigrés). *Shehui kexue* 社会科学 (Journal of social sciences) 7: 59–63.

———. 2007. *Eqiao yinyuejia zai Shanghai (1920s–1940s)* 俄侨音乐家在上海 (1920s–1940s) (Russian émigré musicians in Shanghai, 1920s–1940s). Shanghai: Shanghai yinyue xueyuan chubanshe 上海音乐学院出版社.

Wasserstrom, Jeffrey. 2009. *Global Shanghai, 1850–2010*. New York: Routledge.

Wei, Betty Peh-T'i. 1987. *Shanghai: Crucible of Modern China*. Oxford: Oxford University Press.

Wei Tingge 魏廷格. 1982. "Ding Shande fangwen ji—'Shangyin' zaoqi gangqin jiaoxue ji Ding Shande de gangqin chuangzuo" 丁善德访问记：'上音'早期钢琴教学及丁善德的钢琴创作 (Interview with Ding Shande (Shanghai Conservatory's early piano education and Ding Shande's early piano creativity)). *Zhongguo yinyue* 中国音乐 (Chinese music) 4: 62–64.

Winzenburg, John. 2012. "Aaron Avshalomov and New Chinese Music in Shanghai, 1931–1947." *Twentieth-Century China* 37, no. 1: 50–72.

———. 2013. "Heteroglossia and Traditional Vocal Genres in Chinese-Western Fusion Concertos." *Perspectives of New Music* 51, no. 2: 101–140.

———. 2015. "Musical-Dramatic Experimentation in the Yangbanxi: A Case for Precedence in The Great Wall." In *Listening to China's Cultural Revolution: Music, Politics, and Cultural Continuities*, edited by Paul Clark, Pang Laikwan, and Tsai Tsan-Huang, 189–212. London: Palgrave MacMillan.

———. 2017. "Spanning the Timbral Divide: Tradition, Multiplicity, and Novelty in Chinese-Western Fusion Concerto Instrumentation." In *East-West Musical Encounters: Representation, Reception, and Power Politics in Sino-Western Musical Relations*, edited by Hon-Lun Yang and Michael Saffle, 186–204. Ann Arbor: University of Michigan Press.

Wong, Deborah. 2004. *Speak it Louder: Asian Americans Making Music*. New York: Routledge.

Wordie, Jason. 2007. "Of Borsch and White Russians—Emigres' Legacy to Hong Kong." *South China Morning Post, Post Magazine*, May 6. http://www.scmp.com/article/591788 /borsch-and-white-russians.

"World-Famous Musicians and Dancers Coming to Shanghai." 1928. *North-China Herald and Supreme Court & Consular Gazette*, August 11, 236.

Wu Leyi 吴乐懿. 1994. "Wo de yinyue lucheng: nu gangqin jia Wu Leyi zizhuan." (My musical journey: Female pianist Wu Leyi's autobiography). In *Zhongguo jinxiandai yinyuejia chuan* 中国近现代音乐家傳 (Biographies of contemporary Chinese musicians), vol. 3, edited by Xiang Yanshen, 219–229. Liaoning: Chunfeng wenyi chubanshe 春风文艺出版社.

Wuellner, Guy. 1974. "The Complete Piano Music of Alexander Tcherepnin: An Essay Together with a Comprehensive Project in Piano Performance." DMA dissertation, University of Iowa.

Xi Di 茜蒂. 1941. "Gu sha jing meng guan hou ji" 古刹惊梦观后纪 (Notes after viewing *Incense Shadows*). *Shen Bao* 申報, June 17, 14.

"Xia Guoqiong gangqin duzou shengkuang" 夏国琼钢琴独奏盛况 (The grand occasion of Xia Guoqiong's piano solo recital). 1937. *Shen Bao* 申報, January 25, 15.

"Xiangzhuan huanjing" 香篆幻境 (Incense shadows). 1935. *Shen Bao* 申報, March 12, 11.

Xiang Yansheng 向延生, ed. 1994. *Zhongguo jinxiandai yinyuejia chuan* 中国近现代音乐家傳 (Biographies of contemporary Chinese musicians), 4 vols. Liaoning: Chunfeng wenyi chubanshe 春风文艺出版社.

Xiao Yang 肖阳 and Qian Renping 钱仁平. 2013. "Jiang Dingxian xiansheng yu Guoli yinzhuan" 江定仙先生与"国立音专 (Mr. Jiang Dingxian and the "National Conservatory"). *Huangzhong* 黄钟 (武汉音乐学院学报) (Journal of Wuhan Conservatory of Music) 3: 3–13.

Xiao Youmei 萧友梅. 1928/2004. "Tingguo Shanghai shizhengting dayue yinyuehui hou de ganxiang" 听过上海市政厅大乐音乐队后的感想 (A few thoughts after hearing the Concert of the Shanghai Municipal Orchestra). In *Xiao Youmei quanji* 萧友梅全集 (Complete Writings of Xiao Youmei), 211–213. Shanghai: Shanghai yinyue chubanshe 上海音乐出版社.

———. 1934. "Laiyou Hu Ping Eguo xinpai zuoqujia ji gangqinshi Yalishanda Cheliepunin de lüechuan yu zi zhuzuo de te se" 来游沪平俄国新派作曲家及钢琴师亚历山大·车列浦尔 (Alexandere Tcherepnine) 的略传与其著作的特色 (An introduction to the background and special composition features of modernist Russian composer and pianist Alexander Tcherepnin, now visiting Shanghai and Beiping). *Yinyue zazhi* 音乐杂志 (Music magazine) 3: 1–11.

———. 1935. "Yalishanda Cheliepunin *Wusheng yinjie de ganqin jiaoben juantouyu*" 亚历山大·车列浦尔 五声音阶的钢琴教本卷头语 (Preface to Alexander Tcherepnin's *Piano Study on the Pentatonic Scale*). Shanghai: Yueyun chubanshe 乐韵出版社.

Xiaoshe luocheng jinian kan 校舍落成纪念刊 (Commemorative publication for the completion of the school building). 1935. The volume is titled *Guoli yinyue juanke xuexiao xiaoshe lecheng jinian tekan* 国立音乐专科学校校舍落成纪念特刊 (Special issue to celebrate the completion of the school building of the National Music Institute). Edited by the Conservatory Book Committee. [n.p.] SMAY8-1-468.

Xu Buzeng 许步曾. 1991. "Youtai yinyuejia zai Shanghai (xia)" 犹太音乐家在上海 (下) (Jewish musicians in Shanghai, part 2). *Yinyue yishu (Shanghai yinyue xueyuan xuebao)* 音乐艺术 (上海音樂學院學報) (Journal of the Shanghai Conservatory of Music) 4: 10–16.

———. 1998. "Jews and the Musical Life of Shanghai." In *The Jews of China: Vol. 1: Historical and Comparative Perspectives*, edited by Jonathan Goldstein, 230–238. Armonk, NY: M. E. Sharpe.

———. 2006. "Ji Eluosi Youtai zuoqujia Afuxialuomufu" 记俄罗斯犹太作曲家阿甫夏洛穆夫 (Remembering the Russian Jewish composer Aaron Avshalomov). *Yinyue aihaozhe* 音乐爱好者 (Music lover) 6: 40–44.

———. 2009. "Wu Leyi huiyi enshi Zhahaluofu" 吴乐懿回忆恩师查哈罗夫 (Wu Le Yi and Boris Zakharoff). *Yinyue aihaozhe* 音乐爱好者 (Music lover) 6: 38–41.

Xue Zongming 薛宗明. 2001. "Along Afuxialuomufu de gushi" 阿龙阿甫夏洛穆夫的故事 (Aaron Avshalomov's story). *Yinyue Lan* 音乐览 30: 3–6.

Yang, Hon-Lun. 2012. "The Shanghai Conservatory, Chinese Musical Life, and The Russian Diaspora: 1927–1949." *Twentieth-Century China* 37, no. 1: 73–95.

———. 2013. "Diaspora, Music, and Politics: Russian Musical Life in Shanghai during the Inter-War Period." In *Twentieth-Century Music and Politics*, edited by Pauline Fairclough, 261–278. Farnham: Ashgate.

———. 2017. "From Colonial Modernity to Global Identity: The Shanghai Municipal Orchestra." In *China and the West: Music, Representation, and Reception*, edited by Hon-Lun Yang and Michael Saffle, 49–64. Ann Arbor: University of Michigan Press.

Yang, Hon-Lun, and Neil Edmunds. 2003. "Socialist Realism and Music in the Soviet Union and the People's Republic of China." *BLOK* 2: 70–89.

Yang, Hon-Lun, and Michael Saffle, eds. 2017. *China and the West: Music, Representation, and Reception.* Ann Arbor: University of Michigan Press.

Yang Ning 杨宁. 2015. "Xinnian yinyuehui: wei le xinnian haishi wei le yinyue?" 新年音乐会: 为了新年还是为了音乐? (New Year concert: For New Year or for music?). *Online Blog: A Selection of Critical Mass in Music, Films and Beyond* (January 19). http://digforfire.net/?p=11803. Accessed on January 30, 2016.

Yang Shuzheng 杨树声. 1991. "Keli luowa de shengyue jiaoxue" 克莉罗娃的声乐教学 (The vocal teaching of Krylova). *Yinyue yishu* 音乐艺术 (Journal of the Shanghai Conservatory of Music) 1: 49–54.

Yang Zhe 杨哲. 2005a. "Jiang Chunfang zai kangzhanhou de Shanghai" 姜椿芳在抗战后的上海 (Jiang Chunfang in Shanghai after the war of resistance)." *Zongheng* 纵横 11: 55–57.

———. 2005b. "Jiang Chunfang yu Mei Lanfang, Zhou Xinfang de youyi" 姜椿芳与梅兰芳, 周信芳的友谊 (The friendship of Jiang Chunfang, Mei Lanfang, and Zhou Xinfang). *Yanhuang qiu* 炎黄秋 8: 78–80.

"Yedinym frontom na zashchitu simfonii" (A united front to protect the symphony). 1935. *Shankhaiskaia Zaria*, April 16, 5.

Ying Shizhen 应诗真. 1994. "Weile jianli Zhongguo de gangqin jiaoxue tixi: gangqin jiaoyu jia Yi Kaiji" 为了建立中国的钢琴教学体系—钢琴教育家易开基 (To build China's piano teaching system: Piano educator Yi Kaiji). In *Zhongguo jinxiandai yinyuejia chuan* 中国近现代音乐家傳 (Biographies of contemporary Chinese musicians), vol. 2, edited by Xiang Yanshen, 328–334. Liaoning: Chunfeng wenyi chubanshe 春风文艺出版社.

"Young Composer in Shanghai." 1934. *North-China Daily News*, April 12, 10.

"Young Pianist: Misleading Advertisement." 1939. *North-China Daily News*, December 6, 17.

"Young Pianist Wins Applause at 1st Concert." 1935. *China Press*, April 22, 8.

"Young Russian Pianist May Study In U.S." 1936. *China Press*, April 29, 16.

Yu Shaohua 余少华. 1982. "Zhongguo yinyuejia Xiao Youmei" 中国音乐家萧友梅 (Chinese musician Xiao Youmei). *Mingbao* 明报 17, no. 7: 97–99.

Yu Yixuan. 喻宜萱. 2004. *Yu Yixuan Shengyu Yishu* 喻宜萱声乐艺术 (Yu Yixuan's vocal art). Beijing: Huayue chubanshe 华乐出版社.

"Yuan Mei-yuan to Make Bow to Foreigners." 1933. *The China Press*, May 7, 5.

"Za pianstvo" (For drunkenness). 1929. *Shankhaiskaia Zaria*, February 19, 3.

"Za pianstvo i poproshainichestvo" (For drunkenness and begging). 1929. *Shankhaiskaia Zaria*, April 18, 7.

Zakharoff, Floria Paci. 2005. *The Daughter of the Maestro: Life in Surabaya, Shanghai, and Florence*. New York: iUniverse, Inc.

"Zakrytie sezona" (Closing the season). 1932. *Slovo*, June 1, 4.

Zarrow, Peter, ed. 2006. *Creating Chinese Modernity: Knowledge and Everyday Life, 1900–1940*. New York: Peter Lang.

Zelensky, Natalie K. 2009. "Music in Exile: Constructing the Russian Diaspora in New York Through Russian Popular and Sacred Music." PhD dissertation, Northwestern University.

Zeng Huahui. 2000. *Qierpin yu Jiang Wenye de xiangyu: Erren gangqin zuopin (1934–36) de bijiao yanjiu* 齐尔品与江文也的相遇:二人钢琴作品 (1934–36) 的比较研究 (Tcherepnin's encounter with Jiang Wenye: A comparative study of two people's piano works (1934–36). Taipei: Hanjia chubanshe 汉家出版社.

Zhang Jigao 张继高 et al., eds. 1982. *Xiao Youmei xiansheng zhi shengping* 萧友梅先生之生平 (The life of Mr. Xiao Youmei). Taibei: Yazhou zuoqujia lianmeng zhonghuaminguo zonghui 亚洲作曲家联盟中华民国总会.

Zhang Xiong 张雄. 2010a. "Zhongguo xiandai shengyue jiaoyu de dianji ren Su Shilin" 中国现代声乐教育的奠基人——苏石林 (A founder of China's contemporary vocal music education). *Yinyue aihao zhe* 音乐爱好者 (Music lover) 1: 16–20.

———. 2010b. "Zhuang zai shengyin dong zhen xi dong manhua guoli yin zhuan di yi jie xuesheng yinyue hui" 壮哉声音 动震西东 漫话国立音专第一届学生音乐会 (The earliest students concert of the National Conservatory of Music). *Yinyue aihao zhe* 音乐爱好者 (Music lover) 8: 65–67.

Zhang Yanni 张燕妮. 1990. "Jiang Chunfang tongzhi shenping" 姜椿芳同志生平 (Comrade Jiang Chunfang's life). In *Wenhua lingmiao bozhongren: Jiang Chunfang* 文化灵苗播种人姜椿芳 (A sower of cultural seedlings: Jiang Chunfang), 1–5. Shanghai: Zhongguo wenshi chubanshe 中国文史出版社.

Zhao Xiaosheng 赵晓生. 1994. "Yinshui siyuan: Dingshande Jiaoshou fangtan lu" 饮水思源——丁善德教授访谈录 (To be grateful: Interview with Prof. Ding Shande). *Gangqin yishu* 钢琴艺术 1: 4–8.

———. 1996. "Tongxiang yinyue de shengdian: Wu Leyi jiaoshou fangtan lu" 通向音乐

的圣殿——吴乐懿教授访谈录 (Leading to the temple of music: An interview with Professor Wu Leyi). *Gangqin yishu* 钢琴艺术 2: 4–7.

Zhao Yi. 2015. "Lanxin dajuyuan shangyan jumu yilan biao (1941–1945)" 兰心大戏院上演剧目一览表 (1941–1945) (A list of performance at Lyceum Theater (1941–1945). In *Shanghai zujie yu lanxin da juyuan: dongxi yishu ronghe jiaohui de juchang kongjian* 上海租界与兰心大剧院：东西艺术融合交汇的剧场空间 (Shanghai's International Settlement and Lyceum Theater: A theatrical space for the synergy of East-West arts), edited by Takchiko Ohashi et al., 243–294. Shanghai: Renmin chubanshe 人民出版社.

Zheng, Su. 2010. *Claiming Diaspora: Music, Transnationalism, and Cultural Politics in Asian/Chinese America*. Oxford: Oxford University Press.

"Zhenqiu you Zhongguo fengwei de gangqinqu jiexiao" 征求有中国风味的钢琴曲揭晓 (Announcement of results for the call for piano works with Chinese flavor). 1934. *Yinyue zazhi* 音乐杂志 (Music magazine) 4: 64.

"Zhenshchina kabare i russkaia koloniia" (Women of cabaret and Russian colony). 1933. *Kabare*, no. 1: 2.

"'Zhidovka', premiera 'Sevilskii tsiriulnik' i 'Skazki Gofmana'" ('La Juive,' premiers of 'Sevillan Barber' and 'Hoffman's Tales'). 1938. *Slovo*, January 12, 2.

Zhiganov, Vladimir. 1936. *Russkie v Shankhae* (Russians in Shanghai). Shanghai: Izd. V. Zhiganova.

"Zhizn sodruzhestvo" (Life in the fraternity). 1934. *Ponedelnik*, no. 3–4, n.p.

"Zhizn za tsaria—poslednii raz" (Life for the Tsar—for the last time). 1938. *Slovo*, March 6, 3.

"Zhongguo diyibu yinyueju Meng Jiang Nü" 中国第一部音乐剧孟姜女 (China's first music drama *The Great Wall*). 1945. *Shidai* 时代 135, no. 22: n.p.

"Zhongxi yinyue diyici huizou" 中西音乐第一次会奏 (Chinese and Western music's first meeting in performance). 1933. *Shen Bao* 申报, May 23, 11.

Zhou Xiaoyan 周小燕. 1982. "Shenzhi de huainian—Yi riai Zhongguo de da yinyuejia Qierpin" 深挚的怀念——忆热爱中国的大音乐家齐尔品 (Deeply heartfelt memory: Recalling the great musician Tcherepnin's passion for Chinese music). *Yinyue yishu* 音乐艺术 (Journal of the Shanghai Conservatory of Music) 4: 114–115.

Zhu Ping 朱萍. 1994. "Zhongcheng de zhanshi, xinqin de yuanding: yinyue jiaoyu jia Xiang Yu" 忠诚的战士辛勤的园丁——音乐教育家向隅 (Loyal soldiers and dedicated gardener: Music educator Xiang Yu). In *Zhongguo jinxiandai yinyuejia chuan* 中国近现代音乐家传 (Biographies of contemporary Chinese musicians), vol. 2, edited by Xiang Yansheng, 282–295. Liaoning: Chunfeng wenyi chubanshe 春风文艺出版社.

Zhu Xiaoqi 诸晓琦. 2002. "Lun jindai shanghai de e'qiao shequ" 论近代上海的俄侨小区 (Discussion on contemporary Shanghai's Russian community). *Xueshu yuekan* 学术月刊 11: 61–66.

"Znaete-li Vy svoego uchenika?" (Do you know your pupils?) 1933. *Vechernaia Zaria*, April 1, 4.

INDEX

Page numbers in **boldface** refer to figures and tables.

National Center for Performing Arts
(Beijing), 204, 230n1
National Conservatory of Music:
administration and finances, 129,
222n13; concerts, 38, 126–127, 130, 144–
145, 155, 157; Conservatory Orchestra,
140; enrollment, 130; founding, 127–
128, 205, 221n12; instructors and staff,
1, 75, 116, 129–130, 222n18; location
in Shanghai, 128–129; magazine and
publications, 157, 221n9, 224nn40–
41; and musical life in Shanghai, 3, 35;
names of, 127, 221nn5–6; networks
and connectivity, 2, 156, 210; and New
Chinese Music, 128; organization
and curriculum, 130, 134, 156, 205; in
photographs, 126, 132; Piano Works
Competition, 156–158, 165, 168; Russian
pedagogues, 46–47, 127, 130, 137, 139–
143, 147, 205; students, 46, 126–127, 130–
131, 142–144, 147, 158, 222n23; studied
by Cheung, 211n6. See also Shanghai
Conservatory of Music; Shevtsov, Igor;
Shushlin, Vladimir; Xiao Youmei;
Zakharov, Boris
National Institute of the Arts (Hangzhou),
188
nationalism: Chinese, 128; Russian, 39,
202; transnationalism, 12, 25. See also
cosmopolitanism and nationalism;
Russian heritage
networks, 2, 12, 211nn5–6; Actor Network
Theory, 2, 211n7, 224–225n52
Neuhaus, Heinrich, 131
New Chinese Music, 1, 128, 147, 202, 206,
211n2; piano, 160. See also Tcherepnin,
Alexander
New Culture Movement, 1, 3
New Russian School, 113
newspapers and magazines, 27–28, 29, 31,
52. See also concert reviews; Shanghai
Zaria
New York: Avshalomov, 199, 201, 228n9;
Chinese New Year in, 26; Havsky,
123, 220n29; Russian diaspora in, 10,
Tcherepnin, 156, 166–168, 188
New York Philharmonic Shanghai
partnership, 203

Nie Er: and Avshalomov, 183, 188, 196,
229n16; as leftist, 196; teachers, 74, 141,
143, 215n21, 224n46
nine-step scale, 150, 225n3
North-China Daily News: concert reviews,
120; letters to, 85–86, 122, 219nn12–13
North China Desk Hong List, 71, 214n6,
214n8
Northwest Normal University, 139

Oakes, Vanya, 186, 187, 188
oboists, 65, 67, 74, 75, 217n51. See also
Sarychev, Vladimir; Schvaikowsky, S.
opera houses, 53, 57, 119, 204, 230n4. See
also Carlton Theater; Shanghai Opera
Company
Orchestra of the Alliance Française, 67
Osadchuk, V., 70, 75, **82**
Ouyang Shandao, 197
Ouyang Yuqian, 183

Paci, Mario: accused of collaboration,
198; chamber concerts organized
by, 79, 85; concerts with Russian
choir, 48, 50, 205; conducted special
concerts, 37, **89–97**, 114–115; conductor
of Municipal Band, 63; hiring of
temporary musicians, 63–70, 215n11,
215n16, 215n27, 216n33; and oboist
Schvaikowsky, 76–77, 217n55, 217n64;
piano students, 190; preference for
Italian music, 73, 85, 114, 219n13;
programming, 85, 86, 88–100;
relationships with Russian musicians,
62–63, 73–75, 79–85, 145, 216n46;
salary dispute with Hayek, 67–68;
salary of, 215n21; and Tchaikovsky
performances, 101, 111, 124, 125, 219n5.
See also Shanghai Municipal Orchestra
Paris, 5, 23, 43, 52, 132, 151
Parkes, Henry Francis, 41–42
paternalism, 45, 157
Pathé, 67, 190, 229n25
Pecheniuk, Aleksandr, **72**, **82**, 130, 140
Peking Opera, 147, 165, 184, 193, 194,
228n13. See also Mei Lanfang
pentatonic scale, 15, 159–163, 177, 179
Phedorov (Fedoroff)-Kozmenko, 68–69

ABOUT THE AUTHORS

Hon-Lun Helan Yang is professor of music at Hong Kong Baptist University. She specializes in music of twentieth-century China. Her research interest is both interdisciplinary and cross-cultural, and she has published extensively in topics pertinent to music and identity, politics, migration, diplomacy, censorship, social movement, cultural memory, and historiography. She is the lead author and coeditor of the volume *China and the West: Music, Representation, and Reception* (University of Michigan Press, 2017). Her recent articles will appear or have appeared in such volumes as *The Bloomsbury Handbook of Popular Music and Social Class* (forthcoming), *The Oxford Handbook of Music in China and the Chinese Diaspora* (forthcoming), *The Oxford Handbook of Music Censorship* (Oxford University Press, 2017), *Composing for the State: Music in Twentieth-Century Dictatorships* (Ashgate, 2016), *Liszt and His Legacy* (Pendragon, 2014), *Music and Protest in 1968* (Cambridge University Press, 2013), and *Music and Politics* (Ashgate, 2013). She has published in journals such as *Twentieth-Century Music* (2017), *International Review of Aesthetics and Sociology of Music* (2011), and *Asian Music* (2010).

Simo Mikkonen is senior researcher in the Department of History and Ethnology, University of Jyväskylä (Finland). He specializes in twentieth-century Russian and Eastern European history, cultural and artistic diplomacy, and émigrés. He has published extensively on cultural, international, and transnational East-West connections, particularly from the Soviet perspective, including a monograph *State Composers and the Red Courtiers: Music, Ideology and Politics in the Soviet 1930s* (Mellen, 2009), and edited volumes *Beyond the Curtain: Entangled Histories of the Cold War-Era Europe* (Berghahn, 2015), *Music, Art, and Diplomacy: East-West Cultural Interactions and the Cold War* (Routledge,

2016), and *Entangled East and West. Cultural Diplomacy and Artistic Interaction during the Cold War* (Degruyter, 2018).

John Winzenburg is professor of music at Hong Kong Baptist University, where he conducts the Cantoría Hong Kong. He also appears regularly with the Hong Kong New Music Ensemble. Winzenburg was a Fulbright Doctoral Fellow at the Central Conservatory of Music (CCOM) in Beijing in 2004–2005. Winzenburg's recent research has focused on Chinese-Western "fusion concertos," musical experimentation by Aaron Avshalomov in pre-1949 Shanghai, and new Chinese choral music. His work has been published in *Asian Music*, *CHIME*, the *Journal of the Central Conservatory of Music*, *Journal of Musicological Research*, *Perspectives of New Music*, Palgrave Macmillan, *Twentieth-Century China*, and the University of Michigan Press. Winzenburg is also the editor of the Edition Peters anthology *Half Moon Rising: Choral Music from Mainland China, Hong Kong, Singapore and Taiwan*.